PETERSON'S®

MASTER THE™ GRE® GENERAL TEST

About Peterson's

Peterson's has been your trusted educational publisher for more than 50 years. It's a milestone we're quite proud of as we continue to offer the most accurate, dependable, high-quality educational content in the field, providing you with everything you need to succeed. No matter where you are on your academic or professional path, you can rely on Peterson's for its books, videos, online information, and expert test-prep tools; the most up-to-date education exploration data; and the highest-quality career success resources—everything you need to achieve your education goals. For our complete line of products, visit **www.petersons.com**.

For more information, contact Peterson's, 4380 S. Syracuse St., Suite 200, Denver, CO 80237; call us at 800-338-3282, ext. 54229; or visit us online at **www.petersons.com**.

ISBN-13: 978-0-7689-4608-6

Printed in the United States of America

10 9 8 7 6 5 4 3 2 1 26 25 24

27th Edition

CONTENTS

CONTENTS

Part V: Practice Tests

CONTENTS

Appendixes

Peterson's Updates and Corrections

Check out our website at **www.petersonsbooks.com/updates-and-corrections/** to see if there is any new information regarding the test or any revisions or corrections to the content of this book. We've made sure the information in this book is accurate and up to date; however, the test format or content may have changed since the time of publication.

Credits

Peterson's acknowledges the works featured in *Master the™ GRE® General Test*. Passage excerpts used in the diagnostic and practice tests are taken from the following works:

Whale Primer by Theodore Joseph Walker

Food Remedies by Florence Daniel

The Civil War by James I. Robertson Jr.

Introduction to the Study of the History of Language by Herbert A. Strong

Wolfgang Amadeus Mozart by Mrs. John Lillie

The Art of Perfumery and Methods of Obtaining the Odors of Plants by Piesse

Laughter by James Sully

The Problems of Philosophy by Bertrand Russell

The Appreciation of Music by Thomas Whitney Surette and Daniel Gregory Mason

Applied Psychology for Nurses by Mary F. Porter

Lectures on Painting by Edward Armitage

Elementary Study of Insects by Leonard Haseman

"On Drawing" by A. P. Herbert

The Science of Human Nature by William Henry Pyle

A History of North American Birds, vol. 3 by S. F. Baird, T. M. Brewer, and R. Ridgway

The Prince by Niccolo Machiavelli

Crime: Its Cause and Treatment by Clarence Darrow

The Gourmet's Guide to Europe by Algernon Bastard and Lieutenant Colonel Newnham-Davis

John Francois Millet by Estelle M. Hurll

Federalist Paper #15 by Alexander Hamilton

BEFORE YOU BEGIN

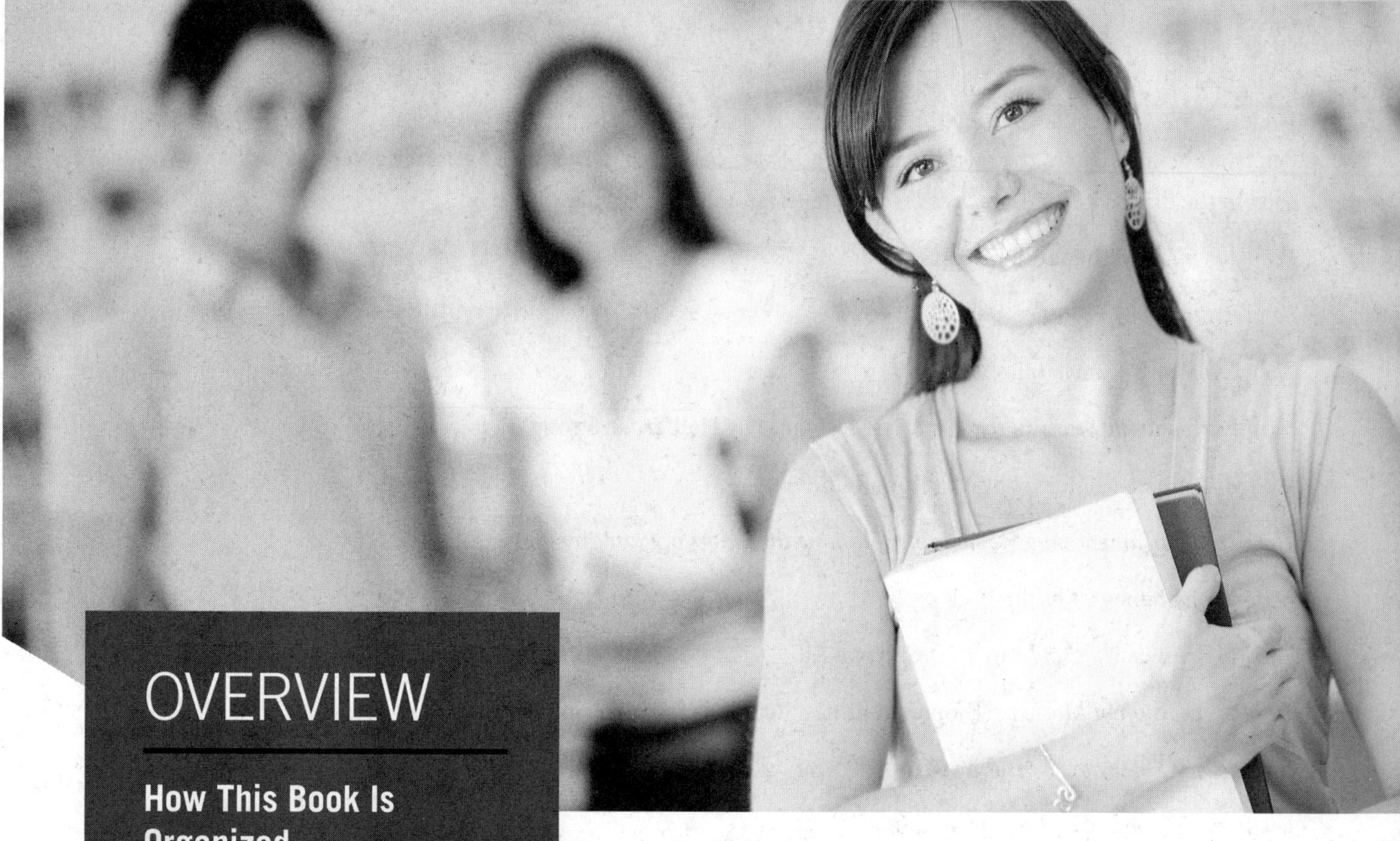

OVERVIEW

- How This Book Is Organized
- Study Features
- Using This Book to Prepare for the GRE General Test
- Peterson's Publications
- Give Us Your Feedback
- You Are Well on Your Way to Success

Peterson's *Master the™ GRE® General Test* is your guidebook for navigating the GRE General Test. Questions on the GRE are designed to evaluate test takers' critical thinking skills in order to effectively predict their overall performance in graduate school.

In the Analytical Writing section,* you'll be asked to evaluate an opinion on an issue and develop an argument to support your views. In the Verbal Reasoning section, you'll find reading comprehension questions that ask you to critique the validity of an author's argument or to identify information that supports an author's argument. Other questions in the Verbal Reasoning section ask you to analyze the context of a sentence or passage and select the best word choice. In the Quantitative Reasoning section, you'll be asked to apply your knowledge of math and other quantitative concepts. An on-screen calculator is available throughout the entire Quantitative Reasoning section. Its purpose is to shift the focus from computation to demonstration of the cognitive processes required to determine the answers.

Peterson's *Master the™ GRE® General Test* will

- walk you through the parts of the test;
- give you strategies to use for each type of question;
- explain how to avoid some common writing problems;
- review basic arithmetic, algebra, geometry, and data analysis;
- help you develop your vocabulary for word-choice questions;
- offer insights to help develop your reading skills; and
- provide simulated practice with one diagnostic and three practice tests.

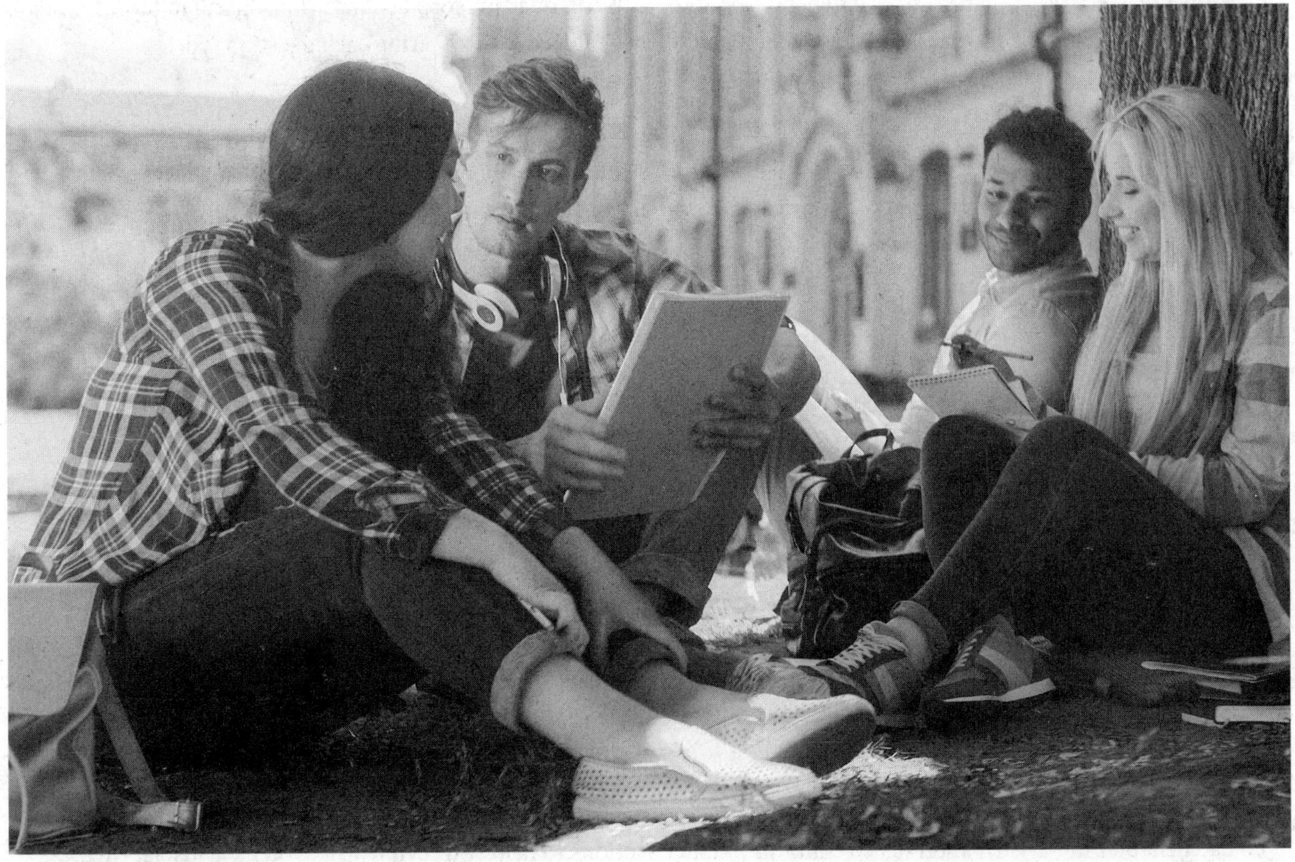

* You may see the term *measure* used in official GRE test descriptions or materials. The test uses this term to refer to the three primary test components—Analytical Writing, Verbal Reasoning, and Quantitative Reasoning—and uses the term *section* to refer to subdivisions within them. In this book, we simplify and use the term *section* to refer to the primary test components.

How This Book Is Organized

Peterson's *Master the™ GRE® General Test* is divided into six parts to facilitate your study:

Part I explains basic information about the GRE General Test and provides an overview with examples of the different question types you'll find on the test. It also offers a diagnostic test to help you identify your areas of strength and those areas where you will need to spend more time in your review sessions. Finally, you'll receive useful tips on how to turn your diagnostic test results into a study plan.

2

Part II explores the Analytical Writing section and offers strategies for developing well-supported and coherent responses to the prompt that you will be required to answer.

3

Part III goes into detail about the different question formats that you will find in the Verbal Reasoning section and offers strategies for answering each question type.

4

Part IV describes the different question formats in the Quantitative Reasoning section and offers strategies to help you tackle difficult questions.

5

Part V contains three full-length practice tests that provide you with simulated practice in taking the GRE General Test under timed conditions.

6

Appendixes A and B offer tips to help you improve your writing. "Appendix A: Common Errors in Grammar and Mechanics" can help you avoid such mistakes as sentence faults, misplaced modifiers, subject-verb agreement issues, and pronoun problems. If misspelled words are a problem for you, check out "Appendix B: Frequently Confused and Confusing Words." Here, you'll find a list of commonly misspelled words, assisting you in presenting a more polished essay in the Analytical Writing section.

Each chapter in Parts III and IV also contains practice sections to help you review what you have just learned.

STUDY FEATURES

This book was designed to be easy to use so that you can locate the information you need. It includes several features to make your preparation easier.

Overviews

Each chapter begins with an overview, listing the topics that are covered in the chapter. This overview allows you to quickly target the areas you are most interested in studying.

Tools to Guide You through the Book

- **Summing It Up** sections at the end of each chapter summarize the most important points covered in the chapter.
- **Tips** provide quick and simple hints to help you select the correct answers for specific types of questions.
- **FYIs** identify characteristics of the testing format or question types that can cause you to make mistakes when you select an answer. FYIs can also warn you about common errors in grammar or in computations and formulas.
- **Alerts** address information about the test structure itself or provide information you need to know.

USING THIS BOOK TO PREPARE FOR THE GRE GENERAL TEST

There are several important things to remember as you work through this book. When taking the GRE General Test, you'll be entering answers by typing on a keyboard or using a mouse. The Analytical Writing measure requires that you compose short responses by typing words, sentences, and paragraphs. The numeric entry questions from the Quantitative Reasoning measure require that you enter numbers into boxes. Other questions require that you select choices by clicking on them with your mouse.

Since you can't answer in this fashion in this book, you'll have to fill in your answers by hand when taking the practice tests and completing the exercises (answer sheets are provided at the end of this book). Some questions in this book may appear in a slightly different form than on the test due to the limitations of print. For instance, answer options will appear with letters before each of them (A, B, C, etc.) in this guide. On the actual test, the answer options may appear as ovals or squares that are not designated by letters. While the way you take the computer-based test may be different than your experience practicing with this book, you can rest assured that this book will nonetheless familiarize you with all the concepts that are likely to be tested.

If you are interesting in supplementing your study with online testing options that mimic the computer-based GRE, check out our online offerings by visiting **www.petersons.com/testprep/gre**.

PETERSON'S PUBLICATIONS

Peterson's publishes a full line of books—career preparation, education exploration, test prep, study skills, and financial aid. You'll find Peterson's titles available for purchase at major retailers or online at **www.petersons.com**. Sign up for one of our online subscription plans and you'll have access to our entire test prep catalog of more than 150 exams plus instructional videos, flash cards, interactive quizzes, and more! Our subscription plans allow you to study at your own pace.

GIVE US YOUR FEEDBACK

Peterson's publications can be found at your local bookstore and libraries, in college libraries and career centers, and at **www.petersons.com**. Peterson's books are also available as ebooks.

We welcome any comments or suggestions you may have—your feedback will help us make educational dreams possible for you and others like you.

YOU ARE WELL ON YOUR WAY TO SUCCESS

By investing in this book, you've officially taken a very important step in your postgraduate education. Peterson's *Master the™ GRE® General Test* will provide the information you need to know and prepare you to score your best on the day of your test.

MASTER THE™ GRE®
GENERAL TEST

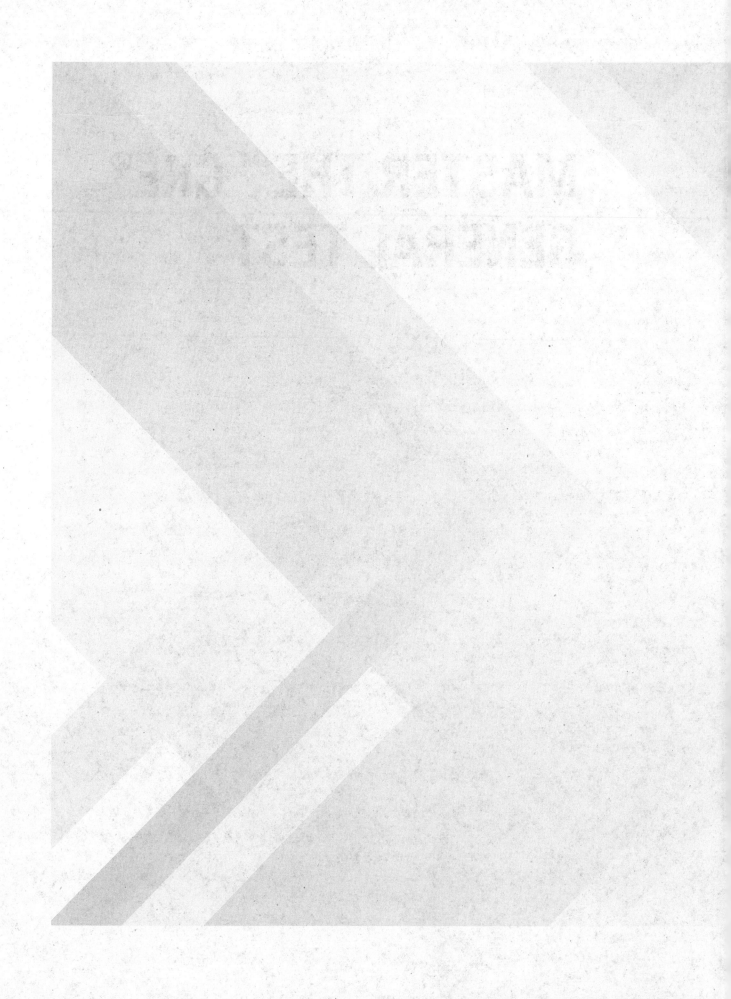

PART I

PREPARING FOR THE GRE

CHAPTER

The Basics of the GRE General Test

THE BASICS OF THE GRE GENERAL TEST

OVERVIEW

- Test Organization and Question Types
- Number of Questions and Time Limits
- Test Tools
- Scoring
- Taking the GRE General Test
- On Test Day
- Summing It Up

The GRE (Graduate Record Examinations) General Test is Educational Testing Service's (ETS's) measure of one's aptitude for graduate or business school. Most often delivered via computer, the test allows for greater user maneuverability and functionality compared to many other standardized tests. For example, you can edit and change what you've written, skip questions and return to them later, and use integrated tools to check your work. While the computer-based test is now the primary way test centers conduct the GRE, a paper version is still available for those who need it as an accommodation.

On the GRE, the Quantitative Reasoning and Verbal Reasoning sections are both computer adaptive. This means that the questions for the second Quantitative Reasoning and Verbal Reasoning sections are based on how well you perform on the first sections. This provides a more personalized assessment of your abilities because the test adjusts to your skill level.

According to ETS, the question types first introduced in 2011 better mirror the reasoning skills that test takers are called on to use in graduate and business school. The topics in the Analytical Writing section, the problems in the Quantitative Reasoning sections, and the passages used as the basis for questions in the Verbal Reasoning sections all simulate the real-world issues and situations that students encounter in their coursework for advanced degrees. Because of such updates, the scores that result from the current GRE General Test are considered by ETS to be "more reliable" than those from any previous iteration.

TEST ORGANIZATION AND QUESTION TYPES

The GRE General Test is divided into three assessment measures: Analytical Writing, Verbal Reasoning, and Quantitative Reasoning. The first section will always be Analytical Writing. The other sections may appear in any order.

Analytical Writing

Analytical Writing assesses your ability to think critically and transform your ideas into well-developed, well-reasoned, and well-supported writing. There is one essay in this section of the test, and it is called the **Analyze an Issue task.** This section requires you to build your own argument either in support of or in disagreement with an opinion, policy, recommendation, or claim. The GRE uses this section to assess your ability to develop and support your own ideas, particularly by drawing upon any relevant evidence that might come to mind. In addition, you will also be expected to sustain well-focused and coherent writing and control the elements of Standard Written English.

The prompt for the Analyze an Issue task presents you with a very brief statement, recommendation, claim, viewpoint, or policy and asks you to agree or disagree with it. No prior knowledge of the issue is required. You can choose to agree or disagree with the issue, as long as you follow the instructions that accompany the premise that the prompt sets up. For example, you might find a prompt and a set of instructions similar to the following wording:

> A nation should require all of its students to study the same national curriculum until they enter college.
>
> *Write a response in which you discuss your views on the policy and explain your reasoning for the position you take. In developing and supporting your position, you should consider the possible consequences of implementing the policy and explain how these consequences shape your position.*

There are six different sets of instructions from which the test makers may choose when forming prompts. These instructions specify the degree or conditions of your agreement or disagreement. Only one set of instructions will be given to direct your response. You may be asked to respond using instructions like the following:

- Discuss the extent to which you agree or disagree with the statement and explain your reasoning for the position you take. In developing and supporting your position, consider ways in which the statement might or might not hold true and explain how these considerations affect your point of view.
- Discuss how much you agree or disagree with the recommendation and describe why. Using specific examples, explain how the circumstances under which the recommendation could be adopted would or would not be advantageous. In developing and supporting your viewpoint, explain how these specific circumstances affect your point of view.

- Discuss how much you agree or disagree with the claim and include the most compelling reasons and/or examples that someone could use to dispute your point of view.
- While addressing both provided viewpoints, discuss which more closely aligns with your own. Explain your reasons for holding this position when providing evidence for your response. As you develop and support your position, be sure to address both viewpoints.
- Discuss how much you agree or disagree with the claim and the reasoning used to support that claim.
- Discuss your viewpoint on the proposed policy and the reasons for your point of view. Take into consideration the potential consequences of implementing the policy and the extent to which these consequences influence your viewpoint in developing and supporting your response.

Each of these prompts requires you to use analytical writing skills in a different way, so plan to pay close attention to the operative words in the instructions. To assist you in your preparation for the GRE General Test, ETS provides access to a pool of all the issues used in the Analytical Writing section. Wording on the actual test may vary slightly, but previewing these topics will give you a general idea of what to expect and a chance to consider claims pertaining to unfamiliar subject matter. To look at the topic pool, visit **https://www.ets.org/pdfs/gre/issue-pool.pdf.**

Verbal Reasoning

The Verbal Reasoning section of the GRE General Test assesses your ability to understand, analyze, and apply information found in the types of reading you will be doing in graduate school. Among the questions you'll find are those that ask you to reason from incomplete data; analyze and draw conclusions; identify authors' assumptions and perspectives; distinguish major and minor points; understand the structure of a text and its interrelated parts; understand the meaning of words, sentences, and passages; and understand multiple levels of meaning.

Three types of questions appear in the Verbal Reasoning section:

- Reading comprehension
- Text completion
- Sentence equivalence

Reading comprehension questions are divided into two types. Multiple-choice questions require you to select either a single answer choice or all correct answers from among a set of options. Select-in-passage questions require you to highlight in a given passage a sentence that fits a certain description.

Multiple-Choice—Select One Answer Choice

For the majority of reading comprehension questions on the GRE General Test, you'll have a list of five answer choices from which to choose. In place of lettered choices, the computer-generated test will provide blank ovals next to answer options. The format will look something like this:

For this question, choose only one answer choice.

The author of the passage would most likely agree with which of the following statements?

◯ Professor Bates did not take into consideration the number of voters who said they would vote but didn't.

◯ Professor Bates did not consider the problems with accuracy inherent in exit polls.

◯ Professor Bates's sample was neither large enough nor random enough.

◯ Professor Bates should have known that plus or minus 10 points was too large a range to be valid.

◯ Professor Bates should not have stopped sampling 10 days before the election, considering how volatile the race was.

Multiple-Choice—Select One or More Answer Choices

The list of multiple-choice options for this question format is limited to three. The answer choices for these question types are preceded by blank squares, not ovals. The instructions will indicate that you should select all answer choices that apply. Anywhere from one to all three choices will be correct. The format will look something like this:

For this question, consider each answer individually and choose <u>all</u> that apply.

According to the critic, what qualities were more evident in her later novels than in her earlier ones?

- ☐ Less social satire
- ☐ More stereotypically drawn characters
- ☐ More dialogue and less description of characters' motivations

Multiple-Choice Question Variations

Within both multiple-choice question formats, you may find questions that use line numbers to refer to a particular line in a passage. Questions with line numbers usually concern vocabulary, such as "In line 4, the word *sterling* most nearly means," followed by a list of possible answers. You may find a passage that highlights two parts in gray and a question that asks you about the two highlighted parts. The arrangement might look something like the following:

Jones's ultimate mistake in the eyes of historians was his disregard of Turner's thesis on the closing of the frontier. However, Jones's own theory was found to be no more penetrating nor half as well supported as he claimed Turner's was. For one thing, Jones's argument was considered weak because he had not consulted the territorial records. His articles tended to lack statistical support, and his conclusions overly generalized from the spotty data that he had used.

Jones's response centered on the fact that he considered his function in life to be popularizing dull and boring history for a popular audience. This won him no friends in academia, but his books about the colorful frontier made him pots of money—like the pot of gold at the end of a rainbow on a rain-soaked prairie—to satirize Jones's florid prose. Jones claimed his wealth evoked jealousy in his peers.

How do the two highlighted sentences help make the author's point that Jones was an egotist?

A. By suggesting that Jones's self-absorption influenced his attitude toward his peers

B. By focusing on negative responses from Jones's peers

C. By highlighting Jones's eventual downfall in academia

Select-in-Passage Questions

Select-in-passage questions ask you to select the sentence in the passage that meets a certain description. To select a sentence, click on any word in the sentence or select the sentence with the keyboard. The question and directions will be set up similarly to the following arrangement:

Rather than allow for a vote on the bill, the senator chose to begin a filibuster that would last for 24 hours and 18 minutes. Senator Thurmond was speaking against the passage of the Civil Rights Act of 1957. Because of the strong emotionalism of the opposition to civil rights for African Americans, the Senate saw another record-breaking filibuster in 1964. Senator Robert Byrd and his colleagues held the Senate floor for 75 hours. Senator Byrd, who came, in time, to renounce his opposition to civil rights legislation, spoke for 14 hours and 13 minutes.

Filibusters against civil rights legislation continued during the 1960s as Southern senators fought to keep the status quo in place. However, the Civil Rights Movement had gained momentum and would not be silenced.

Select the sentence that explains the causal relationship between filibusters and proposed civil rights legislation.

To answer the question, you will need to click in the passage to select your answer choice. Any sentence in the paragraph is fair game to be the answer.

Because this type of question depends upon the use of a computer to select an answer, it cannot be replicated in this book. Instead, a multiple-choice question evaluating an equivalent skill will be shown in its place.

Text Completion Questions

Text completion questions present a passage with up to three missing words. You must select the word that works best for each blank space in the passage, carefully considering its meaning and relation with the entire text. If the passage has one blank to fill in, you will select your answer from a list of five answer choices presented in a column. If the passage has two or three blanks, you will select your answer from a list of three answer choices for each blank, presented in columns. Once you have decided on your answer, click on the cell with that answer. In this book, there will be letters next to the word choices to simulate the format. It will look something like the following:

For this question, choose one answer for each blank. Select from the appropriate column for each blank. Choose the answer that best completes the sense of the text.

A major issue that may slow the (i) _________ of electric cars is the difficulty of charging the batteries. Until or unless local (ii) _________ legislate the installation of charging stations in new construction, at train stations, and in parking lots, (iii) _________ of electric cars say that the general public will not embrace these environmentally friendly vehicles.

Blank (i)	Blank (ii)	Blank (iii)
A. manufacturing	D. municipalities	G. opponents
B. proliferation	E. companies	H. advocates
C. building	F. people	I. myrmidons

Sentence Equivalence Questions

Sentence equivalence questions differ from traditional multiple-choice questions in two significant ways. First, there are six answer choices rather than the usual four or five. Second, you have to choose *two* answers from the list to complete the one answer blank. You are presented with a single sentence that contains one blank space. You must choose two words that both create a coherent sentence when added. Furthermore, these two sentences must convey the same overall meaning. To receive credit for your answer, both answer choices must be correct. The answer choices are preceded by blank squares, not ovals. No partial credit is given if only one of the words is correct.

The direction line for all sentence equivalence questions is the same and is worded something like the following:

For this question, choose two answers that best fit the meaning of the sentence and that result in completed sentences with the same or nearly the same meaning.

The art expert, hired by the potential buyer, was unable to _________ the painting as being from the school of Rembrandt.

☐ authenticate

☐ place

☐ authorize

☐ verify

☐ depose

☐ approve

Quantitative Reasoning

Quantitative Reasoning sections on the GRE General Test measure your ability to understand, interpret, and analyze quantitative information; use elementary mathematical models to solve problems; and apply basic mathematical knowledge and skills. The Quantitative Reasoning section requires basic knowledge in arithmetic, algebra, geometry, and data analysis. On the GRE General Test, the questions draw from a mixture of real-world scenarios and pure mathematics. Often, the questions will take the form of word problems, requiring you to interpret their meaning and extract mathematical models from them.

You will be provided with a simple on-screen calculator, but it is not necessarily required to answer any question. Rather, it should be used to verify or supplement your own mathematical knowledge.

Three types of questions appear in the Quantitative Reasoning section:

- Multiple-choice
- Numeric entry
- Quantitative comparison

Multiple-Choice—Select One Answer Choice

All questions using the multiple-choice—select one answer choice format list five possible answer choices, only one of which is correct. The choices are preceded by an oval to click to select your answer. The question will look something like the following:

For this question, choose one answer choice.

If $y = (x + 8)^2$, then $(-3x - 24)^2$ must equal which of the following?

- ⬭ $-9y^2$
- ⬭ $-3y^2$
- ⬭ $-9y$
- ⬭ $3y$
- ⬭ $9y$

Multiple-Choice—Select One or More Answer Choices

This format may have, as the name states, 1, 2, 3, or more correct answers. Unlike reading comprehension test items that use the multiple-choice—select one or more answers format, questions using this format in the Quantitative Reasoning section may have up to 10 answer options. However, there will always be at least 3 answer choices listed and they will all have blank squares in front of them.

In most instances, the direction line for one of these questions will tell you to "indicate all that apply." However, the direction line may specify the number that you should choose. The following example provides a typical direction line for such a question:

For this question, indicate all the answers that apply.

Which two of the following integers give you a product of less than -54?

- ☐ -9
- ☐ -5
- ☐ 6
- ☐ 9
- ☐ 4
- ☐ -6
- ☐ 5
- ☐ 1

To gain credit for multiple-choice—select one or more answers questions, you need to select all answers that are correct. There is no partial credit for choosing some but not all correct answers.

Numeric Entry Questions

Unlike the other Quantitative Reasoning question formats, numeric entry questions don't have a list of answer choices from which to choose. Instead, you're given a question and one or two answer boxes. If the answer is an integer or decimal, there will be one answer box. If the answer is a fraction, you'll see two stacked answer boxes with a line between them. You'll enter the numerator in the top box and the denominator in the bottom box.

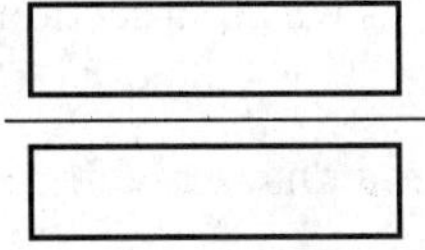

To solve the problem, you'll use the on-screen calculator. If the answer is an integer or decimal, you can use the "Transfer Display" function to enter your answer into the box. If the answer is a fraction, you'll need to type your answer into the two boxes using the keypad.

A numeric entry question will look like the following:

For this question, enter your answer in the box.

If x and y are integers, what is the absolute value of y if $y = -6x + 32$ and $x = -4$?

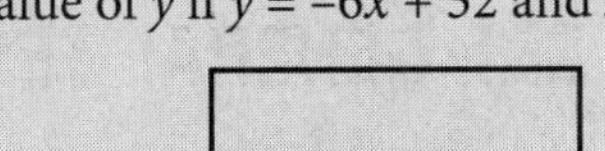

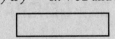

The correct answer is 56. Solve the equation for y using the value –4 for x, so

$y = -6(-4) + 32$

$y = 24 + 32$

$y = 56$

Quantitative Comparison Questions

Quantitative comparison questions present you with two quantities, A and B, in a table with two columns. The objective is to compare the two quantities and choose one of the following answers, which always appear in this order:

A. Quantity A is greater.

B. Quantity B is greater.

C. The two quantities are equal.

D. The relationship cannot be determined from the information given.

Some quantitative comparison questions will have additional information centered above the two columns. This information will help you determine the relationship between the two quantities. Any symbol that appears more than once in a question has the same meaning throughout the question; for example, a symbol in the centered information and in Quantity A will have the same meaning.

A quantitative comparison question will look like the following. Some questions have additional information above the two quantities to use in determining your answer.

For this question, compare Quantity A and Quantity B.

Quantity A	Quantity B
26% of 120	17

A. Quantity A is greater.

B. Quantity B is greater.

C. The two quantities are equal.

D. The relationship cannot be determined from the information given.

Data Interpretation Sets

In addition to the other types of question formats, you'll probably also find at least one group of questions revolving around the same table, graph, or other data representation. These graphics are known as data interpretation sets. All that means is that to answer the two or three questions related to the data on the graphic, you will need to refer to the graphic. Note that quantitative comparison questions are *not* included in data interpretation sets.

NUMBER OF QUESTIONS AND TIME LIMITS

The GRE General Test is divided into five scored sections: one Analytical Writing section, two Verbal Reasoning sections, and two Quantitative Reasoning sections. The test will always begin with the Analytical Writing section. Verbal Reasoning and Quantitative Reasoning sections may follow in any order. The test will take approximately 1 hour and 58 minutes.

The breakdown of scored sections by question and time limit is as follows:

	Number of Sections	Number of Questions	Time per Section
Analytical Writing	1	1 task: Analyze an Issue	30 minutes
Verbal Reasoning	2	Section 1: 12 questions Section 2: 15 questions	Section 1: 18 minutes Section 2: 23 minutes
Quantitative Reasoning	2	Section 1: 12 questions Section 2: 15 questions	Section 1: 21 minutes Section 2: 26 minutes

TEST TOOLS

The test offers two on-screen tools. For the Quantitative Reasoning sections, you'll find an on-screen calculator with the four basic functions—addition, subtraction, multiplication, division—and a square root button. You'll also be able to enter some of the answers directly from the calculator into the answer boxes using a "Transfer Display" function. The calculator is often not necessary because the test places more emphasis on test takers' reasoning skills than on their computational skills.

For the Analytical Writing tasks, you'll be working in an ETS-designed word processing program that will allow you to type, insert and delete text, cut and paste, and undo any of these actions. However, the program doesn't have a spell checker or a grammar checker.

The GRE General Test enables you to move back and forth within a section so you can

- preview and review a section,
- mark questions within a section to return to later, and
- change and edit answers within a section.

SCORING

For the Verbal Reasoning and Quantitative Reasoning sections of the GRE General Test, scores are reported in a range of 130 to 170 points, in 1-point increments. Analytical Writing is reported in half-point increments, using a 0–6 range.

The score delivery time frame for test takers is 8–10 days, and schools may receive scores faster than that, depending upon which delivery method they have chosen. Electronic scores are delivered to schools twice a week.

TAKING THE GRE GENERAL TEST

You can take the GRE General Test once every 21 days, up to five times within any continuous rolling 12-month period (365 days).

Registration

You can register for the GRE General Test online by creating an account on the ETS website. You will receive your score report 8 to 10 days after your test date, so be sure to schedule your test date to allow for delivery of scores and processing by your chosen institutions by their application deadlines.

Registration Fees

At the time of this book's printing, the fee for the GRE is $220. To determine if you are eligible for a fee reduction voucher, visit **https://www.ets.org/gre/test-takers/general-test/register/fees.html.**

Test-Taking Options

You have the option of taking the GRE General Test at one of the more than 1,000 test centers in more than 160 countries, or from the comfort of your own home.

Test Centers: The GRE General Test is administered throughout the year at Prometric test centers and may be offered outside the Prometric network on specific dates. For information about testing dates and locations, visit **https://www.ets.org/gre/test-takers/general-test/schedule.html**.

At Home: The GRE General Test can also be taken at home on your own computer. The at-home test is identical to the test administered at test centers and is offered 24 hours a day, seven days a week. You will be monitored by a human proctor and have your computer scanned as a system check. For more information about taking the GRE General Test at home, go to **https://www.ets.org/gre/test-takers/general-test/register/at-home-testing.html**.

Accommodations are available for GRE General Test takers with disabilities or health-related needs who meet ETS requirements, including assistance with the computer-delivered test and alternative test formats (such as traditional paper-and-pencil, braille, large-print test book, or audio). For a list of available accommodations, visit **https://www.ets.org/gre/test-takers/general-test/register/disability-accommodations.html**. To learn more about the accommodations request process and the resources available to you, visit **https://www.ets.org/disabilities.html**.

ON TEST DAY

There are several rules and restrictions to be aware of on test day. Insufficient identification or policy violations could result in not being able to test, dismissal from the test center, and/or cancellation of your test scores.

The following is a general list of policies you need to know; for a more detailed list, refer to the GRE website (**https://www.ets.org/gre/test-takers/general-test/test-day/test-center-test-day.html**). Be sure to examine the information provided in the *GRE Information Bulletin* (**https://www.ets.org/pdfs/gre/gre-info-bulletin.pdf**) for a comprehensive list of test day policies. Periodically check the website for more updates as test day approaches.

General Test Center Procedures and Regulations

- Dress so that you can adapt to any room temperature; however, clothing is subject to inspection by the test center administrator.
- Friends or relatives who accompany you to the test center will not be permitted to wait in the test center or be in contact with you while you are taking the test. Except for ETS-authorized observers, visitors are not permitted in the testing room while testing is in progress.
- If you have health-related needs that require you to bring equipment, beverages, or snacks into the testing room or to take extra or extended breaks, refer to the accommodations request procedures described in the *2023–2024 Bulletin Supplement for Test Takers with Disabilities or Health-Related Needs*, available at **https://www.ets.org/pdfs/gre/bulletin-supplement-test-takers-with-disabilities-health-needs.pdf**.
- You will be asked to designate up to four score recipients at the test center on the day of the test. If an institution is not listed, ask the test center administrator for the appropriate form to indicate unlisted institutions. Complete the form and turn it in before you leave the test center. The form will not be accepted after you leave the test center.

- If you do not select score recipients on the day of the test or if you would like to send your scores to more than four score recipients, you will need to submit an Additional Score Report request for a fee of $35 per score recipient.
- On occasion, weather conditions or other circumstances beyond the test administrator's or ETS's control may require a delayed start or the rescheduling of your test appointment. If a technical problem at the test center makes it necessary to cancel your test session, or if it is later determined that your scores could not be reported, you will be offered the opportunity to schedule another test appointment free of charge or receive a full refund of the original test fee. Periodically check the website for more updates as test day approaches.

Check-In Procedures and Regulations

ID verification at the test center may include thumbprinting, photographing, videotaping, or some other form of electronic ID confirmation. If you refuse to participate, you will not be permitted to take the test, and you will forfeit your registration and test fees. This is in addition to the requirement that you must present acceptable and valid identification.

If you requested and received an authorization voucher for disabilities or health-related needs from ETS, you must take it with you to the test center.

You will be required to write and sign (not print) a confidentiality statement at the test center. If you do not complete and sign the statement, you cannot take the test and your test fees will not be refunded.

Prohibited Materials

- Food, beverages, tobacco, and e-cigarettes
- Weapons and firearms
- Personal calculators (You will have access to an on-screen calculator while taking the Quantitative Reasoning sections.)
- Cell phones, smartphones (e.g., Androids, iPhones), or other electronic or photographic devices
- All forms of watches, including digital, analog, and smartwatches
- Personal items other than identification documents (Neither ETS nor the test centers assume any responsibility whatsoever for personal items or devices that you choose to bring into the test center. All forms of jewelry except for wedding and engagement rings are prohibited.)

Test Procedures and Policies

- Testing premises are subject to videotaping.
- The test administrator will assign you a seat.
- You may be required to sign the test center log before and after the test session and any time you leave or enter the testing room.
- The test administrator will provide you with scratch paper for use during the test. Scratch paper is not to be used before the test. All paper, in its entirety, must be returned to the test center administrator at the end of the testing session. If you are observed using any document or paper other than the scratch paper given to you by test center staff, it will be confiscated.
- You may not bring your own paper, and you may not remove any paper from the testing room at any time or write on anything other than the paper provided (e.g., the computer or workstation).
- If at any time during the test you have a problem with your computer or for any reason need the administrator, raise your hand.
- If you need to leave your seat at any time, raise your hand; the timing of the section will not stop.
- Because of the essay scoring process, you will not be able to view your scores at the time you test. You can view scores in your ETS account 8–10 days after you take the test.

SUMMING IT UP

- The computer-delivered GRE General Test allows test takers to change and edit answers within each timed section, allowing them to skip and then return to unanswered questions before the allotted time expires. An on-screen calculator and word processing program are included.
- The GRE General Test has three measures: **Analytical Writing, Verbal Reasoning, and Quantitative Reasoning**. Analytical Writing is always first. Verbal Reasoning and Quantitative Reasoning follow Analytical Writing and have two scored sections each, which may come in any order.
- The Analytical Writing section has one task: **Analyze an Issue**. You'll be given one prompt and will not have a choice from which to select.
- All **multiple-choice** questions in the GRE General Test will have answer options preceded by either **blank ovals** or **blank squares**, depending on the question type.
- Verbal Reasoning sections have a mix of **reading comprehension, text completion, and sentence equivalence** questions.
- **Reading comprehension** questions are made up of multiple-choice—select one answer choice; multiple-choice—select one or more answer choices; and select-in-passage questions.
    - **Multiple-choice—select one answer choice** questions, which use the traditional one-answer multiple-choice format, present a list of five answer choices preceded by ovals.
    - **Multiple-choice—select one or more answer choices** questions present only three possible answers, preceded by squares. All three options may be correct, or only one, or only two. Credit is given only if *all* answer choices are correct.
    - **Select-in-passage** questions require test takers using the computer-delivered test to highlight a sentence within the subject passage as the answer.
- **Text completion** questions present a passage with from one to three blanks that must be completed by choosing from a list of possible answers. If the question has only one blank, then five possible choices are provided. If the question has two or three blanks to fill in, there will be a list of only three possible answers for each blank.
- **Sentence equivalence** questions provide six possible answers but only one blank to complete. To answer the question, you must use two words from the list that will complete the sentence so that both versions are similar, or equivalent, in meaning.

- **Quantitative Reasoning** questions may take the form of multiple-choice—select one answer choice; multiple-choice—select one or more answer choices; quantitative comparison; and numeric entry formats.
    - **Multiple-choice—select one answer** is the traditional multiple-choice format and lists five possible answer choices preceded by ovals.
    - **Multiple-choice—select one or more answer** questions list at least 3 answer choices but may have as many as 10 possible answers. The direction line usually says simply to "indicate all that apply." However, some questions may indicate an exact number to select. Credit is given only if *all* answer choices are correct.
    - **Quantitative comparison** questions are set up as two columns, Quantity A and Quantity B, which you must compare and decide if one quantity is greater than the other, if they are equal, or if the relationship can't be determined from the information given. Some questions may provide additional information above the quantities to help you determine your answer.
    - **Numeric entry** questions don't list answer choices. You must calculate your answer using the on-screen calculator and enter it on-screen.
- The test takes approximately **1 hour and 58 minutes** and has the following time limits and questions:

	Number of Sections	Number of Questions	Time per Section
Analytical Writing	1	1 task: Analyze an Issue	30 minutes
Verbal Reasoning	2	Section 1: 12 questions Section 2: 15 questions	Section 1: 18 minutes Section 2: 23 minutes
Quantitative Reasoning	2	Section 1: 12 questions Section 2: 15 questions	Section 1: 21 minutes Section 2: 26 minutes

- The scores for the Quantitative and Verbal Reasoning measures are reported on a scale of 130 to 170 with 1-point increments. The Analytical Writing score is reported on a scale of 0 to 6 with half-point increments.

CHAPTER

Diagnostic Test

DIAGNOSTIC TEST

OVERVIEW

DIRECTIONS FOR THE DIAGNOSTIC TEST

The following diagnostic practice test contains the five scored sections you will encounter on the actual GRE General Test.

On pages 363–369, we've provided sheets for planning and composing your Analytical Writing response, followed by an answer sheet for filling in your responses for the Verbal Reasoning and Quantitative Reasoning sections. Before you begin the test, remove or photocopy these pages.

As on the actual GRE General Test, each diagnostic test section has its own time allocation. During that time period, you may work on only that section. Be sure to use a timer for each section so you can accurately simulate the test-day experience. Total testing time is approximately 1 hour and 58 minutes.

Following the diagnostic test, you will be provided tools to help you assess your response to the Analytical Writing task. An answer key and a comprehensive explanation follow for each test question in the Verbal Reasoning and Quantitative Reasoning sections.

We've provided a Diagnostic Test Assessment Grid at the end of this chapter (page 62) to help you tailor your study plan. This grid points you question by question to the chapters in which you can find the information you need to sharpen your skills in that specific subject area.

Answer sheets for this test can be found on pages 363–369.

SECTION 1: ANALYTICAL WRITING

30 minutes

The time for this Analyze an Issue task is 30 minutes. You must plan and draft a response that evaluates the issue given below. If you do not respond to the specific issue, your score will be zero. Your response must be based on the accompanying instructions, and you must provide evidence for your position. You may use support from reading, experience, observations, and/or coursework.

Some people believe that traveling to and living in numerous places increases one's ability to relate and connect to other people. Others believe that this ability is better cultivated by living in one place and developing a deep understanding of that community.

*Write a response in which you discuss which view more closely aligns with your own position, and explain your reasoning for the position you take. In developing and supporting your position, you should address both of the views presented.**

STOP!

IF YOU FINISH BEFORE THE TIME IS UP, YOU MAY CHECK YOUR WORK IN THIS SECTION ONLY.

* All of the Analytical Writing prompts in the practice tests of this book come directly from the list of prompts for the GRE, which can be found at https://www.ets.org/pdfs/gre/issue-pool.pdf.

DIRECTIONS FOR THE VERBAL REASONING AND QUANTITATIVE REASONING SECTIONS

On test day, you will find information here about the question formats for the Verbal Reasoning and Quantitative Reasoning sections as well as information about how to use the software program. You will also receive important information about how these two sections are scored. Every correct answer earns a point, but points are not subtracted for incorrect answers, so it is better to guess if you aren't sure of an answer than to leave a question unanswered.

All multiple-choice questions will have answer options preceded by either blank ovals or blank squares, depending on the question type.

For your convenience in answering questions and checking answers in this paper-based diagnostic test, answer choices are shown as lettered options. This notation makes it easier to check your answers against the answer keys and explanations.

NOTES

SECTION 2: VERBAL REASONING

18 minutes—12 questions

For each question, follow the specific directions and choose the best answer.

For Questions 1–3, choose one answer for each blank. Select from the appropriate column for each blank. Choose the answer that best completes the sense of the text.

1. Russian author Leo Tolstoy wrote *War and Peace* from an __________ point of view because he wanted to convey what each of his characters was thinking and feeling.

A. accomplished
B. enormous
C. ensemble
D. omniscient
E. acrimonious

2. That Jane Austen's satiric wit is lost on some readers is (i) __________ because it is so (ii) __________ as to become caricature; for example, consider the Rev. Collins in *Pride and Prejudice.*

Blank (i)	Blank (ii)
A. logical	**D.** flashy
B. understandable	**E.** showy
C. inexplicable	**F.** overdrawn

3. One consequence of the desire among modern playwrights to bring (i) __________ to the theater has been the diminution of poetry as a dramatic language. On the other hand, realism in language has brought a (ii) __________ end to rant and rhetoric upon the stage. As one critic wrote, modern playwrights have been pushed to develop plays that are (iii) __________ and convincing when they could no longer rely on "verbal pyrotechnics."

Blank (i)	Blank (ii)	Blank (iii)
A. vibrancy	**D.** welcome	**G.** more forceful
B. verisimilitude	**E.** final	**H.** more cerebral
C. resemblance	**F.** limited	**I.** more believable

For Questions 4–12, choose only one answer choice unless otherwise indicated.

Questions 4 and 5 are based on the following passage.

Over the course of the 20th century, the American suburb evolved from do-it-yourself homes on plots of land at the end of urban rail lines to the most dominant form of prefabricated housing development in the United States. In their current form, American suburbs evolved from what Harvard historian Dolores Hayden has termed "sitcom suburbs." Emerging in the period immediately following World War II, Hayden suggests that most of today's suburban housing development is fashioned on these mid-century suburbs. She argues that their form became a shared visual idea of "suburbia" for Americans through its reflection in the sitcoms of early television.

One of the most influential developers during this period was William J. Levitt. His company, Levitt & Sons, built a suburban housing development called Levittown outside New York City between 1947 and 1951. They pioneered a prefabrication model for quickly and efficiently constructing identical houses on similar sized lots, allowing them to sell for low prices. Once this model proved successful, they created additional Levittowns across the country, and other developers began mimicking their model. Levittown solidified the distinctive look associated with suburbia today: individual homes in a row of individual lots with grass-filled front yards, a space to park your car, and if you're lucky, a white picket fence.

However, the fences weren't the only things white about the sitcom suburbs. The Levittown housing covenants explicitly forbade people of color, Jews, and single women from buying homes. Once an African American family did eventually move into a Levittown in Pennsylvania in the 1950s, they were harassed and threatened. On top of that, the National Housing Act of 1934 had made it standard practice to follow the newly created Federal Housing Administration's (FHA'S) guidelines for issuing mortgage loans, which were in turn informed by the FHA's racially biased practice of redlining.

Redlining was a formalized process to help banks make determinations about mortgage applications. From 1934 onward, maps were created to divide every major city in the United States into sections based on a neighborhood's suitability for housing. Under redlining, neighborhoods with large communities of color were drawn in "red," deeming them least desirable. People consequently couldn't get favorable mortgages for homes in redlined areas, yet they were the only areas with racial covenants that allowed certain populations (mainly people of color) to live there. White families were thus free to take part in expanding suburbanization, while families of color were largely left out. Understanding how redlining contributed to housing segregation along racial lines is therefore critical for understanding the generational wealth gaps that contribute to racial inequality today.

For Questions 4 and 5, consider each answer individually and choose all that apply.

4. The passage suggests that the relationship between suburbanization and wealth inequality is illustrated by which of the following?

   A. The emergence of so-called "sitcom suburbs"

   B. Formalized discrimination through restrictive housing covenants

   C. The FHA's use of redlined maps in determining mortgage eligibility

5. It can be inferred that the author mentions Dolores Hayden's research in lines 3–8 primarily in order to

   A. gesture toward her work on redlining.

   B. lend credibility to their characterization of mid-century suburbanization.

   C. establish a common claim before asserting a counterclaim.

Question 6 is based on the following passage.

Wilarsky: Ever since the federal government classified psychedelic drugs as Schedule I substances in 1973, meaning it was illegal to possess them, it has been difficult for the scientific community to engage in meaningful clinical research about the potential efficacy of these substances in treating a wide range of physical and psychological conditions. Today, this policy is widely regarded as the reason that scientists do not yet have a more nuanced understanding of the therapeutic benefits of psychedelics, which are increasingly proving to be myriad. Luckily, sentiments seem to be shifting in favor of valuing scientific inquiry over outdated notions of propriety regarding what is and is not suitable for therapeutic use. The scientific community should devote more resources to advocacy for decriminalizing psychedelic drugs in order to explore the potential positives that can come from therapeutic use.

Su: While all that is true, there is undeniably a tradeoff that must occur when considering Schedule I psychedelics as therapeutic interventions, especially as concerns patients who have already demonstrated psychological issues or a propensity toward addiction. The fact remains that researchers are largely in uncharted territory when it comes to therapeutic applications of psychedelics generally and psilocybin specifically, so caution must be built into the research model.

For Question 6, consider each answer individually and choose all that apply.

6. Su responds to Wilarsky's argument by doing which of the following?

A. Reiterating the veracity of Wilarsky's evaluation of the benefits of this type of research

B. Challenging Wilarsky's claims regarding the efficacy of psilocybin in clinical applications

C. Highlighting a health and safety concern that must be considered when conducting this type of research

Questions 7–9 are based on the following passage.

The devastating events of the 2012 Dhaka garment factory fire in Bangladesh bear haunting parallels with the 1911 Triangle Shirtwaist Factory fire in New York City. Despite the temporal and geographical distances between these two tragedies, the common thread that connects them is the corporate pursuit of cost-cutting and increased production at the expense of safety standards, leading to catastrophic consequences for workers. The Triangle Shirtwaist Factory fire started on the building's eighth floor; the Dhaka garment factory fire started in its basement. In both fires, workers died from being trapped inside the building or jumping from factory windows because ladders could not reach them. The similar stories of locked exit doors, inadequate fire escapes, and unsafe working conditions echo through time, illustrating the tragic consequences of prioritizing profit over human life.

These tragedies revealed to the public the inhumane working conditions in garment industry shops and their impact on workers. These incidents served as catalysts for heightened awareness and advocacy, prompting discussions on the ethical responsibilities of companies and the need for international collaboration to protect the rights of workers in the garment industry. The Triangle Shirtwaist Factory fire, which killed 146 workers, many of whom were young women, galvanized a wave of labor activism and workplace safety reforms in the United States, resulting in significant advancements in labor laws and workplace safety regulations. The 2012 Dhaka fire, which killed 117 and injured more than 200, raised awareness of the workers' plight. That incident, combined with the Rana Plaza factory collapse in 2013 (1,200 fatalities, 2,500 injured), ignited a global outcry for improved working conditions and labor rights, increased oversight, stricter regulations, and enhanced accountability within the global garment industry. Governments, NGOs, and international bodies responded by pressuring companies to uphold ethical standards and ensure the well-being of workers throughout the supply chain. The labor rights struggle in Bangladesh continues as the government and labor reform entities remain at odds over implementation policies.

For Questions 7 and 8, consider each answer individually and choose all that apply.

7. According to the passage, what parallels exist between the Triangle Shirtwaist Factory fire and the Dhaka garment factory fire?

   A. The fires resulted from corporate cost-cutting and demand for increased production at the expense of the workers' safety.

   B. The workers could not escape during the fires because the doors to the exits were locked.

   C. The fires resulted in significant and immediate advancements in US labor laws and workplace safety regulations.

8. Select the sentence in the passage that does NOT add to the support for the main idea of the passage.

   A. These tragedies revealed to the public the inhumane working conditions in garment industry shops and their impact on workers.

   B. The Triangle Shirtwaist Factory fire started on the eighth floor of the building; the Dhaka garment factory fire started in its basement.

   C. In both fires, workers died from being trapped inside the building or jumping from factory windows because ladders could not reach them.

9. In the passage, "galvanized" (line 14) most nearly means

   A. impeded.

   B. increased.

   C. hurdled.

   D. angered.

   E. incited.

For Questions 10 and 11, choose the two answers that best fit the meaning of the sentence as a whole and result in two completed sentences that are alike in meaning.

10. Green building, that is, the construction of new buildings and the renovation of existing ones to make them eco-friendly, is a fast-growing segment of the construction industry and one that ALLIED Builders hopes to _________ according to its five-year business plan.

A. promote

B. advance

C. capitalize on

D. upgrade

E. utilize

F. endorse

11. The original intention in creating NASA was to explore space, but many of the products people take for granted today, such as cordless power tools and sunglasses with polarized lenses, resulted from _________ research that NASA conducted for the space program.

A. far-reaching

B. wide-ranging

C. innovative

D. unusual

E. cutting-edge

F. conventional

Question 12 is based on the following passage.

Emily Dickinson, a poet virtually unknown in her lifetime, wrote some of the most memorable lines in American poetry. Her poems are instantly recognizable for their brevity (they are often no longer than 20 lines) and their quirky punctuation and capitalization. Her frequent and often idiosyncratic use of the dash serves to emphasize many of her recurrent topics. A great number of Dickinson's almost 1,800 poems deal with the themes of death and immortality, though her poems are also filled with joy and hope. Because of its unusual syntax and use of figurative language—imagery, metaphor, personification—Dickinson's poetry can seem to the uninitiated reader something of a puzzle. Present-day readers would do well to renounce a literal way of reading in order to truly appreciate Dickinson's poetry.

12. The final statement in the passage suggests that the author believes which of the following statements about present-day readers?

 A. Present-day readers should not try to find literal meaning in Dickinson's poetry.
 B. Present-day readers would benefit from developing their ability to interpret figurative language.
 C. Present-day readers should try to figure out what themes were most important to Dickinson.
 D. Present-day readers who try to unlock the mysteries of Dickinson's figurative language are doing themselves a disservice.
 E. Present-day readers need to consider the context in which Dickinson's poetry was written.

STOP!

IF YOU FINISH BEFORE THE TIME IS UP, YOU MAY CHECK YOUR WORK IN THIS SECTION ONLY.

SECTION 3: VERBAL REASONING

23 minutes—15 questions

For each question, follow the specific directions and choose the best answer.

For Questions 1–3, choose one answer for each blank. Select from the appropriate column for each blank. Choose the answer that best completes the sense of the text.

1. Social networking is a marketing tool that many companies are harnessing to sell their products; however, it must be used _________ because the hard sell risks offending potential customers.

A. with ease
B. actively
C. judiciously
D. expeditiously
E. efficiently

2. Garraty states that the problems faced by private colleges in the 1820s and 1830s were of their own making to a degree. Many cities and towns wanted the (i) _________ of hosting a college, but the supply of colleges soon (ii) _________ the demand, that is, the number of potential students.

Blank (i)	Blank (ii)
A. honor	D. outperformed
B. admiration	E. outstripped
C. character	F. outshone

3. The queen is in (i) _________ health, so the prince might have to (ii) _________ the role of king if his mother's health forces her to (iii) _________ the throne.

Blank (i)	Blank (ii)	Blank (iii)
A. robust	D. convey	G. abdicate
B. feeble	E. assume	H. nullify
C. cautionary	F. furnish	I. arbitrate

For Questions 4–15, choose only one answer choice unless otherwise indicated.

Questions 4 and 5 are based on the following passage.

Access to clean drinking water and sanitation systems are crucial global goals. This access constitutes a fundamental health and human dignity issue. Expanding sewage systems will also reduce contamination of soil, rivers, and oceans, thereby promoting biodiversity and decreasing land degradation. Furthermore, access to clean water will reduce geopolitical conflict centered on water rights. In addition, commitment to clean water goals promotes investment in new technologies, such as desalination and water reuse.

The United Nations reported that between 1990 and 2010, more than "2 billion people gained access to improved water sources, and 1.8 billion gained access to improved sanitation"; however, its 2021 global assessment pointed out that 26% of the world population is still struggling for drinking water, 46% for sanitation, and 44% of households are without proper wastewater treatment. The UN continues to spearhead Sustainable Development Goal 6 (SDG6), which aims to ensure global availability and sustainable management of water and sanitation by 2030.

Recognizing that its goal will likely not be met, the UN acknowledges there are factors that slow the progress toward clean water goals. These include environmental disasters, the failure of some countries to set national hygiene standards, inadequate funding or poor absorption of existing funding, lack of skilled labor to implement change, and lack of political will. Only 80% of nations recognize the right to water; only some 50% recognize the right to sanitation.

4. Based on the passage, which of the following is NOT a factor that is delaying progress toward clean water goals?

   A. Failure of some nations to set national hygiene standards

   B. Inability to manage skilled labor resources at water sites

   C. Inadequate funding for global water initiatives

   D. Failure to properly use all available water funding

   E. Reluctance of some nations to consider water as a right

For Question 5, consider each answer individually and choose all that apply.

5. Select the sentence from the passage that is NOT a supporting detail for a central idea.

   A. This access constitutes a fundamental health and human dignity issue.

   B. Expanding sewage systems will also reduce contamination of soil, rivers, and oceans, thereby promoting biodiversity and decreasing land degradation.

   C. Recognizing that its goal will likely not be met, the UN acknowledges there are factors that slow the progress toward clean water goals.

Questions 6 and 7 are based on the following passage.

During World War II, the US system of rationing did not work as planned, not only because it conflicted with personal needs and wants (which had grown during the previous years of deprivation because of the Great Depression and its aftermath), but also because it went against the national character of the American people. This was a nation based on the principle that as long as you have money to spend, nothing is off limits. By limiting each individual's purchasing power, the government had imposed a new economic system that attacked this principle. The emergence of the illegal black market, on the other hand, supported this basic principle of acquisition, or consumerism, for Americans. This is not to deny that many who ran or even patronized the black market were actually motivated by greed, but it does suggest that the individualistic (and frontier) spirit of Americans had not been lost.

6. Select the statement that restates the premise of the author's argument.

   A. Citizens who are normally law-abiding will break the law to satisfy what they consider to be their basic needs and wants.

   B. Americans during World War II acted unlawfully due to circumstances out of their control.

   C. The American system of rationing did not work because Americans circumvented its principles through the practice of the black market.

   D. As long as Americans have enough money to spend, they will spend it however they can.

   E. If the Great Depression had not deprived so many Americans of basic needs and wants, they would not have patronized the black market during World War II.

For Question 7, consider each answer individually and choose all that apply.

7. Which of the following, if it were true, would weaken the author's argument?

   A. During the Great Depression, many Americans found ways to circumvent the law to provide for their families.

   B. A majority of American citizens are law-abiding and will not break the law under any circumstances.

   C. Many Americans continued to patronize the black market after rationing ended.

Questions 8 and 9 are based on the following passage.

The increasing awareness of lighting inefficiency and the billions of dollars of potential annual energy savings that can be achieved by switching to LED lighting have resulted in many government-funded research initiatives around the world. In addition, governments in the United States, Canada, Europe, and Australia have responded to the growing need for energy conservation by passing legislation that regulates or eliminates the sale of incandescent and halogen light bulbs by a certain date. However, though increasing consumers' awareness of the inefficiency of other light sources can help increase the adoption of LED lighting, regulations that focus on enforcing energy-efficient lighting are likely to work better. One example is California's Energy Efficiency Standards for Residential and Nonresidential Buildings, or Title 24, that provides a set of mandatory regulations covering all aspects of new building construction. The Residential Lighting section of Title 24 requires that a high-efficiency light source be used in several areas of the home, including the kitchen and bathrooms, and that all outdoor light fixtures must either use energy-efficient bulbs or be controlled by light and motion sensors.

8. The author lists several countries and continents in lines 3–4 in order to

A. show the places that have been most affected by lighting inefficiency.

B. imply that most countries do not take lighting inefficiency seriously enough.

C. explain that only a minority of governments believe that lighting inefficiency is a problem.

D. prove that legislation to control lighting inefficiency is extremely effective.

E. indicate the governments that have taken initiatives to conserve energy.

9. "Mandatory" (line 9) most nearly means

A. provisional.

B. permanent.

C. predetermined.

D. discretionary.

E. obligatory.

For Questions 10–12, choose the <u>two</u> answers that best fit the meaning of the sentence as a whole and result in two completed sentences that are alike in meaning.

10. If life does exist on other planets, scientists theorize that it would not necessarily _________ life on Earth. For example, depending on the wavelengths of light on the planet, plants could be red, yellow, or green.

A. epitomize

B. mimic

C. illustrate

D. typify

E. imitate

F. reflect

11. Scientists believe that unlocking the genome is _________; it will forever change the way we diagnose, treat, and someday even prevent disease.

A. modernization

B. reforming

C. revolutionary

D. transformative

E. huge

F. corrective

12. Most of the dishes served during the feast were underdone or overcooked, but at least the soup was very _________.

A. thorough

B. palatable

C. vehement

D. appetizing

E. baroque

F. inhospitable

Questions 13–15 are based on the following passage.

Among people who want to make informed choices about what they eat, the issue of whether to buy local or organic food is often debated. The most popular reasons cited for buying organic are to avoid pesticides that harm your health and damage ecosystems, to support a system of agriculture that uses natural fertilizers, and to support more humane animal husbandry practices. The reasons cited for buying local food include supporting the local economy and also buying food that is fresher, has less packaging, and has fewer "food miles," or the distance food has to travel from source to end user. It turns out to be a complicated question, one that can sometimes lead to additional questions that must be answered in order to make a choice. Sometimes the questions are personal ones, such as: What food tastes better? But larger questions can arise, too, such as: How do the choices we make about our food affect the planet?

13. The passage suggests which of the following about whether or not the reader should buy organic or local food?

A. We can never really know which is better.

B. We should try to answer important questions before trying to make that decision.

C. We should figure out which food tastes better.

D. We should try to find other ways to support the local economy.

E. We should buy the food that has the fewest "food miles."

14. Which of the following statements does the passage most clearly support?

A. Buying local or organic food is better than buying food from a big chain supermarket.

B. Buying organic food does not support the local economy.

C. The distance food has to travel is an important consideration when deciding where to buy your food.

D. Animals raised on organic farms are treated more humanely.

E. Food from local farms may have been sprayed with pesticides.

For Question 15, consider each of the three choices individually and choose all that apply.

15. What function does "the distance food has to travel from source to end user" (line 6) serve in the passage?

    A. It is support for the argument for buying local food.

    B. It defines the term "food miles."

    C. It is support for the larger question about how food choices affect the planet.

STOP!

IF YOU FINISH BEFORE THE TIME IS UP, YOU MAY CHECK YOUR WORK IN THIS SECTION ONLY.

SECTION 4: QUANTITATIVE REASONING

21 minutes—12 questions

For each question, follow the specific directions and choose the best answer.

The test maker provides the following information that applies to all questions in the Quantitative Reasoning section of the GRE General Test:

- All numbers used are real numbers.
- All figures are assumed to lie in a plane unless otherwise indicated.
- Geometric figures, such as lines, circles, triangles, and quadrilaterals, *are not necessarily* drawn to scale. That is, you should *not* assume that quantities such as lengths and angle measures are as they appear in a figure. You should assume, however, that lines shown as straight are actually straight, points on a line are in the order shown, and more generally, all geometric objects are in the relative positions shown. For questions with geometric figures, you should base your answers on geometric reasoning, not on estimating or comparing quantities by sight or by measurement.
- Coordinate systems, such as *xy*-planes and number lines, *are* drawn to scale. Therefore, you can read, estimate, or compare quantities in such figures by sight or by measurement.
- Graphical data presentations, such as bar graphs, circle graphs, and line graphs, *are* drawn to scale. Therefore, you can read, estimate, or compare data values by sight or by measurement.

For Questions 1–5, compare Quantity A and Quantity B. Some questions will have additional information above the two quantities to use in determining your answer.

1.

Quantity A	Quantity B
$6\frac{7}{8}$	3.42(2)

A. Quantity A is greater.

B. Quantity B is greater.

C. The two quantities are equal.

D. The relationship cannot be determined from the information given.

Questions 2–3 refer to the diagram below.

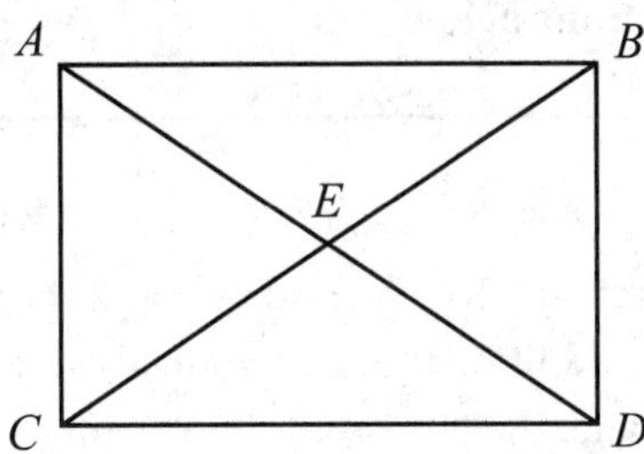

ABDC is a rectangle.

E is the intersection of *AD* and *BC*.

2. | Quantity A | Quantity B |
|---|---|
| the area of triangle *CED* | the area of triangle *AEC* |

A. Quantity A is greater.
B. Quantity B is greater.
C. The two quantities are equal.
D. The relationship cannot be determined from the information given.

3. | Quantity A | Quantity B |
|---|---|
| $m\angle ACD + m\angle CDB$ | $m\angle AEC + m\angle CED$ |

A. Quantity A is greater.
B. Quantity B is greater.
C. The two quantities are equal.
D. The relationship cannot be determined from the information given.

4. $y < x < 0$

Quantity A	Quantity B
$\|x\|$	$\|y\|$

A. Quantity A is greater.
B. Quantity B is greater.
C. The two quantities are equal.
D. The relationship cannot be determined from the information given.

5. Assume *a* is a positive integer and *b* is a negative integer.

Quantity A	Quantity B
$(a + b)^2$	$a^2 + b^2$

A. Quantity A is greater.
B. Quantity B is greater.
C. The two quantities are equal.
D. The relationship cannot be determined from the information given.

DIAGNOSTIC TEST

Questions 6–12 have several formats. Unless the directions state otherwise, choose one answer choice. For Numeric Entry questions, follow the instructions below.

Numeric Entry Questions

The following items are the same for both the actual GRE General Test and the test presented in this book. However, the actual GRE General Test will have additional information about entering answers in decimal and fraction boxes on the computer screen. To take the test in this book, enter your answers in boxes or answer grids.

- Your answer may be an integer, a decimal, or a fraction, and it may be negative.
- If a question asks for a fraction, there will be two boxes. One box will be for the numerator, and one will be for the denominator.
- Equivalent forms of the correct answer, such as 2.5 and 2.50, are all correct.
- Enter the exact answer unless the question asks you to round your answers.

6. A grocery store is having a sale on cherries. Usually, the cost is \$6.99 per pound for cherries. This week, the price is 30% less. How much does a customer save if he purchases 2.5 pounds of cherries this week?

   A. \$2.10

   B. \$5.25

   C. \$4.89

   D. \$17.48

   E. \$4.20

7. A regular six-sided die is rolled three times. What is the probability that each of the three rolls will produce an odd number?

   A. $\frac{1}{2}$

   B. $\frac{1}{3}$

   C. $\frac{1}{6}$

   D. $\frac{1}{8}$

   E. $\frac{1}{216}$

For Question 8, indicate all the answers that apply.

8. Find the next 3 numbers in the sequence.

1, 1, 2, 3, 5, 8, . . .

A. 12

B. 13

C. 14

D. 21

E. 22

F. 33

G. 34

H. 55

9. The position of a particle at time t is given by $s(t) = 8t^2(t + 1)$. Find the position of the particle at time $t = 2$.

A. 32

B. 48

C. 64

D. 84

E. 96

10. Find the value of x.

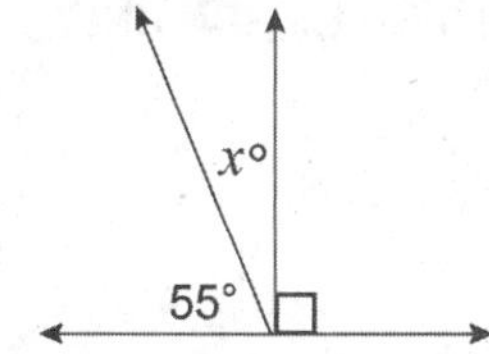

A. 55°

B. 35°

C. 90°

D. 145°

E. 125°

For Question 11, indicate <u>all</u> the answers that apply.

11. Which of the following are factors of 1,200?

A. 8

B. 14

C. 15

D. 75

E. 85

F. 160

G. 250

H. 300

12. If p and q are different prime numbers, what is the greatest common factor of $pq + p$ and $pq + 2p$?

A. p

B. q

C. p^2

D. $p(q + 1)$

E. pq

STOP!

IF YOU FINISH BEFORE THE TIME IS UP, YOU MAY CHECK YOUR WORK IN THIS SECTION ONLY.

SECTION 5: QUANTITATIVE REASONING

26 minutes—15 questions

For each question, follow the specific directions and choose the best answer.

The test maker provides the following information that applies to all questions in the Quantitative Reasoning section of the GRE General Test:

- All numbers used are real numbers.
- All figures are assumed to lie in a plane unless otherwise indicated.
- Geometric figures, such as lines, circles, triangles, and quadrilaterals, *are not necessarily* drawn to scale. That is, you should *not* assume that quantities such as lengths and angle measures are as they appear in a figure. You should assume, however, that lines shown as straight are actually straight, points on a line are in the order shown, and more generally, all geometric objects are in the relative positions shown. For questions with geometric figures, you should base your answers on geometric reasoning, not on estimating or comparing quantities by sight or by measurement.
- Coordinate systems, such as *xy*-planes and number lines, *are* drawn to scale. Therefore, you can read, estimate, or compare quantities in such figures by sight or by measurement.
- Graphical data presentations, such as bar graphs, circle graphs, and line graphs, *are* drawn to scale. Therefore, you can read, estimate, or compare data values by sight or by measurement.

For Questions 1–6, compare Quantity A and Quantity B. Some questions will have additional information above the two quantities to use in determining your answer.

1.

Quantity A	Quantity B
(2.7)(0.3)	$\frac{4}{5}$

A. Quantity A is greater.
B. Quantity B is greater.
C. The two quantities are equal.
D. The relationship cannot be determined from the information given.

2. Let $0 < x < 1$.

Quantity A	Quantity B
x^2	x^3

A. Quantity A is greater.
B. Quantity B is greater.
C. The two quantities are equal.
D. The relationship cannot be determined from the information given.

3. Mary is 6 years older than Stephen. Stephen is $\frac{3}{4}$ of Joe's age. Joe is 16 years old. All three were born in the 21st century.

Quantity A	Quantity B
Mary's birth year	Joe's birth year

A. Quantity A is greater.
B. Quantity B is greater.
C. The two quantities are equal.
D. The relationship cannot be determined from the information given.

4. A try is worth 5 points. A conversion is worth 2 points. A penalty goal is worth 3 points.

Quantity A	Quantity B
3 tries, 2 conversions, 1 penalty	24

A. Quantity A is greater.
B. Quantity B is greater.
C. The two quantities are equal.
D. The relationship cannot be determined from the information given.

5.

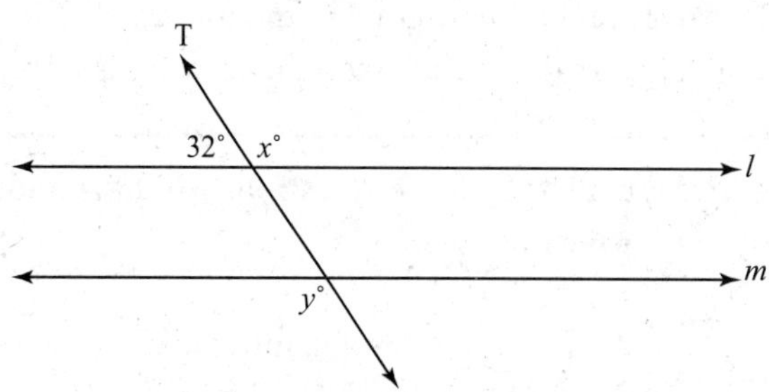

Assume lines l and m are parallel.

Quantity A	Quantity B
x	y

A. Quantity A is greater.
B. Quantity B is greater.
C. The two quantities are equal.
D. The relationship cannot be determined from the information given.

6. $$\frac{y}{x} = 3$$
$$x, y \neq 0$$

Quantity A	Quantity B
x	y

A. Quantity A is greater.

B. Quantity B is greater.

C. The two quantities are equal.

D. The relationship cannot be determined from the information given.

Questions 7–15 have several formats. Unless the directions state otherwise, choose one answer choice. For Numeric Entry questions, follow the instructions below.

Numeric Entry Questions

The following items are the same for both the actual GRE General Test and test presented in this book. However, the actual GRE General Test will have additional information about entering answers in decimal and fraction boxes on the computer screen. To take the test in this book, enter your answers in boxes or answer grids.

- Your answer may be an integer, a decimal, or a fraction, and it may be negative.
- If a question asks for a fraction, there will be two boxes. One box will be for the numerator, and one will be for the denominator.
- Equivalent forms of the correct answer, such as 2.5 and 2.50, are all correct.
- Enter the exact answer unless the question asks you to round your answers.

7. Evaluate the function $f(x) = 5x^3 + 4x^2 + 8x + 1$, when $x = 2$.

A. 73

B. –11

C. 183

D. 117

E. –73

8. A new-model hybrid car gets 45 miles per gallon for city driving and 20% more for highway driving. How many miles per gallon does the hybrid get for highway driving?

A. 34

B. 46

C. 51

D. 54

E. 58

Questions 9–11 refer to the table below.

Number of Children per Family in a Neighborhood	
Number of Children	Number of Families
1	19
2	36
3	21
4+	9
0	15

9. What is the total number of families that have no more than two children?

   A. 19

   B. 36

   C. 55

   D. 70

   E. 81

10. What is the percentage of families that have no children?

    A. 9%

    B. 12%

    C. 15%

    D. 18%

    E. 21%

11. Given that a family has at least one child, what is the probability they have at least three children?

    A. $\frac{21}{100}$

    B. $\frac{21}{85}$

    C. $\frac{3}{10}$

    D. $\frac{6}{17}$

    E. $\frac{11}{17}$

12. In the xy-plane, what is the slope of a line that is perpendicular to the line whose equation is $x + 2y = 5$?

A. -2

B. $-\frac{1}{2}$

C. $\frac{1}{2}$

D. 2

E. 5

13. What is the x-coordinate of the point at which the graphs of the equations $x + 2y = 4$ and $y - x = 2$ intersect?

A. -8

B. -2

C. 0

D. 2

E. 16

For Question 14, choose <u>all</u> the answers that apply.

14. In triangle ABC, the length of side $\overline{AB}$ is 4 centimeters (cm) and the length of side $\overline{BC}$ is 8 cm. Which of the following could be the length of side $\overline{AC}$?

A. 2 cm

B. 4 cm

C. 6 cm

D. 8 cm

E. 10 cm

F. 12 cm

For Question 15, enter your answer in the boxes.

15. Suppose that the circles below are concentric (that is, they share the same center). What is the ratio of the circumference of the smaller circle to the circumference of the larger circle?

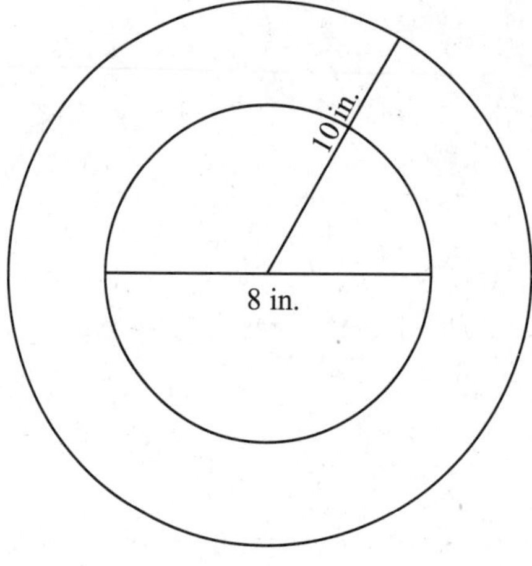

Give your answer as a fraction:

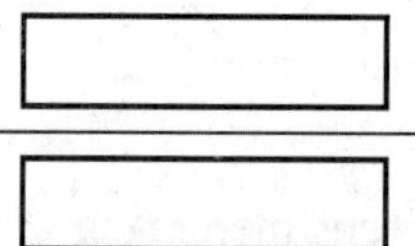

STOP!

IF YOU FINISH BEFORE THE TIME IS UP, YOU MAY CHECK YOUR WORK IN THIS SECTION ONLY.

ANSWER KEYS AND EXPLANATIONS

Section 1: Analytical Writing

To assist you with evaluating your writing, we have provided the following rubric, which is adapted from the official rubric used by ETS.* If you need more assistance evaluating your writing, consider the writing samples for essays at score levels 2, 4, and 6 as provided in Chapter 3.

ANALYTICAL WRITING SCORING RUBRIC SUMMARY

Score Level	Description	Characteristics of a Typical Response
6 Outstanding	A sustained, insightful, organized, detailed analysis of well-developed, complex ideas supported by meaningful evidence and highly persuasive support. Utilizes a wide range of vocabulary and rhetorical methods while demonstrating a superior understanding of the conventions of Standard Written English. Very minor errors may be present but do not impact meaning.	• Presents a distinct and perceptive viewpoint regarding the issue as outlined in the given instructions • Expands meaningfully on the viewpoint with convincing rationales and/or compelling examples • Maintains focus, organization, and clarity while establishing meaningful connections between concepts • Seamlessly and accurately moves between concepts using a range of transitions, word choices, and sentence structures • Exhibits exceptional proficiency with the norms of Standard Written English, even if very minor errors are present
5 Strong	A thoughtful, generally organized, and focused analysis of nuanced ideas supported by sound reasoning and meaningful examples. Uses a range of rhetorical skills and conventions to demonstrate meaningful control of the conventions of Standard Written English. Minor errors may be present but do not impact meaning.	• Presents a lucid and carefully considered viewpoint regarding the issue as outlined in the given instructions • Elaborates on the viewpoint with logically coherent rationales and/or well-chosen examples • Maintains focus and exhibits general organization, establishing suitable connections between ideas • Communicates ideas clearly and effectively, employing fitting vocabulary and varying sentence structures • Exhibits proficiency with the norms of Standard Written English, though occasional minor errors may be present

(continues)

* The GRE General Test: Analytical Writing Measure Scoring," ETS, 2024, https://www.ets.org/gre/test-takers/general-test/prepare/content/analytical-writing/scoring.html.

ANALYTICAL WRITING SCORING RUBRIC SUMMARY (*CONTINUED*)		
Score Level	**Description**	**Characteristics of a Typical Response**
4 Adequate	A competent, considered analysis of meaningful ideas that ventures a main point and supports it with relevant evidence or reasoning. Ideas are organized in a satisfactory manner, clearly conveyed, and supported by adequate control of rhetorical skills and the conventions of Standard Written English. May have some minor errors that impact clarity of meaning.	• Presents a clear viewpoint regarding the issue as outlined in the given instructions • Develops the viewpoint with relevant reasoning and/or examples • Maintains adequate focus and organization • Demonstrates satisfactory command of language to articulate ideas with acceptable clarity • Exhibits general understanding of the norms of Standard Written English, albeit with occasional errors
3 Limited	A somewhat competent analysis that addresses specific required tasks and makes some effort to address main points. Rhetorical skills may be lacking or underdeveloped, and writing may be limited by weak structure, poor organization, or underdevelopment of ideas. Contains some errors that limit clarity of meaning and/or contribute to vagueness.	Exhibits **one or more** of the following concerns: • Shows vagueness or inadequacy in addressing the given instructions, presenting or developing a viewpoint, or both • Demonstrates weakness in employing relevant examples or rationales, or leans heavily on unsupported assertions • Exhibits limited focus and/or organization • Includes issues in language or sentence structure, contributing to lack of clarity • Contains either occasional major errors or frequent minor errors in grammar, usage, and/or mechanics of Standard Written English, impeding comprehension
2 Seriously Flawed	A weak analysis that does not adequately address specific required tasks and/or that is underdeveloped, disorganized, or unclear. Frequent issues with rhetorical skills and/or the conventions of Standard Written English obfuscate meaning and limit clarity. Frequent errors make it difficult to parse.	Exhibits **one or more** of the following concerns: • Exhibits a lack of clarity or serious limitation in addressing the given instructions, developing a viewpoint on the issue, or both • Offers few, if any, relevant rationales or examples to support assertions • Lacks focus and/or organization • Includes serious issues in language or sentence structure, frequently obstructing clarity or contributing to outright confusion • Contains serious errors in grammar, usage, or mechanics that frequently obscure meaning

ANALYTICAL WRITING SCORING RUBRIC SUMMARY (*CONTINUED*)

Score Level	Description	Characteristics of a Typical Response
1 Fundamentally Deficient	A deficient analysis that contains fundamental errors and fails to communicate a meaningful main point. Content may be incomprehensible or extremely difficult to parse and/or may be irrelevant to the task at hand. Frequent and pervasive errors render the analysis incomprehensible or incoherent.	Exhibits **one or more** of the following concerns: • Demonstrates little or no evidence of grasping the given instructions or the issue at hand • Shows minimal or no evidence of the ability to craft an organized response, often appearing disorganized and/or excessively concise • Suffers from severe issues in language and sentence structure, consistently hindering comprehension • Contains widespread errors in grammar, usage, and mechanics, leading to incoherence
0	An analysis that cannot be evaluated because it does not address any aspect of the specified task. It may copy parts of the prompt in lieu of developing concepts or may be written in a foreign language or otherwise incomprehensible.	Exhibits **one or more** of the following concerns: • Demonstrates zero awareness of the given instructions or the issue at hand • Fully off topic • Merely copies the topic • Incomprehensible • Written in a foreign language • Consists only of random keystrokes or nonsensical inputs
NS	Blank essays will receive a score of NS, meaning no score.	

Section 2: Verbal Reasoning

1. D	4. B, C	7. A, B	9. E	11. C, E
2. B, F	5. B	8. B	10. C, E	12. B
3. B, D, G	6. A, C			

1. **The correct answer is D.** In literature, an omniscient point of view is one that features a narrator who has total knowledge of the feelings and thoughts of all characters in the story. *Accomplished* (choice A) means "skillful," and while that word does make grammatical sense in this context, it is not as specific a choice for the context as *omniscient. Ensemble* (choice C) seems to make sense in this context because the author could be dealing with an ensemble of characters, but it does not make grammatical sense as a choice to fill the blank. Neither *enormous* (choice B) nor *acrimonious* (choice E) fit the context.

2. **The correct answers are B and F.** Answer Blank (i): *Understandable* is the best answer choice because it means "capable of being understood." *Logical* (choice A) means "capable of reasoning in a clear and consistent manner," and while it may seem correct, the writer is not reasoning something out so much as stating their opinion. *Inexplicable* conveys an opposite meaning.

   Answer Blank (ii): In choosing answers for text completion items, consider the style and tone of the text. *Overdrawn* means "exaggerated," which fits the meaning and the tone of the sentence. *Flashy* and *showy* (choices D and E) do not match the style and tone. Additionally, both connote something done to draw attention, which is inconsistent with being "lost on some readers."

3. **The correct answers are B, D, and G.** When you have three blanks, context becomes all the more important. Remember, you do not always need to start with Blank (i) if completing another first will help provide context.

   Answer Blank (i): *Vibrancy* (choice A) doesn't make sense in the context because while poetry would add vibrancy to the theater, the sentence states that poetry's position has been diminished in modern plays. Choices B and C are somewhat similar in meaning, but *resemblance* (choice C) doesn't make sense within the sentence as a whole. *Verisimilitude* (choice B), which means "having the appearance of being true or real," is the correct answer by process of elimination.

   Answer Blank (ii): *Final* (choice E) is redundant; an end is final. *Limited* (choice F) doesn't make sense; how can you have a limited end? *Welcome* is the correct answer by the process of elimination, but more importantly because it means "giving pleasure."

   Answer Blank (iii): The phrase that you're looking for needs to balance with the word *convincing.* In this case, *more forceful* means "effective" and is therefore the best choice. *Believable* is a synonym for *convincing*, so choice J would be redundant. There is nothing in the passage to indicate that modern plays should be *more cerebral* (choice H).

4. **The correct answers are B and C.** Both choice B and choice C are mentioned in the context of the author's wider assertion that wealth inequality was exacerbated by the racism that accompanied American suburbanization in the mid 20th century. While the author does discuss the concept of sitcom suburbs in the first paragraph, they do so to set up context for the larger argument about suburbanization and wealth inequality rather than support it directly.

5. **The correct answer is B.** Gesturing both to a known scholar on the topic (Dolores Hayden) and that scholar's credentials (Harvard historian) is a way of lending credibility to their own characterization of mid-century suburbanization. The author does not draw a direct connection between Hayden and redlining (choice A). While they do

use Hayden's research to establish a claim about mid-century suburbanization, they do not do so in service of venturing a counterclaim (choice C).

6. **The correct answers are A and C.** Su reiterates Wilarsky's claims by opening their statement with "While all that is true" (choice A). Su then goes on to highlight that psychological issues or a propensity toward addiction could pose safety risks for those who take psychedelic substances, emphasizing that "caution must be built into the research model." However, Su makes no attempt to challenge Wilarsky's claims that psilocybin is clinically effective; in fact, their implication that research is nonetheless necessary as well as their acknowledgment that Wilarsky's claims are true contradicts the statement made in choice B.

7. **The correct answers are A and B.** Both fires resulted from corporate cost-cutting measures and demand for increased production, which led to unsafe working conditions in the factories that contributed to the tragedies, as indicated in choice B. Choice C is incorrect because it narrows its scope to the United States and asserts immediate change; instead, there was a "global outcry" that did not necessarily spark immediate changes.

8. **The correct answer is B.** The ignition site of the fire is a minor detail that isn't necessary to understand the main idea. Choices A and C are true, but they are incorrect answers because these are important details that *do* clearly support the main idea of the passage, and you are looking for answers that do not.

9. **The correct answer is E.** In this passage, *galvanized* means "incited or spurred on." *Impeded* (choice A) means "hindered," which is the opposite of what occurred. While the word *increased* (choice B) may seem correct, it doesn't match the strong quality implied in the word *galvanized. Hurdled* (choice C) means "jumped over," which doesn't make sense. *Angered* (choice D), while likely true, doesn't mean the same as *incited.*

10. **The correct answers are C and E.** *Capitalize on* and *utilize* mean "take advantage of, make the most of." *Promote* and *advance* (choices A and B) both mean "to put forward, to aid the growth of." In the context of a business plan, the pair doesn't fit the sense. *Upgrade* (choice D) means "to improve," and *endorse* (choice E) means "to approve." These answer choices are not synonyms, and neither are synonyms of the other words in the list.

11. **The correct answers are C and E.** Although you may be confused because the answer choices contain three synonyms—*innovative, unusual,* and *cutting-edge* (choices C, D, and E)—you can eliminate choice D because the characteristic of being unusual is not as strong as being either *innovative* or *cutting edge. Far-reaching* (choice A) and *wide-ranging* (choice B) are synonyms, but the implication from the first part of the sentence is that NASA conducted research related to the space program, so it wasn't doing research over a wide number of fields of study. You can eliminate *conventional* (choice F) because NASA, by the nature of its program, wouldn't be conducting conventional research.

12. **The correct answer is B.** Choice B most closely describes what the author implies: modern readers are not used to figurative language and could have a difficult time making sense of Dickinson's work, though the author suggests they would "do well" to develop the skill. Choice A is incorrect because the author doesn't suggest that modern readers should not look for literal meaning in Dickinson's work, just that it might be a little difficult to do so. The author would likely agree with choice C, but it doesn't reflect the last statement in the passage. Choice D contradicts what the author is implying in the last sentence. Choice E doesn't relate to anything in the passage.

Section 3: Verbal Reasoning

1. C	4. B	7. B, C	10. B, E	13. B
2. A, E	5. C	8. E	11. C, D	14. C
3. B, E, G	6. A	9. E	12. B, D	15. B

1. **The correct answer is C.** The clue to the correct answer is the phrase "hard sell"; the context of the sentence indicates that you need to find the word that means something like "carefully" or "thoughtfully." *Judiciously* means "showing good judgment, being prudent" and matches the sense.

2. **The correct answers are A and E.** Answer Blank (i): *Honor* means "respect, distinction, privilege" and fits the sense of the sentence. *Admiration* (choice B) means "a feeling of pleasure or approval" but doesn't fit in the sentence because the context usually references the source of the admiration, as in something like "towns wanted the admiration of other cities for hosting a college." In this context, however, the use of *admiration* would suggest that the college admires the town, which makes no sense. Choice C is incorrect because none of the many meanings of *character* fits the sense.

   Answer Blank (ii): *Outstripped* means "surpassed, grew greater or faster, and left behind," which fits the sense. Choices D and F are incorrect because a discussion of supply and demand requires a quantitative response, and neither *outperformed* nor *outshone* applies to a quantifiable amount.

3. **The correct answers are B, E, and G.** Answer Blank (i): The sentence indicates that the queen might be forced to give up her position to her son because of her health, so it makes sense that her health is in poor condition. *Feeble* means "poor." *Robust* (choice A) is the opposite of *feeble. Cautionary* (choice C) means "warning" and does not make sense in this context.

   Answer Blank (ii): To take on the role of king is to assume it, so choice E is the best answer.

   Answer Blank (iii): To abdicate a throne is to give it up, which is possibly what the queen will have to do because of her health. *Nullify* (choice H) means "abolish," and it is unlikely she would do away with the throne completely because she was no longer fit to occupy it. *Arbitrate* (choice I) means "judge," which does not make sense.

4. **The correct answer is B.** Choices A, C, D, and E are all mentioned in the passage as factors that are delaying progress toward clean water goals. The passage mentions that not enough skilled labor is available, not that there is a problem in managing skilled labor. Remember, for "NOT" questions, you're looking for the answer choice that *doesn't* fit.

5. **The correct answer is C.** This information, while important, is not a supporting detail; it's a main idea and the topic sentence of the second paragraph. Choices A and B are both important points that support the topic sentence of the first paragraph: access to clean water and sanitation are crucial global goals.

6. **The correct answer is A.** The author's argument is that during the time of rationing, people who wouldn't ordinarily have broken the law did so because they were frustrated at not being able to have the goods they believed they deserved. The author never states choice B in the passage. Choice C restates the facts of what happened, but it doesn't address the author's argument of why it happened. Choice D might seem to be true, but it is not as close a reading of the author's argument as choice A. Choice E might be true, but this is a conclusion based on the facts, and the author never draws this conclusion in the passage.

7. **The correct answers are B and C.** If most Americans are law abiding and would not break the law under any circumstances, then the black market would not exist. Therefore, choice B would weaken the author's argument because most Americans

would not participate in the black market under any circumstances. Furthermore, if most Americans patronized the black market after rationing ended (choice C), that would weaken the argument that Americans only did it as a direct response to rationing. Choice A, by contrast, would strengthen the author's argument.

8. **The correct answer is E.** The author includes the list of countries and continents in lines 3–4 only to indicate the governments that have taken initiatives to conserve energy by passing legislation to regulate or eliminate the sale of incandescent and halogen light bulbs. Choice A is not a strong answer because there is no indication that these places were more affected by lighting inefficiency than others. Choices B and C both imply that most countries do not take lighting inefficiency seriously enough and are incorrect. The list of places does not indicate whether the legislation has been effective, so choice D does not make much sense.

9. **The correct answer is E.** The word *mandatory* means about the same as *obligatory*, meaning "compulsory or required." *Discretionary* (choice D) means "optional," which is the opposite in meaning of the word *mandatory*. All the other options do not fit the context.

10. **The correct answers are B and E.** *Mimic* and *imitate* are synonyms that mean "to copy, to resemble." The words *epitomize* and *typify* (choices A and D) are a synonym pair, meaning "to be a typical example of"—this is not exactly the same as imitating, which better fits the sense. Neither *illustrate* (choice C) nor *reflect* (choice F) have a matching synonym in the set; therefore, neither can be correct.

11. **The correct answers are C and D.** The phrase "forever change" in the second part of the sentence is the clue that identifies *revolutionary* and *transformative* as the words that best fit in the blank, since they both indicate radical change. *Modernization* (choice A) is also a form of change, but it doesn't fit the context. *Reforming* (choice B) may seem correct because it means "to change for the better," but it doesn't have the connotation of radical change that is implied in the sentence. *Huge* (choice E) is a vague word that doesn't indicate the nature of the change. *Corrective* (choice F) implies that something was wrong and needed to be fixed, and that's not implied in the passage.

12. **The correct answers are B and D.** The sentence draws a distinction between the underdone and overcooked dishes served during the feast and the soup. Since dishes that are underdone and overcooked are likely to be unpleasant or difficult to eat, the correct answers should suggest food that is pleasant and easy to eat. *Palatable* and *appetizing* both mean "easy and pleasant to eat." None of the other words could be used to describe a soup that is pleasant to eat.

13. **The correct answer is B.** The author suggests at the end of the passage that the answer is not simple, but that we should ask ourselves questions that could help us make the decision. Choice A seems like the correct choice, but it is much vaguer than choice B. Choices C and E are incorrect because according to the author there are more than just these factors we should consider. Choice D is incorrect because this statement is neither stated nor implied in the passage.

14. **The correct answer is C.** Distance is clearly stated in the passage as one of the things to consider when deciding whether to buy organic or local food (assuming they are not one and the same). Choice A might seem correct, but it is possible to buy organic and local food at big chain supermarkets; therefore, this statement isn't entirely supported by the passage. Choice B makes an assumption that is not necessarily true and is never addressed in the passage. Choices D and E may be partially correct, but neither is supported by the passage as a whole.

15. **The correct answer is B.** The parenthetical clause defines the term *food miles*, and this is its only function in the sentence. The discussion of food miles is one piece of evidence used to support buying locally grown food (choice A), but that's not the function of the definitional clause. Choice C is incorrect for the same reason.

Section 4: Quantitative Reasoning

1. A	4. B	7. D	9. E	11. A, C, D, H
2. C	5. B	8. B, D, G	10. B	12. A
3. C	6. B			

1. **The correct answer is A.**

$$6\frac{7}{8}=6.875$$
$$3.42(2)=6.84$$

Quantity A is greater.

2. **The correct answer is C.** A median of a triangle (or a line through one corner of a triangle and the midpoint of the opposite side) divides the area of the triangle in half. Since *BC* bisects *AD*, it is a median of triangle *ACD*, and so triangle *CED* and triangle *AEC* have equal area.

Alternatively, draw horizontal and vertical lines through point *E* to divide *ABDC* into eight triangles of equal area. Since triangle *CED* and triangle *AEC* each comprise two such triangles, their areas are equal.

3. **The correct answer is C.** Angles in the corners of rectangles are equal to 90°, so any two added together will equal 180°. Angles formed by the bisection of a line by another line equal 180°, so Quantity A is equal to Quantity B.

4. **The correct answer is B.** Since y is less than x, which is less than 0, when we take the absolute values of x and y, y will always be greater than x. Quantity B is greater.

5. **The correct answer is B.** Expanding $(a + b)^2$ yields $a^2 + ab + b^2$, which is greater than $a^2 + b^2$ if ab is positive and less than $a^2 + b^2$ if ab is negative. Since a is positive and b is negative, ab is negative, so Quantity B is greater.

6. **The correct answer is B.** 30% of \$6.99 is \$6.99(0.30) = \$2.10. The customer saves \$2.10(2.5) = \$5.25 this week.

7. **The correct answer is D.** Three of the die's six sides feature odd numbers, so the probability that any given roll will produce an odd number is $\frac{3}{6}$ or $\frac{1}{2}$. Each roll of the die is independent of the others, so the probability that each of the three rolls will produce an odd number is $\frac{1}{2}\times\frac{1}{2}\times\frac{1}{2}$ or $\frac{1}{8}$.

8. **The correct answers are B, D, and G.** You can find the next number by adding the last two numbers in the sequence.

$$5+9=13$$
$$8+13=21$$
$$13+21=34$$

9. **The correct answer is E.** To find the position of the particle at time $t = 2$, evaluate the function $s(t) = 8t^2(t + 1)$ for $s(2)$:

$$\begin{aligned} s(2) &= 8(2)^2(2+1) \\ &= 8(4)(3) \\ &= 96 \end{aligned}$$

10. **The correct answer is B.**

$$90=55+x$$
$$35=x$$

11. **The correct answers are A, C, D, and H.** The prime factorization of 1,200 is $2 \times 2 \times 2 \times 2 \times 3 \times 5 \times 5$. Any portion of this product produces a factor of 1,200. The following are all factors of 1,200:

$$8=2\times2\times2$$
$$15=3\times5$$
$$75=3\times5\times5$$
$$300=2\times2\times3\times5\times5$$

The other choices are not products of only the prime factors of 1,200, so they are not factors of 1,200.

12. **The correct answer is A.** Factor $pq + p$ and $pq + 2p$:

$$pq + p = p(q+1)$$
$$pq + 2p = p(q+2)$$

Since $q + 1$ and $q + 2$ differ by 1, they have no common factors greater than 1. Thus, the greatest common factor of $p(q + 1)$ and $p(q + 2)$ is p.

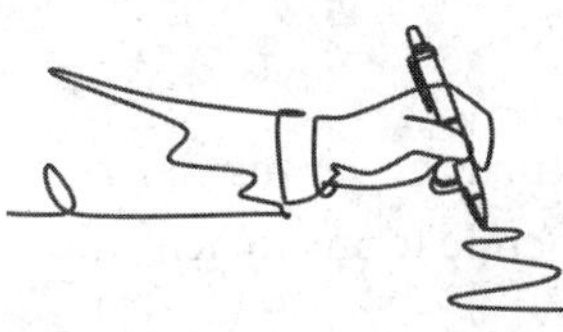

NOTES

Section 5: Quantitative Reasoning

1. A	4. B	7. A	10. C	13. C
2. A	5. C	8. D	11. D	14. C, D, E
3. B	6. D	9. D	12. D	15. $\frac{2}{5}$

1. **The correct answer is A.**

$$(2.7)(0.3) = 0.81 = \frac{81}{100}$$

$$\frac{81}{100} > \frac{80}{100} = \frac{4}{5}$$

Thus, Quantity A is greater.

2. **The correct answer is A.** Raising a number between 0 and 1 to a positive integer power results in a smaller number. For instance, $\left(\frac{1}{2}\right)^2 = \frac{1}{4}$ and $\left(\frac{1}{2}\right)^3 = \frac{1}{8}$. So Quantity A is greater.

3. **The correct answer is B.** Working backwards from Joe's age, we find that Stephen's age is $\frac{3}{4}(16) = 12$, and Mary's age is 12 + 6 = 18. Because Mary is the oldest, she will have a birth year that is less than either Joe's or Stephen's.

4. **The correct answer is B.** Evaluate Quantity A: 3(5) + 2(2) + 3 = 15 + 4 + 3 = 22. Therefore, Quantity B is greater.

5. **The correct answer is C.** Vertical angles are congruent, so $x = 148$. Since l and m are parallel, corresponding angles are congruent. Therefore, y is also 148.

6. **The correct answer is D.** We do not know whether x and y are positive or negative. If $y = 12$, then $x = 4$. If $y = -12$, then $x = -4$. The relationship cannot be determined from the information given.

7. **The correct answer is A.** Evaluate the function:

$$f(x) = 5x^3 + 4x^2 + 8x + 1$$
$$f(2) = 5(8) + 4(4) + 8(2) + 1$$
$$f(2) = 40 + 16 + 16 + 1$$
$$f(2) = 73$$

8. **The correct answer is D.** Turn the verbose language into concise and concrete terms to help you solve this problem.

$$45(0.20) = 9$$
$$45 + 9 = 54$$

9. **The correct answer is D.** Using the information from the table, add the families having 0, 1, and 2 children:

$$19 + 36 + 15 = 70$$

10. **The correct answer is C.** Using the information from the table, there are 19 + 36 + 21 + 9 + 15 = 100 total families and there are 15 families with no children, so the percentage of families with no children is $\frac{15}{100} = 0.15$ or 15%.

11. **The correct answer is D.** There are 100 – 15 = 85 families with children. Of these, 21 + 9 = 30 have at least three children. Thus, if a family with children is chosen at random, the probability that the family has at least three children is $\frac{30}{85} = \frac{6}{17}$.

12. **The correct answer is D.** Since the lines are perpendicular, the product of their slopes must equal –1.

First, rewrite the given equation in slope-intercept form:

$$x + 2y = 5$$
$$2y = -x + 5$$
$$y = \frac{1}{2}x + \frac{5}{2}$$

The given equation's slope is $-\frac{1}{2}$, the coefficient of x. Therefore, the slope is 2.

13. **The correct answer is C.** The point at which the two lines intersect lies on the graph of both equations. Therefore, you have a system of two linear equations, and you're looking for the value of x in the solution to the system.

First, solve the second equation for y:

$$\begin{aligned} y-x&=2 \\ y&=x+2 \end{aligned}$$

Now substitute this expression of y into the first equation:

$$\begin{aligned} x+2y&=4 \\ x+2(x+2)&=4 \\ 3x&=0 \\ x&=0 \end{aligned}$$

14. **The correct answers are C, D, and E.** Let x be the length of side $\overline{AC}$. According to the triangle inequality, x is greater than (and not equal to) the positive difference of the lengths of the other two sides, and it is less than (and not equal to) the sum of the lengths of the other two sides:

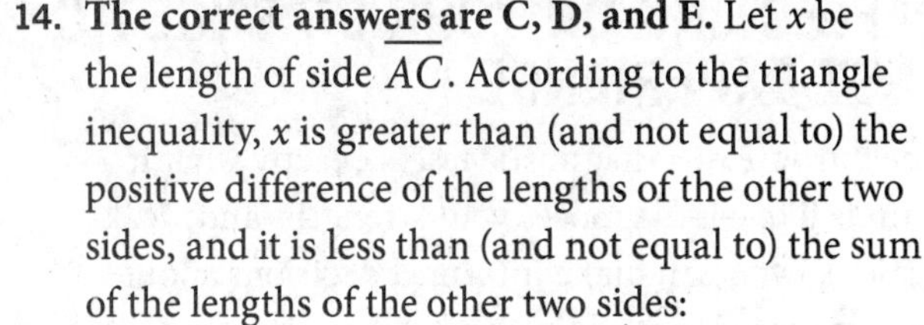

$$\begin{aligned} 8-4<x<8+4 \\ 4<x<12 \end{aligned}$$

15. **The correct answer is $\frac{2}{5}$.** The larger circle has radius 10 inches, so its circumference is $2\pi(10) = 20\pi$ inches. The smaller circle has diameter 8 inches, so its radius is 4 inches. So its circumference is $2\pi(4) = 8\pi$ inches. Therefore, the desired ratio is $\frac{8\pi}{20\pi}=\frac{2}{5}$.

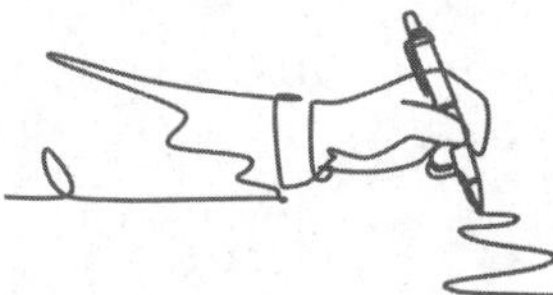

NOTES

REFLECTING ON YOUR DIAGNOSTIC TEST EXPERIENCE

The purpose of a diagnostic test is exactly what it sounds like—it diagnoses your strengths and weaknesses so you can make informed decisions about how you want to study going forward. This section is designed to help you reflect on your performance in the diagnostic test so you can make the most of your study time while preparing for the GRE General Test.

Before we break down how to make a study plan based on your performance in individual test sections, take a moment to reflect on your overall experience during your diagnostic test.

- What went well for you during the diagnostic test? Which categories were easiest for you?
- What did you struggle with during the diagnostic test? Which categories were hardest for you?
- After your experience, what are some things you want to keep in mind as you study?

Diagnostic Test Reflection: Overall	
Diagnostic Test Composite Score: ________	
Reflection Question	**Notes**
What went well for you during the diagnostic test, and which skills were easiest for you to use?	
What did you struggle with during the diagnostic test, or which skills were harder for you to use?	
After your experience, what are some things you might like to keep in mind as you study?	

Diagnostic Test Reflection: Overall (*Continued*)	
Reflection Question	**Notes**
What are some aspects of approaching the GRE for which you are most hoping to build strategies?	
What do you think are the 1–2 things you do best as a test taker?	
What 1–2 improvements could you make as a test taker that would help you most?	
Where did you run out of time? Conversely, where did you end up with extra time?	
Did you answer all the questions? If not, how many did you skip?	

Setting Study Goals

Now that you've reflected on your diagnostic test experience, think about your GRE goals. Are you looking to master a specific skill? Take the test by a specific date? Attain a minimum score, or strive for perfection? No matter what goals you have, it's important to keep them in mind as you study so that you can choose strategies and set up milestones that will help you achieve them. According to ETS research, most test takers prepare for one to three months before taking the GRE General Test. Allotting your time by determining how much time you'd like to spend and how to divide it is an important part of preparing. You'll also want to target your study by determining how much of your allotted time you'd like to dedicate to each subject you need to cover. Decisions regarding allotment and targeting will differ between test takers since everyone comes into the process with different capabilities and opportunities for improvement.

To narrow your study plan focus, look at your diagnostic test scores by category. The following assessment grid shows you exactly where you can find thorough coverage for each question type. Find the question numbers from the diagnostic test that gave you the most trouble and highlight or circle them below. The chapters with the most markings are your ideal starting points on your preparation journey.

Diagnostic Test Assessment Grid		
Section 1: Analytical Writing		
Question Type	**Questions**	**Chapter Reference**
Analyze an Issue	Essay	3
Section 2: Verbal Reasoning		
Question Type	**Questions**	**Chapter Reference**
Text Completion	1, 2, 3	5
Reading Comprehension		
• Analysis/Reasoning/Understanding	4, 6, 7	4
• Details/Main Ideas/Structure	5, 8, 12	4
• Vocabulary/Word Relationships	9	4
Sentence Equivalence	10, 11	6
Section 3: Verbal Reasoning		
Question Type	**Questions**	**Chapter Reference**
Text Completion	1, 2, 3	5
Reading Comprehension		
• Analysis/Reasoning/Understanding	4, 6, 7, 14	4
• Details/Main Ideas/Structure	5, 8, 13, 15	4
• Vocabulary/Word Relationships	9	4
Sentence Equivalence	10, 11, 12	6

Diagnostic Test Assessment Grid (*Continued*)		
Section 4: Quantitative Reasoning		
Question Type	**Questions**	**Chapter Reference**
Quantitative Comparison		
• Algebra	4, 5	9
• Arithmetic	1	9
• Geometry	2, 3	9
Problem-Solving		
• Algebra	9, 12	7, 8
• Arithmetic	6, 11	7, 8
• Data Analysis	7, 8	7, 8
• Geometry	10	7, 8
Section 5: Quantitative Reasoning		
Question Type	**Questions**	**Chapter Reference**
Quantitative Comparison		
• Algebra	2, 6	9
• Arithmetic	1, 3, 4	9
• Geometry	5	9
Problem-Solving		
• Algebra	7, 12, 13	7, 8
• Arithmetic	8	7, 8
• Data Analysis	9, 10, 11	7, 8
• Geometry	14, 15	7, 8

What question type gave you the most trouble?

- Analyze an Issue
- Text Completion
- Reading Comprehension—Analysis/Reasoning/Understanding
- Reading Comprehension—Details/Main Ideas/Structure
- Reading Comprehension—Vocabulary/Word Relationships
- Sentence Equivalence
- Quantitative Comparison—Algebra
- Quantitative Comparison—Arithmetic
- Quantitative Comparison—Geometry
- Problem-Solving—Algebra
- Problem-Solving—Arithmetic
- Problem-Solving—Data Analysis
- Problem-Solving—Geometry

Chapters to focus on first: ___________

Create an Informed Study Schedule

Having analyzed your diagnostic test results, you are now ready to create a study plan. When creating a study plan, your first order of business should be to determine how much time you have to devote to preparation. Figure out how much time you are able to dedicate to preparation and set a reasonable goal for how much studying you would like to do in that time. Then, divide the amount of preparation time you have according to your study priorities.

There are lots of ways to divide your time—the important thing is to consider how much total time you have, make a schedule, and stick to it. Creating a specific study calendar helps remind you that organized studying correlates with a better chance of meeting your score goals. Remember to include variety in your plan (so you don't get too bored with one subject or forget things you study early on) and ample chances to review skills you practiced earlier. Learning is largely about repetition, so you want to give yourself multiple opportunities to review information.

Take a moment to ask yourself the following questions. Then, come up with a study plan that works for you and your goals.

- How much total time can I commit to studying for the GRE?
- How do I want to divide that study time, based on my diagnostic performance?
- What are some of the most important skills I want to work on overall?
- What are some of the most important skills I want to work on for each section?
- When would it be most useful for me to take the practice test(s), given my study style?

Once you have a study plan in place, you are ready to consider how to make the most of your study time.

Consider Your Environment

How and where you prep for your test matters. Creating optimum study conditions will help keep you focused and motivated. How you do so is largely dictated by what has worked for you in the past as well as your current schedule and obligations, but establishing an ideal environment is a key to a successful study session.

As a graduate school candidate, you are no stranger to studying, but it's always a good idea to consider a few factors when you're designing your perfect study environment.

Physical Factors

- **Keep distractions to a minimum.** Your study space should be free of anything that will distract you from the task at hand. This means that cell phones, tablets, and other items that make it difficult to focus should be kept elsewhere.
- **Get comfortable—but not too comfortable.** Your study space should be comfortable enough that you can relax and focus on practice and review, but not so comfortable that you find yourself napping whenever you sit down to study. A good chair and uncluttered desk with the right level of light to keep you engaged are often a better choice than lying down in bed or cozying up on the couch.
- **Gather your tools.** Make sure you have your most effective study tools at hand in your workspace, including this book, paper and pens/pencils, a calculator, a highlighter, and a watch or clock if you're taking a timed practice test. Staying organized will help keep you focused, serious, and motivated.
- **Find a location that works for you.** Do you prepare better alone in your room or in a bustling coffee shop or library? A bit of background noise can be helpful to some and distracting to others. This choice is up to you and should be based on what has worked for you in the past.

Study Style and Preferences

- **Find your ideal time of day.** The time of day during which you study best is an important part of your study environment. If possible, schedule your study sessions at the time of day that matches what naturally works best for you.
- **Pay attention to your mental environment.** Just as important as having the perfect physical study environment is having the right mindset during each study session. Try to leave external worries, stressors, or anxieties outside of your GRE prep since they will only drain your energy and focus. Take a few minutes before each study session to relax, breathe, and clear your mind and thoughts. Sometimes just a minute or two is enough and can make a big difference. When your mind is clear and free from distractions, you'll be much more likely to devote yourself to effective test preparation. Remember that you can also schedule rest days into your study calendar to give your brain time to recharge as necessary.

General Study Strategies

Once you've made a schedule and set your environment, there are some general study strategies that can help you make the most of your prep time.

Don't wait until the last minute—start early! It takes time to move things you review into long-term memory, and the more time you give yourself to learn and review different concepts, the better you'll be able to recall them on test day. Don't cram all your studying into the last minute; instead, come up with a reasonable study calendar early in your test prep process and stick to it.

Spread out your study sessions over time. Few people are served better by a multi-hour cram session than they are by several shorter study sessions spread out over time. Your brain needs time to process what it's learned and then to recall it later, so spreading your studying out across multiple sessions is the best way to allow this to happen.

Study regularly. People need to periodically return to information to ensure that it sticks around in memory, so studying new materials demands that learners complete a periodic review of what they've already learned. Studying regularly leading up to the date of an assessment is the best way to do this and is far more effective than cramming, which offers few opportunities to recall information learned earlier.

Study intensely rather than passively. There is a documented relationship between stress and performance. Low stress situations tend to result in lower performance. High stress situations do the same. But there's a sweet spot where just the right amount of pressure and intensity can improve performance on tasks, especially when learning. For studying, this means that you are far better served by short, intense intervals of studying. Languidly skimming over notes for hours on end will do significantly less than an hour of active retrieval combined with paraphrasing, timed practice questions, or intentional mind mapping. Studying is a question of efficiency, and the most efficient and effective way to study usually involves real effort.

Develop active learning practices. Active learning involves planning, monitoring, and reflecting on your learning process. Here are some tips for active learning:

- Plan out your work time
- Read strategically
- Take some form of notes
- Regularly self-assess
- Spread out your study time
- Keep a regular schedule
- Create something while studying
- Use metacognitive techniques (such as reflective questions) to think about what you've learned so far and how you learned it

Eliminate distractions. Humans can multitask, just not well. Divided attention is often the weakest form of focus. To truly concentrate on a task, you need to isolate what you're learning from other distractions. This ensures proper registration of the information. For many people, language, like song lyrics or background TV noise, is a significant distractor. If your brain struggles to filter out these voices, find a quiet environment and place your phone out of sight. Remember, you don't need to do this for long periods; shorter, intense study sessions (around an hour) are more productive than spending an entire afternoon studying.

Encode new information meaningfully. Whenever we talk about memory, we're talking about a process called encoding, wherein information moves from your senses to be stored for later use. There are any number of tricks and tips for getting information to stick around, but one of the most effective ways is what's called elaborative encoding. When you make information meaningful by connecting it to your own life and interests, the brain more easily stores that information for later use. For example, if you practice a new math concept by thinking about a real-life situation in which you are likely to need it, you are more likely to retain the concept for later retrieval because you've encoded it in a way that holds meaning for you.

Divide tasks and information into chunks. This technique is beneficial for everyone, particularly those with focus issues. Break down topics into smaller, manageable chunks of information rather than tackling larger blocks all at once. Some resources (like this book) may have organizational structures that don't align perfectly with your learning objectives. If a chapter covers too much material or doesn't meet your specific needs, concentrate on individual sections, charts, or exercises. Employ different study strategies for each chunk of information to avoid feeling overwhelmed. Rearrange your notes and study materials based on your own perceived relationships rather than strictly following the resource's structure. Determine what you can realistically cover in a study session and focus solely on that.

Vary topics and weave them together as you learn. Alternate between topics while studying instead of focusing on one at a time. This applies to reviewing and self-quizzing in your notes, as well as practicing questions. When you encounter various types of questions in a sequence (such as simple examples, multiplication, division, addition, and subtraction), you engage different information and strategies, enhancing connections between topics and processes. This interplay improves overall learning. Additionally, explore connections between different fields of study. Consider, for instance, how practicing quantitative skills aids in answering reading questions that involve understanding quantitative data. Reflecting on these connections as you study reinforces concepts in your mind.

Create new materials as you study. To retain and understand information, you need to recall and process as well as apply topics and concepts. Learning about something isn't enough—you need exposure in different forms and in different ways. That usually means doing something with the information you're trying to learn. Often, practice tests are one of the best ways to study, but mixing your methods before you get to the practice test can have positive results. You can do this in the following ways:

- Creating something using the new information, such as forming your own example questions or creating your own mini practice tests
- Developing a visual aid that helps you make sense of new information
- Using different modes (auditory, visual, physical) to study
- Seeking outside sources to expand your research and understanding
- Creating materials that help you engage in repetitive learning (such as flashcards)

Regularly assess your retention and understanding. In this book, we've included Practice Questions sections at the end of the strategies chapters. These sections are designed to assist you with assessing your retention and understanding of the skills assessed on the GRE, but there are lots of other ways to do this as well. Periodically check in with yourself and look for ways to test or elaborate on what you've studied so far. Then, reflect on which skills you've developed well, and which may still need some improvement.

At the end of each study session, review and summarize what you learned. This is yet another form of metacognition that helps you make the most of your study time. By reflecting on what you learned and summarizing new information, you are encoding that new information to give you a better chance of recalling it later. If you can't summarize a concept that you've just learned, then it's a good indicator that you should devote more time to it during a future study session.

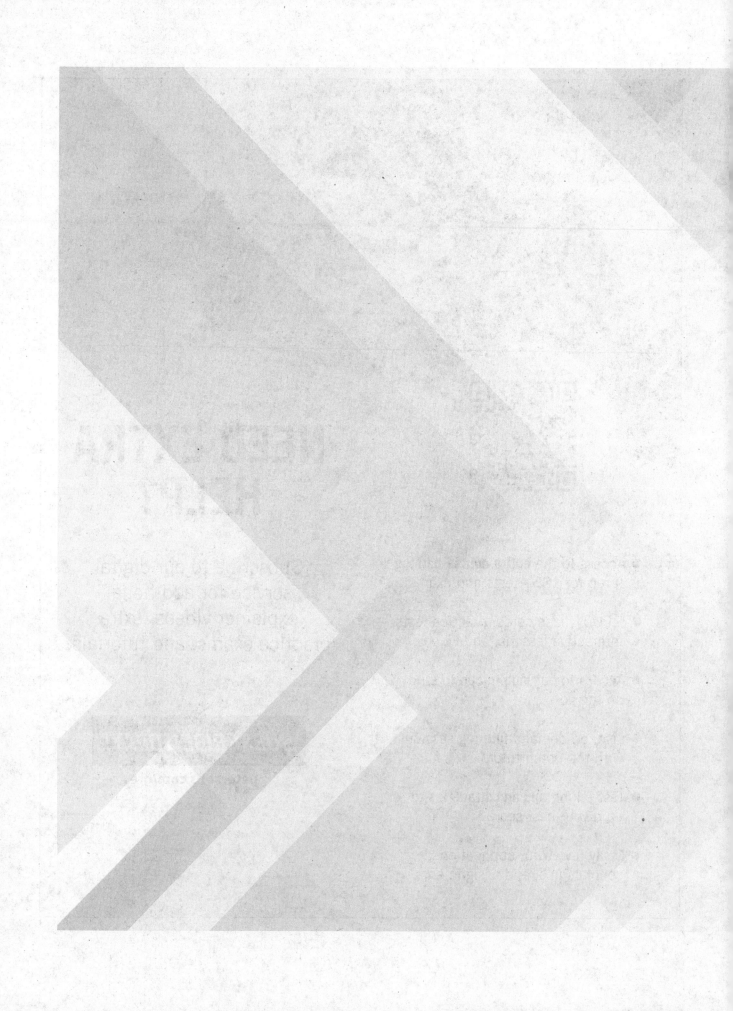

PART II

ANALYTICAL WRITING

CHAPTER

Analytical Writing

ANALYTICAL WRITING

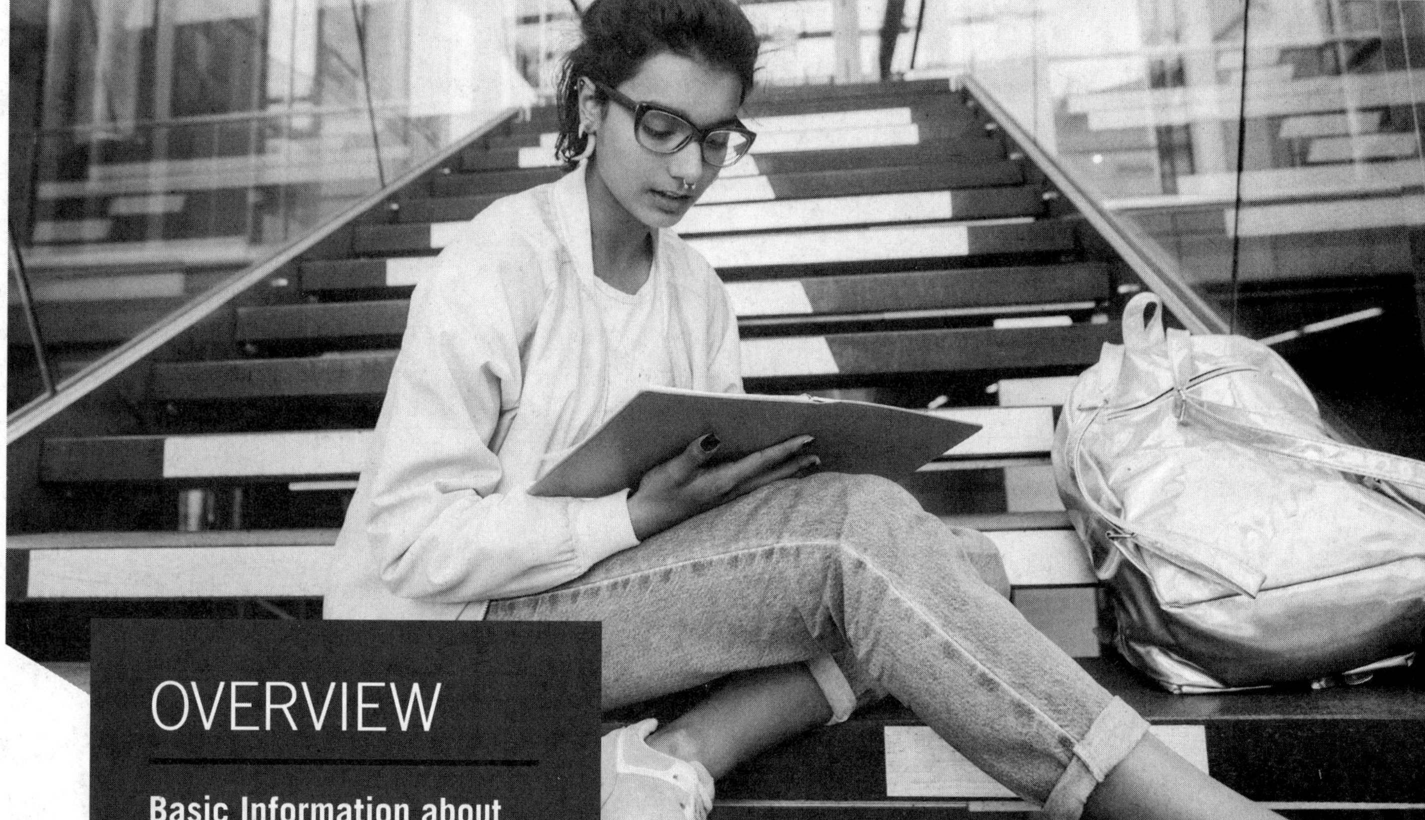

OVERVIEW

The Analytical Writing section of the GRE General Test measures both your ability to think and your ability to write in response to a given prompt. This section assesses how well you can develop and support your own position on a particular issue through the Analyze an Issue task. You are given a single prompt that offers a specific opinion on a topic, sometimes polemic (meaning, subject to dispute or debate) in nature.

To respond to this issue, you'll need to take a position—either agreeing or disagreeing with it—and then defend your position with evidence. As part of that defense, you may be required to counter or account for potential arguments that others might present.

The issue prompt presents you with a brief statement of a general issue and sets the conditions under which you can respond to it. You may agree or disagree with the statement, but you must discuss certain aspects of the issue based on the accompanying instructions. The issue will be one to which anyone can respond, such as whether or not educators or governments should undertake certain actions. The instructions that accompany your prompt will contain important information on how to interact with and respond to the issue.

BASIC INFORMATION ABOUT THE ANALYTICAL WRITING SECTION

The Analytical Writing section is always first in any administration of the GRE General Test. Reviewing the basics of the section in advance, as well as the general organization and development of a response, will help your confidence and your score.

The Prompt

The section presents you with one issue that you may agree or disagree with, but you must do one or the other. While you can make some qualifications for your stance, it is advisable that you pick one side or another rather than taking a neutral stance, as doing so can water down your argument. Remember, the reader will not know your personal thoughts on the issue, so it's okay to choose whichever stance you think will be easiest to argue in writing—it doesn't have to reflect your personal beliefs. The purpose of the section is to measure how well you can stake out a position and develop your reasoning to support it, so choose the stance that will best demonstrate your rhetorical skills.

Typically, the section's statement is quite short. It is usually stated in a single sentence, and it's always of a general nature that anyone could respond to. No special knowledge is required. The Analyze an Issue task is designed to relate to a broad range of topics that can be applied to various situations and allow for different perspectives from the writers.

Below the prompt, you will find instructions that set the conditions for your response. They usually begin with the words "Write a response." The instructions will ask you to (1) take a position, qualifying it, as you want to or need to, by extent or degree; and (2) explain and support your position. The prompt may also ask you to explain your position in relation to one of the following:

- Conditions/circumstances under which the statement of your position might not be true
- Circumstances when the recommendation would not have the intended results
- Likely and major challenges to your position
- Views both for and against your position
- The reasoning on which the claim is based
- The possible consequences of taking action based on your position

The actual wording of the sets of instructions will be somewhat like the following:

- Discuss how much you agree or disagree with the statement, and consider how the statement might or might not always be true and how these considerations affect your point of view.
- Discuss how much you agree or disagree with the recommendation and why. Using specific examples, explain how the circumstances under which the recommendation could be adopted would or would not be advantageous. In developing and supporting your viewpoint, explain how these specific circumstances affect your point of view.
- Discuss how much you agree or disagree with the claim, and include the most compelling reasons and/or examples that someone could use to dispute your point of view.
- While addressing both viewpoints provided, discuss which more closely aligns with your own. Explain your reasoning for holding this position in developing and providing evidence for your response.

- Discuss how much you agree or disagree with the claim and the reasoning used to support that claim.
- Discuss your viewpoint on the proposed policy and the reasons for your point of view. Take into consideration the potential consequences of implementing the policy and the extent to which these consequences influence your viewpoint in developing and supporting your response.

When composing your response, you must take care to focus on the specific requirements in the instructions. You could present a well-reasoned and well-supported position, but if you fail to present views both for and against your position as the prompt asks, you won't earn a high score.

Time Limit and Software

The Analytical Writing section has a time limit of **30 minutes**. This is the same for both the computer- and paper-delivered versions.

The word processing program on the computer-delivered version allows the test taker to use basic functions like cutting and pasting text and undoing actions. A spellchecker and grammar checker are not included. Similarly, those taking the paper-delivered version will not have access to dictionaries or grammar handbooks during the test.

Scoring

The Analytical Writing section has its own rubric. You'll work through this rubric later in this chapter. The section is scored on a scale from 0 to 6. This is the raw score that is reported to graduate schools.

UNDERSTANDING THE SCORING RUBRIC

Your analytical writing section response will be scored on a 6-point scale by two readers. The scale ranges in 1-point increments from 6 to 0. The official ETS rubric can be found at **https://www.ets.org/gre/test-takers/general-test/prepare/content/analytical-writing/scoring.html**. The following table summarizes the rubric.

ANALYTICAL WRITING SCORING RUBRIC SUMMARY

Score Level	Description	Characteristics of a Typical Response
6 Outstanding	A sustained, insightful, organized, detailed analysis of well-developed, complex ideas supported by meaningful evidence and highly persuasive support. Utilizes a wide range of vocabulary and rhetorical methods while demonstrating a superior understanding of the conventions of Standard Written English. Very minor errors may be present but do not impact meaning.	• Presents a distinct and perceptive viewpoint regarding the issue as outlined in the given instructions • Expands meaningfully on the viewpoint with convincing rationales and/or compelling examples • Maintains focus, organization, and clarity while establishing meaningful connections between concepts • Seamlessly and accurately moves between concepts using a range of transitions, word choices, and sentence structures • Exhibits exceptional proficiency with the norms of Standard Written English, even if very minor errors are present

ANALYTICAL WRITING SCORING RUBRIC SUMMARY (*CONTINUED*)		
Score Level	**Description**	**Characteristics of a Typical Response**
5 Strong	A thoughtful, generally organized, and focused analysis of nuanced ideas supported by sound reasoning and meaningful examples. Uses a range of rhetorical skills and conventions to demonstrate meaningful control of the conventions of Standard Written English. Minor errors may be present but do not impact meaning.	• Presents a lucid and carefully considered viewpoint regarding the issue as outlined in the given instructions • Elaborates on the viewpoint with logically coherent rationales and/or well-chosen examples • Maintains focus and exhibits general organization, establishing suitable connections between ideas • Communicates ideas clearly and effectively, employing fitting vocabulary and varying sentence structures • Exhibits proficiency with the norms of Standard Written English, though occasional minor errors may be present
4 Adequate	A competent, considered analysis of meaningful ideas that ventures a main point and supports it with relevant evidence or reasoning. Ideas are organized in a satisfactory manner, clearly conveyed, and supported by adequate control of rhetorical skills and the conventions of Standard Written English. May have some minor errors that impact clarity of meaning.	• Presents a clear viewpoint regarding the issue as outlined in the given instructions • Develops the viewpoint with relevant reasoning and/or examples • Maintains adequate focus and organization • Demonstrates satisfactory command of language to articulate ideas with acceptable clarity • Exhibits general understanding of the norms of Standard Written English, albeit with occasional errors
3 Limited	A somewhat competent analysis that addresses specific required tasks and makes some effort to address main points. Rhetorical skills may be lacking or underdeveloped, and writing may be limited by weak structure, poor organization, or underdevelopment of ideas. Contains some errors that limit clarity of meaning and/or contribute to vagueness.	Exhibits **one or more** of the following concerns: • Shows vagueness or inadequacy in addressing the given instructions, presenting or developing a viewpoint, or both • Demonstrates weakness in employing relevant examples or rationales, or leans heavily on unsupported assertions • Exhibits limited focus and/or organization • Includes issues in language or sentence structure, contributing to lack of clarity • Contains either occasional major errors or frequent minor errors in grammar, usage, and/or mechanics of Standard Written English, impeding comprehension

(continues)

ANALYTICAL WRITING SCORING RUBRIC SUMMARY (*CONTINUED*)		
Score Level	**Description**	**Characteristics of a Typical Response**
2 Seriously Flawed	A weak analysis that does not adequately address specific required tasks and/or that is underdeveloped, disorganized, or unclear. Frequent issues with rhetorical skills and/or the conventions of Standard Written English obfuscate meaning and limit clarity. Frequent errors make it difficult to parse.	Exhibits **one or more** of the following concerns: • Exhibits a lack of clarity or serious limitation in addressing the given instructions, developing a viewpoint on the issue, or both • Offers few, if any, relevant rationales or examples to support assertions • Lacks focus and/or organization • Includes serious issues in language or sentence structure, frequently obstructing clarity or contributing to outright confusion • Contains serious errors in grammar, usage, or mechanics that frequently obscure meaning
1 Fundamentally Deficient	A deficient analysis that contains fundamental errors and fails to communicate a meaningful main point. Content may be incomprehensible or extremely difficult to parse and/or may be irrelevant to the task at hand. Frequent and pervasive errors render the analysis incomprehensible or incoherent.	Exhibits **one or more** of the following concerns: • Demonstrates little or no evidence of grasping the given instructions or the issue at hand • Shows minimal or no evidence of the ability to craft an organized response, often appearing disorganized and/or excessively concise • Suffers from severe issues in language and sentence structure, consistently hindering comprehension • Contains widespread errors in grammar, usage, and mechanics, leading to incoherence
0	An analysis that cannot be evaluated because it does not address any aspect of the specified task. It may copy parts of the prompt in lieu of developing concepts or may be written in a foreign language or otherwise incomprehensible.	Exhibits **one or more** of the following concerns: • Demonstrates zero awareness of the given instructions or the issue at hand • Fully off topic • Merely copies the topic • Incomprehensible • Written in a foreign language • Consists only of random keystrokes or nonsensical inputs
NS	Blank essays will receive a score of NS, meaning no score.	

FYI

If you are taking the computer-delivered test, your response may be scored by only one reader and then by *e-rater*, ETS's computerized program designed to identify essay components related to proficiency in writing. A second reader is used only if a large discrepancy exists between the scores given by the first reader and e-rater.

The following summaries indicate the basic characteristics of an essay at each scoring band.

6 Points

To earn 6 points, your response should have these characteristics:

- A clear, focused position on the issue and an overall response to the specific writing task that is thorough, cogent, and sophisticated
- Fully developed, persuasive support for the position, including but not limited to particularly apt or well-chosen examples, facts, and other illustrations, as well as any explanations that clearly and effectively link the support to the specific requirements of the writing task
- A rhetorically effective method of organization, such as one that organizes support by order of importance and saves the most effective reasons for last; connections between and among ideas are logical and may also be as subtle as they are effective
- A formal grace that is a product primarily of well-constructed, varied sentences and exact and rhetorically effective word choices
- Adherence to almost all the conventions of Standard Written English, including grammar, usage, and mechanics; errors, if any, should be minor

5 Points

To earn 5 points, your response will likely have these characteristics, though it may exceed one or more of them yet fall short on another:

- A clear, focused position on the issue and a thoughtful, complete response to the specific writing task
- Persuasive support for the position, including but not limited to examples, facts, and other illustrations, as well as explanations that clearly link the support to the specific requirements of the writing task
- An effective method of organization with logical connections between and among all ideas
- Well-constructed, varied sentences and appropriate word choices that help create clarity as well as interest
- Adherence to almost all the conventions of Standard Written English, including grammar, usage, and mechanics; errors, if any, should be minor

4 Points

To earn 4 points, your response will have these characteristics:

- A clear position on the issue and a generally complete response to the specific writing task
- Support for the position, as well as an explanation that links the support to the specific requirements of the writing task
- A logical method of organization

- Sentences and word choices that generally create clarity
- General adherence to the conventions of Standard Written English; some errors may occur

3 Points

Your response will earn only 3 points if it has *one or more* of the following characteristics:

- A generally clear position and a response to the specific writing task that may be limited in scope or marred by occasional vagueness, extraneous detail, repetition, or other flaws
- Limited or inadequate support for the position or a limited or inadequate explanation that links the support to the specific requirements of the writing task
- Lapses in organization or confusing organization, and/or lack or misuse of transitional words and phrases
- Sentences and word choices that occasionally interfere with clarity
- One or more errors in the conventions of Standard Written English that are so significant that they obstruct meaning

2 Points

Your response will earn only 2 points if it has *one or more* of the following characteristics:

- A wandering, unclear, or limited response characterized by an unclear or not fully articulated position and a response to the specific writing task that is limited or inadequate in scope or marred by vagueness, extraneous detail, repetition, or other flaws
- Inadequate support and explanation
- Confusing organization and/or general lack or misuse of transitional words and phrases
- Sentences and word choices that interfere with clarity
- Repeated errors in the conventions of Standard Written English that are so significant that they obstruct meaning

1 Point

Your response will earn only 1 point if it has *one or more* of the following characteristics:

- An unclear position and almost no response to, or minimal understanding of, the specific task
- A total lack of support or only illogical or flawed support for the main point or points; a total lack of explanation or only illogical or flawed explanation of the main points of your argument in relation to the specific details of the task
- No pattern of organization or confusing organization
- Sentences and word choices that interfere with clarity
- So many errors in the conventions of Standard Written English that they obstruct meaning throughout the response

0 Points

Your response will earn 0 points under the following circumstances:

- The response does not answer the task in any way.
- The response is written in a foreign language.
- The response simply copies the argument.
- The response is not legible.
- The response is nonverbal.

Looking at these criteria, you can infer that understanding the following four tasks or conditions is crucial if you wish to achieve a favorable score.

1. You must meet the requirements stated in the prompt completely.
2. You need a clear statement of your position; substantial, thoughtful support; and explanations that link your support to the specific task requirements.
3. You can make minor errors in grammar, usage, and mechanics without seriously jeopardizing your score, but remember that errors in these areas can affect the clarity of your writing, so be sloppy at your own peril.

4. The length of your response is not necessarily a deciding factor in your score, but completeness is. Don't assume that brevity is always a virtue. According to the rubric, you'll have to produce a response of sufficient length to support your position in adequate, if not dense, detail. Although there is no magic number for success, aim to make at least three points in favor of your position—and aim to elaborate them fully.

TIP

To keep your writing organized, consider a divided thesis in parallel structure. This looks something like stating your stance and two to four elements of your argument in the order you plan to present them. For example: "It is important for educators to consider the needs of students with disabilities because it contributes to more equitable outcomes, enriches the classroom environment, and builds trust between teachers and students." This type of thesis statement previews the order in which the argument will unfold, lending clarity.

DEVELOPING YOUR RESPONSE

In addition to keeping track of time—and using it wisely—there are some priorities that you can set and skills you can review and practice to help you write a successful response. Obviously, it takes time to develop superior writing skills that assure you a score of 6; however, staying focused on a few simple guidelines can add a point or more to your score. Think about putting these recommendations to work for you.

State a Thesis, and State It Early

Don't make your reader guess what side of the issue you're on. A thesis statement that makes your view on the issue unmistakable should appear somewhere in the first paragraph. Don't worry about being too obvious or even leading off with your thesis. If you're not sure where in the first paragraph to place it, the final line of the paragraph is always a good bet, since it sets up a transition to your first major point. Of course, you must be sure that the thesis is clear and that it adequately reflects the content that follows.

Use a Standard Pattern of Organization

ETS makes it clear that test takers don't necessarily need to employ a standard pattern of organization to succeed. But think critically about that advice—a lack

TIP

If you're taking the paper-delivered test and there is enough space on the sheets of paper, write on every other line. That will leave you space to insert additions and neatly make deletions. If your handwriting isn't legible, try printing, but practice ahead of time so that you can print quickly and legibly.

TIP

Using a standard pattern of organization has an added benefit. If you decide ahead of time how to set up your response, you can save time when faced with writing the actual response on test day.

of necessity for standardization does not necessarily mean that standard patterns of organization are a bad idea. In fact, standardizing how you organize your response will make it easier to stay on topic given the time restrictions of the task. A standard pattern of organization helps to lead your reader smoothly from point to point. In addition, such patterns help create fluency.

Order Paragraphs Effectively

Once you've got your overall structure, you'll need to figure out how to arrange your ideas within that structure so that your paragraphs flow in logical order. Possibly the best organizational model and one of the easiest to conceive on the fly during a timed essay involves arranging your topics by order of importance. For example, you could order the paragraphs in the body of your response from the least important reason to the most important reason. This technique often results in a strong or memorable ending. Alternatively, you could start with the most important reason and then introduce less important reasons as you move along. While this may not create as impactful a conclusion, it's a smart way to organize things if you're worried about running out of time, since it ensures that your main points are up front in the essay. As you work through practice essays, toy with different approaches to see which work for you.

In crafting your paragraphs, don't begin the first two body paragraphs with something like "The first reason in support of my thesis is" and "The second reason in support of my thesis is." Similarly, don't just end with a cliched "In conclusion" or "As I have said." Use meaningful transitional words and phrases that are tailored to the types of points you're making. They can provide a smooth link from one paragraph to another—and from one sentence to another—by identifying and emphasizing the relationships between ideas. In its analysis of the scoring of sample papers, as well as in its rubrics, ETS stresses the value of transitional words and phrases. In addition to helping you create coherence, transitions can help you vary the beginnings of your sentences. Well-crafted transitions can also make your writing stand out against the hundreds of more routine responses that a reader will encounter as they score essays.

Transitions

Review the following lists of transitional words and phrases, and use them as you practice writing responses to the tasks in the practice tests. The more you practice using these transitional words and phrases, the easier it will be to use them as you write the actual response on the GRE General Test.

Transitions That Introduce or Link Opinions and Reasons		
because	evidently	indeed
besides	for this reason	on the other hand
by comparison	furthermore	since
consequently	however	therefore
Transitions That Introduce or Link Examples		
for example	in this case	one type
for instance	in this situation	to illustrate this point
Transitions That Create Emphasis or Add Information		
after all	furthermore	more important
again	in addition	moreover
besides	indeed	similarly
certainly	in fact	what's more
Transitions That Introduce Opposing Views		
although this may be true	naturally	on the other hand
even though	nevertheless	undeniably
evidently	notwithstanding	unquestionably
it may be said	of course	without a doubt

Use a Standard Pattern of Paragraphing

To help you internalize how to structure an essay under timed conditions, try working with a traditional paragraph structure as you develop the paragraphs within the body of your response.

- **Topic sentence:** The topic sentence states the main idea of the paragraph. In the context of the Analytical Writing section, the topic sentence of each body paragraph can state a reason that supports your point of view or a likely challenge, or reason, against your point of view. For example, if you're arguing that it is, in fact, a reasonable policy to insist that visitors to the nation's museums in Washington, DC, pay an entrance fee, a topic sentence might suggest that by having to pay, people will place a greater value on their visit. If you are moving from one topic to another, you may need to include a transition in your topic sentence.
- **Support and development:** Once you've written the topic sentence for your paragraph, you have several choices for how to develop the rest of the paragraph. You can choose restriction (a qualification or other way of narrowing and focusing the topic sentence), explanation, and/or evidence. Your job in this part of the paragraph is to make your topic sentence convincing by developing it with supporting points. Generally, you'll want to make claims and then support them with evidence, examples, or reasoning. For example, if you were discussing paid entry to national museums in Washington, DC, you might talk about how families who traveled far to visit for a long weekend might not come if they had to pay for two adults and several children at three museums. You could emphasize the loss of firsthand access to our nation's history for those children and how seeing, for example, the original Constitution can foster patriotism. Try to make this part of your paragraph full and dense with detail. When you make a claim or assertion, try to include at least one sentence of support.
- **Final summary or clincher statement:** This last sentence is optional in body paragraphs, but can give a final rhetorical punch to the paragraph.

It can also help you transition from the topic at hand to the topic that follows. When concluding a paragraph, you could ask a rhetorical question or restate the idea of the paragraph in a fresh way. What you want is a way to give final emphasis to the idea developed in the paragraph. If you can't think of an original and effective clincher, don't add anything to the paragraph. Go on to the next paragraph, using a transition.

- If, however, this is the final paragraph in your response, search hard for a memorable final statement. You want to end your response in a way that gives closure to your thoughts and emphasizes your points. You could rephrase the thesis, summarize the main points, or direct the reader to a larger issue. The concluding paragraph should tie up all loose ends so that the reader doesn't finish with a sigh of "so what?" If you're rushed for time, even a single concluding sentence is better than no concluding paragraph at all.

Successful paragraphs can certainly deviate from this order. The important thing to keep in mind, however, is that paragraphs are themselves discrete units of discourse that require organization. It's not enough to organize the paragraphs of your essay logically. The sentences of each paragraph must be organized logically too.

Develop Each Paragraph Fully

A huge factor in the success or relative failure of your essay will be the kinds and amount of support you provide. Unless you are doing so to quickly tack a concluding sentence onto your essay at the last minute, never write a one-sentence paragraph. If you have two-sentence paragraphs, the chances are good that they need more substance. Of course, you can't just add words for the sake of adding words, nor should you repeat yourself. You will need more examples, illustrations, or other evidence, combined with explanations that relate them back to the topic sentence or thesis and connect them to the next ideas. If your paragraphs lack details, ask yourself if you can add any of the following:

- **Facts and sources:** Facts are always the best choice for support. Statistics are one kind of fact that lends credibility to an argument. You aren't expected to pull sophisticated facts and statistics out of the air on the GRE General Test. But you may know some general facts or statistical trends. Incorporate as many facts as you can, but make sure that your analysis and explanation take center stage. If you simply cite facts with no commentary of your own, it allows the reader less space to consider your argumentative skill.
- **Examples:** Multiple examples or illustrations of an idea will add substance and support to a position. Use examples generously to support your points; they are usually very effective appeals to

TIP

The overall structure of an essay is not dissimilar from the structure of a good paragraph. Use the first paragraph to introduce your topic, grab your reader's attention, and preview your argument with a thesis statement. Use the body paragraphs to present different aspects of your argument and provide meaningful supporting details and evidence. Use the final paragraph to restate your thesis statement in different words and "clinch" your argument with a meaningful final thought.

FYI

An overstuffed paragraph can be just as distracting as one that lacks sufficient detail. If you find a paragraph getting longer than about 10 sentences, it may be time to move to a new one. Moreover, if you have a significant shift in topic, approach, or perspective, that's generally a good time for a new paragraph. Aim to have your paragraphs each represent a complete thought.

reason. Ideally, you would want to have at least one significant example in each body paragraph. If you use multiple examples (and you should whenever possible), just make sure to adequately couch them within the scope of your own analysis. Your argumentative acumen is the focal point of your score. Use examples in service of your own thought; deploy them to demonstrate the strength of your stance.

- **Authoritative opinions or human interest:** You may not be able to call a quote to mind, yet you may recall a famous person's idea or point of view about your topic. For example, for a response on whether government should fund the arts, you might paraphrase the chair of the National Endowment for the Arts on the value of arts to the economy or a local restaurant owner on how much the theater down the street drives business to her establishment. Similarly, you could refer to a novel or artistic movement in support of an argument concerning more abstract concepts such as creativity or beauty. Note that sometimes these kinds of quotations or opinions might appeal more to emotion than to reason. In some cases, appeals to emotion are as effective as appeals to reason, but the latter often prove more potent.
- **Observations:** Your own firsthand observations about life can be useful evidence of a point of view. In fact, since you cannot use source material on the GRE General Test, this type of evidence can be quite useful, as it is available to you in abundance. In fact, on a timed essay, where the reader knows that you don't have access to research materials to support your point, observations are considered all the more valid as evidence. Observations may appeal to either reason or emotion.
- **An anecdote:** Occasionally, a brief story not only enlivens your writing but also adds evidence. Use an anecdote to illustrate some general truth such as how schools rely on parent volunteers. This is another technique that should be used sparingly—most likely just once in a response. Like observations, anecdotes may appeal to either reason or emotion; occasionally, they appeal to both. An additional benefit is their potential to grab the reader's attention. Remember that your audience may have read dozens of similar essays (if not more) in a single sitting. Anecdotes could help your response "pop" and stand out. That said, an overreliance on anecdotes can cause a response to be cloying, so deploy them judiciously.
- **Drawing from your strengths:** In most cases, you have a clear idea of what field you wish to pursue in graduate school. If possible, draw from your experience in your chosen field. For example, let's say that you are given a polemic quote that says, "Beauty is always less important than functionality." If you have a background in art, you might be able to draw from theories on aesthetics to support your stance on this issue. If you have worked in the biological sciences, you could perhaps turn to the evolutionary function of visual attraction in flowers.

These are just a few examples of how you could approach such an abstract topic. The point is that writing from your comfort zone often leads to greater confidence in what you say. While your reader will not know your own research background, you can still invoke a sense of authority if you draw from what you know best. There are cases where it could be hard to connect your background knowledge to a prompt. In these situations, it's best to avoid using examples that only tangentially connect to the prompt at hand. However, if you can organically introduce evidence from your own research, it often will be a great strength.

Take Care with Tone and Person

ETS makes no mention of tone in its scoring rubrics. Nevertheless, you should strive to sound reasonable. You may be forceful and impassioned at the same time, but don't cross the line into harangue or diatribe. The most successful arguments rely on valid reasoning and sophisticated support, both of which can be undercut by an overly strident voice. Consider the kind of tone that would be acceptable in an academic setting and try not to stray too far from it.

Similarly, ETS makes no mention of person. Because you are striving to sound academic, using the third person is your safest bet, but there may be times when you might want to, or should, incorporate the first person (*I, me, my, myself, mine*) in your essay. For instance, if you're incorporating an anecdote or personal observations, that's an acceptable time to shift to the first person perspective, particularly since these types of evidence are expected on timed essays. It's certainly better to say *I* or *me* than to try to maintain the third person by referring to yourself as "this writer" or in any other self-conscious way. That said, refer to yourself only as necessary and don't, for example, use obvious lead-ins such as "In my humble opinion." You also don't need to hedge assertions with statements like "I think that" or "I believe." The fact that you are the one writing the essay makes it clear that you are sharing your thoughts and beliefs, so assert them with confidence rather than hedging.

As Time Permits, Add Extras

Should you take time for style or craft? Yes, by all means, once you've got the substance of your ideas completely down on paper. (Of course, it's much easier for computer-delivered test takers to follow this advice than paper-delivered test takers.) Be sure, however, to view all the following as add-ons. You can have, for example, the most interesting and well-written introduction in the world and not do well on the task if you don't have time to develop the key points that support your opinion, or you don't have time to answer the task fully because you never deal with the key challenges to your position. Get to the most important parts first, then add flourishes to make your essay pop.

Interest-Grabbing Opening

If you have time, create an interesting lead by posing a question or offering a surprising or startling fact, or craft a formal introduction that establishes some background or context for your position. As a review of the sample essays from ETS shows, you can succeed without crafting a formal opening, but doing so can make your writing seem more polished if you have time for it.

TIP

If you think you might use the first person in your response, brush up on when to use *I* (subject) versus *me* (object) and when to use *myself* appropriately (either as a reflexive or intensive pronoun).

Apt Word Choice

As time permits, you should also review and revise your word choice:

- Avoid simple, overused words such as *very, really, good, bad, interesting, fun, great, awesome, incredible, and unbelievable.*
- Replace state of being verbs, such as *was* and *are*, with active verbs.
- Edit out clichés. (For example, don't begin an essay on dogs with "A dog is man's best friend.")
- Whenever you know a more precise, forceful, or connotatively rich word that will accurately convey your meaning, use it, BUT don't go for the big word just because it's big. No one needs to say *pulchritudinous* instead of *beautiful*.

Varied Sentence Structure

If you want a 6, you have to show some style by varying your sentences. There are many ways to do this:

- Intersperse an occasional short sentence in a paragraph of long sentences.
- Vary the types of your sentences by occasionally inserting a question where appropriate. (A word of caution: Avoid exclamatory sentences and exclamation points. These are almost never appropriate.)
- Vary your sentences by structure, using compound, complex, and simple sentences.
- Create sentence variation by beginning sentences in different ways; that is, make sure all sentences in a paragraph don't begin with "The" followed by the subject. Begin sentences with conjunctions, prepositions, and transitions.

A Final Word of Advice

Think of the organization for your response as the box that holds a product you're trying to sell. Although the box is necessary, chances are you won't sell that prouct —no matter how good it is—in a plain cardboard box. Instead, you'll need to package it in a way that commands attention. That's why you must also strive for qualities such as original and sophisticated word choice, sentence variation, and rhetorical devices in your essay. A plain essay is good enough for an average score, but ETS readers will not give a score of 5 or 6 to a plain cardboard box, metaphorically speaking.

CREATING YOUR WRITING PLAN

You'll have just 30 minutes to read and respond to the Analyze an Issue task prompt. But don't just read the prompt and start writing. You need a plan to attack the task, and that plan has three parts: prewriting, drafting, and proofreading. Of the 30 minutes, set aside 2 to 3 minutes at the end to review and proofread your response. The bulk of the 30 minutes—say, 23 minutes or so—should be spent in the actual writing of your response. The first 4 to 5 minutes should be spent in planning and prewriting.

Prewriting

The prewriting part of your writing plan has three steps that will help you focus on the task, gather your ideas, and plan the development of your response. Because your time is so short, you may be tempted to overlook prewriting. This is inadvisable for several reasons. First, with prewriting, you're testing your position to see if it will work; that is, in the few minutes you spend prewriting, you will be finding out whether you have good ideas or not. Completing this step gives you an opportunity to refine and add nuance to your ideas before you start writing. Second, organization is dependent on ideas. If you have a few ideas jotted down when you start to write, it will be much easier to order your ideas effectively. It's a trick that experienced writers use because it's much easier to start writing with a short list of ideas in front of you than no ideas at all.

TIP

Those taking the computer-delivered test will be given scrap paper for making notes, so if you're taking the computer version, consider jotting down the key requirements of the instructions. If you're taking the paper-delivered test, you may want to underline the key requirements.

Step 1: Restate the Prompt

Don't overlook this first step. Be sure the issue is clear to you by stating it in your own words.

Step 2: Think About Reasons on Both Sides of the Issue

Understanding and being able to develop both sides of the issue are necessary in crafting a successful response. There are two main reasons for this. First, you don't need—nor are you expected—to express your truest feelings. Instead, you need to choose the side of the issue for which you can present the most convincing, well-developed argument of your own. Second, to be successful with most variations of the prompt, you need to anticipate and refute the opposing point of view.

Step 3: Jot a Quick Write

A quick write can look like a mind map, an outline, a set of bullet points, or any other visual representation of the ideas you plan to discuss. Begin by briefly identifying your position on the issue and then listing reasons that support your position. Strive for the most persuasive reasons. Then, connect different pieces of support to the points you plan to make.

If the specific instructions ask for challenges, both sides of the issue, advantages or disadvantages, or other considerations related to the opposite viewpoint, list reasons that could be given to oppose your position.

The flow of ideas won't come in any particular order, so reread your quick writing and number the reasons in the order that you want to use them. You may also find that some ideas don't fit with the rest of your ideas, or that you have too many ideas, or some are weak. Don't be afraid to cross off those that don't fit or are less convincing so you can focus on those that will prove most fruitful.

Drafting

Because of your time limitation, you will likely be revising and drafting simultaneously. To get the most of your actual writing time, keep the following priorities in mind.

Answer the Task

Be sure that you answer the task. This may seem obvious, but in the hurry to write down your ideas, don't let your ideas take you on a tangent or protracted line of thinking that doesn't respond to the issue and the task. Even though you have a quick write to work from, new ideas will come as you write. Go back to the last few lines of the prompt to be sure you're not only agreeing or disagreeing with the issue, but also addressing both points of view, citing and refuting possible challenges, or doing whatever else the task specifically requires you to do.

Organize Your Response

The following pattern is a standard, or traditional, way to organize your overall response. It smoothly guides your reader through your response by eliminating confusion and guesswork. In addition, it helps to create fluency—or the illusion of it. If you're a writer who has trouble with organization, this pattern gives you a structure to develop your ideas around:

- **Opening paragraph:** Thesis or clear statement of your position
- **Body paragraph 1:** Reason 1 for your position, fully explained and supported
- **Body paragraph 2:** Reason 2 for your position, fully explained and supported
- **Body paragraph 3:** A statement of the most effective counterargument, an acknowledgment of its reasonableness, and your fully explained and supported response; or any other specific and developed point needed to address the writing task instructions
- **Closing paragraph:** Reason 3 (another key challenge or another main point) that directly responds to the specific writing instructions; support as needed; plus a detail, statement, question, or other device that delivers closure

Suppose you use this pattern of organization. How do you decide what reason to use first, second, and third? Often, the best way to organize points for an argument is by order of importance. You could choose your most significant reason to be first or last. If you use your most powerful—that is, strongest—support as the third and final point, your readers will take away from your response your most impressive piece of argument.

Provide Ample, Thoughtful, Well-Developed Support

Developing sufficient support is the key element for success in the analytical writing section. The most foolproof method of organization you can use in an issue essay is to begin with a clear statement of your opinion in your opening. Then, develop each well-chosen point of support paragraph by paragraph.

Link Ideas Clearly

Your organization doesn't have to be traditional or based in any way on typical instruction in college writing classes, but it does have to be logical and help to create overall coherence. Based on reviewing sample analyses, ETS values transitional words and phrases, so link paragraphs and ideas appropriately as you write. Also, don't overlook the value of a topic sentence in providing an organizational boost to your essay.

Consider Style

If you're aiming for a top score, vary your sentences and word choices. Rubric criteria specifically call for varied, well-constructed sentences; for this test, they are an important index of your sophistication as a writer. ETS readers are also looking for appropriateness, precision, and rhetorical effectiveness in word choice.

Proofreading

When you go back over your essay in the 2 or 3 minutes you may have remaining, keep the following priorities in mind, which are based on the scoring rubric:

- **Check your thesis:** Make sure you've stated it and that it's clear. Make sure it also adequately reflects the content of your essay.
- **Look for omitted words:** When you're writing in a hurry, it's easy to leave out words. One omitted word can, however, destroy the clarity of an entire sentence, and sentence clarity is an important rubric criterion.
- **Check for sentence faults:** At this stage, you want to make certain that you eliminate any ineffective fragments, run-on sentences, fused sentences, or comma splices. This is because poor grammar can obscure your meaning and bring down your score.
- **Don't spend much time on spelling or commas:** Keep in mind that the rubric doesn't mention spelling. Generally, if the reader can tell what word you were trying to spell, they will consider this a "minor error." Likewise, a missing comma here or there shouldn't affect your score unless the lack of it obscures meaning.

TIP

A run-on sentence consists of two independent clauses joined without punctuation; for example, *A run-on sentence looks like this it detracts from meaning.* Fix it by making the two clauses separate sentences, making one clause dependent on the other, using a semicolon, or adding a comma and a coordinating conjunction. See Appendix A for more on correcting sentences.

FYI

Make sure your thesis statement matches the essay you actually wrote! Most people start with the thesis statement and then develop their argument from there. However, many tend to warp or change their argument throughout the writing process. When proofreading, go back to your initial thesis statement and make sure it matches the essay you ended up with. If it doesn't, change the thesis to match what you did write.

If you need help reviewing some of the most important conventions of Standard Written English that are likely to come up when writing and proofing your essay, see Appendix A (page 346).

A FINAL NOTE OF CAUTION

ETS wants its computer-delivered test takers to know that their responses will be subject to analysis by software that searches for similarities to published information. It warns that it will "cancel" a score if it contains any unacknowledged use of sources. In addition, ETS will cancel a response if an essay or any part of it has been prepared by another person. Finally, a score will be canceled if it includes language that is "substantially" similar to the language in one or more other test responses. Be aware that any entity that claims to prewrite essays for memorization is also on ETS's radar. If readers suspect that you have memorized a prewritten essay, even one that you have adapted to your prompt, your essay may be flagged.

SUMMING IT UP

- The Analytical Writing section is always presented first in the administration of the GRE General Test. The time limit is **30 minutes**.
- The Analytical Writing section measures how well you can develop and support your own position on an issue through the **Analyze an Issue task**.
  - The Analyze an Issue task prompt will be accompanied by a set of instructions that establishes the conditions or requirements for the response.
  - Issues are general in nature, and no special knowledge is required to analyze and form an opinion.
- The Analyze an Issue task is scored against a rubric using a 0 to 6 range in 1-point increments. The Analytical Writing score is reported on a scale ranging from 0 to 6 in half-point increments.
- The Analytical Writing section uses specially designed word processing software that allows the user to insert and delete text, cut and paste text, and undo actions. There is no spelling or grammar checker.
- Follow these steps to organize your Analyze an Issue task:
  - State the thesis early.
  - Use a standard pattern of organization, namely order of importance.
  - Order paragraphs effectively.
  - Use a standard pattern of paragraphing—topic sentence, support and development, final summary statement—and include transitions.
  - Develop each paragraph fully—use facts, authoritative opinions or human interest, observations, anecdotes, and examples.
- Your writing plan should consist of the following steps:
  1. **Prewriting:** Restate the prompt, formulate support for both sides of the issue, and jot down ideas.
  2. **Drafting:** Answer the task, organize your response, provide well-developed support, link ideas clearly, and consider style, tone, and person.
  3. **Proofreading:** Check your thesis, look for omitted words, and check for sentence faults. (While you shouldn't spend time on spelling or minor mechanical errors, remember that misspelled words and faulty punctuation can detract from meaning.)

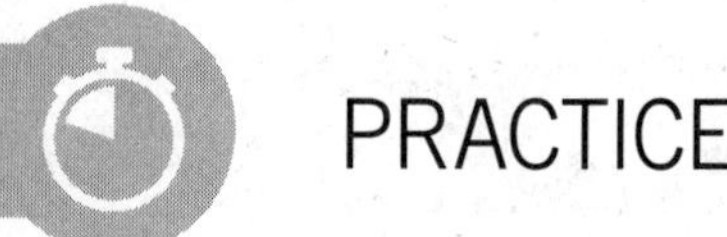

PRACTICE

ANALYTICAL WRITING

Use this prompt as a practice opportunity and compare your response with the samples, scoring, and analyses that follow. You will need to use your own paper to complete the quick write and create your response.

Time yourself and follow these 6 steps. On the real test, you will have 30 minutes.

1. Read the prompt.
2. Follow the prewriting steps.
3. Stop! Compare your quick write with the sample quick write that follows the prompt to see different ideas (perhaps more sophisticated, perhaps less) that you might not have thought of.
4. Draft your response.
5. Read each model that follows the sample quick write. You will be given examples of essays at a score of 6, 4, and 2 to help you gauge how the rubric translates to real-life writing. Determine the positive and negative qualities of each sample response before you read its scoring analysis.
6. Score your response against the rubric on pages 74–76. Be honest in your analysis, using the sample essays to help you determine how a reader might evaluate your writing.

Analyze an Issue Task

No field of study can advance significantly unless it incorporates knowledge and experience from outside that field.

*Write a response in which you discuss the extent to which you agree or disagree with the statement and explain your reasoning for the position you take. In developing and supporting your position, you should consider ways in which the statement might or might not hold true and explain how these considerations shape your position.**

* All of the Analytical Writing prompts in the practice tests of this book come directly from the list of prompts for the GRE, which can be found at https://www.ets.org/pdfs/gre/issue-pool.pdf.

Sample Quick Write

The 6-point response to this prompt began with just 3 minutes of prewriting and planning. It looked like this:

Tentative Thesis Statement: While outside knowledge and experience isn't strictly required for every field to advance, very few fields would not benefit from interdisciplinary thinking.

- Knowledge is multifaceted (1)
    - It's hard to have new ideas in a bubble
    - Different perspectives = complexity
    - Other fields have new ways of looking
- ~~Some knowledge more valuable?~~
- Critics would say that most fields require specificity (3A)
    - Outside ideas can "water down" clarity (?)
    - Specified knowledge is more important
    - ~~Infighting between disciplines?~~
- Saying "no field" is too limiting—some can advance without it but most can't ⟶ this is my opinion I want to argue, include in thesis
- ~~More true for humanities than STEM?~~
- Interdisciplinary thinking is more equitable (2)
    - Some fields are dominated by men, historically white, etc.
    - ~~Confirmation bias~~
- Challenges (4)
    - People presenting uneducated opinions as having equal weight to experts (4c if time)
    - Experts being listened to less in general (4a)
    - Expert ideas require specific knowledge that so few people have (4b)
    - ~~waste time that could be spent among peers?~~
- The important thing is being able to have dialogues (5 if time, lead into conclusion)
    - You don't necessarily need ideas from elsewhere, but there should be more talk across disciplines

Making Your Plan Work

In many ways, the success of the 6-point response based on this prewriting is due to some of the thought processes demonstrated in this quick write plan. First, it has information both on how the writer will support their own position as well as challenges they will address and ideas on how critics might respond to their own argument. Second, notice that the writer decides not to develop every single idea generated in the prewriting. The writer makes a judgment to develop ideas that they believe can be treated with deeper analysis or are less predictable answers to the prompt. They also rank their ideas by order of importance, and indicate some that they will include only if they have time for additional writing. Third, the writer has clearly used the quick write to ensure they have notes on every aspect of the argument required by the prompt.

TIP

Note how specific the quick write is. This helps to provide a good foundation for developing a response that is grounded in specific details to support any generalizations that you choose to make in your argument.

TIP

Using or developing shorthand writing skills could prove very useful during prewriting, as it will allow you to get a lot of ideas on paper quickly.

Return to this planning guide after you read the sample 6-point model that follows. Notice how the prewriting does not reflect the exact order of the essay's eventual organization. Note also that there are more details than the quick write includes. Once the writer began to write, ideas began to flow, affirming the idea that writing is a generative process. This should be a comforting fact to remember as you prepare. You don't need to list every single one of your ideas in a quick write; believe that more ideas will come as you write. However, it's also important to check your quick write against the task instructions to make sure that your flow of ideas isn't taking you off the track of responding accurately and adequately to the task.

Furthermore, you don't want to spend the kind of time on the prewriting process that extensive planning would require. The main goal of prewriting during a timed writing test is to be sure that you've got good points to make before you begin your writing. If you don't, quickly scratch out your first plan and make another.

Model 1: 6 points out of 6

As human knowledge advances, so does our capacity for recognizing the patterns and congruences that link discrete fields of study. Emergant fields like neuroscience and cultural ecology illuminate the ways that fields of study once thought disparate, like the humanities and the hard sciences, have more in common than scholars of the past might have first realized. There can be no doubt that all fields are ultimately enriched by recognizing where their threads intertwine within the tapestry of academic study. While it may be a stretch to say that no field of study could advance significantly without incorporating knowledge or experience from outside the field, it is true that virtually all fields of study would benefit from adopting interdisciplinary approaches. Interdisciplinary approaches help fields expand by potentiating new perspectives, ensuring more equitable approaches, and creating opportunities for dialogue and innovation.

There's a popular saying that goes something like "the definition of insanity is doing the same thing and hoping for different results." Yet this is so often the approach that many fields of study take. Methods and theories are time tested, canonized, and elevated as vaunted knowledge, often making it harder for new ideas to gain a foothold. The result is the creation of different academic bubbles, wherein researchers interact primarily with other researchers from their own field—an echo chamber can be the only result. Different fields have their own ways of approaching the same topics, and expanding study to include more of those approaches ultimately supports a more nuanced approach to knowledge.

Expanding approaches is also the key to creating more equitable fields of study. When tried and true methods and thinkers are privileged, the inevitable power imbalances that govern the world at large play out in terms of whose ideas are valued and canonized and what types of players get to make an impact. Too often this means fields of study privileging opportunities and renown for those with the most power before anyone else. While critics of this position might assert that outside ideas water down the clarity of academic fields, it is also true that such a "watering down" usually involves the introduction of perspectives that have historically been ignored. Inviting dialogue with a wider range of fields also means inviting dialogue with a greater variety of people, all of whom have something to contribute. Consider, for instance, the contributions made by those in disability studies, women's studies, and race and ethnic studies to fields like medicine and psychology, helping both of the latter account for a wider range of human experiences.

As fields of study embrace interdisciplinary thinking, they also gain new opportunities for dialogue and innovation. No one field can master human knowledge, but numerous fields working in concert can illuminate larger patterns that would be impossible to recognize from a single vantage point. For example, when art historians first started working with forensic scientists, chemists, and archaeologists, they were able to develop better methods for identifying the age and history of art works via techniques like carbon dating. Opportunities like this one are myriad, provided different fields of study are willing to work together.

Our world is ever changing, and the paradigms that different fields of study use to make sense of our world must shift with it. While it may be possible that some fields of study can advance considerably in isolation, there is no doubt that interdisciplinarity is a valuable tool for expanding knowledge in virtually all fields. The problems that the world faces are likely to only get more complicated, but so too will our knowledge of how the world works become more complex. Working together, rather than apart, is our best bet at continuing to advance knowledge.

Scoring Analysis

This response scores 6 out of 6 for the following reasons:

- **It answers the task.** With care and considerable sophistication, this response not only gives cogent reasons for agreeing with the statement but also responds thoughtfully to potential challenges by acknowledging critics and recognizing that while they agree with the basic premise, it may not apply in every single case.
- **It is well supported.** Support for their position is abundant and they draw on their own ideas, experiences, and past knowledge to offer cogent examples, such as those about art historians and carbon dating, or the role that women's and disability studies have played in psychology and medicine.
- **It is well organized.** The writer uses the opening paragraph to state and qualify the position by venturing a specific thesis statement. They then use subsequent, discrete, and well-constructed paragraphs to counter challenges and reinforce the position. All ideas lead logically and smoothly to a satisfying conclusion.
- **It is fluid, precise, and graceful.** The capable prose includes short sentences that are interspersed with longer ones for dramatic effect. Advanced word choices include *congruences, equitable,* and *myriad.* The tone and style help the reader form an opinion of the writer as objective and thoughtful.
- **It observes the conventions of Standard Written English.** There may be some minor errors present, such as the misspelling of *emergent* as "emergant." This error does not impact meaning and would therefore have no effect on one's score unless it was one of numerous similar errors.

Other observations: You can see how the prewriting helped this writer with their essay, but their argument evolved as they wrote. Consequently, the writer ends up creating a more specific thesis than the tentative thesis they wrote during prewriting. The writer also addresses critics or challenges to the stance well enough to still qualify for a 6, but the essay would be even stronger with more direct analysis of potential challengers to the stance the writer takes, Nonetheless, because this essay is well organized, thorough, and demonstrates a strong command of vocabulary and syntax, it would be considered a strong candidate for a score of 6. ETS readers do not expect perfection in 30 minutes, nor do they expect you to cover every single aspect of your topic. What they do expect, however, are intelligent, well-supported, well-organized, and fluent responses within the time constraints.

How a score of 5 would differ: Essays that receive a score of 5 are not that different from those that score a 6, but typically lose points for one of the following reasons:

- Too many small errors or more than one large error in grammar or conventions
- Diminished argument clarity
- Not long enough to sufficiently answer all aspects of the prompt
- Too few transitions to guide the reader between ideas
- No clear statement of the argument in the first paragraph, even if it can be inferred from the rest of the essay

Model 2: 4 points out of 6

In our modern age its apparent that different fields of study share common ground. Emerging areas like neuroscience and cultural ecology show that the humanities and hard sciences aren't as differentiating as once thought. It's clear that acknowledging these connections benefits all disciplines. While it might be a stretch to say no field can advance without incorporating outside knowledge, most would benefit from interdisciplinary approaches.

Many fields of study stick to familiar methods and theories, making it hard for new ideas to emerge. This leads to academic bubbles where researchers only engage with others in their field. When people think in a bubble there can also be confirmation bias. Embracing diverse approaches allows for a more nuanced understanding of subjects. More ideas are better than just some.

Expanding approaches promotes fairness, in academia. When traditional methods are favored, it reinforces existing power dynamics. For instance, more men having power than women. However, incorporating perspectives historically ignored can lead to richer dialogue and better insights. For example, disciplines like medicine and psychology have benefited from input from disability studies and women's studies.

Interdisciplinary thinking encourages coming up with new ideas and having new discussions. No single field can grasp the entirety of human knowledge, but collaboration can reveal patterns that would be hard to otherwise spot. What field wouldn't benefit from seeing how another one looks at things? For instance, art historians working with scientists have developed better methods for dating artworks like with carbon dating, for instance.

As the world progresses, we will need to come up with new ways to make sense of our expanding world. Some might think that sticking to your own field is important, but they are probably looking over some of these benefits. While some fields may be able to progress in isolation, it's pretty clear that interdisciplinary collaboration is essential for advancing knowledge in most disciplines. Working together is vital for progress now and in the future.

Scoring Analysis

This response scores 4 out of 6 for the following reasons:

- **It answers the task.** This response clearly takes a position and supports the position. It is less effective on responding to the possible challenges to that position.
- **It supports the position well but is limited in terms of explaining and countering challenges.** Examples are appropriate and various, but responses to likely challenges are not as clearly explained or developed as they should be—in fact, they're limited primarily to a vague statement in the final paragraph. Examples given are also vague and could have been better incorporated.
- **It is organized but lacks transitions.** This essay is organized enough that it might even be close to a 5; however, it lacks transitions that would help the reader make even more sense of how elements are combined. The vague thesis statement also does little to preview how the essay will be organized.
- **It is generally clear.** Most points are clear, but there are a few points when the author introduces an idea and doesn't expand on it or situate it with their other ideas. For instance, in paragraph 2: "When people think in a bubble there can also be confirmation bias." This sentence is inserted into the middle of the paragraph without any analysis to help situate it for the reader.
- **It observes the conventions of Standard Written English.** There are several minor flaws, such as spelling errors, missing or misplaced commas, and sentence fragments, but they do not significantly interfere with meaning. They do, however, help contribute to the score of 4, since there are enough of them to start to slightly interfere with meaning (e.g., the use of *differentiating* instead of *different*).

Other observations: While the general ideas in this essay are about as strong as those in the example for a score of 6, the writer could have done more to arrange them together meaningfully. Sentence structure and word choices are also more basic throughout the essay—the writer could have improved the sophistication of their writing by including more details, varying sentence structure more, and using a wider range of vocabulary. More should have been done to address challenges to the main idea or to explain why critics might think differently. Vague statements throughout also weaken the argument (e.g., "More ideas are better than just some"). In general, the writer would have benefitted from saving more time for proofreading. The response is an adequate length but is on the short side of average.

How a score of 3 would differ: Essays that receive a score of 3 are not that different from those that score a 4, but typically lose points for one of the following reasons:

- Grammatical errors, minor or major, that have begun to interfere with meaning but not significantly so
- Neutral, vague, or inadequately articulated position that may cause a reader to struggle to determine what the argument is right away
- Not long enough to sufficiently answer all aspects of the prompt
- Repetitive ideas or phrasing
- Missing a thesis statement and/or topic sentences to guide the reader through the argument
- Issues with organization that diminish meaning

Model 3: 2 points out of 6

As humans learn more, it seems like different subjects are connected somehow. So it would probably indeed be good for different fields. Like how neuroscience and cultural ecology show that humanities and hard sciences have things in common. It might be good to notice these connections, but some people might not agree. The answer is probably in the middle of both sides.

Maybe there is a benafit to keeping to your own methods. They work for a reason and people in the field know them. Lots of subjects stick to what they know, which makes it hard for new ideas to come up in the field. This makes little groups in the academic world where researchers only talk to each other. If you are only talking to your little group, then you won't have new ideas. But also, only those in the group are specialists, and know what they need to know to have expert opinions, so its complicated. Experts still need to be able to talk to other experts from the same field. Maybe looking at things in different ways could help us understand better but maybe not every field, it really depends on many factors.

Using different methods might make things more fair in academia. The usual ways tend to help people who already have power, which isn't fair. Bringing in ideas from different groups might make discussions more open and give better insites. For example, medicine and psychology have improved because of ideas from other fields. Sometimes, this doesn't work though, and we need to do better at bringing things together, like the methods used and who does what. You can't throw out what is already known, you still have to keep important ideas or its backward progress.

Working together between fields could help with talking about big ideas and making new stuff happen in a field. No single subject knows everything, but when they work together, we might find out things we didn't know before. It's possible. For example, artists and scientists have made better ways to figure out how old art is, and, this wasn't available before.

As people learn more, we need new ways to understand what we know. Some subjects can keep going on their own, but most need to work together. Teamwork is important for making progress and understanding more. A different way of doing things exists.

Scoring Analysis

This response scores 2 out of 6 for the following reasons:

- **It answers the tasks, but not clearly.** At times, the writer seems to take one position before taking another, sometimes even swapping stances mid paragraph (as in paragraph 2). Consequently, it's difficult to tell what their argument even is, though they do seem to lean more toward agreeing with the prompt statement.
- **It lacks support.** The assertions are either not backed up or are backed up with extremely simple or inadequate support. Where examples are given, they are vague, as in "medicine and psychology have improved because of ideas from other fields."
- **It is poorly written.** While the length is adequate, the writer doesn't use the space well. They are repetitive at points and vague at others. The paragraphs themselves are organized but tend to hop around between ideas. No single idea is explored in depth.
- **It contains errors in the conventions of Standard Written English.** There are several minor grammatical errors that add to the overall impression that this piece was poorly conceived and written. Misplaced commas, sentence structure errors, misspellings, and more all diminish the writer's ability to communicate effectively.

Other observations: This writer could probably have scored an extra point or more by paying close attention to their own argument. They do make some attempts to address the challenges that the prompt raises, but the way they go about doing so makes it seem like they are flip-flopping between stances. Creating a clear argument, separating out criticisms from support, and using the organizational structure of the essay more intentionally would all be ways to improve the score.

How a score of 1 would differ: Essays that receive a score of 1 are not that different from those that score a 2, but typically lose points for one of the following reasons:

- Grammatical errors, minor or major, that interfere with meaning and make it difficult to parse the writer's stance at all
- Only minimal association with the prompt
- Complete lack of support or only illogical or flawed support for the main point or points; may be lacking any kind of organization
- Confusing organization within which it is not possible to find a pattern
- Not long enough to sufficiently answer all aspects of prompt
- Repetitive ideas or phrasing
- Missing a thesis statement and/or topic sentences

If a score does not answer the prompt at all, answers only in a foreign language, or otherwise fails to address the given prompt, it will be given a score of NS: No Score.

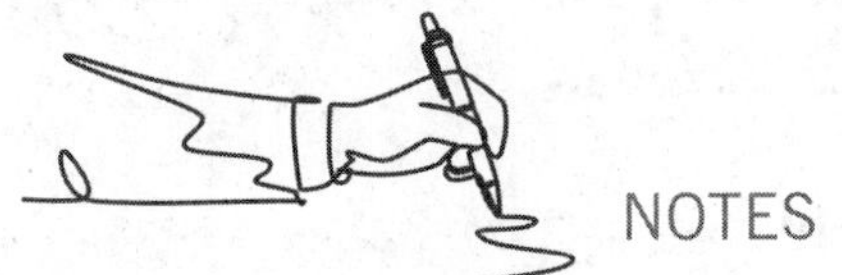

NOTES

PART III

VERBAL REASONING

CHAPTER

Reading Comprehension Questions

READING COMPREHENSION QUESTIONS

OVERVIEW

- Basic Information about Reading Comprehension Question Types
- Active Reading
- Strategies for Multiple-Choice Questions
- Strategies for Select One or More Answer Choices Questions
- Strategies for Select-in-Passage Questions
- Summing It Up
- Practice: Reading Comprehension Questions
- Answer Key and Explanations

This chapter describes the reading comprehension questions on the GRE General Test. Most reading comprehension questions on the GRE are multiple-choice questions—select one answer choice. However, you will also encounter two other question types: multiple-choice questions—select one or more answer choices and select-in-passage questions. In addition to basic information about the reading comprehension questions, Chapter 4 offers useful strategies to help you answer reading comprehension questions in all three formats quickly and competently.

4

BASIC INFORMATION ABOUT READING COMPREHENSION QUESTION TYPES

The reading comprehension questions on the Verbal Reasoning section of the GRE General Test assess your ability to understand, analyze, and apply information found in the types of reading you will encounter in graduate school. About half the questions on the verbal section of the GRE General Test are reading comprehension questions.

The Passages

There are approximately 10 reading comprehension passages on the GRE General Test. They are based on information found in a wide range of scholarly and everyday sources from nonfiction books to popular periodicals to scholarly journals. Content areas represented include the arts and humanities, physical sciences, biological sciences, social sciences, business, and daily topics.

The passages may be from one to several paragraphs in length and can range from 100 words to as many as approximately 450 words. Most, however, will be one paragraph; only one or two will be longer. Some passages will inform, while others will analyze. Some will argue a point and seek to persuade. As in all real-world writing, a single passage may reflect more than one mode of exposition.

Each reading comprehension question on the computer-delivered test appears on a separate screen with the passage on which it is based. If the passage is too long to display legibly on a single screen, as in the case of multiparagraph passages, you will be able to scroll through the passage without changing screens.

Directly before the start of the passage is a statement of how many questions each passage has. For example:

Questions 1–3 are based on the following passage.

Direction lines appear in the question sets telling you how many answers to select. Examples include the following:

- **For Questions 1–3, choose only <u>one</u> answer choice unless otherwise indicated.**
- **For Question 2, consider each answer individually and choose <u>all</u> that apply.**

These direction lines may appear before the entire question set or may appear directly before a specific question. Pay careful attention so that you know how many answers you need to select.

ALERT

All multiple-choice questions in the computer-delivered test will have answer options preceded by either blank ovals or blank squares, depending on the question type. The paper-delivered test will follow the same format of answer choices but will use letters instead. For your convenience, the letters A, B, C, D, etc., are used for the answer choices in this book. This way, it is easier to check your answers against the answer key and explanations.

Question-and-Answer Formats

Each passage is followed by one to three questions. There are three formats that questions and answers may take for reading comprehension questions:

Multiple-choice questions—select one answer choice

Multiple-choice questions—select one or more answer choices

Select-in-passage

Most reading comprehension questions ask you to select one answer from a list of five possible answer choices. The answer choices for this type of multiple-choice question will be preceded by *ovals* in the computer-delivered test.

You will find a few multiple-choice questions that ask you to select one or more answers from a list of three possible choices. One, two, or all three answers may be correct. You must select all the correct possibilities to earn credit for that question. The answer choices for these questions are preceded by *squares*.

On the computer-delivered test, you will find only a few select-in-passage questions that will ask you to select a sentence or a paragraph in the passage as your answer. Because this type of question depends on the use of a computer, it will not appear on the paper-delivered test. Instead, an equivalent multiple-choice question will be used in its place.

Skills

The questions on the GRE General Test are meant to assess the preparedness of potential graduate school students. Therefore, you will find questions that ask you to use the skills and abilities that are expected of students in graduate school. To answer questions on the reading comprehension section, you will need to be able to

- identify or infer the main idea, or major point, of a passage;
- distinguish between main and subordinate ideas (*major* and *minor* points, in GRE test parlance);
- summarize information;
- reason from incomplete data to infer missing information;
- determine the relationship of ideas to one another and/or to the passage in which they appear;
- analyze a text;
- draw conclusions from information;
- identify the author's assumptions or perspective,
- identify the strengths and weaknesses of a position;
- develop and assess alternative ideas; and
- determine the meaning of individual words, sentences, and paragraphs, and of longer pieces of writing.

Some questions require you to use more than one skill at a time. For example, you might need the main idea to answer a question, but to find it, you might have to distinguish between main ideas and subordinate or supporting details. Or, you might have to find a relationship between ideas by both inferring information about main and subordinate ideas and using structural clues to understand meaning.

Recurring Question Types

The list of skills may seem daunting, but when put in the context of actual questions, they will seem much more familiar. For example, the question "Which of the following best restates the author's point of view?" asks for the main idea of the passage. To find it, you may need to infer it, or it may be directly stated—though probably not in a graduate-level piece of writing.

You will find that certain categories of questions recur among the reading comprehension questions. The common question types follow.

Main Idea Questions

These questions require you to identify or infer the main idea (or major point), summarize the passage, draw conclusions from complete or incomplete information about the main idea, and infer relationships between the main idea and subordinate details. You will find this to be a common question type, both in this book and on the GRE General Test. Examples of various main idea question formats include the following:

- Which of the following does the passage most clearly support?
- What was the underlying cause of the financial crisis?
- What qualities of the painter's style most influenced the critic's view?
- The passage implies that the president's actions were based on . . .
- Select the sentence that restates the premise of the author's argument.
- Which of the following would be a suitable title for the passage?

Supporting or Subordinate Details Questions

These questions ask you to identify subordinate details, infer subordinate details, summarize the passage, draw conclusions about subordinate details, or infer relationships between two or more subordinate details. Question formats may be similar to the following:

- The passage mentions financial regulations in order to . . .
- You can infer that the president's actions were based on . . .
- The passage notes each of the following causes EXCEPT . . .
- Based on the passage, which of the following was excluded from the experiment?
- The passage suggests that which set of data is the more compelling?
- The purpose of the sentence "Yet a close look . . . continents" is to . . .
- Select the sentence that restates the author's claim.

Author's Perspective Questions

To answer these questions, you may need to infer the author's attitude or tone or deduce the author's unstated assumptions. Not every question that mentions the author—or even the author's beliefs—is a perspective question. The question may, for example, be a main idea question, such as the next-to-last example under Main Idea Questions. Questions related to the author's perspective may be similar to the following:

- What was the underlying cause of the financial crisis, according to the author?
- The author attributes the early experimental results to . . .
- You can infer from the passage that the author believes that . . .
- The author of the passage most likely agrees with which historian's view as described in the passage?
- Select the sentence that best describes the author's attitude toward critics of Darwin.

Authorial Intent Questions

Authorial intent questions are similar to those regarding an author's perspective. The main difference is that they gauge your ability to understand the implicit intention of a passage. In other words, you will be asked to identify the author's goal for writing a passage in a certain manner. Often, this requires you to infer the intended audience of a passage while simultaneously analyzing how the author intends to engage them. The questions might also ask you to identify why the author refers to specific sources or data within the analysis. Questions related to authorial intent may be similar to the following examples:

- You can infer that the author references a study from (specific journal) in order to . . .
- Through this passage, you can infer that the author intends to . . .
- The author most likely included the quotation in paragraph 2 in order to . . .

Argumentative Analysis Questions

These questions task you with analyzing and articulating rhetorical strategies in arguments. Typically, they follow a very specific format, and this causes them to stand out from other question types. The passage will take the form of an argumentative exchange or dialogue. The first part will be an argumentative proposal, and the second will be a rebuttal. Passages will look similar to the following:

> **Adams:** If we look at Shakespeare's *King Lear*, we can find several compelling correlations with Geoffrey of Monmouth's *Historia Regum Brittanniae*. The latter contains the earliest historical account of King Leir of Britain. Given the similarities between Shakespeare's and Geoffrey of Monmouth's accounts, we can conclude that *Historia Regum Brittanniae* was Shakespeare's sole inspiration for *King Lear*.
>
> **Baretta:** That's not necessarily true. While there are clear similarities between the two works, *King Lear* also deviates from Geoffrey of Monmouth's account in significant ways. For example, Cordelia's death in *King Lear* follows a completely different timeline than that of *Historia Regum Brittanniae*. In fact, Shakespeare's rendering bears more similarity to Edmund Spenser's account of Cordelia's death in *The Faerie Queene*. It's likelier that Shakespeare used a variety of sources for his play rather than adhered to a single, authoritative source.

The questions will ask you to determine what strategies are at play in the counterargument. For example, these strategies can include pointing out spurious correlations, uncovering incorrect information, identifying misused generalizations, and analyzing inconsistencies, among others. Questions concerning argumentative analysis may look similar to the following:

- Baretta responds to Adams's assertion by employing which of the following strategies?
- Baretta identifies which of the following flaws in Adams's argument?

Application Questions

These test items ask you to evaluate the strengths and weaknesses of an argument, develop alternative explanations, hypothesize about the relationship of new ideas to stated or implied ideas, and use structural clues to determine or infer meaning. As their name suggests, these questions will often require you to apply or build on what you have already identified or inferred about the main idea, the supporting details, or the author's perspective in earlier questions in the set for a particular passage and then apply that information to a different idea or situation. Application questions may resemble the following:

- Which of the following, if it were true, would weaken the author's argument?
- Select the sentence that best describes the opinions of the anthropologists who actually examined the skeleton.
- What is the primary purpose of the two groups of highlighted words?
- Which of the following is most similar in reasoning to the ideas expressed in the final sentence?
- According to the passage, which is the correct sequence of events?

Word Meaning Questions

These questions are easy to spot because they're accompanied by line numbers to help you quickly pinpoint the word and the context. They require you to infer the meaning of a word from the specific context in which it appears. The phrase "specific context" is important because words have different meanings in different subject areas and as different parts of speech. Examples of word meaning questions include the following:

- "Verisimilitude" (line 6) most nearly means . . .
- In the passage, "obfuscate" means . . .

TIP

If you are running out of time, you could go through remaining passages looking for word meaning questions. To answer these, read the question, the sentence referred to in the question, and the sentences immediately before and after the sentence.

ACTIVE READING

This is a timed test, and you will feel the pressure of the clock. Nevertheless, you should still adjust your reading rate so that you're reading every passage with concentration and active participation. This can be hard to do when the clock is ticking, but it's your best bet to improve your comprehension, and it is especially good advice when the content is unfamiliar to you.

Simply slowing down as you read won't help you all that much. You need to focus on and actively participate in what you are reading. You should:

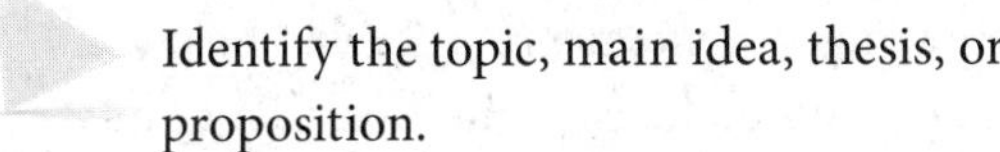

Identify the topic, main idea, thesis, or proposition.

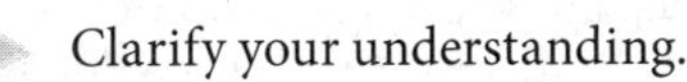

Clarify your understanding.

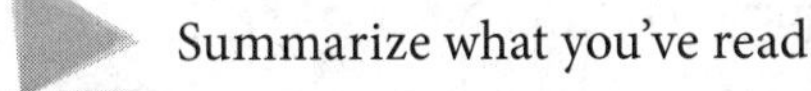

Summarize what you've read.

To help you understand the process, skim the following reading comprehension passage to get an idea of its topic, main idea, and details.

Sculptor Henry Moore (born 1898) achieved prominence in the 1930s with his earliest recumbent figures. An English abstractionist, Moore has also been associated with romantic feeling in the relationship of his biomorphic forms to nature. His sculptures, which often consist of large flowing, rhythmic masses united by a common base, have been called universal shapes by art historian Brian McAvera, who credits them with subconscious appeal to our essential humanity. Yet this characterization is not entirely comforting, for the biomorphic figures, many of which are suggestive of the female figure, can both soothe and disturb as they evoke motherhood, sexuality, or even a surreal anxiety. Moreover, Moore can be said to have explained and celebrated the void as much as he explored the body in his sculptures, which, as time marched forward and his fame grew, came to be modeled rather than carved and more the product of mass-production techniques than of exacting attention to every inch of every surface.

Identify the Topic, Main Idea, Thesis, or Proposition

The more unfamiliar the subject matter of the passage is, the more basic your approach must be. Furthermore, working step by step to find meaning can help you focus. Determine the main idea first. If you can't identify the main idea, then start by identifying the simple subject, or topic, of the passage. For example, the topic of Passage 1 is the sculptures of Henry Moore.

To get from topic or subject to thesis, main idea, or proposition, ask yourself what the author is saying about the topic or subject. If you can establish only part of that thesis, main idea, or proposition, do as much as you can. For example, you might begin identifying the thesis of Passage 1 as

> The author is saying that Henry Moore's sculptures consist of large flowing masses, some of which are figures that both comfort and disturb.

Clarify Your Understanding

There are a variety of techniques for clarifying understanding. One is to ask and answer questions as you read. For example, you might ask yourself what a concept means or the meaning of a word in the context of the passage. As you read Passage 1 on Henry Moore, you might ask yourself what *biomorphic* means. At least one question on the reading comprehension test is almost certain to be about the meaning of a key word. Often, this word will convey a meaning that is specific to the context. Again, if you can establish only part of that meaning, do at least that much, using knowledge of word parts, context clues, or other applicable strategies. For example,

> In the passage, the term *biomorphic* seems to have a specific meaning that is related to shapes, figures, and nature. The word part *bio* suggests humans or animals; the word part *morph* suggests forms or shapes.

Another way to clarify understanding is by stopping to restate or paraphrase information. This usually involves rereading the previous sentence or, perhaps, a couple of sentences. For example, you might stop and ask yourself exactly what the second sentence in the passage is saying. Restate whatever you can. Don't worry if you can't restate everything. Your thinking might be something like the following:

> The second sentence of the test passage says that Moore's work was abstract; that is, he didn't represent things as they really are. It says his shapes are biomorphic, or forms of humans and animals. It says his sculptures had a relationship to nature.

Summarize

Quickly summarize the passage to yourself after you have read it, but before you begin answering the question(s). This strategy can also help you clarify your understanding.

STRATEGIES FOR MULTIPLE-CHOICE QUESTIONS

The GRE General Test reading comprehension passages have widely varied purposes, structures, and content, and, unfortunately, there is no single strategy that can guarantee success with all. In addition to active reading, the following 10 general strategies will help you answer reading comprehension multiple-choice questions, whether you need to select one answer choice or one or more answer choices:

- Restate the question.
- Try answering the question before you read the answer choices.
- Read all the answers before you choose.
- Compare answer choices to each other and the question.
- Avoid selecting an answer you don't fully understand.
- Choose the *best* answer.
- Pay attention to structure and structural clues.
- Don't select an answer just because it's true.
- Substitute answer choices in word meaning questions.
- Choose the answer that *doesn't* fit for EXCEPT questions.

TIP

The GRE General Test design supports the following test-taking strategies: (1) pacing yourself using the on-screen clock, (2) skipping and returning to questions, and (3) answering every question in each section. Take advantage of these features.

This list may seem like a huge number of strategies to remember and use on test day, but there are two things to remember about the strategies:

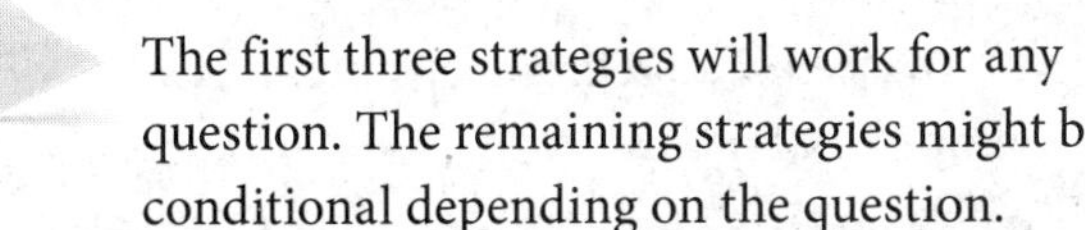

- The first three strategies will work for any question. The remaining strategies might be conditional depending on the question.

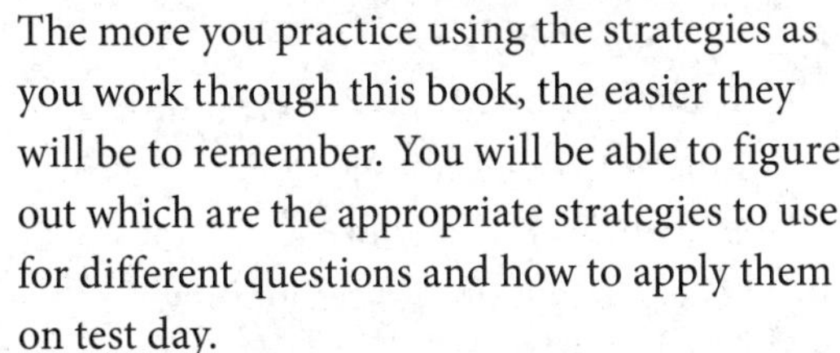

- The more you practice using the strategies as you work through this book, the easier they will be to remember. You will be able to figure out which are the appropriate strategies to use for different questions and how to apply them on test day.

For the first six strategies in this section, you will focus on a single reading comprehension passage and a single question. There is an additional strategy later in the chapter for multiple-choice questions—select one or more answer choices. You may want to use a sticky note or other bookmark to mark this page with the passage and the question so that you can refer back to it easily.

Question 1 is based on the following passage.

Sculptor Henry Moore (born 1898) achieved prominence in the 1930s with his earliest recumbent figures. An English abstractionist, Moore has also been associated with romantic feeling in the relationship of his biomorphic forms to nature. His sculptures, which often consist of large flowing, rhythmic masses united by a common base, have been called universal shapes by art historian Brian McAvera, who credits them with subconscious appeal to our essential humanity. Yet this characterization is not entirely comforting, for the biomorphic figures, many of which are suggestive of the female figure, can both soothe and disturb as they evoke motherhood, sexuality, or even a surreal anxiety. Moreover, Moore can be said to have explained and celebrated the void as much as he explored the body in his sculptures, which, as time marched forward and his fame grew, came to be modeled rather than carved and more the product of mass-production techniques than of exacting attention to every inch of every surface.

For Question 1, choose only <u>one</u> answer choice.

The passage suggests that the main quality of Moore's work is most nearly which of the following?

A. A romantic presentation of human or animal forms

B. An attempt to reinvent abstraction as a mirror of nature

C. A soothing evocation of the often-recumbent female figure

D. A blend of artisan craft and mass production techniques

E. A use of flowing forms with universal appeal but diverse response

If you come across a passage like this that is totally unfamiliar to you—whether it is about fine arts, political geography, or any other subject—don't leap to the conclusion that the passage is too difficult for you. Proceed logically by using your strategies. Remember that all questions can be addressed using only the information provided in the passage—you do not need outside knowledge to succeed.

You may be tempted to "mark" a passage like this to come back to later without giving it an active reading. Use this strategy only if you are still stumped after having given the passage a purposeful, focused reading and having at least attempted to answer one or more of the questions.

If you save a passage with three questions for later, and you are doing a typical test with 20 questions, you have just delayed answering approximately 15 percent of the test. Putting off large chunks of the test until later can lead to increased anxiety. Saving, returning, and, most of all, rereading also eats into your precious time. Sometimes, you may have no choice, but you should give the passage and its questions a good try first.

1. Restate the Question

Here again is the question that accompanies the passage on Henry Moore.

For Question 1, choose only <u>one</u> answer choice.

The passage suggests that the main quality of Moore's work is most nearly which of the following?

- **A.** A romantic presentation of human or animal forms
- **B.** An attempt to reinvent abstraction as a mirror of nature
- **C.** A soothing evocation of the often-recumbent female figure
- **D.** A blend of artisan craft and mass production techniques
- **E.** A use of flowing forms with universal appeal but diverse response

In addition to verifying what you must select, paraphrase or restate the question to be sure that you know what you are being asked to find:

- The question asks which is the most important quality of Moore's work, according to the author.
- You need to find and weigh all the characteristics of Moore's work that are presented in the passage and decide which is most important. In short, you are looking for the main idea, or topic, of the passage.

2. Try Answering the Question Before You Read the Answer Choices

This strategy is especially useful when you feel confident that you understand the passage, but it can also work when you feel unsure of your understanding. By trying to answer the question in your own words first, you can get part of the way toward the correct answer. When you check the answers, you might find an answer that's the same as your idea, but in different words. This could likely signal that you are on the right track. If no answer is even close to yours, you've likely missed the point. Coming up with your own answer or a partial answer is, in fact, a way to clarify your understanding in relation to the specific question you must answer.

ALERT

Don't rely on outside information to answer questions. Base your answers solely on the information in the passage. You may know that Romanticism was an art style in the late 18th century, but in this passage *romantic* is used in its 20th-century sense.

Again, returning to Question 1, come up with the best answer you can before you begin to eliminate choices. For example, you might come up with the following:

> The passage emphasizes forms and shapes that suggest humans or animals and their effects on the viewer. The viewer has an immediate recognition because the shapes are "universal," but recognition doesn't always mean comfort or a good feeling.

3. Read All the Answers Before You Choose

After you've developed some idea of the correct answer, read all the answer choices listed. Don't simply read the first one and choose it if it seems correct. Take the time to review all answer choices so you can be positive that you've selected the best one. Keep in mind that a well-constructed test will have answers that are close approximations of the correct answer.

ALERT

Reading all the answers is especially important for multiple-choice questions that require you to select one or more answer choices. Pay attention to all directions that indicate how many choices you should select.

4. Compare Answer Choices to Each Other and the Question

Suppose you eliminate three answer choices, but you cannot eliminate one of the two remaining. If you are crunched for time, you can make your best guess at this point. If you have time, however, don't guess before you try this strategy: compare the choices to each other and to the question. The following is based on Question 1 and assumes that you've eliminated choices B, C, and D:

- Choice A is very different from choice E. Choice A does get to the heart of Moore's work by mentioning human or animal—or biomorphic—forms. Yet it calls them "romantic," an idea that a later detail about mass production seems to refute. In comparison, choice E also presents the fundamental idea of forms while incorporating more of the fundamental facts: first, that the forms are universal, and second, that they evoke diverse responses, which the passage explains can range from soothed to disturbed.
- The question asks for a main quality. Choice E encompasses the notions of universal appeal; of abstract, flowing forms; and of "diverse" responses of the viewer. In comparison, the key word in choice A seems to be "romantic," which, in the context of the passage, is a less important quality that is not developed, or is perhaps even contradicted or limited, by the author. Therefore, **the correct answer is E.**

5. Avoid Selecting an Answer You Don't Fully Understand

Again, suppose you have eliminated three choices, but you're at a loss to eliminate one of the two remaining answers. As you reread the choices, avoid selecting the one that is more confusing or unintelligible to you. You might work your way through your dilemma something like this:

- Choice A is hard to understand. The passage implies that a romantic feeling is evoked by Moore's forms, but the term *romantic* isn't really ever defined in the passage, and it seems to relate to only some of his work.
- Choice E is easier to understand and also clearly sums up more of the ideas in the paragraph. Therefore, choice E is more likely to be correct.

6. Choose the *Best* Answer

Once again, suppose you have been able to eliminate three choices but are having trouble eliminating one of the two remaining answers. As you try to choose, remember that your goal is to select the *best* answer. Therefore, if both answers appear reasonable or possibly correct to you, your task is to choose the better—more reasonable—of the two.

- Choice E sums up the ideas in the paragraph. It summarizes essential or main qualities of Moore's work: universality, abstract forms, and diverse response.

- On the other hand, choice A seems as if it could possibly be correct, but it definitely doesn't sum up most of the main ideas that the passage's author attributes to Moore.
- You're looking for the main idea of the passage, so choice E is more likely to be correct (because it encompasses more key information).

For the next four strategies, you will focus on a multi-paragraph passage and four questions to learn to apply the strategies. Once again, it is probably wise to mark the passage for easy reference as you try out the various strategies.

Passage 2 differs in two significant ways from the first passage you read. First, it has four paragraphs. While most passages you encounter on the test will be a single paragraph in length, at least one passage is likely to be longer. Second, notice also that this passage contains some information highlighted in gray. You can safely assume that this must be important information.

For Questions 2–6, choose only one answer choice unless otherwise indicated.

Questions 2–6 are based on the following passage.

Americans take a profound interest in wildlife, as long as that wildlife is in other people's backyards. American Audubon societies strive mightily to save Central America's jaguar, while schoolchildren across the nation focus on China's endangered panda and the African elephant. But when it comes to America's own most pressing wildlife problem, deer, the public is curiously—and dangerously—somnolent.

Adaptable to a wide range of habitats, including the paved roads and manicured, pesticide-rich lots of suburban America, white-tailed deer live in at least part of every state except for, possibly, Hawaii, Alaska, and Utah. And just about everywhere, as their numbers increase yet their habitat decreases, the animals are wreaking havoc: destroying public and private landscape; eating row crops and nursery stock; and, most significantly, carrying with increasingly alarming frequency tick-borne pathogens that cause Lyme disease, babesiosis, and other newly emerging diseases.

While states pretend to deal with these animals by establishing hunting seasons to harvest populations, as well as by offering information on control, the problem escalates. One reason for this may be that deer populations were endangered in the 1930s and brought back, leading wildlife agencies to trumpet the success of "sustainable hunting." Another more disturbing reason may be that Americans think deer are cute. Called "charismatic" animals on at least one website, tick-infested deer are seemingly beloved for their fluffy white tails; their large, dark eyes; their lithe and graceful prancing motions; and, perhaps most of all, their reticence or retreat in the face of human contact.

But what are the economics of cuteness? Just a few annual costs include $2 billion borne by US farmers and 150 human fatalities plus $3.8 billion in insurance payouts to drivers who hit deer. Additionally, there's the approximately $11,000 per case of Lyme disease—and all of these costs will rise dramatically as deer populations grow. These costs alone show the necessity of stopping deer in their tracks.

Now, read Question 2.

2. What function do the two groups of highlighted words serve in this argument?

   A. The first anticipates the argument's conclusion; the second provides support for that conclusion.

   B. The first supports the proposition or opinion; the second states the proposition or opinion.

   C. The first presents the proposition or opinion; the second presents the final support for the proposition or opinion.

   D. The first serves as an intermediate conclusion; the second serves as a definitive conclusion.

   E. The first presents the argument; the second restates and reinforces the argument.

7. Pay Attention to Structure and to Structural Clues

When you read actively, you should be drawing a conclusion about the author's purpose. Many passages inform, but the purpose of this particular passage is to persuade. As part of reading actively, you should also be looking for the main idea, proposition, or thesis of the passage. The viewpoint of this passage is that more must be done to stop the problems caused by deer.

TIP

Before you try any other strategy, remember to eliminate any answer that you know is wrong. Each of the answers has two parts. Each part characterizes one group of highlighted words. If you can eliminate either part of the answer choice, the whole answer is wrong.

Once you know you are reading a persuasive piece—an argument, in other words—and once you determine the thesis or proposition, begin the work of tracing the argument's development and separating claims from evidence, opinions, and judgments.

- The first highlighted segment presents a series of effects caused by deer; these facts support the opinion that strong measures are necessary to stop the problems caused by deer.
- The second highlighted segment states an opinion.

TIP

Make a mental note of transitional words and phrases as you read. Transitions can show time order, add information, indicate cause and effect, and show comparisons and contrasts.

Persuasive writing is often organized inductively to lead the reader through a process of reasoning. With this method of organization, the conclusion often presents the opinion for the first time. It may also draw a final conclusion or present a clincher statement that reinforces the opinion or proposition. Therefore, while a proposition, or thesis, may be stated at the beginning of an argument both for clarity and clout, stating it at the end of an argument, as if it were the most logical conclusion possible, is also rhetorically effective.

- The first highlighted segment presents facts about the dangerous and costly effects of deer as supporting evidence for the idea that stronger measures for controlling deer are necessary.
- The intermediate claim "the animals are wreaking havoc," which leads up to the facts and signals a list with its closing colon, suggests that support for the claim will follow.
- The factual claims about land destruction, crop damage, and disease are evidence that supports the intermediate claim as well as the conclusion drawn by the final sentence, and the final sentence clearly states the proposition, or argument. Therefore, **the correct answer is B.**

Sometimes, structural clues reveal the writer's thinking over the course of an entire paragraph. For example, a passage from the GRE General Test online sample questions reveals the following structure, embedded in it:

- Sentence 1: "According to . . ."
- Sentence 2: "In this view . . ."
- Sentence 3: ". . . however . . ."

These clues tell you that you're reading one view—stated and explained in sentences 1 and 2. In sentence 3, you're reading its rebuttal or some significant qualification of it (beginning with *however*) in the remainder of the paragraph.

In another sample passage, there are no structural clues until the passage's midway point:

- Sentence 4: "It follows that . . ."
- Sentence 6: "Therefore, . . ."

These clues tell you that you're most likely reading an argument.

The GRE General Test showcases the following type of question more than once in its practice materials. This question type tests your ability to understand a passage's argumentative structure. Furthermore, it tasks you with understanding how the argument would be modified by the introduction of new information.

Which of the following, if it were true, would most seriously weaken the argument?

A. Expenditures for landscape damages include losses of plantings and foundations, as well as costs of fencing, netting, and repellents.

B. Controversial deer culling proposals tend to elicit organized resistance from anti-hunting constituencies.

C. The highest cost of automobile accidents involving deer is reported by the states of Pennsylvania and Michigan, with annual price tags of $343 million and $339 million, respectively.

D. In its most recent report, the Centers for Disease Control and Prevention states that 95% of all cases of Lyme disease originated in just 13 states.

E. Hunting in the United States, mainly deer, generates some $67 billion in business revenues and creates approximately 1 million jobs annually.

To correctly answer this question, you must first find the relationship between a hypothetical or an alternative idea and the ideas in the passage. This is an application question because you're applying information from one situation to other situations. You will use a variety of reading comprehension skills to answer the question, including making inferences, drawing conclusions, and evaluating hypotheses.

The argument is that stronger measures are needed to stop the problems presented by the white-tailed deer in America.

- You can eliminate choice A because this information supports the idea that damage to the landscape from deer is significant and costly.
- You can eliminate choice B because it neither weakens nor strengthens the argument; instead, it heads off in a new direction by anticipating, but not countering, opposition to the thesis.
- Choice C is incorrect because it adds increased specificity to the cost of crashes with deer, which is already reported in paragraph 4 and strengthened by this information.
- Choice D is tempting, but also incorrect, because this fact does not necessarily clash in any way with facts in the passage that point to the increasing incidence and cost of Lyme disease.
- Choice E shows the great economic benefit of deer. This idea contradicts the thesis, or controlling opinion. Therefore, **the correct answer is E.**

8. Don't Select an Answer Just Because It's True

You want to choose an answer because it answers the question. Some answers may be true, but that doesn't mean that they answer the question. Restating the question is especially useful for determining this. It will help you to anchor your thoughts before you dive into the verbiage of the answer choices.

The passage suggests which of the following as a cause of American insensitivity to the problems created by white-tailed deer?

A. White-tailed deer thrive even in conditions that are seemingly hostile to them.

B. Americans prefer to focus on the wildlife issues of other countries and continents.

C. Hunting has proven to be an inadequate means of controlling the deer population.

D. A self-congratulatory stance derived from past wildlife management efforts prevails.

E. The white-tailed deer does not pose equal threats in every state in the nation.

The correct answer is D. Remember to read all the answer choices before you choose one.

- Choice A is true, but the author does not suggest it as a cause of insensitivity.
- Even though the statement in choice B is used to open the argument, the author never states a cause-effect relationship between this focus and insensitivity to the problems posed by deer. Instead, the author suggests the irony of the two coexisting attitudes, so choice B is incorrect.
- While the author implies the truth of choice C, that hunting has been an inadequate means of control, hunting is not given as a reason for insensitivity.
- Paragraph 3 presents two key reasons why the deer problem escalates and, by implication, goes unsolved. Choice D is true, but keep reading to the end of the answer choices.
- While passage facts permit the reader to infer the truth of choice E (How can states without deer be as threatened by them as states with them?), it does not suggest this as a reason for failure to deal with the problems presented by deer.

Each of the five answer choices has some truth to it. But only choice D correctly answers the question of cause, because it's consistent with the cause-effect relationships stated or implied by the passage.

9. Substitute Answer Choices in Word Meaning Questions

Word meaning questions may appear more than once on the GRE General Test. The context in which the word is used will help you choose the correct answers. Reading the answer choices may not be enough to get you to the correct answer because often a word will have several meanings and you need to find the meaning of the word as it is used in the passage. To do this, substitute each answer choice for the word in the passage.

In the passage, "lithe" (line 17) most nearly means

A. light.

B. supple.

C. alacritous.

D. labored.

E. ambulatory.

The correct answer is B.

You may already know that *lithe* means "nimble, supple, or graceful." If you don't know its meaning, however, you could substitute each answer choice in the sentence: "Called 'charismatic' animals on at least one website, tick-infested deer are seemingly beloved for their fluffy white tails; their large, dark eyes; their _________ and graceful prancing motions; and, perhaps, most of all, their reticence or retreat in the face of human contact."

- While lithe movements might appear light, this is not the full, exact, or correct meaning of *lithe*, so choice A is incorrect.
- Neither were the movements described as quick, so the word *alacritous* (choice C) doesn't work.
- The context suggests movements that are the opposite of labored, so you can eliminate *labored* (choice D).
- Choice E doesn't work because *ambulatory* means "capable of movement" and does not describe the movement itself.

As you can see, the answer choices may contain relatively obscure or complex words. It is important that you brush up on vocabulary in preparation for the test. Aim to learn new words of graduate-level complexity.

10. Choose the Answer That *Doesn't* Fit for EXCEPT Questions

You may find one or two EXCEPT questions on the GRE General Test. These questions ask you to find the answer choice that *doesn't* answer the question. In other words, you're looking for the wrong answer as your right answer.

TIP

Remember to use other strategies for multiple-choice questions, such as restating the questions and trying to come up with answers on your own.

All the following support the claim of "cute," likable, or endearing deer EXCEPT their

A. association with nursery stock.

B. physiognomy.

C. agility.

D. seeming shyness.

E. avoidance of human beings.

The correct answer is A.

The article mentions damage to nursery stock as evidence of the problems caused by deer, so choice A does not support the claim of cuteness. Choices B, C, D, and E are developed with details about the appearance and behavior of deer. The passage touches on physiognomy, or facial appearance, with details about the deer's eyes, agility is implied by descriptive details about movement, and shyness and avoidance are expressed by the passage details of "reticence" and "retreat." Only choice A fails to support the claim.

STRATEGIES FOR SELECT ONE OR MORE ANSWER CHOICES QUESTIONS

You will find a few multiple-choice questions on the GRE General Test that may require one or more answers to be correct. We say "may" because only one answer may be correct, or two, or all three choices. The direction for the question will state that you are to choose "all that apply." If you choose only choice A, and choice C is also correct, you won't get credit for the question. To get credit, you need to select "all that apply."

The multiple-choice—select one or more answer choices questions typically have only three choices listed as possible answers. Each choice is preceded by a square rather than an oval. For your convenience in checking answers, we have used A, B, and C to signal the answer choices in this book.

The major strategy that you need to remember for answering questions that use the format of multiple-choice questions—select one or more answer choices is *to choose an answer that answers the question on its own.*

Choose an Answer That Answers the Question on Its Own

Each answer choice must answer the question on its own. Don't make the mistake of thinking that because there may be more than one answer, combining partial answer choices gives you a complete answer. Always assess each answer as a stand-alone. Is it accurate? Is it complete? Then move on to the next answer and ask yourself the same questions.

Question 7 is based on the following passage.

Telematics, a science that will, conceivably, by the year 2025, allow every car to be connected to the internet, should be used to stop or significantly reduce the 1.48 million crashes now estimated to result from texting or other cell phone use while driving. Through a combination of GPS and knowledge of individual drivers' habits and their typical locations during the day, gathered in part from mobile carriers, telematics has the potential both to block handheld use of phones and texting, as well as to shut down a driver's phone when a text or call comes in. While insurance companies as well as many mobile carriers have become ardent opponents of texting while driving, a network-level technology solution, not to mention the Big Brother–style encroachment on civil rights, gives significant pause. Will millions of lives hang in the balance, then, until the self-driving car makes the issue moot?

For Question 7, consider each answer individually and choose <u>all</u> that apply.

7. The second-to-last sentence, "While insurance . . . significant pause." (lines 16–22) serves which of the following purposes in the passage?

   A. It counters the argument expressed in the first sentence.

   B. It provides evidence for the positive effect of telematics.

   C. It suggests the limitation of freedom imposed by telematics.

The correct answers are A and C.

The first sentence argues that telematics should be employed to cut the accident rate resulting from cell phone use and texting. Although the second-to-last sentence begins with a kind of reassertion of the thesis, that sentence mainly brings up a problem with telematics, or the "network-level solution" involving mobile carriers: drivers being monitored and controlled "Big Brother" style. Therefore, the second-to-last sentence counters—or raises a point in opposition to—the first sentence, so choice A is correct. Choice B is incorrect because the next-to-last sentence does not supply evidence and is mainly about a negative consequence. However, choice C is correct because ultimately, the use of telematics described here is a surveillance system that curtails the freedom of the driver.

STRATEGIES FOR SELECT-IN-PASSAGE QUESTIONS

Select-in-passage questions ask you to choose a sentence within a passage as the correct answer. You will have a direction line, but no listing of multiple-choice answers (unless you're taking the paper-delivered test).

FYI

Select-in-passage questions appear as multiple-choice questions on the paper-delivered test; however, the strategies presented for answering this question type still apply.

Any sentence in the entire paragraph is fair game for the answer. To make your choice, click on any part of the sentence that you determine to be the answer. The entire sentence will be highlighted and registered as your answer.

Similar to answering multiple-choice—select one or more answer choices questions, you need to assess each sentence in the passage as a stand-alone sentence.

Match the Sentence to the Information

The GRE General Test information materials note two facts about select-in-passage questions. First, a select-in-passage question contains the description of a sentence—content, tone, purpose, author's perspective, or similar aspect. In answering the question, you must look for the sentence that contains that information. In other words, *match the sentence to the information*. However, you should not select a sentence if any part of the information in the sentence doesn't match the question.

This relates to the second caveat for select-in-passage questions: a question may not necessarily describe all aspects of the sentence for the sentence to be the correct answer. Sentences in the passages may be long and complicated. A question may focus on one or two aspects of a sentence. The sentence you choose just can't *contradict* the description in the question.

Question 8 is based on the following passage.

Georg Wilhelm Friedrich Hegel (1770–1831) is one of the most prominent German philosophers of all time. Though his dense works are notorious for giving today's philosophy students headaches, his complex ideas were so revolutionary that they founded the basis of most modern philosophy, including serving as inspiration to prominent thinkers like Karl Marx, Søren Kierkegaard, and Michel Foucault. Hegel developed a way of thinking known as the dialectic, which involved investigating how contradictions between two seemingly true things, termed a *thesis* and an *antithesis*, can reveal an even higher level of truth. The process of thinking through the contradiction between thesis and antithesis and its implications was known as the "Hegelian dialectic," and the idea was that engaging in dialectical thinking helped advance knowledge over time.

Hegel's most illustrative example of the dialectic involves the idea of power. The concept is often termed the "master/slave" dialectic, and it describes a dialectical thought process that imagines the power dynamic that would exist between an enslaved person and the person who enslaves them. Sometimes also referred to as the "lordship and bondage" dialectic, the concept is essentially that the two cannot exist without each other. Let's call the thesis the idea that a person cannot be enslaved without another person forcing them to do so. No one would choose to be a slave, most likely, so they can only become one if someone else exerts power over them. Meanwhile, the antithesis is the idea that the person who forces another person to be their slave cannot feel that sense of power over another without a person to force into slavery. Their existence as "master" over a slave only happens so long as the slave exists. Therefore, the power of one does not exist without the antithetical power of the other. This master/slave dialectic is thus meant to reveal a greater truth about the nature of power and can be considered a platonic model of the Hegelian dialectic more generally conceived.

For Question 8, choose only <u>one</u> answer choice.

In which sentence does the author state the main idea of the passage?

A. The second sentence ("Though his dense . . . Michel Foucault.")

B. The third sentence ("Hegel developed . . . level of truth.")

C. The fourth sentence ("The process . . . over time.")

D. The fifth sentence ("Hegel's most . . . of power.")

E. The sixth sentence ("The concept . . . enslaves them.")

The correct answer is D.

Each of the sentences indicated by the answer choices helps provide important context for the main idea, but only choice E states the main idea plainly. Do not be distracted by answers that provide only partial context for the main idea, such as choices B and C, which provide key information on the concept of the Hegelian dialectic, and choice E, which provides details to clarify the thesis statement made in choice D.

SUMMING IT UP

- There are approximately eight reading comprehension passages on the Verbal Reasoning sections of the GRE General Test.
- Most passages will be one paragraph in length, though you will find one or two passages that have multiple paragraphs.
- Passages may be informational, analytical, or persuasive.
- There are three formats for questions:
    1. Multiple-choice—select one answer choice
    2. Multiple-choice—select one or more answer choices
    3. Select-in-passage
- Multiple-choice—select one answer choice questions are preceded by ovals. Multiple-choice—select one or more answer choices questions are preceded by squares in the computer-delivered version of the test.
- Multiple-choice—select one answer choice questions are followed by a list of five possible answer options. Multiple-choice—select one or more answer choices questions are followed by a list of only three answers.
- The select-in-passage questions on the computer-delivered test will require students to choose a sentence within the passage to highlight as the answer. For students taking the paper-delivered version, the select-in-passage questions will be in the form of multiple-choice—select one answer questions.
- Answer all questions based only on the information contained in the passage.
- You will find that certain types of questions recur among the reading comprehension questions: main idea (major point), supporting details (minor points), author's perspective, authorial intent, argumentative analysis, application, and word meaning.
- Remember to use the following active reading strategies when reading the passages:
    1. Identify the topic, main idea, thesis, or proposition.
    2. Clarify your understanding.
    3. Summarize what you've read.

- The following strategies can be helpful for both kinds of multiple-choice questions:
  1. Restate the question.
  2. Try answering the question before you read the answer choices.
  3. Read all the answers before you choose.
  4. Compare answer choices to each other and to the question.
  5. Avoid selecting an answer you don't fully understand.
  6. Choose the *best* answer.
  7. Pay attention to structure and structural clues.
  8. Don't select an answer just because it's true.
  9. Substitute answer choices in word meaning questions.
  10. Choose the answer that *doesn't* fit for EXCEPT questions.

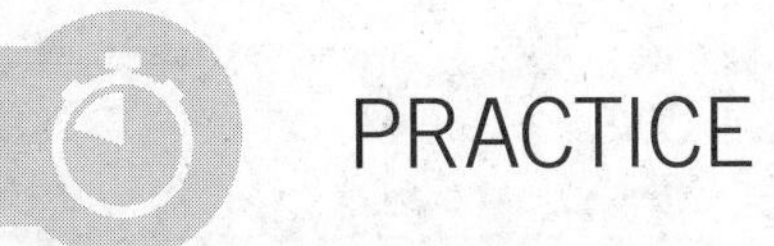

READING COMPREHENSION QUESTIONS

For Questions 1–15, choose one answer choice unless otherwise directed.

Question 1 is based on the following passage.

Ploha: Prenatal dietary supplements are key to maternal and neonatal health, offering essential nutrients like folic acid, iron, and DHA that support fetal development and maternal well-being. Studies link these supplements to lower risks of preterm births and developmental issues in infants, and also to combating maternal anemia. Ensuring that all pregnant women have access to these supplements is crucial for a healthy start for both mothers and babies.

Moelmann: Emphasizing prenatal supplements overlooks the adequacy of a balanced diet, which can meet most nutritional needs during pregnancy. Overreliance on supplements may ignore the potential for adverse effects from excessive intake and divert attention from broader health determinants, such as quality health care access and mental health support. A personalized approach to prenatal care is vital.

1. Moelmann responds to Ploha by doing which of the following?

   A. Offering a critical perspective on the efficacy of prenatal dietary supplements

   B. Recounting an anecdote regarding their personal experience with prenatal dietary supplements

   C. Advising caution regarding overreliance on prenatal dietary supplements in place of commonsense measures like monitoring one's diet

   D. Listing numerous reasons why prenatal dietary supplements can actually be detrimental

   E. Questioning the science Ploha used to reach their conclusion

Questions 2–4 are based on the following passage.

One question about whale behavior that remains somewhat unanswered is—how much rest do whales require? There have been indications that the California gray whale in the lagoons of Lower California may rest a good deal. However, the question of sleep during the long migration or on the feeding grounds has not been answered, and as yet attempts to determine this have been hardly more than preliminary tries. In order to succeed at this venture, observers must be able to remain close enough to the whales at night to be within sound of the spouts. Limited visibility at night, and the amount and direction of the boat's drift, make it difficult to keep contact with a whale spouting only once every 4 to 15 minutes. The scientists who sail with the whalers to study whales are too busy with the daily catch to consider this problem of how much a whale sleeps. Occasionally, a whale is struck by a ship during the night, and this is considered as indirect evidence that the whale was asleep on the surface.

—Excerpt from *Whale Primer* by Theodore Joseph Walker

For Questions 2 and 3, consider each answer individually and choose all that apply.

2. Which sentence in this passage clearly reflects the author's perspective on a question posed earlier in the passage?

   A. Sentence 3 ("However, the question . . . preliminary tries.")

   B. Sentence 4 ("In order to succeed . . . the spouts.")

   C. Sentence 7 ("Occasionally, a whale . . . on the surface.")

3. It can be inferred from the passage that the author believes that

   A. scientists should be much more careful when studying sleeping whales.

   B. more work is required to determine how much whales rest.

   C. how much whales rest is not a main concern of scientists who study whales.

4. Which of the following, if it were true, would weaken the correlation the author draws between whales sleeping and instances of whales being struck by ships?

   A. Whales do not stray far from their young at night.

   B. Whales communicate with each other by making a variety of expressive sounds.

   C. Whales can suffer a variety of injuries when ships strike them, and many have been killed by oncoming ships.

   D. Whales mistake the sounds of ships with communicative noises made by other whales.

   E. Whales tend to only suffer minor injuries when struck by small vessels.

Questions 5–7 are based on the following passage.

The banana is invaluable in inflammation of all kinds. For this reason, it is very useful in cases of typhoid fever, gastritis, peritonitis, etc., and may constitute the only food allowed for a time.

Not only does it actually subdue the inflammation of the intestines but, in the opinion of at least one authority, as it consists of 95 percent nutriment, it does not possess sufficient waste matter to irritate the inflamed spots.

But great care should be taken in its administration. The banana should be *thoroughly sound and ripe*, and all the stringy portion carefully removed. It should then be mashed and beaten to a cream. In severe cases I think it is better to give this neat, but if not liked by the patient a little lemon juice, well mixed in, may render it more acceptable. It may also be taken with fresh cream.

—Excerpt from *Food Remedies* by Florence Daniel

5. In the passage, "administration" (line 6) most nearly means

A. distribution.
B. authority.
C. enforcement.
D. supervision.
E. committee.

6. The writer most likely mentions typhoid in this passage in order to

A. explain how bananas are used to treat inflammation.
B. cast doubt on assumptions about the effectiveness of bananas as a treatment.
C. reinforce the idea that bananas can be used to treat inflammation.
D. provide an example of a condition that bananas may help treat.
E. introduce the main topic of the passage.

7. In the passage, what is the primary purpose of the italicized words?

A. They indicate a specific name of a banana variety used to treat inflammation.
B. They provide details about the preparation of bananas when treating inflammation.
C. They contradict the idea that any banana can be used to treat inflammation.
D. They support the idea that bananas are very effective remedies for inflammation.
E. They are details crucial to the use of the banana as a remedy for inflammation.

Questions 8 and 9 are based on the following passage.

Few nations have been as unprepared for a full-scale war as was the United States in 1861. The US Army consisted of barely 17,000 men. Most of the soldiers were stationed at remote outposts on the western frontier. To make matters worse for the Union, a large number of army officers who had been born in the South and educated at West Point resigned from the army and offered their services to the Confederacy.

The US Navy was in an equally bad state. It had performed little duty since the War of 1812. The navy had a total of 90 ships, but only 42 of them were in active service at the outbreak of civil war. Of this number, 11 fell into Confederate hands with the capture of the naval base at Norfolk, Virginia, in April 1861. The remaining vessels were scattered around the world. Moreover, 230 of 1,400 naval officers joined the forces of the Confederacy.

At the beginning of the Civil War, the North seemed to possess every advantage:

(1) 23 Northern states aligned against only 11 Southern states. (Maryland, Kentucky and Missouri were slave states, but they remained in the Union. Also, the western counties of Virginia revolted and formed their own state when the Old Dominion cast her lot with the Confederacy.)

(2) The population of the Northern states was approximately 22,000,000 people. The Southern states had only 9,105,000 people, and one-third of them (3,654,000) were slaves. The great difference in population, plus a steady flow of European immigrants into the Northern states, gave the Union tremendous manpower. Over 2,000,000 men served in the Federal armies, while no more than half that number fought for the South.

—Excerpt from *The Civil War* by James I. Robertson Jr.

For Question 8, consider each answer individually and choose all that apply.

8. The sentence "At the beginning . . . every advantage" (line 10) serves which of the following purposes in the passage?

A. It indicates how certain statistics do not guarantee a particular conclusion.

B. It states an assumption that a conclusion previously stated in the passage contradicts.

C. It makes an assertion that supports the conclusions previously stated in the passage.

9. Which of the following statements does the passage most clearly support?

A. The Confederacy was composed exclusively of disloyal soldiers.

B. Fighting a war shortly before 1861 may have benefited the Union.

C. Overconfidence was fatal to the Union army.

D. Its population advantage was crucial to the Union's victory.

E. The Union would have lost the Civil War without immigration.

Questions 10 and 11 are based on the following passage.

A full history of the development of language would demand an exact knowledge of all the groups of sound ever uttered or heard, and of all the ideas awakened by such sound-groups and symbolized by them. The impossibility of attaining any such knowledge is obvious; it is, however, possible for us to get a general idea of the play of the forces at work in the vast and complex series of processes involved in the development of language. A part only of these operating forces is cognizable by our senses. Speaking and hearing are two of the processes which can be apprehended; and, again, the ideas, or pictures, called up by language, and those which, though unspoken, pass through our consciousness, are to some extent capable of cognition. But one of the greatest triumphs of modern psychology is the proof, due to its agency, of the unconscious activity of the human mind. All that has once been present to our consciousness remains as a working factor in unconsciousness. Power consciously acquired by exercise in consciousness may be translated into power operating and manifesting itself unconsciously. The mind forms from the groups of ideas with which it is stored, psychological groups, such as sound-groups, sequences of sounds, sequences of ideas, and syntactical combinations. Strong and weak verbs, derivatives from the same root, words fulfilling identical functions, such as the different parts of speech, associate themselves into groups; and again the plurals of nouns, their different cases, their different inflections, and even entire clauses of similar construction or similar cadence, group themselves in the same way. These groups arise naturally, automatically, and unconsciously, and must not be confused with the categories consciously drawn up by grammarians; though the two, of course, must frequently coincide.

These groups must obviously be in a constant state of change, some growing weaker from the fact that they are strengthened by no fresh impulse, and some being strengthened and, it may be, changed by the accession of new ideas which ally themselves therewith. It must not be overlooked also that, as each person's mind is differently constituted, the groups of his linguistic ideas will take a development peculiar to himself; even though the sources whence the groups take their rise should be identical, yet the elements which go to form the groups will be introduced differently and with different intensity in the case of each individual.

—Excerpt from *Introduction to the Study of the History of Language* by Herbert A. Strong

10. The author of the passage would most likely consider which of the following ideas most similar to the mental processes mentioned in lines 11–16?

A. The instinctual love for one's own family.

B. The natural fear of dangerous animals such as poisonous snakes.

C. The innate understanding of what different facial expressions mean.

D. The ability to learn to speak, read, and write different languages.

E. The capability of remembering a wide variety of vocabulary words.

11. Which of the following, if it were true, most seriously undermines the first statement in the final paragraph?

A. When children fail to practice certain elements of language, they tend to lose their understanding of those elements.

B. Speaking regularly helps children to maintain their ability to understand different elements of language instinctively.

C. A study of 17,000 children revealed that they learned foreign languages more effectively if they started at the age of 11 rather than the age of 8.

D. While children do learn much of language instinctively, they must also study grammar since there are often elements of language that contradict intuition.

E. Some children maintain complete fluency even if they neither use nor are exposed to certain elements of language for a long time.

Questions 12–14 are based on the following passage.

Wolfgang Amadeus Mozart was born at Salzburg in 1756. His father had possessed musical talent, but in him it was genius. At three years of age he learned to play; before he was five he had composed a great many little melodies, which his father wrote down for him. I remember seeing in the studio of an English artist in London, himself the son of a great musician, a picture representing the baby Mozart, a charming little figure, leading a visionary choir of angels. It seemed to me the very embodiment of what Mozart must have been as a child—beautiful, fascinating, angelic, and a musician to his very soul.

His sister Anna, or "Nannerl," as she was called, also played marvelously, and when the children were very young their father started with them on a concert tour, during which they played in London. Everywhere they went they were fêted and caressed in a way which would have spoiled even Mozart's sweet, sunny nature, but for his father's watchful care.

Innumerable presents were made them, some of rich jewelry. This their father insisted upon keeping in a box, only allowing them to take it out on rare occasions and enjoy looking at it for a little while.

It was during that London visit that the father fell ill. They were in lodgings in Chelsea, which was then an open country with blooming gardens and green lanes. The little Mozarts had to keep very quiet during this illness of their father's. The harpsichord was closed, and the children took to running about the pretty suburban place, no doubt enjoying the rest from practicing. But it was during this enforced idleness that Mozart composed his first symphony (Opus 15). He was then in his tenth year. Think of the amount of scientific knowledge as well as the genius the boy must have possessed! Soon after, they gave more concerts, playing among other things duets for four hands on the harpsichord, which was then (in 1765) a great novelty.

—Excerpt from *Wolfgang Amadeus Mozart* by Mrs. John Lillie

12. It can be inferred that the author judges which of the following characteristics as most clearly defining or epitomizing Mozart?

A. Mozart's creative brilliance

B. Mozart's physical attractiveness

C. Mozart's genius in all fields

D. Mozart's ability to win admirers

E. Mozart's graciousness when receiving gifts

13. It can be inferred that Mozart's father was tolerant of all the following aspects of his son EXCEPT

A. his son's love of performing music.

B. his son's interest in writing his own music.

C. his son's desire to keep gifts.

D. his son's potential to become spoiled.

E. his son's desire to travel.

14. In the passage, "figure" (line 5) means

A. number.

B. calculate.

C. appearance.

D. leader.

E. celebrity.

Question 15 is based on the following passage.

I have recently made some experiments with oil of lemons, of which the following is a short account:—

Being constantly annoyed by the deposit and alteration in my essence of lemons, I have tried various methods of remedying the inconvenience.

I first tried redistilling it, but besides the loss consequent on distilling small quantities, the flavor is thereby impaired. As the oil became brighter when heated, I anticipated that all its precipitable matter would be thrown down at a low temperature, and I applied a freezing mixture, keeping the oil at zero for some hours. No such change, however, took place.

The plan which I ultimately decided upon as the best which I had arrived at, was to shake up the oil with a little boiling water, and to leave the water in the bottle; a mucilaginous preparation forms on the top of the water, and acquires a certain tenacity, so that the oil may be poured off to nearly the last, without disturbing the deposit. Perhaps cold water would answer equally well, were it carefully agitated with the oil and allowed some time to settle.

—Excerpt from *The Art of Perfumery and Methods of Obtaining the Odors of Plants* by Piesse

15. According to the information in this passage, in what order would these steps in the process of obtaining the essence of lemons most likely take place?

A. combine oil and water, allow to settle, remove excess oil

B. distill lemons, redistill them, heat

C. boil water, add oil, shake vigorously

D. shake oil and water together, remove mucilaginous preparation

E. shake oil and boiling water together, drain oil, steep

ANSWER KEY AND EXPLANATIONS

1. C	4. D	7. E	10. C	13. D
2. A	5. A	8. A, B	11. E	14. C
3. B, C	6. D	9. B	12. A	15. A

1. **The correct answer is C.** Moelmann does not outright reject the efficacy of prenatal dietary supplements but does suggest that the benefits of these vitamins may be overstated, particularly since many of the same results can be achieved with a balanced diet. Therefore, it is reasonable to infer that Moelmann is advising caution regarding overreliance on prenatal supplements. You can eliminate choices A, D, and E because each implies that Moelmann is being more critical than the passage suggests. Choice B is incorrect because the passage does not contain a personal anecdote.

2. **The correct answer is A.** Sentence 3 indicates that the author's perspective on the only question asked in the passage—"how much rest do whales require?"—is that it is not yet possible to determine an answer to that question at all. Choices B and C offer some supporting details for the topic of whales at rest, but neither sentence indicates anything about the amount of rest or whether that amount can be determined.

3. **The correct answers are B and C.** Evidence in the passage supports both choices B and C. The statement that California gray whales "*may* rest a good deal" and the even more inconclusive statement about how long whales rest during long migrations support choice B. The statement that "scientists who sail with the whalers to study whales are too busy with the daily catch to consider this problem of how much a whale sleeps" supports choice C. Although the author mentions that sleeping whales are occasionally struck by ships, the lack of judgment about such accidents means there is insufficient support for choice A.

4. **The correct answer is D.** If whales are confused by the noises ships make as they traverse open waters, one could infer that the whales that are struck by ships are drawn to those ships out of confusion, rather than that they are sleeping near the surface. The other answer choices do not refer to any specific evidence in the passage. The author never discusses the relationship of whales to their young or how whales communicate with each other, so choices A and B are irrelevant. The author is less concerned with the damage that ships cause than he is with what ships striking whales says about whales' sleeping habits, so choices C and E are incorrect.

5. **The correct answer is A.** The word *administration* has a number of meanings, but only the word *distribution* makes sense in this particular context since the author is referring to the "distribution" of bananas to patients. A remedy, such as bananas, is not usually "enforced," so the word *enforcement* (choice C) is not as strong an answer as choice A. When applied to bananas, most of the other answer choices do not make sense. A banana cannot have authority (choice B), provide supervision (choice D), or serve as a committee (choice E).

6. **The correct answer is D.** The author mentions typhoid in the context of various conditions that may involve inflammations that bananas may help treat. Typhoid is only mentioned as an example; it is not used to explain anything, so choice A is not the best answer. Choice B is the opposite of the author's intention in writing the passage as a whole. Typhoid is mentioned as an example, not something that reinforces any idea, so choice C is inaccurate. The main topic of the passage is

how bananas may be used to treat inflammation; typhoid is not the main topic. Therefore, choice E is incorrect.

7. **The correct answer is E.** Italics are often used for emphasis, so it is likely that the details in italics are especially crucial when choosing the right bananas for treating inflammation. While certain titles are italicized, the italicized words in this passage do not comprise a specific title or name, so choice A is inaccurate. The italicized words refer to the selection of bananas, not the preparation of them, so choice B is incorrect. Choice C implies that the author intends to make a counterargument, but there is no evidence of that. Choice D implies that the italicized words support an argument, which they do not.

8. **The correct answers are A and B.** In the first paragraph, the author explains how the Union was at a severe disadvantage at the beginning of the Civil War, yet this sentence indicates that the Union seemingly had several consequential advantages over the Confederacy. This supports both choice A and choice B. Choice C is the opposite of those conclusions, so it should be eliminated.

9. **The correct answer is B.** The author mentions that the lack of war since the War of 1812 had left the Union navy unprepared, so it is logical to assume that a war fought shortly before the Civil War may have remedied this problem. While the author indicates that many soldiers disloyal to the Union decided to join the Confederacy instead, choice A is an extreme conclusion. While the supposed Union advantages the author describes may seem to support choice C, the fact that the author never implies that the Union lost the war makes choice C a weak answer. Choices D and E reach very specific conclusions that the information in this passage does not support.

10. **The correct answer is C.** In lines 11–16, the author basically explains that humans come to understand different aspects of language without specifically learning them first. Of the answer choices, this is most similar to understanding what different facial expressions mean without learning their meanings first. While the information in lines 11–16 does deal with instinct on a certain level, it is more about understanding than emotions, such as love and fear, so choice C is a better answer than choices A and B. Lines 11–16 deal with intuitive understanding rather than formal learning, so choice D is incorrect. Choice E focuses on memory rather than instinctive understanding.

11. **The correct answer is E.** The first sentence of the final paragraph states with some certainty that elements of language will be lost if not exercised, but the variable introduced in choice E undermines that certainty. Choices A and B support rather than undermine the first statement of the final paragraph. Choices C and D have little to do with that statement at all.

12. **The correct answer is A.** While the author draws attention to numerous positive qualities she feels Mozart possessed, the author seems mainly interested in Mozart's ability to play and write wonderful music, which are aspects of Mozart's creative brilliance. The author does refer to Mozart as "beautiful" and "angelic," which supports the idea that the composer was physically attractive, but the author mentions these qualities only in passing and focuses more on Mozart's music than his looks. Therefore, choice B is not the best answer. The author does refer to Mozart as a "genius," but she does not imply that Mozart was a genius in all fields, so choice C is not the best answer. The author also describes Mozart's ability to win admirers, but this, too, is less important than Mozart's music, so choice D is not the best answer either. How Mozart reacted when receiving gifts is never discussed in this passage, so there is no support for choice E.

13. **The correct answer is D.** According to the second paragraph, Wolfgang Amadeus Mozart may have become spoiled "but for his father's watchful care." This implies that his father took measures to ensure Mozart did not become spoiled because this would be intolerable. Because Mozart's father took him on a tour of performance, the reader can infer that his father tolerated young Mozart's love of performing music (choice A) and desire to travel (choice E). There is no evidence that Mozart's father did not think his son should compose his own music, so choice B is not the exception we are looking for. While Mozart's father was afraid his son might become spoiled and only let his son view the gifts he received occasionally, he did allow young Mozart to keep those gifts, so choice C is also not the exception we are looking for.

14. **The correct answer is C.** While each answer choice can be used as a synonym for the word *figure*, the word *appearance* makes the most sense in this particular context since it describes how someone looks in a painting. *Figure* does not refer to a number (choice A) in this context. *Figure* is clearly used as a noun, not as a verb as the word *calculate* (choice B) suggests. While Mozart would become a leader (choice D) and celebrity (choice E) in his later days, these words do not suit the context of line 5 as well as *appearance* does.

15. **The correct answer is A.** According to the final paragraph of the passage, the method for obtaining the essence of lemons using either boiling or cold water would be to (1) combine the oil and water, (2) allow to settle, and (3) remove excess oil. Choice B describes a failed process described in the third paragraph. Choice C relates only part of the process. Choice D suggests removing the mucilaginous preparation, though this is contraindicated in the passage. Choice E places the steps in the wrong order.

CHAPTER

Text Completion Questions

5

TEXT COMPLETION QUESTIONS

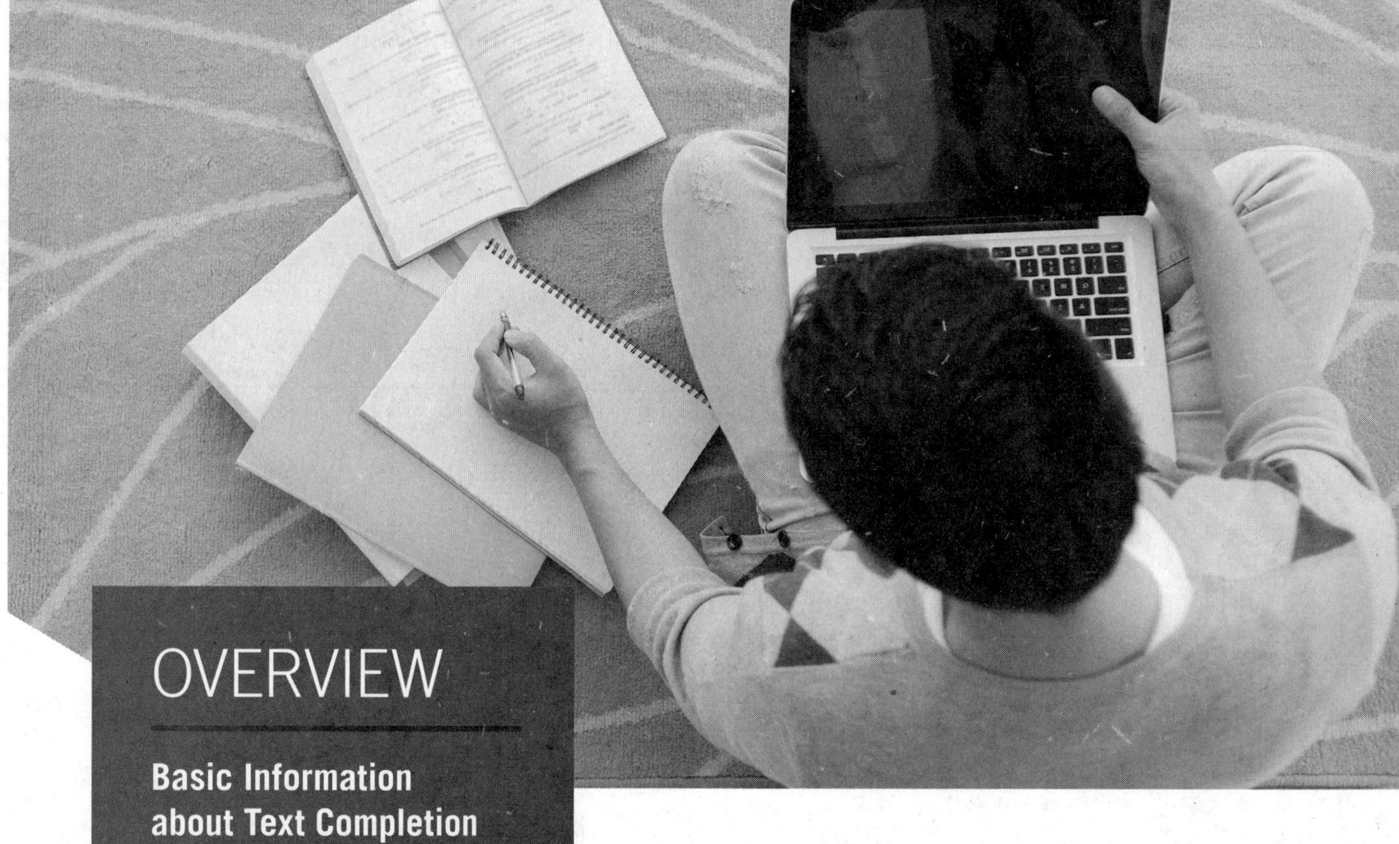

OVERVIEW

Text Completion questions evaluate your skill in choosing appropriate words or phrases to complete blanks in a passage. These questions ask you to rely on the context of the passage to form a logical and meaningful sentence. Chapter 5 describes question formats for the text completion questions on the GRE General Test and provides an overview of strategies to help you answer this question type.

5

BASIC INFORMATION ABOUT TEXT COMPLETION QUESTIONS

The text completion questions on the GRE General Test assess your ability to actively interpret and evaluate what you read and to supply words and phrases whose meanings are consistent with the ideas presented. You can expect to see about two to four text completion questions, interspersed with other test items, in the Verbal Reasoning section.

The text completion items (and the sentence equivalence items) test your vocabulary. To do well on these questions, you will need to have a robust vocabulary. However, not all the words are a test of the size of your vocabulary. Some items will involve words that are close in meaning or that represent an unusual meaning of a familiar word. The text completion items also test your reading comprehension skills, and you may have to apply your knowledge of grammar and usage to select the best answers.

TIP

Sign up for supplemental test prep at **www.petersons.com/gre** for a variety of flash cards to help you improve your vocabulary.

Passages and Question Formats

Unlike the reading comprehension questions, the text completion items follow a predictable format. Overall, the text completion passages are much less intimidating and require less time than reading comprehension passages. Text completion passages are also shorter than reading comprehension passages, making them easier and quicker to read.

Here is a quick overview of how text completion items will be presented:

- Each text completion passage consists of one to five sentences, and each sentence will have one to three blanks.
- If there is only one blank, there will be five answer choices.
- If there are two or three blanks, there will be three answer choices per blank.
- There is only one correct answer per blank.

Regardless of the number of blanks, each question is worth 1 point. You must correctly answer all the blanks for a test item to earn a point for that question.

The Direction Line and Answer Choices

The directions for text completion items will look something like this:

For Questions 1–10, choose <u>one</u> answer for each blank unless otherwise indicated. Select from the appropriate column for each blank. Choose the answer that best completes the sense of the text.

STRATEGIES FOR TEXT COMPLETION QUESTIONS

Throughout this chapter, we will cover the different strategies you can use to answer text completion questions. The first four strategies are commensense reminders; the last four strategies ask you to apply what you learned in English composition classes.

- Try answering the question before you read the answer choice(s).
- Focus on one blank at a time.
- If there is more than one blank, complete the blanks in the order that makes sense to you.
- Check your answer(s) in place.
- Use structural clues.
- Consider tone and style.
- Consider grammar and usage.
- Avoid selecting a word or phrase that you don't fully understand or is unfamiliar.

TIPS

Remember that there is no penalty for wrong answers. If you cannot decide on an answer even through the process of elimination, make your best guess based on what you do know.

If time is running out and you still have several questions to answer, go quickly through the test looking for text completion and sentence equivalence questions. They're quicker to answer than reading comprehension questions, and a point is a point, no matter what question you answer to earn it.

Try Answering the Question Before You Read the Answer Choice(s)

When reading a passage, first try to get a clear sense of what the passage is about. Then, before you read the answer choices, fill in the answer blank(s) in your own words. What you come up with doesn't need to be overly complex; it just needs to be a word or words that capture the meaning of the sentence. With your answer in mind, check the list of answers and choose the one that best matches your idea.

Try this now with Question 1.

For Question 1, choose one answer for the blank. Choose the answer that best completes the sense of the text.

1. Emerging African democracies of the 1960s and 1970s faced insurmountable problems that ranged from lack of infrastructure to borders that ignored ethnic conflict: in fact, these __________ governments were destined to fail.

A. despotic
B. ephemeral
C. incompetent
D. deteriorating
E. fledgling

The correct answer is E.

If you try to fill in the blank before you read the answers, you might come up with the word *new,* as cued by the word *emerging.* Your next step is to review the answer choices for a synonym to the words *new* or *emerging. Fledgling* means "young and inexperienced," which suggests the meaning of *new. Fledgling* is most often applied to birds leaving the nest and trying their wings for the first time, just as the new democracies referred to in the passage were beginning to grow, develop, or "take flight" in a metaphorical sense.

Focus on Only One Blank at a Time

Most of the text completion items will present you with either two or three blanks to fill. When you have multiple blanks to fill, concentrate on one blank at a time. Try out this strategy as you read the following two-blank item.

For Question 2, choose one answer for each blank. Select from the appropriate column for each blank. Choose the answer that best completes the sense of the text.

2. A major part of the body's immune system, the lymphatic system, is responsible for producing, maintaining, and distributing lymphocytes (white blood cells that attack bacteria in blood and take the form of T cells and B cells) in the body as well as for defending the body against pathogens. Besides removing waste, dead blood cells, and toxins from cells and the tissues between them, the lymphatic system works in concert with the circulatory system to deliver oxygen, nutrients, and hormones from the blood to the cells. The (i) _________ role of the lymphatic system in fighting disease and maintaining homeostasis (ii) _________.

Blank (i)	Blank (ii)
A. crucial	D. must not be trivial
B. autonomous	E. cannot be gainsaid
C. hypothetical	F. will not be equivocated

The correct answers are A and E.

Starting with the first blank might lead you to a word that conveys the importance or centrality of the lymphatic system, like *key*, *major*, *necessary*, or *central*. Reading down the list of answers for Blank (i), you find the word *crucial* (choice A), which means "key" or "essential," so this is the correct answer for Blank (i). Read all the answer choices for Blank (i) just to be sure *crucial* is the best choice. Once you complete the first blank, it's usually easier to come up with the second answer. For example, it makes no sense to say that "the crucial role must not be trivial." Neither does it make sense to say that "the crucial role will not be equivocated," meaning "using vague language." Therefore, the correct answer for the second blank is choice E, "cannot be gainsaid." Even if you didn't know that *gainsaid* means "denied," focusing on the context provided by the first blank would help you arrive at the correct answer.

If There Is More Than One Blank, Complete the Blanks in the Order That Makes Sense to You

Don't assume that you need to fill in the first blank first, the second blank second, and so on. Start by filling in the blank that is easiest or most obvious to you. Try this strategy now with the following three-blank item.

For Question 3, choose one answer for each blank. Select from the appropriate column for each blank. Choose the answer that best completes the sense of the text.

3. Those calling for the regulation of commodities trading are, at best, uninformed. Instead of (i) _________ traders for spikes in prices of wheat, oil, and metals, legislators would be wiser to consider how speculators help to create (ii) _________ by injecting cash into markets—which contributes to market efficiency. Furthermore, legislators who are gung ho to rein in traders might bother to note that speculators have little or no effect on the production, and only (iii) _________ effect on the consumption, of goods.

Blank (i)	Blank (ii)	Blank (iii)
A. regulating	D. liquidity	G. minimal
B. scapegoating	E. activity	H. negative
C. ostracizing	F. inventory	I. lasting

The correct answers are B, D, and G.

Maybe you read the passage and know that injecting, or moving, cash into markets creates liquidity, so you mark choice D for Blank (ii). With *liquidity* in place for Blank (ii), you can now move back to Blank (i) or on to Blank (iii). In either case, you can use the concept of liquidity to help you make sense of the rest of the passage. The more words you fill in, the easier it will be to come up with the answer that is most difficult for you. For the record, the correct answer for Blank (i) is *scapegoating* (choice B), which means "blaming unfairly." The correct answer for Blank (iii) is *minimal* (choice G).

You will revisit Question 3 and read a more detailed analysis later in this chapter.

Check Your Answer(s) in Place

Once you've chosen your answer(s), reread the question quickly with the answers in place. All the words collectively should create a unified whole—the meanings should all work together, everything should be grammatically correct, and the tone and style should be consistent.

Use Structural Clues

In many text completion items, passages are structured in a way that can help you determine the correct answer. These structures include sentences and paragraphs that compare, contrast, restate, show causes and/or effects, and present the main idea and supporting details. Some passages will contain "signposts," which are signal or transitional words and phrases to help you understand the meaning of the passage or the relationship of ideas within that passage.

You can use the following types of structural clues to determine meaning and fill in the blanks of text completion questions. Note that, in some cases, a single sentence or passage may contain more than one type of structure and structural clue. The following clues can help you identify answers:

- Restatement
- Cause and effect
- Contrast
- Structure of comparison or similarity
- Main idea and details

Restatement

Restatement is a presentation of an idea in words other than those used the first time the idea is presented, an amplification or clarification of an idea, or the presentation of an example of the idea. A sentence or passage that uses restatement will most often have two independent clauses joined by a colon, a semicolon, or a correlative conjunction, like *moreover*. Alternatively, a restatement might take the form of two sentences, the second of which begins with a signal word for restatement.

Depending on the restatement structure used, one of the following will be apparent:

- Sentence 2 or clause 2 uses different words to express the meaning of sentence 1 or clause 1.
- Sentence 2 or clause 2 amplifies or clarifies sentence 1 or clause 1. This is more likely than simple repetition of an idea in other words.
- Sentence 2 or clause 2 exemplifies sentence 1 or clause 1. That is, sentence 2 or clause 2 provides a single example or illustration.

Signals for Restatement		
Among the words and phrases that can signal restatement relationships are the following:		
for example	in other words	that is
for instance	in short	this means

You may have to infer the words and phrases that signal restatement, amplification, clarification, or illustration. For an example of restatement, we'll look again at Question 1. You should be able to identify a restatement signal before you read the analysis that follows the question.

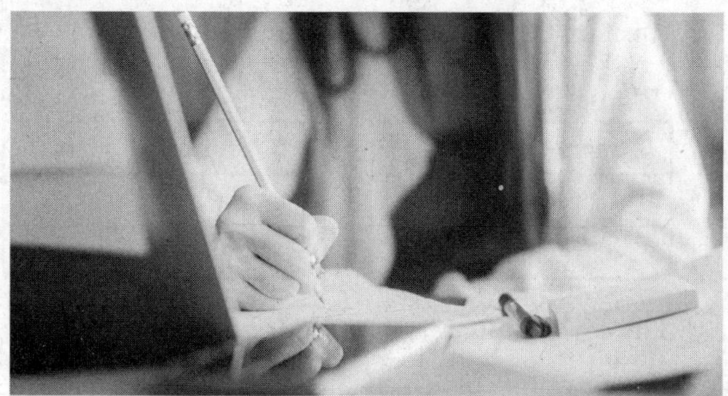

For Question 1, choose one answer for the blank. Choose the answer that best completes the sense of the text.

1. Emerging African democracies of the 1960s and 1970s faced insurmountable problems that ranged from lack of infrastructure to borders that ignored ethnic conflict: in fact, these __________ governments were destined to fail.

A. despotic
B. ephemeral
C. incompetent
D. deteriorating
E. fledgling

The correct answer is E.

A thought process to work through Question 1 might look like this:

- Note that the signal phrase "in fact," along with the way the second clause rephrases or amplifies the first, signals a restatement.
- Knowing that you're working with restatement, you should then restate, paraphrase, or summarize the item. Focus on the central idea of the passage, and eliminate extraneous wording. For this passage, you would concentrate on the two main clauses and eliminate the clause that begins with "that ranged from . . . ." You might arrive at this summary: "New African governments faced huge problems; these __________ governments could do nothing to avoid failure."
- The omission of extra words shows how the word that fits the blank must be a synonym for *emerging* or *new*, or it must in some way express a similar meaning.
- To arrive at the correct answer, use the process of elimination. The first four choices are not synonyms for *new*, nor do they evoke something new. Therefore, the correct answer is *fledgling* (choice E).

Go back to Question 1, and drop out the words "in fact." Reread the passage without those words and you'll see that you're still dealing with restatement, even though it's not as apparent.

Cause and Effect

A sentence or passage with a cause-and-effect structure expresses the reason(s) someone did something or something occurred and the result(s) of an action or event. A cause-and-effect relationship can be expressed in one sentence or in a longer passage.

Cause-and-Effect Signals	
Cause-and-effect relationships may or may not include signal words. Among the words and phrases that can signal cause-and-effect relationships are the following:	
as a result	since
because	so
consequently	so that
for	therefore
in order to	thus
reason why	why

Sometimes, you will have to infer cause-and-effect relationships. For example, Question 4 begins with the infinitive phrase "To defeat the English." You can and should reasonably infer that this phrase means "[In order to] defeat the English," or "[Because he wanted to] defeat the English." This is your first step.

For Question 4, choose one answer for the blank. Choose the answer that best completes the sense of the text.

4. To defeat the English, Metacomet, whom the English called King Philip, knew he had to bring disparate and sometimes warring groups together into a __________.

A. regiment
B. community
C. legation
D. confederation
E. hierarchy

The correct answer is D.

An analysis of Question 4 could take the following shape:

- Once you know that you're working with cause and effect, start by restating, paraphrasing, or summarizing the item in a way that reflects your understanding of the cause-and-effect relationship. For example, you might arrive at this loose paraphrase or summary: "In order to defeat the English, Metacomet had to bring together different and warring groups into a __________."
- This summary leaves out the clause "whom the English called King Philip" because it is extraneous to the cause-and-effect relationship. Doing so makes it clear that the reason, or cause, for bringing together the groups was defeat of the English. Therefore, the word that goes into the blank must name a group that can defeat someone or something. That immediately leaves out the all-too-peaceable *community* (choice B) as well as the diplomatic and also peaceful *legation* (choice C). It also leaves out *hierarchy* (choice E); a hierarchy alone wouldn't accomplish the job of defeating someone.
- Using cause-and-effect clues in this case quickly narrows down the possible choices to *regiment* (choice A) and *confederation* (choice D).
- To reach the correct answer, try a general strategy, like comparing two answers against each other and against the passage. A regiment is a discrete unit within an army, so its scope is too narrow. A confederation brings many different groups together, which is the point of the sentence.

Contrast

A sentence or passage with a contrast structure expresses differences. This commonly used structure is probably very familiar to you.

Contrast Signals	
Like other structures, contrasts of information may or may not include signal words. Among the words and phrases that can be used to signal contrasts are the following:	
although	instead
as opposed to	nevertheless
but	on the contrary
by contrast	on the other hand
conversely	otherwise
however	still
in contrast	unlike
in spite of	

Oftentimes, you'll need to infer contrasts or the words and phrases that signal them. Question 5, however, does contain a contrast word.

For Question 5, choose one answer for the blank. Choose the answer that best completes the sense of the text.

5. Judging by the various glances exchanged, the statistics Mai offered during the meeting struck everyone in attendance as __________; later, however, she managed to authenticate most of them in her expansive written analysis.

A. valid
B. inconsequential
C. spurious
D. unexpurgated
E. superfluous

The correct answer is C.

An analysis of the contrast relationship in Question 5 might look like this:

- Once you have identified the structure as a contrast, you can then restate, paraphrase, or summarize the item in a way that reflects your understanding of the contrast relationship. For example, you might arrive at this paraphrase: "The glances showed people thought Mai's statistics were __________; later, her analysis showed they were authentic."
- This loose paraphrase makes it clear that the answer must express the opposite, or near opposite, of *authentic*.
- Through the process of elimination, choices A, B, D, and E should all be ruled out because they don't show or suggest the opposite of *authentic*. *Valid* (choice A) means "just, producing the desired results, or legally binding," which is somewhat similar to *authentic*. *Inconsequential* (choice B) is incorrect because it isn't the opposite of *authentic*. *Unexpurgated* (choice D) refers to not removing offensive material from something. *Superfluous* (choice E) means "unnecessary, more than what is required." Therefore, *spurious* (choice C), meaning "false," is the correct answer.

Try rereading the passage after eliminating the signal word *however* to come up with an alternative way in which a contrast passage might appear.

Structure of Comparison or Similarity

Like a sentence or passage expressing contrasting ideas, a sentence or passage expressing a comparison or similarity should be familiar to you. This structure expresses how two or more things are alike.

Comparison Signals	
Among the words and phrases that can signal a comparison are the following:	
also	like
and	likewise
another	moreover
as	same
by the same token	similarly
in comparison	too
in the same way	

For Question 6, choose one answer for the blank. Choose the answer that best completes the sense of the text.

6. Debussy is regarded as the germinal musical impressionist who created color through the use of individual instruments in the orchestra; by the same token, Monet's use of blocks of color, in lieu of line, was a(n) __________ influence on impressionism in art. There, however, the similarity between the two "impressionists" ends.

A. imperative
B. seminal
C. discernable
D. super
E. formidable

The correct answer is B.

An analysis of the comparison in Question 6 could look something like this:

- Note that the signal phrase "by the same token" and the word *similarity* indicate a comparison.
- The next step is to restate, paraphrase, or summarize the item in a way that reflects your understanding of the comparison relationship or structure. For example, you might arrive at this summary: "Debussy had great influence in music because of his use of color; likewise, Monet was a(n) _________ influence in art because of how he used color."
- This summary significantly reduces the original phrasing to focus on the comparison. It also shows that the correct answer must be an adjective that suggests great influence.
- At this point, you can use the process of elimination. Choice A should be eliminated because *imperative* means "absolutely necessary." *Discernable* (choice C) can also be eliminated because the similarity suggests that Monet had more than a discernable, or noticeable, influence on art; he had a great influence. *Super* (choice D), which can mean "particularly excellent," is too informal for this passage. *Formidable* (choice E), while suggesting a meaning that fits, does not exactly match the meaning expressed by the first clause. The context makes it clear that the effect of each artist on his discipline was not only significant but also influential. *Seminal* (choice B) is the only word that conveys something formative or something that shaped, influenced, or decided what was to come.

Now try analyzing Question 6 without the signal words in the passage.

If you look back at Question 1, you'll see that it could also be approached as a comparison, but without any signal words. Structures can be combined or overlapped in a single sentence or passage. Your task is not to identify the "right" structure but to identify and use structures that will best help you find the answer.

Main Idea and Details

As an organizing structure, main ideas and details consist of more than one sentence. The main idea may be stated at the beginning of the passage, in the middle, or at the end. It may also be implied through the details in the passage. Although passages might contain signal words and phrases like "for example" to help you identify details, you will probably have to infer the main idea based on the content of the passage.

Take another look at Question 2. See if you can identify its main ideas and details before you read the analysis.

For Question 2, choose one answer for each blank. Select from the appropriate column for each blank. Choose the answer that best completes the sense of the text.

2. A major part of the body's immune system, the lymphatic system is responsible for producing, maintaining, and distributing lymphocytes (white blood cells that attack bacteria in blood and take the form of T cells and B cells) in the body as well as for defending the body against pathogens. Besides removing waste, dead blood cells, and toxins from cells and the tissues between them, the lymphatic system works in concert with the circulatory system to deliver oxygen, nutrients, and hormones from the blood to the cells. The (i) _________ role of the lymphatic system in fighting disease and maintaining homeostasis (ii) _________.

Blank (i)	Blank (ii)
A. crucial	D. must not be trivial
B. autonomous	E. cannot be gainsaid
C. hypothetical	F. will not be equivocated

The correct answers are A and E.

To help you answer a text completion question, consider this analysis of the main idea and supporting details in the passage for Question 2:

- Start by finding the main idea (the last sentence) and the details that support it (everything that precedes the last sentence).
- Then, restate, paraphrase, or summarize the part or parts of the passage containing the blank or blanks you must fill in. For example, you might arrive at this summary: "The _________ part played by the lymphatic system in the body _________."
- This summary depends on the details for correct completion, so now reread the details. The details explain the various and important roles the lymphatic system plays in the body. Therefore, the first blank must have to do with importance or being essential.
- The word that comes closest in meaning to *important* is *crucial. Crucial* (choice A) is the correct answer for Blank (i).
- To complete Blank (ii), work with the more complete version of your summary: "The crucial part played by the lymphatic system in the body _________." If you come up with your own answer for this blank, you might say "cannot be (or must not be or will not be) denied." Therefore, look for the answer choice that means "denied." In this case, "cannot be gainsaid" (choice E) is correct.

If you don't know the meaning of all the words—or even if you do—remember to use the process of elimination. *Trivial* (choice D) doesn't mean "denied." Neither does *equivocated* (choice F). So even if you don't know that *gainsaid* (choice E) means "denied," by the process of elimination, it must be the correct answer.

Consider Tone and Style

Although this strategy won't apply to every passage, some passages will carry a distinctive tone that can help you infer meaning. For example, the author's attitude may be sympathetic, indignant, questioning, mournful, celebratory, or praising. If there is an obvious tone, it might be a clue to the words that belong in the blanks. Look again at Question 3, and see if you can identify the tone of the passage for Blanks (i) and (ii).

For Question 3, choose one answer for each blank. Select from the appropriate column for each blank. Choose the answer that best completes the sense of the text.

3. Those calling for the regulation of commodities trading are, at best, uninformed. Instead of (i) _________ traders for spikes in prices of wheat, oil, and metals, legislators would be wiser to consider how speculators help to create (ii) _________ by injecting cash into markets—which contributes to market efficiency. Furthermore, legislators who are gung ho to rein in traders might bother to note that speculators have little or no effect on the production, and only (iii) _________ effect on the consumption, of goods.

Blank (i)	Blank (ii)	Blank (iii)
A. regulating	D. liquidity	G. minimal
B. scapegoating	E. activity	H. negative
C. ostracizing	F. inventory	I. lasting

The correct answers are B and D.

An analysis of the question based on tone would be something like this:

- The critical, almost indignant, tone of this passage is signaled by two groups of words that denigrate legislators: "at best, uninformed" and "legislators who are gung ho to rein in traders."
- This critical tone tells you that the author probably won't use moderate or measured word choices. Instead, to be consistent with the tone of the passage, you might consider words with strong negative connotations. Of all the answer choices, *scapegoating* (choice B) has the most negative connotation. It is, in fact, the correct answer for Blank (i).
- While the author's tone may not necessarily provide any clues for the second blank, consider the context of the topic: finance. What kind of financial asset is cash considered? *Liquidity* (choice D) is the obvious choice for Blank (ii).

Considering the author's style might also help you choose the correct answer. Read Question 6 again, but this time pay attention to the writer's style.

For Question 6, choose one answer for the blank. Choose the answer that best completes the sense of the text.

6. Debussy is regarded as the germinal musical impressionist who created color through the use of individual instruments in the orchestra; by the same token, Monet's use of blocks of color, in lieu of line, was a(n) _________ influence on impressionism in art. There, however, the similarity between the two "impressionists" ends.

A. imperative
B. seminal
C. discernable
D. super
E. formidable

The correct answer is B.

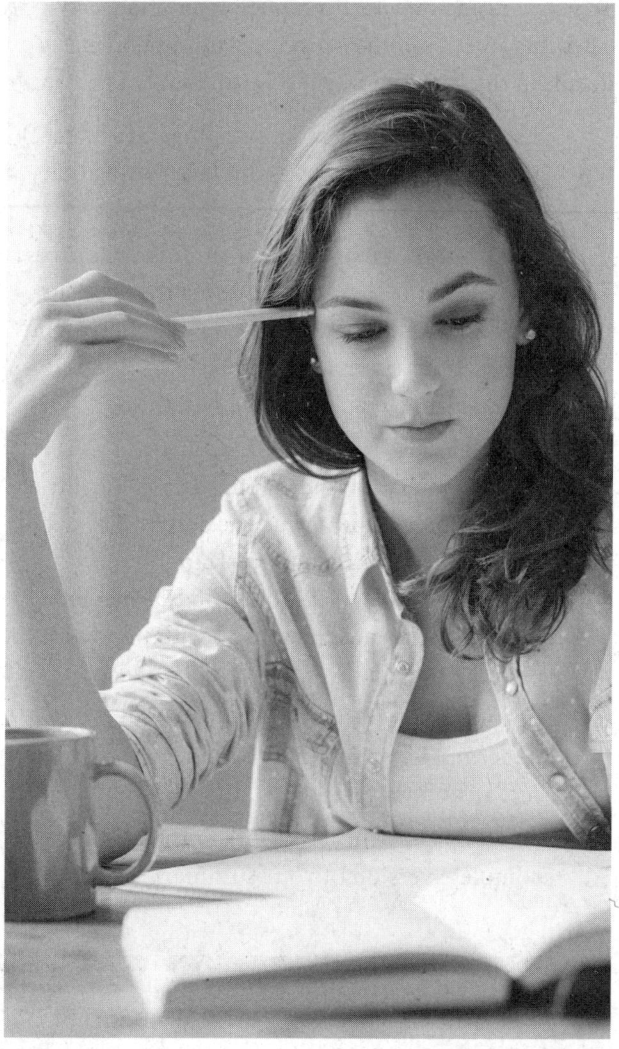

The style of the passage is formal and academic; therefore, the correct answer must match that style. A quick read-through of the answer choices reveals *super*. Though it means "particularly excellent" and might seem correct at first, *super* is likely too informal for the style of this passage, so choice D can be eliminated. That leaves you with four other choices, so you can use the process of elimination to select the best answer.

Use Grammar and Usage

You can eliminate some answer choices because they violate the rules of grammar or do not fit the context or structure of the sentence. Let's take another look at Question 3, Blank (iii).

For Question 3, choose <u>one</u> answer for each blank. Select from the appropriate column for each blank. Choose the answer that best completes the sense of the text.

3. Those calling for the regulation of commodities trading are, at best, uninformed. Instead of (i) _________ traders for spikes in prices of wheat, oil, and metals, legislators would be wiser to consider how speculators help to create (ii) _________ by injecting cash into markets—which contributes to market efficiency. Furthermore, legislators who are gung ho to rein in traders might bother to note that speculators have little or no effect on the production, and only (iii) _________ effect on the consumption, of goods.

Blank (i)	Blank (ii)	Blank (iii)
A. regulating	D. liquidity	G. minimal
B. scapegoating	E. activity	H. negative
C. ostracizing	F. inventory	I. lasting

The correct answer is G.

Notice that both *negative* and *lasting* require the article *a* before them. Only *minimal* fits in the space as it is worded. Therefore, *negative* (choice H) and *lasting* (choice I) must both be eliminated.

SUMMING IT UP

- Text completion questions assess your ability to interpret and evaluate what you read and supply words or phrases whose meaning is consistent with the ideas presented.
- On text completion questions, there are one to three blanks that you must fill in.
- Test items that have one blank offer a list of five options. Test items with two or three blanks offer lists of three options for each blank.
- Some test items will revolve around words that are close in meaning or ask for an unusual meaning of a familiar word. Some items may involve less-familiar words.
- Passages for the text completion test items tend to have lighter concept loads than those for reading comprehension questions on the GRE General Test.
- The following strategies for answering text completion questions involve both common sense and knowledge gained in English composition classes:
    - Try answering the questions before you read the answer choice(s).
    - Focus on only one blank at a time.
    - If there is more than one blank, complete the blanks in the order that makes sense to you.
    - Check your answer(s) in place.
    - Use structural clues (restatement, cause and effect, contrast, comparison, main idea, and details).
    - Consider tone and style.
    - Consider grammar and usage.

PRACTICE

TEXT COMPLETION QUESTIONS

For Questions 1–10, choose one answer for each blank. Select from the appropriate column for each blank. Choose the answer that best completes the sense of the text.

1. Because the witness was so __________, the attorney issued a subpoena to guarantee that she would show up in court to testify.

A. reliable
B. steadfast
C. clandestine
D. passé
E. capricious

2. Much to the teacher's __________, she was unable to get the unruly students to settle down.

A. chagrin
B. reproof
C. tincture
D. symmetry
E. caterwauling

3. While they have reputations for being fierce hunters, many bears are actually (i) __________ creatures who are as likely to munch on pine cones or mushrooms as they are to (ii) __________ fish from streams.

Blank (i)	Blank (ii)
A. carnivorous	D. lope
B. omnivorous	E. seize
C. herbivorous	F. graze

4. The children began singing the tune with such startling (i) __________ that the adults could not (ii) __________ their own delighted laughter.

Blank (i)	Blank (ii)
A. alacrity	D. inaugurate
B. poignancy	E. actualize
C. dolefulness	F. repress

5. The banker was so exasperated with years of dealing with (i) _________ matters that she (ii) _________ to find another line of work.

Blank (i)
A. plagiaristic
B. titanic
C. pecuniary

Blank (ii)
D. resolved
E. demurred
F. repudiated

6. Because the instructor failed to (i) _________ the assignment effectively, the students remained utterly (ii) _________.

Blank (i)
A. elucidate
B. muddle
C. elongate

Blank (ii)
D. clinched
E. bewildered
F. indubitable

7. As of this writing, Grover Cleveland has the (i) _________ of being the only person to be elected US president on two (ii) _________ occasions. Cleveland first (iii) _________ office in 1885 when he became the 22nd president of the United States. Then in 1893, he also became the United States' 24th president.

Blank (i)
A. odium
B. mortification
C. distinction

Blank (ii)
D. ensuing
E. lateral
F. nonconsecutive

Blank (iii)
G. assumed
H. sundered
I. dissevered

8. She had always been an extremely (i) _________ woman, so no one was (ii) _________ when she announced that she would be going into business for herself. In fact, more than a few people offered to invest in her budding (iii) _________.

Blank (i)
A. enterprising
B. ignominious
C. esoteric

Blank (ii)
D. left in the lurch
E. thrown for a loop
F. bent out of shape

Blank (iii)
G. firmament
H. tether
I. venture

9. Alexander Hamilton was chief among the founding fathers in working to replace the (i) __________ national government in accordance with the Articles of Confederation with a more (ii) __________ system. In composing the majority of the essays and articles known as *The Federalist Papers,* Hamilton effectively ratified the once (iii) __________ Constitution.

Blank (i)	Blank (ii)	Blank (iii)
A. intermittent	D. inexplicable	G. mercurial
B. ineffectual	E. potent	H. problematic
C. pedantic	F. demonstrative	I. obsequious

10. In the Northern Hemisphere, when a mature tropical cyclone has developed in the range of 180 degrees and 100 degrees, it is (i) __________ as a typhoon. (ii) __________, there is no difference between a typhoon, a cyclone, and a hurricane in any terms other than location. Where the storm occurs is the sole factor in its (iii) __________

Blank (i)	Blank (ii)	Blank (iii)
A. lauded	D. In essence	G. countenance
B. excoriated	E. However	H. semblance
C. categorized	F. Furthermore	I. designation

ANSWER KEY AND EXPLANATIONS

1. E	3. B, E	5. C, D	7. C, F, G	9. B, E, H
2. A	4. A, F	6. A, E	8. A, E, I	10. C, D, I

1. **The correct answer is E.** The word in the blank should define someone who may or may not show up to testify. This implies an unreliable or unpredictable nature, and *capricious* means "unpredictable." *Reliable* and *steadfast* are the opposite of *unpredictable*, so choices A and B can be eliminated. *Clandestine* (choice C) means "secretive," which does not really suit this particular context. *Passé* (choice D) means "old-fashioned," which makes no sense in this context.

2. **The correct answer is A.** The word in the blank refers to something the teacher possesses, which is probably a noun. Therefore, the verb *caterwauling* (choice E), meaning "wailing," can be eliminated because it is not functioning as a noun in this context. The other answer choices are all nouns. The best noun for this context is *chagrin*, which means "annoyance," since having to cope with a room full of unruly students would probably be annoying for a teacher. *Reproof* (choice B) means "criticism," and it is uncommon to use the phrase "much to one's reproof." The remaining answer choices would make no sense in this context since *tincture* (choice C) means "color" and *symmetry* (choice D) means "balance."

3. **The correct answers are B and E.** Blank (i): For the first blank, you'll need a contrast to assumptions about fierce hunters. Since a fierce hunter would probably be a meat eater or carnivore, a contrast to that idea is needed. Choice B fits the bill since *omnivorous* means "eating both meat and plants." Consequently, *carnivorous* (choice A) can be eliminated. *Herbivorous* (choice C), meaning "eating only plants," can also be eliminated as the sentence makes it clear that bears do eat meat, such as fish.

   Blank (ii): A verb suggesting hunting is necessary, and *seize* means "catch," which is what hunters or fishers do. Choice D would make no sense in this context, since *lope* means "jog." Choice F does not make sense either, since to *graze* is "to eat grass."

4. **The correct answers are A and F.** Blank (i): A term that suggests an approach causing "delighted laughter" is needed here. *Alacrity* means "enthusiasm." Enthusiastic singing can prompt an audience to laugh with delight. *Poignancy* (choice B) means "sadness" or "regret," and a song sung with poignancy would likely stir feelings of sadness instead of delight. So would *dolefulness* (choice C), which means "unhappiness."

   Blank (ii): The second blank suggests a failure to stop a sudden reaction to something delightful, and *repress* means "stop." *Inaugurate* means "start," so choice D is the opposite of the correct answer. *Actualize* (choice E) means "bring into reality," which would also be the opposite of the correct answer.

5. **The correct answers are C and D.** Blank (i): The correct answer for the first blank should have some connection to banking, and *pecuniary* refers to financial matters. *Plagiaristic* means "related to illegal copying," so choice A does not make much sense in this context. Neither does choice B, since *titanic* means "massive."

   Blank (ii): A word suggesting the making of a firm decision is needed, and that is what *resolved* is. The other answer choices simply do not make sense in this context, since *demurred* (choice E) means "objected" and *repudiated* (choice F) means "rejected."

6. **The correct answers are A and E.** Blank (i): The first blank should suggest something an instructor is expected to do, and an instructor should clarify, or *elucidate*, lessons so that students are not confused. *Muddle* (choice B) means "confuse" and should be eliminated. *Elongate* (choice C) means "lengthen," which does not make sense in this context.

   Blank (ii): The negative effect of the instructor's failure to clarify is needed, and that effect would be a class full of confused, or *bewildered*, students. *Clinched* (choice D) does not make sense in this context, since it means "confirmed." Choice F can be eliminated, since *indubitable* means "unquestionable."

7. **The correct answers are C, F, and G.** Blank (i): When someone is the only person to achieve something, they are distinct from all others, so *distinction* is the best answer. Choices A and B do not make sense in this context, since *odium* means "horribleness" and *mortification* means "embarrassment."

   Blank (ii): The years that Cleveland was president show that he was not reelected in immediate succession to his first term, and *nonconsecutive* means "not in direct order." *Ensuing* (choice D) means "following," which is the opposite of the correct answer. *Lateral* (choice E) means "on the side," which does not make sense in this context.

   Blank (iii): A verb implying the taking of a position is needed, and *assumed* means "took." *Sundered* (choice H) means "split." *Dissevered* (choice I) also means "split." Neither word makes sense in this context.

8. **The correct answers are A, E, and I.** Blank (i): The word on the first blank should support the idea of a woman who goes into business for herself, and *enterprising* means "ambitious" or "showing resourcefulness." The other answer choices do not make sense in this blank since *ignominious* (choice B) means "embarrassing" and *esoteric* (choice C) means "obscure."

   Blank (ii): An idiomatic phrase meaning "surprised" is needed, and that is what *thrown for a loop* is. The other idioms do not mean "surprised." *Left in the lurch* (choice D) means "left out," and *bent out of shape* (choice F) means "upset."

   Blank (iii): A word suggesting a new business project is needed. *Venture* means "business project." The other answer choices do not make sense in this context. *Firmament* (choice G) means "sky," and *tether* (choice H) means "connector."

9. **The correct answers are B, E, and H.** Blank (i): The first blank requires a word that suggests something that needs to be replaced. Such a thing might be *ineffectual*, which means "not effective." Something *intermittent* (choice A) happens irregularly, so it is a less logical answer than choice B. *Pedantic* (choice C) means "finicky," and a government is generally not described as finicky.

   Blank (ii): The opposite of *ineffectual* is needed for the second blank, and that is what *potent* is. *Inexplicable* (choice D) means "unable to be explained," which is not the opposite of *ineffectual*. Neither is *demonstrative* (choice F), which means "affectionate."

   Blank (iii): A word is needed that implies the problems the former Constitution suffered prior to improvement. *Problematic* means "troubled." *Mercurial* (choice G) means "unpredictable," which is not a problem a document like the Constitution would have. *Obsequious* (choice I) means "flattering," and a document cannot be flattering.

10. **The correct answers are C, D, and I.** Blank (i): The first blank requires a word suggesting a specific label, and *categorized* means "labeled." Since a typhoon is a negative force, it is not likely to be *lauded* (choice A), which means "celebrated."

While *excoriated* (choice B), meaning "criticized," makes more sense than *lauded*, something uncontrollable like the weather is less likely to be criticized than it is to be simply labeled, so choice C remains the best answer choice.

Blank (ii): A transitional phrase or word suggesting something essential is needed, and that is what *In essence* is. *However* (choice E) implies a contradiction. *Furthermore* (choice F) suggests an elaboration or the revelation of additional information about a previously discussed matter.

Blank (iii): The third blank refers back to the label of typhoon and requires a synonym for the word *label*, which is what *designation* is. *Countenance* (choice G) means "face," and *semblance* (choice H) means "trace."

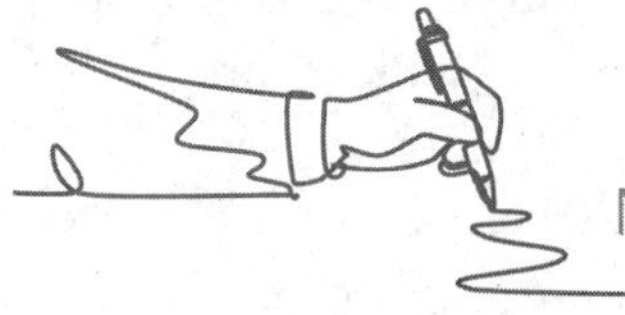

NOTES

CHAPTER

Sentence Equivalence Questions

SENTENCE EQUIVALENCE QUESTIONS

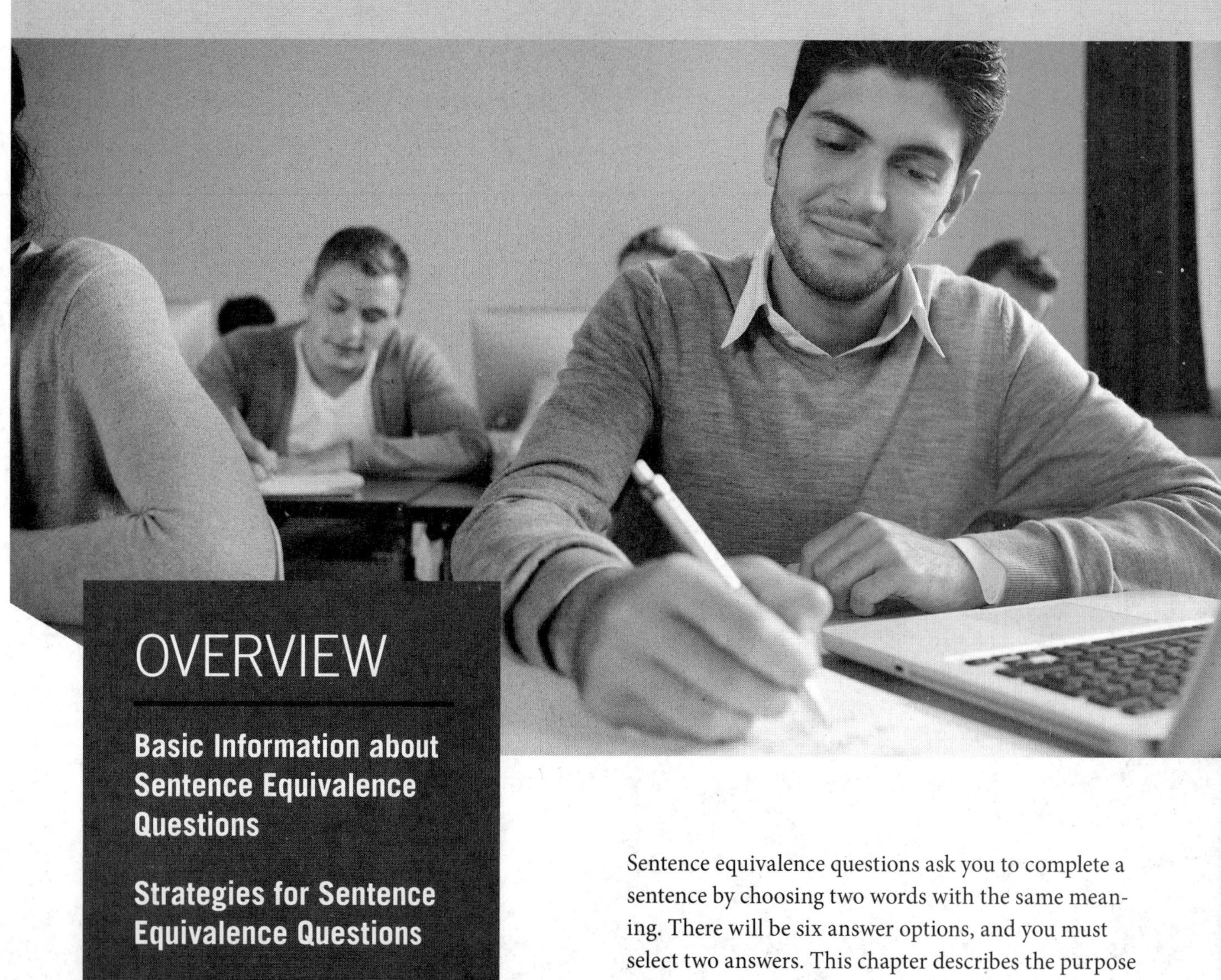

OVERVIEW

Sentence equivalence questions ask you to complete a sentence by choosing two words with the same meaning. There will be six answer options, and you must select two answers. This chapter describes the purpose of the sentence equivalence test items and offers strategies to help you answer these questions correctly.

BASIC INFORMATION ABOUT SENTENCE EQUIVALENCE QUESTIONS

Like text completion items, sentence equivalence questions on the GRE General Test assess your ability to both interpret what you read and supply words whose meanings are consistent with the ideas presented in the test items. Unlike text completion items, however, sentence equivalence items place more emphasis on the meaning of the completed sentence.

Also, like text completion items, sentence equivalence items test your vocabulary. Therefore, having a robust vocabulary will be helpful, but that's not the only way to score points. Learning and using a few key strategies can help you as well.

Question Format

Each sentence equivalence question follows the same format: you'll be presented with a single sentence with one blank, followed by six answer choices. From the six options, you must choose two answers. Choose two answers that have a similar (equivalent) meaning so that they both complete the sentence with a similar (equivalent) meaning.

The directions for sentence equivalence questions will look something like this:

For Questions 1–2, choose the two answers that best fit the meaning of the sentence as a whole and result in two completed sentences that are alike in meaning.

You can expect to see three to five sentence equivalence items in the Verbal Reasoning section. These items are interspersed with the other items in each of the two scored verbal sections of the test. Sentence equivalence items generally require the least time and effort of all the question types in the Verbal Reasoning section.

Selecting Answers

To earn credit for a sentence equivalence test item, you must choose both correct answers. Choosing only one correct answer of the pair doesn't get you any points.

Because the sentence equivalence questions are less time-consuming than reading comprehension items, they are easier to revisit. Consider completing reading comprehension and text completion items first and saving the sentence equivalence questions for the end. When you're running out of time, go through the section and look for any unanswered sentence equivalence questions so that you can answer them quickly and get more points.

STRATEGIES FOR SENTENCE EQUIVALENCE QUESTIONS

Many of the strategies we've discussed for approaching reading comprehension and text completion questions apply to sentence equivalence questions as well. Strategies can be grouped into two categories: general commonsense ideas and specific language strategies you learned in English composition classes. The first group includes the following three strategies:

1. Read the item stem first.
2. Come up with your own answer.
3. Check your answers in place.

More specific language strategies include the following:

1. Use signal words and structural clues.
2. Don't commit to the first pair of synonyms you see.
3. Examine connotations.
4. Consider grammar and usage.

ALERT

Remember, answer choices that are preceded by a square on the computer-delivered test indicate that there is more than one correct answer.

Notice how these strategies are integrated into the approaches for answering each of the sample items in this chapter.

Read the Item Stem First

Read through the entire sentence before you do anything else, so that you can get a clear sense of what it's about. The answers are deliberately structured with multiple pairs of synonyms and with terms having close meanings that might appear correct at first glance, so make sure that you understand the meaning of the incomplete sentence.

Come Up with Your Own Answer

Coming up with your own answer before you read the answer choices can be a helpful approach in responding to sentence equivalence items. Try this now with Question 1 below.

For Question 1, choose the two answers that best fit the meaning of the sentence as a whole and result in two completed sentences that are alike in meaning.

Jade could not keep her negativity or aggression to herself; it seemed that everywhere she went, some kind of ________ ensued.

A. kerfuffle
B. insurgency
C. insurrection
D. rebellion
E. demonstration
F. disturbance

The correct answers are A and F.

Working through the answer process might look like this: Read the sentence first and try to figure out your own answer. Using this strategy, you come up with either the word *problems* or the word *difficulty.* Then look for a pair of words in the list that mean the same as, or close to the same as, *problems* or *difficulty. Kerfuffle* means "disturbance" or "minor outburst or tumult." It is a state of commotion rather than complete uproar like choices B, C, and D. A kerfuffle is not so intense or serious as an insurgency, insurrection, or rebellion. In the context of the completed sentence, *disturbance* means the same thing. Therefore, the correct answers are *kerfuffle* (choice A) and *disturbance* (choice F). For the record, *demonstration* connotes a protest, usually large in nature, so choice E is also incorrect.

Check Your Answers in Place

Remember that the answers must create equivalence, so the last step is to evaluate the meaning of the completed item. To do this, read the item twice—first filling in the blank with the first answer you have chosen, and the second time with the second answer. Ask yourself whether the two sentences have the same meaning. If the meanings differ, you'll need to go back and revisit the other answer options.

Use Signal Words and Structural Clues

Many sentence equivalence items will include transitions—signal words and phrases—such as *consequently, because, on the other hand, although, moreover, however,* and *in fact.* These words signal a relationship between ideas in the sentence. Pay close attention to them. They can help you decide whether the answer should show cause and effect, contrast, comparison, or restatement. Examples of signal words for different types of structures follow.

RESTATEMENT SIGNALS

Words and phrases that can signal restatement relationships include the following:

for example	in other words	that is
for instance	in short	this means
in fact	namely	thus

CAUSE-AND-EFFECT SIGNALS

Cause-and-effect relationships may or may not include signal words. Words and phrases that can signal cause-and-effect relationships include the following:

as a result	in order to	so that
because	reason why	therefore
consequently	since	thus
for	so	why

CONTRAST SIGNALS

Like other structures, contrasts of information may or may not include signal words. Words and phrases that can be used to signal contrasts include the following:

although	however	on the contrary
as opposed to	in contrast	on the other hand
but	in spite of	otherwise
by contrast	instead	still
conversely	nevertheless	unlike
despite	nonetheless	yet

COMPARISON SIGNALS

Words and phrases that can signal a comparison include the following:

also	in comparison	moreover
and	in the same way	much like
another	just as	same
as by contrast	like	similarly
by the same token	likewise	too

Not all test items for sentence equivalence will have signal words and phrases. You'll need to recognize clues to organizational structures, such as restatement and cause and effect, without the help of transitional words and phrases.

To practice identifying and using structural clues, read Question 1 again and then read through the analysis that follows based on the sentence's restatement structure.

For Question 1, choose the two answers that best fit the meaning of the sentence as a whole and result in two completed sentences that are alike in meaning.

Jade could not keep her negativity or aggression to herself; it seemed that everywhere she went, some kind of _________ ensued.

A. kerfuffle

B. insurgency

C. insurrection

D. rebellion

E. demonstration

F. disturbance

The correct answers are A and F.

The second part of the sentence (what follows the semicolon) amplifies the information in the first part (the part preceding the semicolon). No signal word or phrase is present. Structural analysis shows that the pair of words you are looking for must name something that results from negativity or aggression. *Insurgency* (choice B), *insurrection* (choice C), and *rebellion* (choice

TIP

A sentence or passage that uses restatement in a sentence equivalence test item will most often have two independent clauses joined by a colon, a semicolon, or a correlative conjunction, such as *moreover*.

D) go well beyond negativity or aggression. They don't express the same minor degree of problem, commotion, or upset conveyed by the first part of the sentence, so you can eliminate them. *Demonstration* (choice E) is typically used in conjunction with a large group, so it is incorrect as well. Negativity and aggression might both lead to a disturbance. The only synonym or near synonym on the list for *disturbance* is *kerfuffle*. Therefore, the correct answers are *kerfuffle* (choice A) and *disturbance* (choice F).

It's also reasonable to see this sentence as a cause-and-effect relationship. The following is one way you might work through the sentence looking for an effect of Jade's attitude:

- If you begin by restating the item with cause and effect in mind, you might arrive at this paraphrase: "Because Jade could not keep her negativity or aggression in check, she caused some kind of _________ everywhere she went."
- Structural analysis helps you determine that the pair of words you are looking for must name something that results from negativity or aggression.
- The rest of the analysis is the same as above, so the correct answers are *kerfuffle* (choice A) and *disturbance* (choice F).

Don't Commit to the First Pair of Synonyms You See

You might think it's a good idea to just find a pair of synonyms among the answer choices as quickly as you can and move on to the next item. However, many answer sets contain more than one pair of synonyms. As the test maker warns, even if a word is a synonym for the correct choice, it doesn't necessarily lead to the same meaning in the completed sentence. Two words may be synonyms, but they may have different connotations.

Look at Question 1 again:

For Question 1, choose the two answers that best fit the meaning of the sentence as a whole and result in two completed sentences that are alike in meaning.

1. Jade could not keep her negativity or aggression to herself; it seemed that everywhere she went, some kind of _________ ensued.

A. kerfuffle

B. insurgency

C. insurrection

D. rebellion

E. demonstration

F. disturbance

The correct answers are A and F.

The first pair of synonyms in the list of answer choices for Question 1 is *insurgency* and *insurrection* (choices B and C). The meaning of these words, however, suggests a much bigger situation than just one person's negativity or aggression. Note also that choices B, C, and D

ALERT

Two words that are frequently confused are *connotation* and *denotation*. *Connotation* is an idea or meaning suggested by a word. *Denotation* is the literal meaning of a word.

are similar. If you chose two answers just by looking for pairs of synonyms, you would end up with several answers that seem correct but are actually incorrect upon further examination.

Examine Connotations

In choosing answers, think about the connotations that the words carry. As you read Question 2, for example, consider the meaning of the word *walked.*

For Question 2, choose the two answers that best fit the meaning of the sentence as a whole and result in two completed sentences that are alike in meaning.

Kierkegaard said that he had "walked himself into his best thoughts"; in fact, research links exercise with heightened states of _________ experience.

A. examining

B. pensive

C. thoughtful

D. meditative

E. generative

F. contemplative

The correct answers are D and F.

The walking in this sentence led to thinking, so it was likely solitary and prolonged walking. Now consider the connotations of the answer choices. Even though *pensive* and *meditative* are synonyms, they don't result in equivalence in the sentence. *Pensive* (choice B) suggests a deep or melancholy thoughtfulness—an inward kind of experience that would not necessarily be generative. Similarly, *contemplative* and *thoughtful* are synonyms. *Contemplative* (choice F) carries connotations of prolonged thought, which might happen during a long walk. However, *thoughtful* (choice C) doesn't have that connotation, so you can eliminate it. *Generative* (choice E) must be eliminated because there is no similar word that would result in equivalence. *Examining* (choice A) is also incorrect in terms of usage and has no synonym here. Through elimination, that leaves *meditative* (choice D) and *contemplative* (choice F) as synonyms that have similar connotations.

Consider Grammar and Usage

As with the text completion items, the words you select for sentence equivalence must result in correct grammar and standard usage when inserted into the sentence. Look again at Question 2 and the first answer choice.

For Question 2, choose the two answers that best fit the meaning of the sentence as a whole and result in two completed sentences that are alike in meaning.

Kierkegaard said that he had "walked himself into his best thoughts"; in fact, research links exercise with heightened states of _________ experience.

A. examining

You can eliminate choice A because even though the form of the word *examining* seems like it could be an adjective, it results in an ambiguous and nonstandard usage in the sentence, as in ". . . research links exercise with heightened states of examining experience."

SUMMING IT UP

- Sentence equivalence test items assess your ability to interpret what you read and supply words whose meanings are in line with the ideas presented in the test items.
- The emphasis is on the meaning of the complete sentence.
- Each sentence equivalence test item is a single sentence with one blank, followed by six answer choices. From the six answer choices, you must select two answers for the question that will result in two sentences with a similar—equivalent—meaning.
- Both answer choices must be correct in order to earn credit for the question.
- Commonsense strategies for answering sentence equivalence questions are as follows:
    - Read the item stem first.
    - Come up with your own answer.
    - Check your answers in place.
- More specific language strategies include the following:
    - Use signal words and structural clues.
    - Don't commit to the first pair of synonyms you see.
    - Examine connotations.
    - Consider grammar and usage.

PRACTICE

SENTENCE EQUIVALENCE QUESTIONS

For Questions 1–10, choose the two answers that best fit the meaning of the sentence as a whole and result in two completed sentences that are alike in meaning.

1. Tourists regularly visited the _________ volcano without any fear of being caught amid a sudden disaster.

   A. quiescent

   B. efficacious

   C. operative

   D. exertive

   E. expedient

   F. dormant

2. The _________ man delighted in inciting his followers into sharing his grim view of humanity.

   A. magnanimous

   B. unflappable

   C. opprobrious

   D. contemptuous

   E. imperturbable

   F. solicitous

3. Certain types of music can have a downright _________ effect when heard during stressful times.

   A. symphonic

   B. lilting

   C. consonant

   D. palliative

   E. aggravating

   F. mollifying

4. The thief _________ the man into revealing all of his personal financial information.

   A. chastised

   B. deluded

   C. bickered

   D. assuaged

   E. hoodwinked

   F. cogitated

5. Although I vowed never to leave my job, I _________ after receiving an offer for a new position that I simply could not refuse.

   A. obliged

   B. capitulated

   C. betrothed

   D. opined

   E. presupposed

   F. conceded

6. Threatening the child with punishment was not the _________ to bad behavior her parents hoped it would be.

   A. incitement

   B. stimulation

   C. deterrent

   D. deferment

   E. disincentive

   F. reduction

7. She received a well-deserved patent for her ______ invention.

   A. ingenious
   B. shrewd
   C. applicable
   D. insoluble
   E. invective
   F. negligible

8. Bored with living in a small town, my family decided to relocate to a more ________ city.

   A. glamorous
   B. derelict
   C. forlorn
   D. relinquished
   E. populous
   F. inhabited

9. Mr. Donnelly tends to be ________, so be ready for an argument if you engage him in conversation.

   A. acquiescent
   B. reticent
   C. stilted
   D. contentious
   E. perturbed
   F. factious

10. Only the most ________ person would believe anything that duplicitous man says.

   A. hesitant
   B. credulous
   C. skeptical
   D. dupable
   E. credible
   F. leery

ANSWER KEY AND EXPLANATIONS

1. A, F	3. D, F	5. B, F	7. A, B	9. D, F
2. C, D	4. B, E	6. C, E	8. E, F	10. B, D

1. **The correct answers are A and F.** An active volcano would likely make tourists afraid to visit it, so a volcano that does not cause fear should be inactive. Both *quiescent* and *dormant* mean "inactive." Choices B, C, and D are the opposites of the correct answers since *efficacious* means "effective," *operative* means "active" or "working," and *exertive* means "using power." Choice E simply does not make sense in this context since *expedient* means "convenient."
2. **The correct answers are C and D.** The correct answers should describe a person who enjoys stirring feelings of hatred for other people, and such an individual would be opprobrious and contemptuous, since both words mean "hateful." Choices A and F are the opposites of the correct answers since *magnanimous* means "generous," and *solicitous* means "caring." Choices B and E both mean "calm," and while neither *unflappable* nor *imperturbable* would make the sentence nonsensical, they do not fit its meaning as well as choices C and D.
3. **The correct answers are D and F.** The correct answers should imply an emotional effect since the sentence draws a correlation between music and how it affects one's feelings. Since the feelings in question are stressful feelings, the correct answers should either suggest the calming or intensifying of stress, and *palliative* and *mollifying* both refer to something that calms. While *aggravating* (choice E) refers to the intensifying of stress, and could be used in the blank, there is no other answer choice that shares its meaning, so it cannot be the correct answer. The other answer choices all describe aspects of music but do not imply anything about how music affects feelings. *Symphonic* (choice A) means "orchestral," *lilting* (choice B) means "swinging," and *consonant* (choice C) means "harmonious."
4. **The correct answers are B and E.** The sentence describes a criminal tricking a victim, and the words *deluded* and *hoodwinked* both mean "tricked." The other answer choices do not have that meaning. *Chastised* (choice A) means "criticized," *bickered* (choice C) means "argued," *assuaged* (choice D) means "lessened," and *cogitated* (choice F) means "thought."
5. **The correct answers are B and F.** The first part of this sentence suggests something contradicted by its second part. Therefore, the correct answers should suggest a change of mind. *Capitulated* and *conceded* both mean "gave up." The other answer choices do not suggest such an action. *Obliged* (choice A) means "agreed," *betrothed* (choice C) means "married," *opined* (choice D) means "expressed an opinion," and *presupposed* (choice E) means "assumed."
6. **The correct answers are C and E.** Parents would likely try to prevent a child from misbehaving, and the parents in this sentence apparently failed to accomplish that. Therefore, the correct answers should mean "prevention," and that is what both *deterrent* and *disincentive* mean. *Incitement* (choice A) and *stimulation* (choice B) are both opposites of "prevention." *Deferment* (choice D) means "postponement," and parents would want to prevent bad behavior rather than simply postpone it. Similarly, they would want to prevent, not reduce, bad behavior, so *reduction* (choice F) would not work.

7. **The correct answers are A and B.** Only original works receive patents, and the most original inventions are clever. *Ingenious* and *shrewd* both mean "clever." The other answer choices do not make sense in this context. *Applicable* (choice C) means "appropriate," *insoluble* (choice D) means "mysterious," *invective* (choice E) means "tirade," and *negligible* (choice F) means "insignificant."
8. **The correct answers are E and F.** The correct answers should suggest the opposite of life in a small town, which typically has a small population. Therefore, the correct answers should suggest a large population, which is what *populous* and *inhabited* do. A big city is likely more glamorous than a small town, but no other answer choice shares a meaning with choice A. *Derelict* (choice B) means "abandoned," which is the opposite of the correct answers. *Forlorn* (choice C) means "pitiful," and not many people want to move to a pitiful place. Choice D does not make sense in this context since *relinquished* means "surrendered," and one would not describe a place as "surrendered."
9. **The correct answers are D and F.** In this sentence, Mr. Donnelly is defined by his tendency to argue, so the correct answers should be synonyms of *argumentative*. That is what both *contentious* and *factious* are. The other answer choices do not suggest an argumentative nature. *Acquiescent* (choice A) means "agreeable," which is the opposite of *argumentative*. So is *reticent* (choice B), which means "reserved" or "quiet." *Stilted* (choice C) means "stiff," and *perturbed* (choice E) means "anxious."
10. **The correct answers are B and D.** The correct answers should suggest a person who easily believes what an untrustworthy person says. *Credulous* and *dupable* both mean "easily fooled." *Hesitant* (choice A), *skeptical* (choice C), and *leery* (choice F) all mean the opposite of "easily fooled." *Credible* (choice E) means "believable."

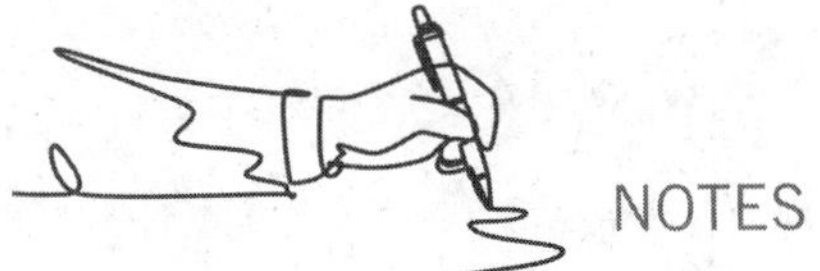

NOTES

PART IV

QUANTITATIVE REASONING

CHAPTER

Multiple-Choice Questions

MULTIPLE-CHOICE QUESTIONS

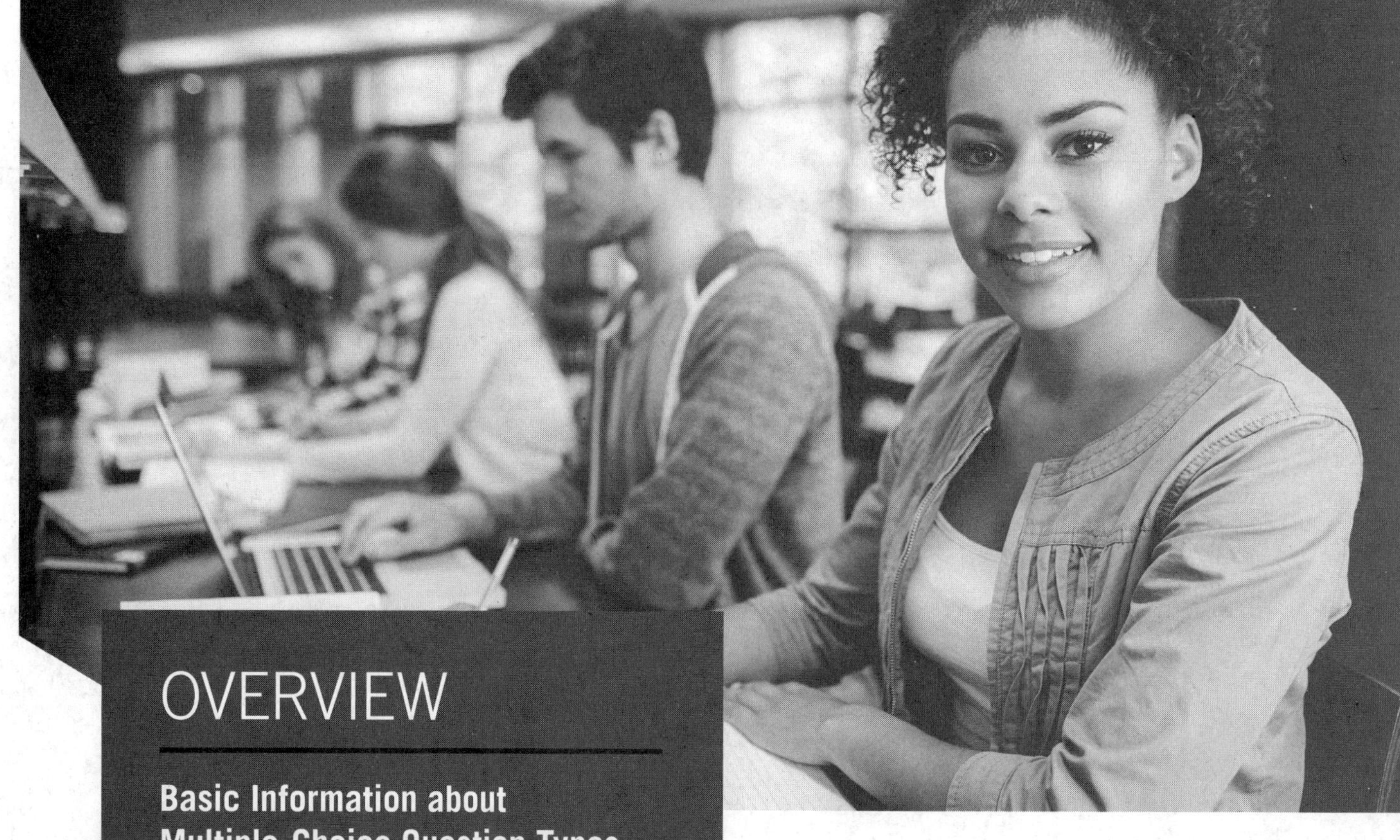

OVERVIEW

The Quantitative Reasoning section of the GRE General Test evaluates test takers' understanding of basic math concepts in arithmetic, algebra, geometry, and data analysis and their ability to apply these concepts to analyze and interpret real-world scenarios. This may sound daunting if you haven't studied math for several years, but working through the strategies and the practice questions in this and the next two chapters should reassure you that the math on the GRE General Test is not that difficult.

This chapter will introduce you to the two types of multiple-choice questions found on the GRE General Test and provide strategies that will help you answer these questions correctly and quickly.

BASIC INFORMATION ABOUT MULTIPLE-CHOICE QUESTION TYPES

On the GRE General Test, there are two formats for multiple-choice questions:

1. Multiple-choice questions—select one answer choice
2. Multiple-choice questions—select one or more answer choices

You may find multiple-choice questions as stand-alone items, or they may be part of a group of questions that refer to the same tables, graphs, or other forms of data presentation. In the latter case, they are known as data interpretation questions.

Multiple-Choice Questions—Select One Answer Choice

Most multiple-choice questions on the GRE General Test follow a familiar format in which you select one answer choice. These questions are accompanied by five answer choices, each with an oval beside it. These questions have only one correct answer, as you would surmise from the name.

Multiple-Choice Questions—Select One or More Answer Choices

The items that the GRE sometimes calls multiple-choice questions—select one or more answer choices are accompanied by a varying number of answer choices. Each answer choice has a square beside it, which is a reminder that the question is a multiple-choice question that may have more than one correct answer, as the name suggests.

The following notes apply to questions that ask for one or more answer choices:

- The number of answer choices is not always the same—though typically you will see at least three choices.
- The number of correct answer choices is also not always the same. It may be that only one answer choice is correct, or two, or three, or all of them.
- Usually, the question asks you to select all correct answer choices. Sometimes, though, a question will instruct you to select a certain number of answer choices—in which case, of course, you should select exactly that number of choices.

In order to answer a question of this type correctly, you must select all the correct answer choices, and only those.

- You do not get any credit if you select some, but not all, of the correct answer choices.
- You do not get any credit if you select the correct number of answer choices, but not all the choices you have selected are correct. (That is, if three out of five answer choices are correct, and you select two of the correct ones as well as an incorrect one, you don't get any credit.)

Although in this book we refer to answer choices as A, B, C, and so on, the answer choices are not labeled on the actual computer-delivered GRE General Test. The oval or square beside each answer choice is blank.

ALERT

Remember that ovals next to answer choices mean that the correct answer consists of a single choice, whereas square boxes next to the answer choices mean that the correct answer consists of one or more answer choices.

MATH CONVENTIONS

The test maker provides the following information that applies to all questions in the Quantitative Reasoning section of the GRE General Test:

- All numbers used are real numbers.
- All figures are assumed to lie in a plane unless otherwise indicated.
- Geometric figures, such as lines, circles, triangles, and quadrilaterals, *are not necessarily* drawn to scale. That is, you should *not* assume that quantities, such as lengths and angle measures, are as they appear in a figure. You should assume, however, that lines shown as straight are actually straight, points on a line are in the order shown, and more generally, all geometric objects are in the relative positions shown. For questions with geometric figures, you should base your answers on geometric reasoning, not on estimating or comparing quantities by sight or by measurement.
- Coordinate systems, such as *xy*-planes and number lines, *are* drawn to scale. Therefore, you can read, estimate, or compare quantities in such figures by sight or by measurement.
- Graphical data presentations, such as bar graphs, circle graphs, and line graphs, *are* drawn to scale. Therefore, you can read, estimate, or compare data values by sight or by measurement.

The On-Screen Calculator

The GRE General Test provides you with an on-screen calculator. You may use the calculator at any point during the Quantitative Reasoning sections, but you may find it particularly useful with the numeric entry questions. Before we talk about how you may use the calculator, let's discuss when you should and should not use it.

In general, you should use the on-screen calculator if you need to perform difficult calculations. However, most calculations on the GRE General Test are not that complicated, so most of the time you will not need the calculator. In particular, you *should not use* it in the following cases:

- When the required calculations are simple to perform mentally or on scratch paper
- When you need to give the answer as a fraction rather than a decimal in either numeric entry or multiple-choice questions
- When estimating will suffice (for instance, in certain quantitative comparison or data interpretation questions)

The following are a few notes on using the calculator. Learn them before test day to relieve some of the stress you may experience on that day.

- Unlike some other calculators, this one follows the order of operations. So, for instance, if you type in the sequence "1 + 3 × 5 =" the calculator will yield 16 as the answer because it will perform the multiplication of 3 by 5 first and then add 1 to the result. If, however, you need to compute (1 + 3) × 5 instead, then you must type the entire sequence including parentheses. Alternatively, you may type "1 + 3 =" followed by "× 5 =." However, it is easy to make mistakes if you try to perform a lengthy combination of operations as a single sequence on the calculator. It may be better to perform each individual computation on its own, use your scratch paper to note intermediate results, and then perform new computations on these results. In the above example, calculate 1 + 3 first, note the result (4) on your scratch paper, clear the calculator display by pressing the "C" button, and finally calculate 4 × 5.
- When you click the memory sum button ("M+"), the number in the calculator display is placed in the calculator's memory bank, and the letter "M" appears to the left of the display. When you later click "M+" again, the number in the calculator's display is added to the number in the memory bank. When you click the memory recall button

ALERT

If you are taking the paper-delivered test, don't take your calculator to the test site since you won't be allowed to use it. You will be given a calculator to use for the test.

("MR"), the number in the calculator's memory bank at that time appears in the display area. The memory clear button ("MC") clears the memory.

- In numeric entry questions, you may click the calculator's "Transfer Display" button to transfer the number displayed on the calculator to the answer box. You cannot use the transfer display feature if the answer is a fraction. Note that if you click the Transfer Display button on a question that asks you to round your answer to a certain degree of accuracy, you may need to edit the number in the answer box so that it is appropriately rounded up or down.

STRATEGIES FOR SELECT ONE ANSWER CHOICE QUESTIONS

Reviewing the math principles that are covered in the GRE General Test is an important part of preparing to take the test. However, using test-specific strategies can help you move through the test more quickly and with greater confidence. The following four strategies work especially well for multiple-choice questions that require only one answer:

1. Pick and plug numbers.
2. Work backward from the answer choices.
3. Turn verbose or abstract language into concise and concrete wording.
4. Estimate.

Pick and Plug Numbers

Picking and plugging numbers can be a useful strategy if

- a question and its answer choices contain variables, but you're not certain how to solve the question directly;
- you are dealing with a question about percentages, or
- you are not certain about a particular number property—such as whether the product of two odd numbers is odd or even.

Apply the strategy by

- picking simple numbers so that calculations are reasonable,
- plugging these numbers into the answer choices, and
- eliminating any choices that don't produce the desired result.

ALERT

For specific examples of how to use the on-screen calculator, see *GRE® Guidelines to Using the On-Screen Calculator* at **https://www.ets.org/content/dam/ets-org/pdfs/gre/on-screen-calculator-guidelines.pdf.**

For Question 1, choose one answer choice.

Susan can run $2x$ miles in y hours. In 75 minutes, how many miles will Susan run?

A. $\frac{5y}{8x}$

B. $\frac{2x}{75y}$

C. $\frac{150x}{y}$

D. $\frac{5xy}{2}$

E. $\frac{5x}{2y}$

The correct answer is E.

You can solve this question directly. If Susan runs $2x$ miles in y hours, then she runs $\frac{2x}{y}$ miles per hour. Thus, in 75 minutes (that is, in $\frac{5}{4}$ hours) she will run $\frac{2x}{y}\times\frac{5}{4}=\frac{5x}{2y}$ miles.

If you don't feel comfortable solving directly, there is an alternative way to solve. Let $x = 4$ and $y = 1$. Susan can run 8 miles in 1 hour (60 minutes), so in 75 minutes Susan will run 10 miles: one-and-a-quarter as many miles as she can run in 1 hour. Now, plug the values $x = 4$ and $y = 1$ into the answer choices and see which of them yield(s) 10.

$\frac{5\times1}{8\times4}=\frac{5}{32}$ Eliminate.

$\frac{2\times4}{75\times1}=\frac{8}{75}$ Eliminate.

$\frac{150\times4}{1}=600$ Eliminate.

$\frac{5\times4\times1}{2}=10$ This option is a possibility. Keep this in mind and move on to solve option E.

$\frac{5\times4}{2\times1}=10$ This option is also possible.

Since two answer choices produce the desired result, you need to check these choices again. Pick different numbers to plug in for the variables—say, $x = 6$ and $y = 2$. Susan runs 12 miles every 2 hours, or 6 miles per hour. Therefore, in 75 minutes, Susan will run 7.5 miles.

$\frac{5\times6\times2}{2}=30$ Eliminate.

$\frac{5\times6}{2\times2}=7.5$ Correct.

Picking numbers can be a useful backup tool if you're not confident that you can solve a question directly. However, when it comes to percentage increase/decrease problems, it is not only a good backup but an excellent way to find the right answer even more quickly than if you were solving directly. Consider the following example:

For Question 2, choose one answer choice.

Mariah sold her biology textbook to her friend Jayden for a 40% discount compared with the price she paid to buy it. After completing his class, Jayden sold the book on the internet for 20% more than the price he paid Mariah for the book. The price for which Jayden sold the book is what percentage of the price that Mariah paid?

A. 40

B. 60

C. 72

D. 80

E. 120

The correct answer is C.

Pick the number $100 to represent the amount that Mariah paid to buy the book. She sold the book to Jayden for a 40% discount off $100, or $100 – $40 = $60. Jayden turned around and sold it for 20% more than the $60 he paid, so he sold the book for $72. To solve, calculate what percentage of $100 (the price Mariah paid to buy the book) $72 is (the price Jayden got when he sold it).

$$\frac{72}{100}=\frac{x}{100}\Rightarrow x=72$$

Work Backward from the Answer Choices

If there are numbers in the answer choices, and if, to solve directly, you need to work through some complicated equations, you may choose to work backward from the answer choices.

For Question 3, choose one answer choice.

In Forestburg, the first $30,000 of someone's annual income is taxed at the rate of 5%, while any income over $30,000 is taxed at the rate of 10%. If in a certain year Betty paid $2,100 in Forestburg city taxes, what was her income that year?

A. $32,000

B. $33,000

C. $34,000

D. $35,000

E. $36,000

The correct answer is E.

In this example, you can turn the information in the question into an equation, and then solve that equation directly. Or you can go straight to the answer choices, and, since the choices are listed from least to greatest, begin with choice C, the middle one. If Betty's income had been $34,000, then she would have paid $\frac{5}{100}\times \$30,000+\frac{10}{100}\times \$4,000=\$1,500+\$400=\$1,900$.

This amount is too low, so Betty must have earned more than $34,000. You can eliminate choices A and B in addition to choice C, because the amounts given are less than choice C. Next, check choice D. If Betty's income had been $35,000, then she would have paid $\frac{5}{100}\times \$30,000+\frac{10}{100}\times \$5,000=\$2,000$. This amount is also too low, so you can eliminate choice D. By working backward from the answer choices, you are left with choice E as the correct answer.

Turn Verbose or Abstract Language into Concise and Concrete Wording

Sometimes it seems as though test makers are trying to confuse you with wordy questions. Don't worry! You can always turn excessive verbiage into diagrams or mathematical expressions that are easier to understand and work with.

For Question 4, choose one answer choice.

Diana prepared a certain amount of a chemical solution and stored it in 10 right-cylindrical containers, each with a diameter of 8 inches and a height of 8 inches. Alternatively, she could have stored the same amount of the solution in 40 right-cylindrical containers, each with the same height as one another and with a radius of 2 inches. What is the height of one of these alternative containers? (Assume the sets of containers are completely filled with the solution in both cases.)

A. 4

B. 8

C. 10

D. 16

E. 40

The correct answer is B.

Begin by writing down the given information, removing the clutter of any extraneous words. The dimensions of the first set of containers are $r=\frac{8}{2}=4$ and $h=8$. The dimensions of the second set of containers are $r'=2$ and h'.

TIP

These are the two most important strategies for you to follow: (1) always read questions carefully, and (2) reword confusing questions into concise and concrete language. You need to understand what a question is asking to answer it correctly.

The volume of the solution equals 10 times the volume of each of the initial containers: $V_{total} = 10\pi r^2 h$. The volume also equals 40 times the volume of each of the alternate containers: $V_{total} = 40\pi(r')^2 h'$. Equate these two expressions: $10\pi r^2 h = 40\pi(r')^2 h'$.

Next, substitute the values of r, h, and r': Eliminate π from both sides of the equation and calculate the two squares: $10 \times 16 \times 8 = 40 \times 4h'$. Divide both sides by 160: $h' = 8$.

Estimate

Estimating is a very valuable strategy for data interpretation questions as well as for quantitative comparisons. However, even in regular multiple-choice questions with a single correct answer, estimating may help—especially if you're running out of time.

For Question 5, choose one answer choice.

Sixty percent of the 25 professors in a certain university's engineering department are male. If two male professors retire and two female professors are hired, what percentage of the department's professors will be male? (Assume no other changes in the engineering faculty.)

A. 48

B. 52

C. 56.5

D. 60

E. 68

The correct answer is B.

It's best to solve this question directly. However, you should also note that, after the changes, the engineering department will have fewer male professors than it had before, but it will still have the same total number of professors. The percentage of its faculty that is male should drop from the original 60%. Thus, you can eliminate answer choices D and E because they are greater than or equal to 60%.

To solve this directly, first find the number of male professors before the changes:

$$\frac{60}{100} = \frac{x}{25} \Rightarrow x = \frac{60 \times 25}{100} \Rightarrow x = 15$$

After the changes, the department still has 25 professors, but this time 13 of them are male. Set up a proportion in order to turn 13 into a percentage:

$$\frac{13}{25} = \frac{x}{100} \Rightarrow x = 52.$$

STRATEGIES FOR SELECT ONE OR MORE ANSWER CHOICES QUESTIONS

Remember that the number of answer choices is not always the same for this multiple-choice format. You might have three answers to choose from—the basic number of choices—or more. The number of correct answers that you can be asked to choose varies as well. If you don't choose all the correct answers, you will not get credit for the correct answers that you do choose.

Unlike with multiple-choice questions that require only one answer, picking numbers may not always be a useful strategy when you aren't told how many correct answer choices there are. Estimating can be very useful, especially in data interpretation questions, as you'll see later in this chapter. Turning verbose language into

TIP

If you decide to skip a question, make sure you click the "Mark" button, so you can find it quickly on the Review screen later. Remember: There's no wrong-answer penalty, so don't leave any questions unanswered!

something concise and concrete is always a helpful strategy in mathematics. That said, the following strategies and notes are specific to multiple-choice questions with one or more correct answer choices:

- Calculate the least and greatest possible values.
- Make sure you're answering the correct question.
- Think through data sufficiency questions.

Calculate the Least and Greatest Possible Values

On some questions, it is helpful to calculate what the least and greatest possible values for the answer choices are, and then eliminate any choices that do not fit within that range.

For Question 6, indicate all the answers that apply.

A kiosk sells only the following snacks: cookies for \$1.50 each, ice-cream bars for \$2.50 each, and chips for \$1.00 each. Clara bought four snacks at the kiosk. Which of the following could be the total amount that she paid?

Indicate all such amounts.

A. \$3.50

B. \$4.00

C. \$4.50

D. \$6.50

E. \$8.50

F. \$10.50

The correct answers are B, C, D, and E.

Start by calculating the least and greatest possible values to limit your options. If Clara bought four bags of chips, the cheapest item, then she spent \$4. Thus, all answer choices that are an amount less than \$4 are incorrect, so you can eliminate choice A. If she bought four ice-cream bars, the most expensive item, then she spent \$10. Thus, all answer choices that feature an amount greater than \$10 are incorrect, and you can eliminate choice F.

You're left with the middle four answer choices, and indeed, all four of them are possible: \$4 (choice B) represents a purchase of four bags of chips; \$4.50 (choice C) represents a purchase of three bags of chips and one cookie; \$6.50 (choice D) represents a purchase of two cookies, one bag of chips, and one ice-cream bar; and \$8.50 (choice E) represents a purchase of three ice-cream bars and one bag of chips.

Pay attention to which questions require you to work backward from the answer choices. Do not start by calculating all the possible amounts that Clara could have spent because the answer choices do not have to list all of these amounts, only some of them. For instance, Clara could have spent \$7.50 if she had bought two ice-cream bars, one cookie, and one bag of chips. However, \$7.50 is not one of the answer choices—so you don't want to waste your time making calculations that are unnecessary.

Make Sure You're Answering the Correct Question

This is always sound advice, of course, but it is of particular importance in answering questions with one or more correct answer choices. Most of these questions ask you to select all the correct answer choices.

However, you may also come upon a question that asks you to select a specific number of answer choices. You must read the questions carefully to be sure of what to do.

For Question 7, indicate all the answers that apply.

If p is a prime number, then the product of which two of the following numbers must be the square of an integer?

A. $\frac{1}{p}$

B. $\sqrt{p}$

C. p^2

D. p^3

The correct answers are A and D.

Since you know that the product of only two of the answer choices is a perfect square, you may not need to check all the possible combinations. When you find the two answer choices that work, you can stop and move on to the next question. In this case, if you noticed early on that the product of $\frac{1}{p}$ and p^3 is p^2, a perfect square, you won't have to consider any other products.

TIP

While you're verifying that you're answering the correct question, also make sure to double-check your work.

Think Through Data Sufficiency Questions

Historically, the GRE has included questions that require you to evaluate the sufficiency of given data. While this question type has mostly been removed in the current GRE, you may still encounter questions that require you to use the same skills.

Example 8 is a data sufficiency question: a question that asks you to determine whether each answer choice is sufficient on its own to provide a definitive answer to the question. Sometimes, a data sufficiency question is of the yes/no variety (as is the case with this example). For such questions, an answer choice is sufficient if

- it provides a positive answer,

OR

- it provides a negative answer.

For Question 8, indicate all the answers that apply.

Angela is five years older than Melissa, who is two years younger than Heather. Which of the following statements individually provide(s) sufficient additional information to determine whether Heather is older than 23 years old?

Indicate all such statements.

A. Angela is 27 years old.

B. Melissa is younger than 21 years old.

C. Heather is twice as old as Melissa was 10 years ago.

The correct answers are A, B, and C.

Begin by reviewing the information in the question. If Angela is five years older than Melissa, and Melissa is two years younger than Heather, then Angela is three years older than Heather. It helps to write out these relationships as equations:

$$A = M + 5$$

$$H = M + 2$$

$$A = H + 3$$

Answer choice A: If Angela is 27 years old, then Heather is 24 years old—in other words, Heather is older than 23 years old. Answer choice A is sufficient.

Answer choice B: This tells you that Melissa is younger than 21 years old. Since $H = M + 2$, Heather is younger than 23 years old. Answer choice B is sufficient, as well.

Answer choice C: Write out this statement as an equation:

$$H = 2(M - 10) \Rightarrow$$
$$H = 2M - 20$$

You now have two equations that relate H and M (the other one is $H = M + 2$). These two equations are distinct —that is, one is not a multiple of the other—so it is possible to solve these equations and find a unique solution for H and M. Therefore, the third answer choice is also sufficient.

STRATEGIES FOR MULTIPLE-CHOICE QUESTIONS IN DATA INTERPRETATION SETS

In each Quantitative Reasoning section, you should expect to see one set of questions that are grouped together and refer to the same data presentation—such as a graph or table. The questions will be either multiple-choice (both types) or numeric entry. The following strategies are helpful in solving data interpretation sets:

- Scan the data quickly.
- Make sure you're answering the correct question.
- Estimate.

The last two are useful for all types of questions in the Quantitative Reasoning section.

Quickly Scan the Data

When you first encounter a data interpretation set, scan the data in order to get a general idea of the information presented. Just as you do when reading a Reading Comprehension passage, don't waste time on the details. There will be time for the details when you look at the actual questions. Rather, note the following:

- What kind of data—such as sales figures, population trends, etc.—are presented?
- Do the graphs/tables give actual values or percentages?
- If more than one table or graph is presented, how are they related? For instance, does one table give actual values, whereas the other gives percentages?
- What units are used (for example, millions vs. billions of dollars)?
- Are there any notes above or below the data that give additional information?

Make Sure You're Answering the Correct Question

Don't make careless mistakes when considering the questions. If a question asks about June sales figures, don't look in the July column of the table by mistake. If you're asked to find a percentage, don't look for or calculate actual values.

The following is a straightforward bar graph. It compares enrollment by male and female students majoring in science, engineering, and mathematics. The information is presented in real numbers.

TIP

Since the GRE General Test does not penalize wrong answers, educated guessing is a great strategy to use and could raise your score.

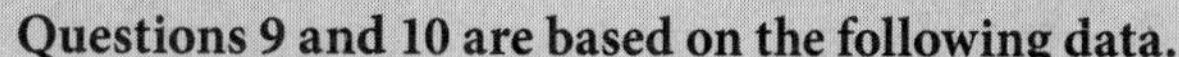

Questions 9 and 10 are based on the following data.

NUMBER OF STUDENTS AT UNIVERSITY K MAJORING IN SCIENCE, ENGINEERING, AND MATHEMATICS

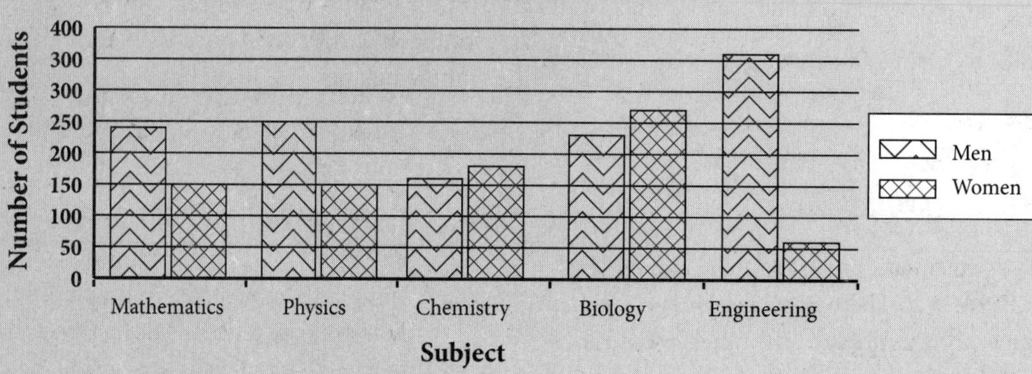

For Question 9, choose <u>one</u> answer choice.

If a total of 12,049 students are enrolled in University K, approximately what percentage of these students is majoring in engineering?

A. 0.5

B. 3

C. 3.5

D. 17

E. 20

The correct answer is C.

This question is not particularly difficult, as long as you don't make any careless mistakes. Make sure you look at the bars representing the engineering majors, not any of the other four sets of bars. Also, make sure you consider both male and female engineering majors, not just male or just female students.

The number of male engineering majors is approximately 355. The number of female engineering majors is approximately 70. Thus, the total number of engineering majors is approximately 425. Solve a proportion in order to find what percentage of the total student population 425 is:

$$\frac{425}{12,049} = \frac{x}{100} \Rightarrow x = 3.53$$

Estimate

For some questions, you only need to find approximate values. Don't waste time performing exact calculations if you don't have to. Remember that graphs are drawn to scale, so you can use them to estimate values. Consider the following:

For Question 10, indicate all the answers that apply.

Which of the following statements about science majors at University K must be true?

Indicate all such statements.

A. The absolute value of the difference between male and female physics majors is greater than the absolute value of the difference between male and female mathematics majors.

B. More students, male and female, majored in biology than in engineering.

C. The number of students who majored in mathematics is closer to the number of students who majored in physics than it is to the number of students who majored in biology.

The correct answers are A, B, and C.

Answer choice A: From the graph, you can tell that there are slightly more male physics majors than male mathematics majors, but about the same number of female physics majors as female mathematics majors. You don't need to worry about their exact numbers. The visual evidence is sufficient to tell you that when you subtract the number of female physics majors from the number of male physics majors, you get a larger number than you do when you subtract the number of female mathematics majors from the number of male mathematics majors. Answer choice A is true.

Answer choice B: The number of students who majored in biology was approximately 225 (male) + 275 (female) = 500. In question 9, you approximated the number of engineering students as 425. Again, the visual evidence is sufficient, even if your estimates are not perfect. Answer choice B is true.

Answer choice C: Once again, you can estimate from the graph that the number of students who majored in mathematics is slightly less than 400, which is similar to the number of students who majored in physics. You've already estimated the number of students who majored in biology as 500. Thus, answer choice C is true as well.

SUMMING IT UP

- There are two types of multiple-choice questions on the Quantitative Reasoning section of the GRE General Test:
  - **Multiple-choice—select one answer choice**
  - **Multiple-choice—select one or more answer choices**
- Multiple-choice questions may be structured separately, or they may be part of a **data interpretation set**, which includes several questions built around a presentation of data, such as a table or graph.
- Multiple-choice questions that require only one answer have five answer choices to select from. Each answer choice is preceded by an **oval**.
- Multiple-choice questions that ask for one or more answer choices are accompanied by a varying number of answer choices. These answer choices are preceded by **squares**, not ovals, as a signal to choose one or more answer choices.
- Strategies that are useful for all math questions are as follows:
  - Make sure you're answering the correct question.
  - Skip and come back to questions—used sparingly.
- Strategies specific to **multiple-choice questions—select one answer choice** include the following:
  - Pick and plug numbers.
  - Work backward from the answer choices.
  - Turn verbose or abstract language into concise and concrete wording.
  - Estimate.
- Strategies specific to **multiple-choice questions—select one or more answer choices** are as follows:
  - Calculate the least and greatest possible values.
  - Make sure you're answering the correct question.
- Strategies for **data interpretation sets** include the following:
  - Scan the data quickly.
  - Make sure you're answering the correct question.
  - Estimate.

PRACTICE

MULTIPLE-CHOICE QUESTIONS

For Questions 1–15, unless the directions state otherwise, choose one answer choice.

1. The sum of the squares of two consecutive positive even integers is 100. What is the sum of the two integers?

   A. 8

   B. 10

   C. 14

   D. 48

   E. 100

2. Every year, between 20% and 30% of the graduating class at Ochen University are engineering majors. If this year there are 1,182 graduating students who are engineering majors, which of the following is a possible value for the total number of students in the graduating class?

   Indicate all possible answers.

   A. 3,000

   B. 4,000

   C. 5,000

   D. 6,000

   E. 7,000

3. If x is an even positive integer and y and z are negative odd integers, which of the following cannot be a positive even integer?

   A. $\frac{xy}{z}$

   B. $x + y + z$

   C. $y - z$

   D. $\frac{x}{y}$

   E. xyz

4. If a card is picked at random from a standard 52-card deck, what is the probability that the card is either red or a queen?

   A. $\frac{1}{2}$

   B. $\frac{1}{13}$

   C. $\frac{15}{26}$

   D. $\frac{7}{13}$

   E. $\frac{1}{26}$

5. The average age of the men in a chess club is 52.

   The average age of the women is 40. If there is at least one man and at least one woman, and the club consists of at least twice as many men as women, which of the following could be the average age of all the men and women in the club?

   Indicate all possible answers.

   A. 47

   B. 48

   C. 49

   D. 50

   E. 51

   F. 52

   G. 53

6. The population of a city increases by at most 20,000 people per year. If the current population is 700,000, by how many years from now can the population have grown by 12%?

Indicate all possible answers.

A. 3

B. 4

C. 5

D. 8

E. 10

F. 12

7. In a bag of 20 candies, 25% of them are red, 30% are blue, 20% are green, and 25% are yellow. If 1 red candy, 2 blue candies, 3 green candies, and 4 yellow candies are added to the bag, what percentage of the candies will be red?

A. 35%

B. 25%

C. 20%

D. 17.5%

E. 10%

8. If a and b are fractions such that $b > a$ and $ab > b - a$, which of the following could be the graph of $a < x < b$?

Indicate all possible answers.

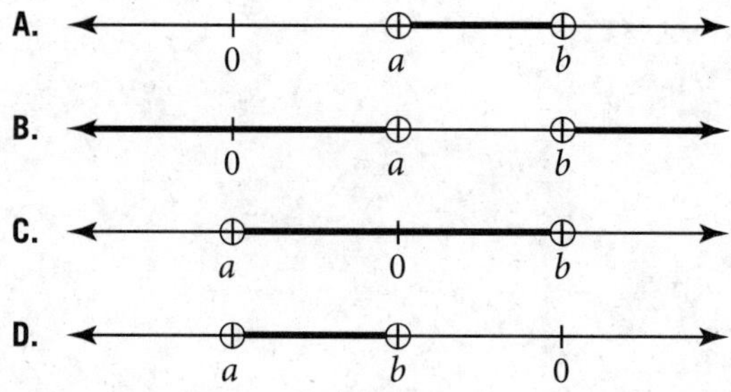

9. Tickets to a play were sold at a cost of $22 for each adult ticket and $12 for each child ticket. If a total of 125 tickets were sold for $2,480, what was the difference between how many adults and how many children attended the play?

A. 125

B. 98

C. 71

D. 27

E. 10

10.

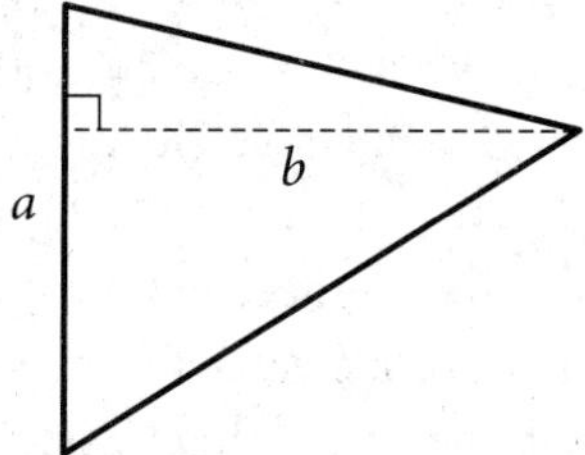

The area of the triangle above is 28. If a and b are both integers, which of the following can be the value of a?

Indicate all possible answers.

A. 2

B. 3

C. 4

D. 5

E. 6

F. 7

Questions 11–13 are based on the following data.

Education Level and Smoking Status for 612 People

Education Level	Smoking Status		
	Smoker	Nonsmoker	Total
No post-secondary education	61	126	187
Some college	21	92	113
Undergraduate degree	15	233	248
Graduate degree	6	58	64
Total	103	509	612

11. Which level of education is associated with the lowest percentage of smokers?

A. No post-secondary education

B. Some college

C. Undergraduate degree

D. Graduate degree

E. Both undergraduate and graduate are equal

12. If a person is chosen at random from among the surveyed population, what is the probability that the person will both have a graduate degree and be a nonsmoker?

A. $\frac{58}{64} = \frac{29}{32}$

B. $\frac{233}{612}$

C. $\frac{58}{509}$

D. $\frac{58}{612} = \frac{29}{306}$

E. $\frac{6}{612} = \frac{1}{102}$

13. Given that a person is a smoker, what is the probability that they have no post-secondary education?

A. $\frac{61}{103}$

B. $\frac{61}{126}$

C. $\frac{61}{184}$

D. $\frac{187}{612} = \frac{11}{36}$

E. $\frac{103}{612}$

14. 

A circle is inscribed in a square, as shown. If the perimeter of the square is *P*, what is the area of the shaded region in terms of *P*?

A. $\left(\frac{4+\pi}{64}\right)P^2$

B. $\left(\frac{4-\pi}{4}\right)P$

C. $\left(\frac{1-\pi}{64}\right)P^2$

D. $\left(\frac{4-\pi}{4}\right)P^2$

E. $\left(\frac{4-\pi}{64}\right)P^2$

15. If x is a solution of the equation $x^2 + 2x - 15 = 0$, then x cannot be a solution of which of the following equations?

A. $2x - 6 = 0$

B. $x^2 + 11x + 30 = 0$

C. $x^2 - 4x - 5 = 0$

D. $x^3 + 2x^2 - 15x = 0$

E. $x^2 + 3x - 18 = 0$

ANSWER KEY AND EXPLANATIONS

1. C	4. D	7. C	10. A, C, F	13. A
2. B, C	5. B, C, D, E	8. A, D	11. C	14. E
3. D	6. C, D, E, F	9. C	12. D	15. C

1. **The correct answer is C.** If x is an even integer, then the next even integer is $x + 2$. The sum of their squares is $x^2 + (x + 2)^2$, and this must be equal to 100:

$$\begin{aligned} x^2 + (x+2)^2 &= 100 \\ x^2 + x^2 + 4x + 4 &= 100 \\ 2x^2 + 4x - 96 &= 0 \\ 2(x^2 + 2x - 48) &= 0 \\ 2(x-6)(x+8) &= 0 \\ x &= 6, -8 \end{aligned}$$

Since the integers are positive, $x = 6$ is the only solution. This is the smaller integer, so the sum of the two integers is $x + (x + 2) = 6 + 8 = 14$.

Choice A is incorrect since 8 is only one of the two integers, not their sum. Choice B is incorrect since 6 is the smaller of the two integers, not the larger. Choice D is incorrect since 48 is the product of the two numbers rather than their sum. Choice E is incorrect since 100 is the sum of the squares of the numbers, not the sum of the original numbers.

2. **The correct answers are B and C.** Let x be the total number of students in the graduating class. If this year's engineering majors represent 20% of the class, then the equation $0.2x = 1{,}182$ yields $x = 5{,}910$. On the other extreme, if 1,182 is 30% of the class, then $0.3x = 1{,}182$, and $x = 3{,}940$. Therefore, the size of the graduating class must be between 3,940 and 5,910. Choices B and C are the only choices that fall within this range. Choice A is too low, while choices D and E are too high.

3. **The correct answer is D.** The question asks which choice cannot be a positive even integer. Therefore, even a single example of values for x, y, and z that make an answer choice into a positive even integer makes the choice incorrect.

For choice A, consider $x = 2$, $y = -9$, and $z = -3$. Then $\frac{xy}{z} = \frac{2(-9)}{-3} = \frac{-18}{-3} = 6$, which is a positive even integer. For choice B, consider $x = 4$, $y = -1$, and $z = -1$. Then $x + y + z = 4 + (-1) + (-1) = 2$, which is a positive even integer. For choice C, consider $y = -1$, $z = -3$. Then $y - z = -1 - (-3) = 2$, which is a positive even integer.

For choice E, any values will make the expression a positive even integer, since yz will always be positive, and then multiplying by an even number will make the product even. For choice D, however, notice that a positive number is being divided by a negative number. This could possibly turn out to be an even integer, but it will always be negative—never positive. Therefore, choice D is the correct answer.

4. **The correct answer is D.** In a standard deck of 52 cards, there are 26 red cards and 4 queens. This seems to give a total of 30 cards that satisfy the question. However, two of the queens are red, so these have been double counted to arrive at the total of 30. Adjusting for this by subtracting 2 gives a total of 28 cards satisfying the condition given. The probability is therefore $\frac{28}{52} = \frac{7}{13}$.

Choice A is the probability of getting a red card. Choice B is the probability of getting a queen. Choice C is the probability obtained by adding the red cards and the queens but forgetting to subtract 2 for the double counting. Choice E is the product of the individual probabilities, but they should be added, not multiplied.

5. **The correct answers are B, C, D, and E.** Since the men have a higher average age, the overall age will increase as the number of men increases. The smallest possible ratio of men to women is 2:1.

   With this ratio, the average age for the entire club would be $\frac{2\times52+1\times40}{3}=\frac{144}{3}=48$. This shows that the average age for the entire club will be at least 48. It also certainly cannot be 52 or above, since 52 is what it would be if the club had only men and the question clearly says that there is at least one woman. The possible answers are B, C, D, and E. Choice A is too low, while choices F and G are too high.

6. **The correct answers are C, D, E, and F.** Twelve percent of the initial population of 700,000 is $0.12 \times 700{,}000 = 84{,}000$. If the population grows at the maximum rate of 20,000 people per year, the population will have increased by 80,000 after four years, which is not quite 12% of 700,000. Thus, answer choices A and B are too low. After five years, however, the population could have grown by up to 100,000, so the population could have increased by 12% in five years or more. The choices that satisfy this condition are C, D, E, and F.

7. **The correct answer is C.** The number of red candies in the original bag is 25% of 20, or 5. A single red candy is added, so there are now 6 red candies. A total of $1 + 2 + 3 + 4 = 10$ candies are added, so there are $20 + 10 = 30$ candies in the bag at the end. Therefore, the percentage of candies in the bag that are red is 6 out of 30, or 1 out of 5, which is 20%.

   Choice A is simply the sum of the red percentages from the original and new candies. Choice B is the percentage of red candies from among the original candies and does not take the new candies into account. Choice D is the average of the red percentages for the new and old candies; since they are not based on the same total, the percentages cannot simply be averaged. Choice E is the percentage of red candies from among the new candies but does not take the original ones into account.

8. **The correct answers are A and D.** Since $b > a$ is equivalent to $b - a > 0$, and since $ab > b - a$, it follows that $ab > 0$. Thus, a and b are either both positive or both negative. If they are both positive, the graph resembles choice A. If they are both negative, the graph resembles choice D. Choice B is incorrect since x is supposed to be between a and b. Choice C is incorrect since it shows a as a negative value and b as a positive value, which would make $ab < 0$.

9. **The correct answer is C.** Let a be the number of adult tickets sold and c the number of child tickets sold. Then $a + c = 125$, and $22a + 12c = 2{,}480$. This system can be solved using substitution or elimination. Using substitution, first solve the first equation for a: $a = 125 - c$. Then substitute this into the second equation and solve:

$$
\begin{aligned}
22(125-c)+12c &= 2{,}480\\
2{,}750-22c+12c &= 2{,}480\\
2{,}750-10c &= 2{,}480\\
-10c &= -270\\
c &= 27
\end{aligned}
$$

   Now substitute this value back into the first equation, to find a:

$$
\begin{aligned}
a+27 &= 125\\
a &= 98
\end{aligned}
$$

   Therefore, 98 adults and 27 children attended the play. The difference between these values is $98 - 27 = 71$.

Choice A is the total number of attendees. Choice B is the number of adults, not the difference between the number of adults and the number of children. Similarly, choice D is the number of children. Choice E is the difference in cost between an adult ticket and a child ticket, not the difference in how many of each attended.

10. **The correct answers are A, C, and F.** The area of the triangle is given by $\frac{1}{2}ab$. If this is equal to 28, then $ab = 56$. Since a and b are both integers, they must both be factors of 56. Among the answer choices, the factors of 56 are 2 (choice A), 4 (choice C), and 7 (choice F). Choices B, D, and E are not factors of 56.

11. **The correct answer is C.** Find the approximate percentage of the people in each education category who are smokers.

    No post-secondary education: $\frac{61}{187} \approx 33\%$

    Some college: $\frac{21}{113} \approx 19\%$

    Undergraduate degree: $\frac{15}{248} \approx 6\%$

    Graduate degree: $\frac{6}{64} \approx 9\%$

    The lowest percentage of smokers is in the undergraduate degree category. Note that the percentage is calculated by dividing the number of smokers by the total number of people in that category. The number of nonsmokers does not directly appear in the calculation. Additionally, even though the number of smokers is smallest in the graduate degree category, it does not represent the lowest percentage.

12. **The correct answer is D.** The number of people who have graduate degrees and are nonsmokers is 58. The total population in this setting consists of 612 people. Therefore, the probability is $\frac{58}{612} \approx 0.0948$.

    Choice A incorrectly assumes that the person is selected from among those with a graduate degree. Choice B is the result of mistakenly using the number of nonsmokers who have undergraduate degrees rather than graduate degrees. Choice C is the result of incorrectly assuming that the person is selected from among those who are nonsmokers. Choice E is the result of using the number of smokers with graduate degrees in the calculation rather than nonsmokers.

13. **The correct answer is A.** There are 103 smokers, and of these, 61 have no post-secondary education. Therefore, the probability is $\frac{61}{103} \approx 0.5922$. Notice that the denominator is 103, not 612. Since we are given information that the person is a smoker, we restrict ourselves to only that column of the table. Choice B is the ratio of smokers to nonsmokers among those with no post-secondary education. Choice C is the probability that someone with no post-secondary education is a smoker. Choice D is the overall probability that a randomly chosen person has no post-secondary education, but it is not restricted to smokers. Choice E is the probability that a randomly chosen person is a smoker.

14. **The correct answer is E.** Since the perimeter of the square is P, each side has length $\frac{P}{4}$. The area of the square is therefore $\frac{P}{4} \times \frac{P}{4} = \frac{P^2}{16}$. The radius of the circle is half of the side length of the square, or $\frac{P}{8}$. Since the area of a circle is given by πr^2, the area of this circle is $\pi\left(\frac{P}{8}\right)^2 = \frac{\pi P^2}{64}$. The shaded area is the difference between the area of the square and the area of the circle. This is $\frac{P^2}{16} - \frac{\pi P^2}{64}$. Factoring

out P^2 and combining the fractions with a common denominator leaves $\left(\frac{1}{16}-\frac{\pi}{64}\right)P^2=\left(\frac{4-\pi}{64}\right)P^2$.

Choice A is the result of adding the areas of the square and circle, rather than subtracting them. Choice B is the result of using P as the area of the square rather than its perimeter. Choice C is the result of forgetting to obtain a common denominator when combining the fractions. Choice D is the result of incorrectly using P as the side length of the square rather than its perimeter.

15. **The correct answer is C.** The factors of $x^2 + 2x - 15$ are $x + 5$ and $x - 3$, so the solutions are $x = -5$ and $x = 3$. If a polynomial $p(x)$ does NOT have either $x + 5$ or $x - 3$ as factors, then neither of these values can be a solution of $p(x) = 0$.

Factor the polynomials on the left side of each equation given in the answer choices. For choice A, the polynomial factors as $2(x - 3)$, so one of the factors we are looking for is present. Similarly, choice B factors as $(x + 5)(x + 6)$, choice D factors as $x(x + 5)(x - 3)$, and choice E factors as $(x + 6)(x - 3)$, so these all contain at least one of the factors we are looking for. Choice C, however, factors as $(x - 5)(x + 1)$. Neither of these is one of the factors from above, so neither -5 nor 3 is a solution of this equation.

NOTES

CHAPTER

Numeric Entry Questions

NUMERIC ENTRY QUESTIONS

OVERVIEW

This chapter describes the answer format for numeric entry questions and provides the following three useful strategies for solving this question type:

1. Turn verbose or abstract language into concise and concrete wording.
2. Make sure you're answering the correct question.
3. Round correctly.

Like multiple-choice questions, numeric entry questions may be stand-alone items, or they may be part of a data interpretation set: a group of questions that refer to the same tables, graphs, or other forms of data presentation. Strategies for data interpretation, other than estimating, apply to numeric entry questions as well.

Remember that you can always skip a question and return to it if you find that you're having trouble figuring out what the question is asking, or if you think it will take too long to answer.

8

ANSWER FORMAT FOR NUMERIC ENTRY QUESTIONS

Numeric entry questions do not offer any answer choices from which you can choose. Rather, they present you with a question and

- one answer box, if the answer is an integer or decimal, or
- two answer boxes, if the answer is a fraction.

Use your keyboard to input your answer in the appropriate answer box. If the answer is a fraction, type the numerator in the top box and the denominator in the bottom box.

Entering Answers

Here are a few instructions for entering answers with which you should familiarize yourself before you take the test. Knowing how to enter answers will ease some of the stress you may experience on test day.

- To erase a numeral in the answer box, use the "backspace" key.
- To enter a negative sign, type a hyphen.
- To remove the negative sign, type the hyphen again.
- To enter a decimal point, type a period. Note that you cannot use decimal points in fractions.
- Equivalent forms of the answer, such as 2.5 and 2.50, are all correct.
- You do not need to reduce fractions to lowest terms.

A REMINDER ABOUT USING THE ON-SCREEN CALCULATOR

The on-screen calculator can be especially useful in answering numeric entry questions. One feature that can save you a few seconds—and keep you from making an entry mistake—is the "Transfer Display" function. You may click this button to transfer the number displayed on the calculator to the answer box. However, you cannot use the "Transfer Display" feature if the answer is a fraction.

Note that if you click "Transfer Display" on a question that asks you to round your answer to a certain degree of accuracy, you may need to edit the number in the answer box so that it is appropriately rounded up or down.

STRATEGIES FOR NUMERIC ENTRY QUESTIONS

Because numeric entry questions don't provide any answer choices, you will not be able to use some of the strategies—such as working backward from the answer choices and eliminating incorrect ones—that are helpful on multiple-choice questions. On the other hand, you will not be tempted by trap answer choices, meaning those that are the result of using incorrect processes or faulty computations. Let's review what you can—and should—do to answer numeric entry questions correctly.

ALERT

For a money question, the dollar symbol will appear to the left of the answer box. Don't worry about entering it—you can't. You can only enter numbers, a decimal point, and a negative sign in the answer boxes for numeric entry questions.

Turn Verbose or Abstract Language into Concise and Concrete Wording

Remember to write out equations or draw diagrams when the question does not provide any, as this will help you get a clearer picture. In this respect, numeric entry questions are no different from multiple-choice questions.

For Question 1, enter your answer in the box.

Dominic bought a pair of shoes for \$90, two T-shirts for \$20 each, and four pairs of socks. If he paid 8% sales tax on the entire purchase, and if the total amount of the tax he paid was \$12, what was the cost of each pair of socks?

\$ [ ]

The correct answer is \$5.

Instead of trying to think this through in the abstract, write out the information you have as an equation. Let S be the cost of each pair of socks. Then, before tax, Dominic paid $\$90 + 2 \times \$20 + 4S$. The amount of tax he paid was 8% of $\$90 + 2 \times \$20 + 4S$, or $\frac{8}{100}(\$90 + 2 \times \$20 + 4S)$. Equate this to \$12 and solve for S:

$$\frac{8}{100}(\$90 + 2 \times \$20 + 4S) = \$12$$

$$\frac{2}{100}(\$90 + 2 \times \$20 + 4S) = \$3$$

$$\frac{2}{100}\$130 + \frac{2}{100}4S = \$3$$

$$\frac{2}{100}4S = \$0.4$$

$$S = \$5$$

Make Sure You're Answering the Correct Question

Your worst enemy on numeric entry questions, especially if you feel you have to race against the clock, is a careless mistake—such as confusing the diameter for the radius or giving an answer in the wrong units (e.g., minutes instead of hours, or feet instead of inches). To avoid such mistakes, always read the question carefully and double-check your work.

For Question 2, enter your answer in the box.

What is the median of the first 10 positive integers?

[ ]

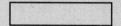

The correct answer is 5.5 (or equivalent).

TIP

An equivalent form of the correct answer 5.5, such as 5.50 and 5.500, will be considered correct. This is especially useful to remember when answering questions for which the answer is a fraction. You might enter this as 8/10 and someone else might enter it as 4/5. Both will be counted as correct unless you are specifically told to reduce it.

TIP

One way to be sure that you are answering the right question is to double-check your answer against the question. Did you solve for the correct variable and the proper units?

This is not a hard question, but one that invites two kinds of careless mistakes. When a question asks for the mean, median, or mode, make sure you don't mistakenly calculate the wrong one. Second, don't answer hastily. In this case, don't answer "5," thinking that the middle number among the first 10 positive integers will be 5. After more reasoned thinking, you would realize that because there are 10 numbers—that is, an even number of numbers—the median will be the average of the middle two numbers: 5 and 6.

For Question 3, enter your answer in the boxes.

If 12 of the 20 members of Springfield's city council are male and the rest are female, what is the ratio of female council members to male council members?

Give your answer as a fraction.

The correct answer is $\frac{8}{12}$ (or any equivalent fraction).

Here you are asked to find a part-to-part ratio: female-to-male council members. Do not provide a part-to-whole ratio (e.g., female-to-total council members), or the wrong part-to-part ratio (male-to-female council members). If there are 20 council members and 12 are male, the remaining 8 are female. The ratio you're looking for is $\frac{8}{12}$. Since fractions do not need to be reduced to lowest terms, you do not need to reduce $\frac{8}{12}$ to $\frac{2}{3}$.

Round Correctly

Sometimes, a numeric entry question will ask you to round your answer to a certain degree of accuracy. Once you've performed the necessary calculations, don't lose sight of that instruction. For instance, if you're asked to round your answer to the nearest integer, and your calculations yield 13.6, type "14" in the answer box.

Make sure, however, that you don't round any numbers until the very end. For instance, let's say that in the process of computing the answer, you have to multiply 11.2 by 3. That product is 33.6, which, rounded to the nearest integer, is 34. However, if you had rounded 11.2 down to 11 before performing the final calculation, you would have answered 33, which would have been incorrect.

For Question 4, enter your answer in the box.

In 2017, the sales of The Cranston Computer Company, a manufacturer of desktop and laptop computers, increased by 20% compared with 2016. In 2018, Cranston's sales decreased by 20% compared with 2017. Cranston's 2016 sales were what percentage of its 2018 sales?

Give your answer to the nearest tenth.

 %

The correct answer is 104.2% (or equivalent).

Pick the number 100 to represent the company's sales in 2016.

Then, the 2017 sales were 120 and the 2018 sales were $120-\frac{20}{100}(120)=96$.

Now you need to find what percentage 100 (the 2016 sales) is of 96 (the 2018 sales). Set up and solve a proportion, remembering that you need to round your answer to the nearest tenth of a percent:

$$\frac{100}{96} = \frac{x}{100}$$
$$x = \frac{10{,}000}{96}$$
$$x = 104.\overline{16}$$

Note that the calculator will give you the answer as 104.16667, and this is the number that will be placed into the answer box if you use the calculator's "Transfer Display" feature. In that case, you must then click inside the answer box and change "104.16667" to "104.2." If you don't, your answer will be marked incorrect.

TIP

Always read questions carefully. Reading carefully and turning confusing questions into concise and concrete wording may be the two most important strategies you can use. You need to understand what a question is asking in order to answer it correctly.

SUMMING IT UP

- Numeric entry questions do not offer lists of possible answers. Instead, you will be presented with a question and one or two answer boxes.
    - If the answer should be an integer or a decimal, there will be one answer box.
    - If the answer should be in the form of a fraction, there will be two answer boxes, one over the other for the numerator and denominator.
- Some numeric entry questions may be part of a data interpretation set.
- The screen will show a calculator for you to use.
    - To erase numerals in an answer box, use the "backspace" key.
    - To enter a negative sign, type a hyphen; to erase a negative sign, type the hyphen again.
    - To enter a decimal point, use a period.
- Equivalent forms of an answer are correct.
- Fractions don't need to be reduced to lowest terms, but some directions may instruct you to round decimals up or down.
- The three specific strategies to use for solving numeric entry questions are the following:
    - Turn verbose or abstract language into concise and concrete wording.
    - Make sure you're answering the correct question.
    - Round correctly.

PRACTICE

NUMERIC ENTRY QUESTIONS

For Questions 1–10, enter your answer in the boxes.

1. A cylindrical cake has a diameter of $\frac{16}{\sqrt{\pi}}$ inches and a height of 3 inches. If the cake is sliced into equal sixths, what is the volume of one slice in cubic inches?

   [ ] cubic inches

2. Jayla earns a weekly salary of $450 selling electronics and earns a commission that is calculated as x% of the sale price of the items she sells. Last week she made $1,250 in sales and earned a total of $520. What is the value of x?

   [ ]

3. If a and b are integers, define the operation $\otimes$ by $a \otimes b = ab + 1$ and the operation $\odot$ by $a \odot b = 2a - b$. What is the value of $5 \odot (2 \otimes 3)$?

   [ ]

4. Working alone, Janet can build a picnic table in 4 hours, and Jack can build a picnic table in 2 hours. If they work together, how many minutes will it take for them to build two picnic tables?

   [ ] minutes

5. A jar contains 60 marbles, a quarter of which are blue. If 2 marbles are chosen at random, what is the probability that neither is blue? Express your answer as a fraction.

   [ ]

6. In the list of numbers below, no number appears more than once:

   26, 14, 40, 13, k.

   If the median of the list is 26, what is the smallest possible integer value of k?

   [ ]

Questions 7 and 8 refer to the following chart.

Distribution of 200 Cars in a Parking Lot

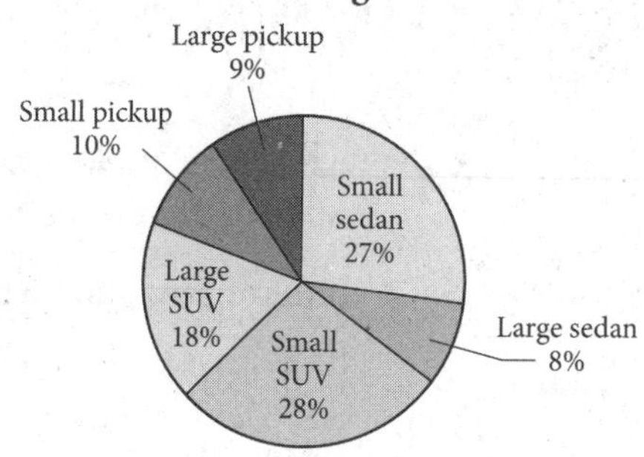

7. How many sedans are in the parking lot?

   [ ]

8. The following table shows the average fuel efficiency, in miles per gallon, of each type of vehicle.

Vehicle Type	Average MPG
Small sedan	34
Large sedan	26
Small SUV	28
Large SUV	22
Small pickup	23
Large pickup	16

   What is the average fuel efficiency, in miles per gallon, of all SUVs in the parking lot? Give your answer to the nearest tenth.

   [ ] miles per gallon

9. A rectangular lot measures 35 feet (ft.) by 42 ft. The owner wants to pave the lot and enclose it with a fence. If the cost of paving the lot is $1.50 per square foot (sq. ft.) and the cost of fencing is $3.25 per foot, what is the total cost, in dollars, of completing this project?

   $ [ ]

10. What is the largest prime number less than 65?

   [ ]

ANSWER KEY AND EXPLANATIONS

1. 32	3. 3	5. $\frac{33}{59}$	7. 70	9. 2,705.5
2. 5.6	4. 160	6. 27	8. 25.7	10. 61

1. **The correct answer is 32.** The volume of a cylinder is given by the formula $V = \pi r^2 h$, where V is the volume, r is the radius, and h is the height. Since the diameter of the cake is $\frac{16}{\sqrt{\pi}}$ inches, its radius is $\frac{8}{\sqrt{\pi}}$ inches. Substituting the values given, we find that the total volume of the cake is 192 cubic inches:

$$V = \pi r^2 h$$

$$V = \pi\left(\frac{8}{\sqrt{\pi}}\right)^2 (3)$$

$$V = \frac{64\pi(3)}{\pi}$$

$$V = 192$$

Thus, the volume of one slice is $\frac{192}{6}$, or 32 cubic inches.

2. **The correct answer is 5.6.** Since \$520 – \$450 = \$70, Jayla's commissions account for \$70 of her total earnings. To calculate what percent 70 is of 1,250, divide $\frac{70}{1{,}250} = 0.056 = 5.6\%$. Therefore, $x = 5.6$.

3. **The correct answer is 3.** First calculate $2 \otimes 3$, since it is in parentheses. Using the formula given for $\otimes$, calculate $2 \otimes 3 = 2(3) + 1 = 7$. Now replace $(2 \otimes 3)$ with 7 and use the formula for $\odot$ to calculate $5 \odot (2 \otimes 3) = 5 \odot 7 = 2(5) - 7 = 3$.

4. **The correct answer is 160.** Since Janet can build a table in 4 hours, she builds at a rate of $\frac{1}{4}$ tables per hour. Similarly, Jack builds a rate of $\frac{1}{2}$ tables per hour. Combined, they build at a rate of $\frac{1}{4} + \frac{1}{2} = \frac{3}{4}$ tables per hour. At this rate, it will take $\frac{2}{\left(\frac{3}{4}\right)} = \frac{8}{3}$ hours to build two tables. Multiply by 60 to convert to minutes: $\frac{8}{3} \times 60 = 160$.

5. **The correct answer is $\frac{33}{59}$.** Suppose the marbles are removed one at a time. Since one-quarter of the marbles in the jar are blue, the probability that the first randomly chosen marble is not blue is $\frac{3}{4}$. In that case, of the 59 marbles remaining, $59 - \frac{60}{4} = 59 - 15 = 44$ are not blue. Therefore, the probability that neither of the 2 randomly selected marbles is blue is $\frac{3}{4} \times \frac{44}{59} = \frac{33}{59}$.

6. **The correct answer is 27.** Put the numbers other than k in order: 13, 14, 26, 40. Since the median is 26, k must fit into the list to the right of the 26. It cannot be equal to 26, since the list has no duplicates, and it must be an integer. Therefore, the smallest value it can have is 27.

7. **The correct answer is 70.** The small and large sedans account for 27% + 8% = 35% of all 200 cars, and 35% of 200 is 70.

8. **The correct answer is 25.7.** The average fuel efficiency for all SUVs in the parking lot is the weighted average of the fuel efficiencies given for small and large SUVs, weighted by the percentage of SUVs in the parking lot of each type. Since SUVs account for 28% + 18% = 46% of all cars in the lot, this value can be used as the

denominator. Thus, the average fuel efficiency of all SUVs in the parking lot is equivalent to $\frac{28(0.28)+22(0.18)}{0.46}=\frac{11.8}{0.46}$, or $\frac{1,180}{46}$ miles per gallon. Rounded to the nearest tenth, $\frac{1,180}{46}=25.7$.

9. **The correct answer is 2,705.5.** The area of the lot is 35(42) = 1,470 sq. ft. The cost to pave it is therefore 1,470($1.50) = $2,205. The perimeter is 2(35) + 2(42) = 154 ft., so the cost of the fencing is 154($3.25) = $500.50. The total cost is $2,205 + $500.50 = $2,705.50, or 2,705.5 dollars.

10. **The correct answer is 61.** Start listing numbers from 64 and counting down. 64 is not prime since it is divisible by 2. 63 is not prime since it is divisible by 3. 62 is not prime since it is divisible by 2. 61, however, is a prime number. To see this, try to divide 61 by all integers starting at 2 and going up until you reach 8, since at that point you have passed the square root of 61. A remainder of 1 is left when 61 is divided by 2, 3, 4, 5, or 6 and a remainder of 5 is left when it is divided by 7.

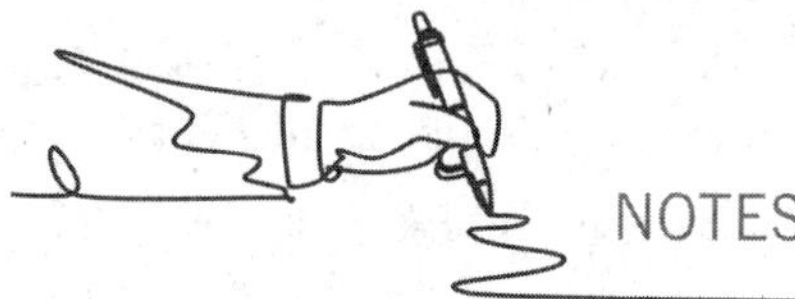

NOTES

CHAPTER

Quantitative Comparison Questions

QUANTITATIVE COMPARISON QUESTIONS

OVERVIEW

In this chapter, you will find an introduction to the quantitative comparison questions that you will encounter on the GRE General Test, as well as a discussion of strategies to help you answer those questions quickly and competently. A few of these strategies will be familiar to you from the chapters on multiple-choice questions and numeric entry questions. Most, however, are specific to answering quantitative comparison questions. The strategies are as follows:

- Pick and plug numbers.
- Simplify the quantities.
- Avoid unnecessary calculations.
- Estimate.
- Redraw the figure.
- Recognize when the answer cannot be "The relationship cannot be determined."

What you won't find in the quantitative comparison section of the GRE General Test are data sets. Each quantitative comparison question is a stand-alone item.

BASIC INFORMATION ABOUT QUANTITATIVE COMPARISON QUESTIONS

Quantitative comparisons present you with two quantities, A and B. Your task is to compare the quantities and choose one of the following answers:

A. Quantity A is greater.

B. Quantity B is greater.

C. The two quantities are equal.

D. The relationship cannot be determined from the information given.

These answer choices, *in this exact order*, appear with all quantitative comparison questions. Memorize the answers in order, so you don't waste time reading them for each question.

On the official GRE General Test, these answer choices are not labeled A, B, and so on. They are merely listed in this order, each with an oval to its left. For your convenience in this book, we've labeled the ovals A, B, C, and D.

Here are two other points of information to remember:

- Some questions feature additional information centered above the two quantities. You should use this information to help you determine the relationship between the two quantities.
- Any symbol that appears more than once in a question (e.g., one that appears in Quantity A and in the centered information) has the same meaning throughout the question.

STRATEGIES FOR QUANTITATIVE COMPARISON QUESTIONS

In addition to the strategies explained here, remember that you can always skip and return to a question. You will need to click the "Mark" button so that you can find the question quickly in the "Review" screen when you are ready to give it another try. However, you can only go back to a question in the section you are currently working on.

Pick and Plug Numbers

Picking and plugging numbers to represent variables is a powerful strategy if you are asked to compare expressions that contain variables. You pick numbers to represent the variables, and then plug these numbers into the expressions given in Quantities A and B. Work quickly, but also thoroughly. Depending on the question, you should choose

- not only positive, but also negative numbers;
- not only integers, but also fractions (in particular, fractions between 0 and 1, and 0 and –1); and/or
- the numbers 1 and 0.

For Question 1, compare Quantity A and Quantity B. This question has additional information above the two quantities to use in determining your answer.

$$\frac{x}{y}=3$$

$$y \neq 0$$

Quantity A	Quantity B
x	y

A. Quantity A is greater.

B. Quantity B is greater.

C. The two quantities are equal.

D. The relationship cannot be determined from the information given.

The correct answer is D.

First, rewrite the centered information as $x = 3y$, which is easier to work with.

This question features variables in both quantities, so picking numbers is likely to get you to the right answer quickly. Choose different numbers for y and see what results you get for x; also determine the relationship between the two quantities. To keep track of the results, draw a table on your scratch paper.

y		x
1	<	3
2	<	6
$\frac{1}{3}$	<	1

So when y equals 1, x equals 3; when y equals 2, x equals 6; and when y equals $\frac{1}{3}$, x equals 1. In all three cases, x is greater than y, so you may be tempted to conclude that Quantity A will always be greater than Quantity B. However, you have not yet tested a sufficient variety of numbers, so you should not jump to a conclusion yet. (In fact, testing $y = 2$ was a waste of time because there was no reason to think that it would have yielded a different result than did $y = 1$.) In order to be thorough, you should also test numbers that have some different properties.

y		x
−1	>	−3

In this example, picking a negative number for y results in y being greater than x. Because you have now found at least one instance in which x is greater than y, as well as at least one instance in which y is greater than x, you are finished.

For Question 2, compare Quantity A and Quantity B. This question has additional information above the two quantities to use in determining your answer.

$$\frac{x}{y} = 3$$

$$y \neq 0$$

Quantity A	Quantity B
$\lvert x \rvert$	$\lvert y \rvert$

A. Quantity A is greater.

B. Quantity B is greater.

C. The two quantities are equal.

D. The relationship cannot be determined from the information given.

The correct answer is A.

This question is similar to Question 1, but there is one important difference. You are now being asked to compare the absolute values of the two variables, not the variables themselves.

Again, start by rewriting the centered information in the following form:

$$x = 3y$$

Pick numbers again.

y	x	$\lvert y \rvert$		$\lvert x \rvert$
1	3	1	<	3
−1	−3	1	<	3
$\frac{1}{3}$	1	$\frac{1}{6}$	<	$\frac{1}{2}$

This time, because the absolute values eliminate the minus signs, the pattern that emerges is reliable. Because x equals 3 times y and because you're asked to compare the absolute values of x and y, no matter what value you pick for y, the absolute value of x will always be greater than the absolute value of y.

When to Use (and Not to Use) Pick and Plug

Picking numbers is a useful strategy, but you should keep in mind that it doesn't always answer the question definitively.

- It is best used when it quickly reveals two different relationships between the quantities, in which case you have proved that the answer is choice D.
- It is also helpful if the possible values that the variables may take are few, and you are able to test them all.

However, if the possible values that the variables may take are infinite—or if they are finite, but too many for you to check in any reasonable amount of time—then you cannot use this strategy alone to answer the question. Even if you test many numbers, all of which produce the same result, it's entirely possible that some other numbers, which you have not yet tested, may produce a different result.

That said, even in such a case, picking numbers may be useful if you are stuck and do not know how to proceed. After you've picked a few numbers and examined the results, you may notice a pattern that you may not have noticed previously and that will help you compare the quantities.

Simplify the Quantities

Sometimes, test-item writers present you with expressions—either in the two quantities or in the centered information—that appear complicated, thus making your job harder. In such cases, you can help yourself by

- simplifying each quantity in order to make it easier to evaluate on its own;
- manipulating one quantity in such a way as to make it easier to compare with the other quantity; or
- simplifying the centered information so that you end up with a new piece of information that's easier to interpret.

For Question 3, compare Quantity A and Quantity B.

Quantity A	Quantity B
$4x^2 - 8x + 4$	$(2x - 2)^2$

A. Quantity A is greater.

B. Quantity B is greater.

C. The two quantities are equal.

D. The relationship cannot be determined from the information given.

The correct answer is C.

As written, these quantities are hard to compare. However, you can manipulate either quantity so that it resembles the other one. For instance, if you distribute Quantity B, you get

$$(2x - 2)^2 = 4x^2 - 8x + 4$$

Thus, Quantity A is the distributed form of Quantity B, so the two quantities are equal.

For Question 4, compare Quantity A and Quantity B. This question has additional information above the two quantities to use in determining your answer.

$$-1 < x < y < 0$$

Quantity A	Quantity B
xy	$\frac{x}{y}$

A. Quantity A is greater.

B. Quantity B is greater.

C. The two quantities are equal.

D. The relationship cannot be determined from the information given.

The correct answer is B.

In this question, you should simplify the two quantities together in order to arrive at something that's easier to compare. Start by assuming that one quantity is larger than the other, and simplify the inequality until you arrive at a statement that you can evaluate. If that statement is correct, then your initial assumption was correct. If that statement is incorrect, your initial assumption was incorrect. Let's see this process at work.

Begin by assuming that Quantity A is larger than Quantity B:

$$xy > \frac{x}{y}$$

Next, cancel x from both sides of the inequality—that is, divide both sides by x. You can do this for two reasons: first, because $x \neq 0$, division by x is permissible; second, because $x < 0$, you know that division by x will reverse the sign of the inequality. (If you don't know whether a variable is positive or negative, you cannot multiply or divide both sides of the inequality by that variable.) So you are left with $y < \frac{1}{y}$.

Now evaluate whether this statement is correct or not. Since y is a fraction between 0 and –1 (such as $-\frac{1}{2}$), its reciprocal will also be a negative number, but one smaller than –1 (such as –2). Thus, y is greater than $\frac{1}{y}$ and the inequality $y < \frac{1}{y}$ is incorrect. This means that the initial assumption that Quantity A is larger than Quantity B was also incorrect.

Since it turns out that $y > \frac{1}{y}$, you should reverse the sign of the inequality for each one of the prior steps, thus arriving at $xy < \frac{x}{y}$.

Eliminating Terms When Simplifying Quantities

This example also illustrates another helpful tool you can use when you simplify two expressions together. You can eliminate any term that appears on both expressions, as long as you keep the following rules in mind:

- You can add or subtract any term to or from both quantities. For instance, if both quantities feature the term $3y$, you can subtract it from both of them.
- You can multiply or divide both quantities by any nonzero term, as long as you know whether this term is positive or negative.

Avoid Unnecessary Calculations

Remember that you do not always need to find the exact value of the two quantities in order to compare them. This will save you time.

For Question 5, compare Quantity A and Quantity B.

Quantity A	Quantity B
The average (arithmetic mean) of all odd integers between 10 and 30	The average (arithmetic mean) of all even integers between 11 and 31

A. Quantity A is greater.

B. Quantity B is greater.

C. The two quantities are equal.

D. The relationship cannot be determined from the information given.

The correct answer is B.

To answer this question, you could, of course, list all the odd integers between 10 and 30, add them up, and find their average in order to determine the exact value of Quantity A. Then you could do the same for the even integers in Quantity B. However, that would be a very time-consuming process. Luckily, you don't have to do all that.

Instead, think about what the two quantities are. Quantity A is the average of 10 integers, starting with the number 11 and ending with the number 29. Quantity B is also the average of 10 such integers, this time starting with 12 and ending with 30. Notice that both quantities feature the same number of terms.

Next, you should note that the smallest term in Quantity B is larger than the smallest term in Quantity A; the second smallest term in Quantity B is larger than the second smallest term in Quantity A; and so on, for each of the 10 terms in the two quantities, since in both cases the numbers increase by 2.

Thus, the sum of the terms in Quantity B is larger than the sum of the terms in Quantity A, and, therefore, the average of the terms in Quantity B is also larger than the average of the terms in Quantity A. No further work is needed.

Estimate

One particular way to avoid unnecessary calculations is estimating.

For Question 6, compare Quantity A and Quantity B.

Quantity A	Quantity B
$65 \times \frac{6}{5}$	47% of 130

A. Quantity A is greater.

B. Quantity B is greater.

C. The two quantities are equal.

D. The relationship cannot be determined from the information given.

The correct answer is A.

Avoid the temptation to use the calculator. As a quantitative comparison, the question asks you to compare the two quantities, not to evaluate them fully.

First, look at Quantity A. The fraction $\frac{6}{5}$ is greater than 1. That means that Quantity A is greater than 65. Stop there for the moment, and move on to Quantity B.

Quantity B features a number that is less than 50% of 130. 50% of 130 is 65, so Quantity B is less than 65.

In other words, Quantity A is greater than 65, whereas Quantity B is less than 65, which means that Quantity A is greater than Quantity B.

Redraw the Figure

Remember that geometric figures on the GRE General Test are not necessarily drawn to scale. When in doubt, you can always redraw a figure on your scratch paper, altering any quantities such as side lengths or angle measures that have not been defined fully. Doing so may reveal additional information about the figure that may not have been obvious from the figure that the test maker provided.

For Question 7, compare Quantity A and Quantity B. This question has additional information above the two quantities to use in determining your answer.

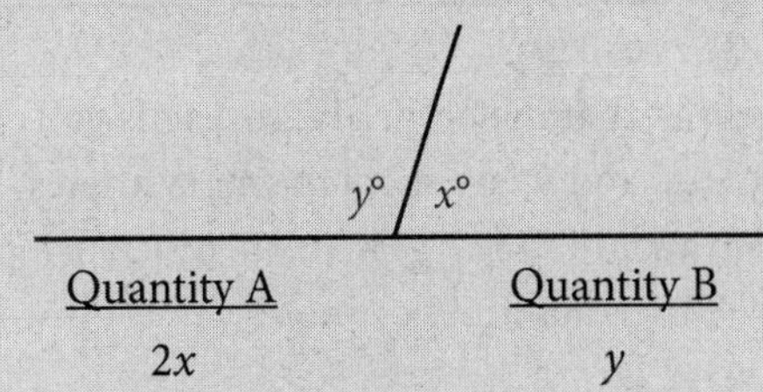

Quantity A	Quantity B
$2x$	y

A. Quantity A is greater.

B. Quantity B is greater.

C. The two quantities are equal.

D. The relationship cannot be determined from the information given.

The correct answer is D.

TIP

Redrawing the figure can be useful in answering other types of questions as well.

As the figure is drawn, you may be tempted to assume that $x°$ is an acute angle and $y°$ is an obtuse angle. Further, you may be tempted to estimate the value of the two angles and try to compare the two quantities that way. Don't!

The figure is not necessarily drawn to scale, and you have no further information to help you evaluate the angles. You can redraw the figure on your scratch paper in order to see this latter point visually:

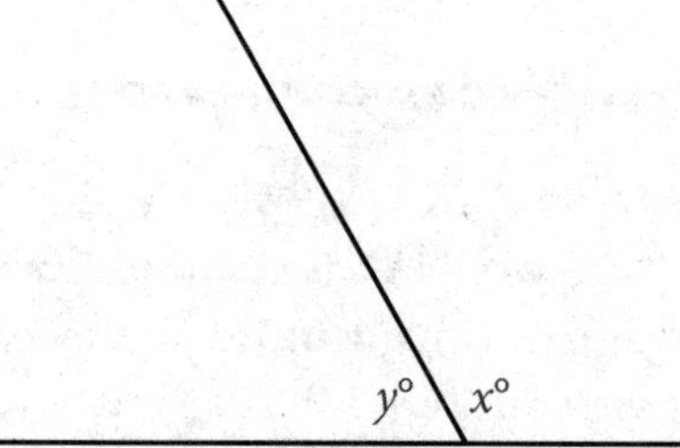

The only thing that the original figure tells you definitively is that $x°$ and $y°$ are supplementary angles—that is, that they add up to 180°. Thus, the relationship between the two quantities cannot be determined.

Recognize When the Answer Cannot Be "The relationship cannot be determined."

The answer in a quantitative comparison question cannot be that the relationship cannot be determined if the two quantities are defined fully. That happens in the following cases:

- When there are no variables in either quantity
- When there are variables, but each of the variables may take only one value

For Question 8, compare Quantity A and Quantity B. This question has additional information above the two quantities to use in determining your answer.

$$x - 3 = 2$$

$$3y = x + 7$$

Quantity A	Quantity B
x	y

A. Quantity A is greater.

B. Quantity B is greater.

C. The two quantities are equal.

D. The relationship cannot be determined from the information given.

The correct answer is A.

Even though the quantities feature variables, these variables are defined absolutely because of the two equations in the centered information. The first equation yields a unique value for x, and that value, when substituted into the second equation, yields a unique value for y. Because both quantities are fully defined, a definitive comparison between them is possible. In this case, $x = 5$ and $y = 4$.

SUMMING IT UP

- Quantitative comparison questions present two quantities, A and B, that you must compare. To select an answer, you choose one answer from the following list:

  A. Quantity A is greater.

  B. Quantity B is greater.

  C. The two quantities are equal.

  D. The relationship cannot be determined from the information given.

- Some questions feature additional information centered above the two quantities. You should use this information to help you determine the relationship between the two quantities.
- Any symbol that appears more than once in a question (e.g., one that appears in Quantity A and in the centered information) has the same meaning throughout the question.
- Specific strategies for quantitative comparison questions include the following:
  - Pick and plug numbers.
  - Simplify the quantities.
  - Avoid unnecessary calculations.
  - Estimate.
  - Redraw the figure.
  - Recognize when the answer cannot be "The relationship cannot be determined."
- Data interpretation sets are not used for quantitative comparison questions.

PRACTICE

QUANTITATIVE COMPARISON QUESTIONS

For Questions 1–15, compare Quantity A and Quantity B. Some questions will have additional information above the two quantities to use in determining your answer.

1. $x^2 = y^3$

Quantity A	Quantity B
x	y

A. Quantity A is greater.
B. Quantity B is greater.
C. The two quantities are equal.
D. The relationship cannot be determined from the information given.

2. $x = 60$

Quantity A	Quantity B
x	$2y$

A. Quantity A is greater.
B. Quantity B is greater.
C. The two quantities are equal.
D. The relationship cannot be determined from the information given.

3.

Quantity A	Quantity B
47% of 250	125

A. Quantity A is greater.
B. Quantity B is greater.
C. The two quantities are equal.
D. The relationship cannot be determined from the information given.

4. List A: x, y, z

List B: x, x, y, y, z, z

Quantity A	Quantity B
The average of the numbers in list A	The average of the numbers in list B

A. Quantity A is greater.
B. Quantity B is greater.
C. The two quantities are equal.
D. The relationship cannot be determined from the information given.

5. $0 < x < 1$ and $1 < y < 2$

Quantity A	Quantity B
$x + y$	xy

A. Quantity A is greater.

B. Quantity B is greater.

C. The two quantities are equal.

D. The relationship cannot be determined from the information given.

6.

Quantity A	Quantity B
$(x + 2)^2 + (y - 3)^2 + 5$	$x^2 + y^2 + 4x - 6y + 18$

A. Quantity A is greater.

B. Quantity B is greater.

C. The two quantities are equal.

D. The relationship cannot be determined from the information given.

7.

Quantity A	Quantity B
$\lvert x \rvert$	$\lvert x + 1 \rvert$

A. Quantity A is greater.

B. Quantity B is greater.

C. The two quantities are equal.

D. The relationship cannot be determined from the information given.

8. Martin has an older sister, Val, and a younger sister, Luiza.
In two years, Val will be twice as old as Martin.

Quantity A	Quantity B
The average of all three siblings' ages	The average of Val and Luiza's ages

A. Quantity A is greater.

B. Quantity B is greater.

C. The two quantities are equal.

D. The relationship cannot be determined from the information given.

9. The radius of circle C is 50% greater than the radius of circle A, and the radius of circle B is 50% less than the radius of circle C.

Quantity A	Quantity B
The area of circle A	The area of circle B

A. Quantity A is greater.
B. Quantity B is greater.
C. The two quantities are equal.
D. The relationship cannot be determined from the information given.

10. A bag contains x black marbles and y red marbles, with at least one marble of each color.

Quantity A	Quantity B
The probability of drawing a black marble and then a red marble, with replacement	The probability of drawing a black marble and then a red marble, without replacement

A. Quantity A is greater.
B. Quantity B is greater.
C. The two quantities are equal.
D. The relationship cannot be determined from the information given.

11. A fair six-sided die is rolled until a 6 occurs.

Quantity A	Quantity B
The probability that the die is rolled at most thrice	The probability that the die is rolled four times or more

A. Quantity A is greater.
B. Quantity B is greater.
C. The two quantities are equal.
D. The relationship cannot be determined from the information given.

12. $x > 1$

Quantity A	Quantity B
$\frac{x^{50} - x^{49}}{x - 1}$	x

A. Quantity A is greater.

B. Quantity B is greater.

C. The two quantities are equal.

D. The relationship cannot be determined from the information given.

13.

Quantity A	Quantity B
The least common multiple of 6 and 9	The greatest common factor of 36 and 54

A. Quantity A is greater.

B. Quantity B is greater.

C. The two quantities are equal.

D. The relationship cannot be determined from the information given.

14. A triangle has two sides of lengths 2 centimeters (cm) and 3 cm.

Quantity A	Quantity B
The area of the triangle in cm^2	3

A. Quantity A is greater.

B. Quantity B is greater.

C. The two quantities are equal.

D. The relationship cannot be determined from the information given.

15. p is a prime number.

Quantity A	Quantity B
The number of positive integer factors of $2p^3$	9

A. Quantity A is greater.

B. Quantity B is greater.

C. The two quantities are equal.

D. The relationship cannot be determined from the information given.

ANSWER KEY AND EXPLANATIONS

1. D	4. C	7. D	10. B	13. C
2. C	5. A	8. B	11. B	14. D
3. B	6. C	9. A	12. A	15. B

1. **The correct answer is D.** Consider the numbers that are both squares and cubes of integers, such as 1 or 64. If $x = -1$ and $y = 1$, then $x^2 = y^3 = 1$ and x is less than y. If $x = 8$ and $y = 4$, then $x^2 = y^3 = 64$ and x is greater than y. Therefore, the relationship between x and y cannot be determined from the information given.
2. **The correct answer is C.** Since x and y combine to make a right angle, $x + y = 90$. But $x = 60$ is given, so $y = 90 - 60 = 30$. Therefore, $2y = 60$, which is the same as x.
3. **The correct answer is B.** There is no need to actually calculate 47% of 250. Instead, note that it is less than 50% of 250, which is 125. Therefore, 125 is larger than 47% of 250.
4. **The correct answer is C.** The average of the numbers in list B is as follows:

$$\frac{x+x+y+y+z+z}{6}$$
$$=\frac{2x+2y+2z}{6}$$
$$=\frac{2(x+y+z)}{6}$$
$$=\frac{x+y+z}{3}$$

But this is exactly the average of the numbers in list A, so the two quantities are equal.
5. **The correct answer is A.** Since x is between 0 and 1, multiplying a positive number by it will produce a smaller positive number. This means that xy is smaller than y. On the other hand, both x and y are positive, so adding them together produces a number that is larger than either one, so $x + y$ is larger than y. Therefore, Quantity A is greater.
6. **The correct answer is C.** Expand the expression given as Quantity A:

$$(x+2)^2+(y-3)^2+5$$
$$=x^2+4x+4+y^2-6y+9+5$$
$$=x^2+y^2+4x-6y+18$$

This is the same as Quantity B.
7. **The correct answer is D.** Although at first glance it may seem that Quantity B is always greater, this is in fact only true if x is greater than -0.5. If x is any value less than -0.5, then Quantity A will actually be larger.

For example, if $x = -1$, then $|x| = 1$, and $|x + 1| = |0| = 0$. Since we don't know the value of x, the relationship between these quantities cannot be determined.
8. **The correct answer is B.** The average of Val and Luiza's ages—even if Luiza is a newborn—must be at least half of Val's age. In two years, Val will be twice as old as Martin, so Martin's age is currently less than half of Val's. Thus, the average of Val and Luiza's ages is greater than Martin's age. When Martin's age is factored in, the average decreases, so the average age of all three siblings is less than the average of Val and Luiza's ages.
9. **The correct answer is A.** The formula for the area of a circle is $A = \pi r^2$. To figure out which quantity is greater, we need to figure out which circle has a larger radius.

Let r_A, r_B, and r_C represent the radii of circles *A*, *B*, and *C*, respectively. Then the given information tells us that $r_C = 1.5r_A$ and $r_B = 0.5r_C$. Substituting $r_C = 1.5r_A$ into the latter equation shows that $r_B = 0.5(1.5r_A) = 0.75r_A$, so that the radius of circle *B* is 75% of the radius of circle *A*. In particular, circle *A* has the larger radius, so Quantity A is greater.

10. **The correct answer is B.** The probability of drawing a black marble and then a red marble with replacement is $\frac{x}{x+y} \times \frac{y}{x+y}$. The probability of drawing a black marble and then a red marble without replacement is $\frac{x}{x+y} \times \frac{y}{x+y-1}$, where the denominator of the second factor has the term −1 since the first marble drawn is not replaced. In both cases, the first factor is the same. Comparing the second factors, the denominator in the latter situation is smaller, which means the fraction is larger. Therefore, Quantity B is greater.

11. **The correct answer is B.** The die is rolled four times or more if a 6 does not occur in the first three rolls. Since the die is fair, the probability that no 6 occurs in the first three rolls is $\frac{5}{6} \times \frac{5}{6} \times \frac{5}{6} = \frac{5^3}{6^3} = \frac{125}{216}$. Half of 216 is 108, so this probability is greater than 0.5. Therefore, the probability that the die is rolled four or more times is greater than the probability that the die is rolled at most thrice.

12. **The correct answer is A.** Factor Quantity A: $\frac{x^{50} - x^{49}}{x-1} = \frac{x^{49}(x-1)}{x-1}$. Since $x > 1$, $x - 1$ cannot be 0, so it can be canceled from the numerator and denominator, leaving x^{49}. Now again, since $x > 1$, multiplying it by itself produces larger and larger numbers, so $x^{49} > x$. Therefore, Quantity A is greater.

13. **The correct answer is C.** Calculate each quantity. The prime factorizations of 6 and 9 are $6 = 2 \times 3$ and $9 = 3 \times 3$, so their least common multiple is $2 \times 3 \times 3 = 18$. The prime factorizations of 36 and 54 are $36 = 2 \times 2 \times 3 \times 3$ and $54 = 2 \times 3 \times 3 \times 3$, so their greatest common factor is $2 \times 3 \times 3 = 18$. The two quantities are equal.

14. **The correct answer is D.** If the triangle happens to be a right triangle with the sides of length 2 cm and 3 cm meeting at the right angle, then the area would be 3 cm^2. However, if those two sides do not meet at a right angle, the area of the triangle will be less than 3 cm^2. Therefore, the relationship between these two quantities cannot be determined.

15. **The correct answer is B.** The only prime factors of $2p^3$ are 2 and p, so any positive integer factor of $2p^3$ is either 1 or a combination of 2 and p. Listing these out, we find that the positive integer factors of $2p^3$ are 1, p, p^2, p^3, 2, $2p$, $2p^2$, and $2p^3$. (Note that if $p = 2$, then $p^2 = 2p$ and $p^3 = 2p^2$.) Since $2p^3$ has at most eight positive integer factors, Quantity B is greater.

PART V

PRACTICE TESTS

CHAPTER

Practice Test 1

PRACTICE TEST 1

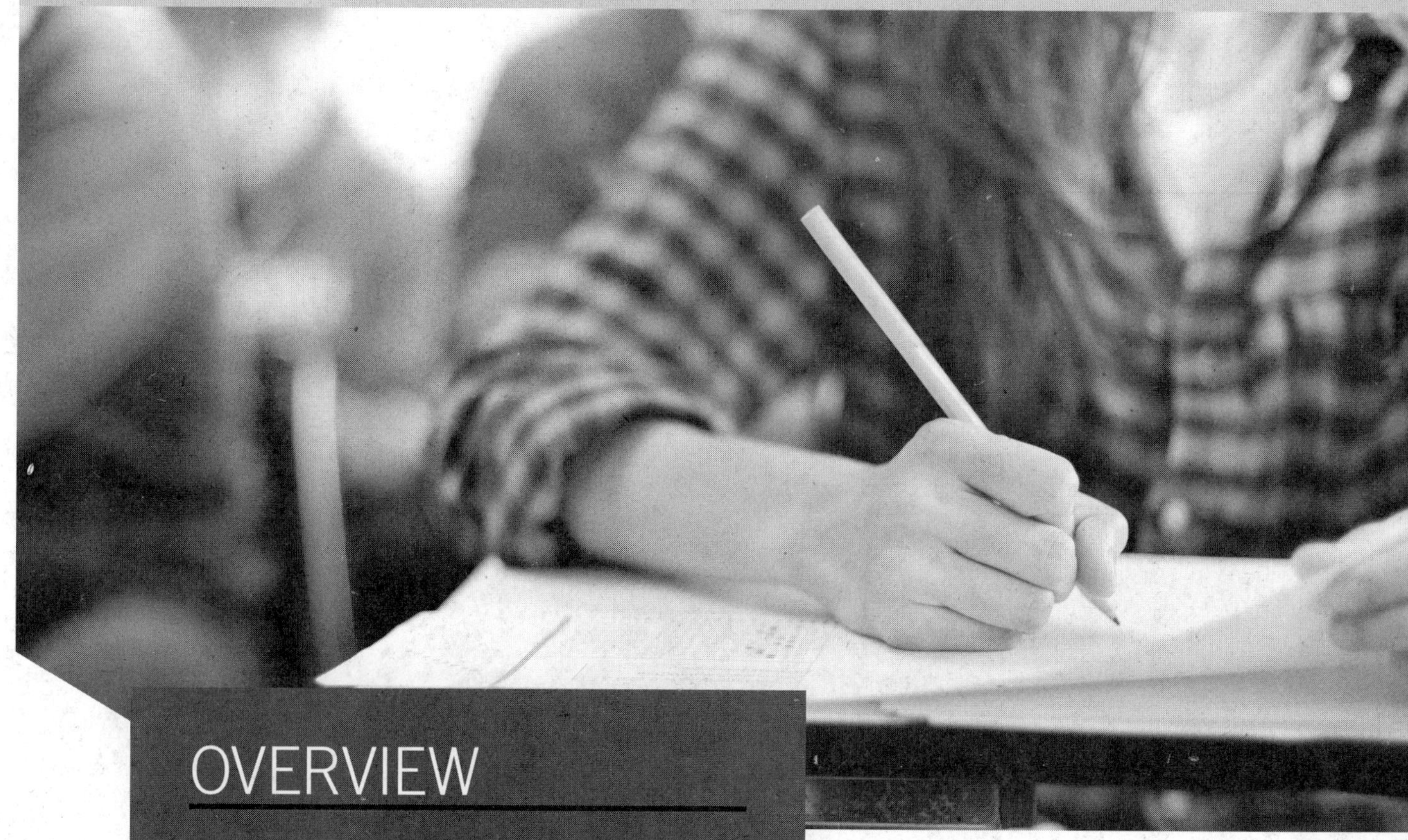

OVERVIEW

10

DIRECTIONS FOR PRACTICE TEST 1

Practice Test 1 contains the five scored sections you will encounter on the actual GRE General Test.

On pages 371–377, we've provided sheets for planning and composing your Analytical Writing response, followed by an answer sheet for filling in your responses in the Verbal Reasoning and Quantitative Reasoning sections. Before you begin the test, remove or photocopy these pages.

As on the actual GRE General Test, each test section has its own time allocation. During that time period you may work on only that section. Be sure to use a timer for each section so you can accurately simulate the test-day experience. Total testing time is approximately 1 hour and 58 minutes.

Following Section 5, you will be provided tools to help you assess your response to the Analytical Writing task. An answer key and a comprehensive explanation follow for each test question in the Verbal Reasoning and Quantitative Reasoning sections.

Answer sheets for this test can be found on pages 371–377.

SECTION 1: ANALYTICAL WRITING

30 minutes

The time for this Analyze an Issue task is 30 minutes. You must plan and draft a response that evaluates the issue given below. If you do not respond to the specific issue, your score will be zero. Your response must be based on the accompanying instructions, and you must provide evidence for your position. You may use support from reading, experience, observations, and/or coursework.

Educators should find out what students want included in the curriculum and then offer it to them.

*Write a response in which you discuss the extent to which you agree or disagree with the statement, and explain your reasoning for the position you take. In developing and supporting your position, you should consider ways in which the statement might or might not hold true and explain how these considerations shape your position.**

STOP!

IF YOU FINISH BEFORE THE TIME IS UP, YOU MAY CHECK YOUR WORK IN THIS SECTION ONLY.

* All of the Analytical Writing prompts in the practice tests of this book come directly from the list of prompts for the GRE, which can be found at https://www.ets.org/pdfs/gre/issue-pool.pdf.

DIRECTIONS FOR THE VERBAL REASONING AND QUANTITATIVE REASONING SECTIONS

On test day, you will find information here about the question formats for the Verbal Reasoning and Quantitative Reasoning sections as well as information about how to use the software program. You will also receive important information about how these two sections are scored. Every correct answer earns a point, but points are not subtracted for incorrect answers, so it is better to guess if you aren't sure of an answer than to leave a question unanswered.

All multiple-choice questions will have answer options preceded by either blank ovals or blank squares, depending on the question type.

For your convenience in answering questions and checking answers in this paper-based practice test, answer choices are shown as lettered options. This notation makes it easier to check your answers against the answer keys and explanations.

NOTES

SECTION 2: VERBAL REASONING

18 minutes—12 questions

For each question, follow the specific directions and choose the best answer.

For Questions 1 and 2, choose one answer for each blank. Select from the appropriate column for each blank. Choose the answer that best completes the sense of the text.

1. After years of (i) _________, the workers finally decided to go on strike to obtain the pay they deserved. As the protest grew increasingly (ii) _________, security officers became concerned that it could erupt into violence.

Blank (i)	Blank (ii)
A. activism	D. placid
B. antagonism	E. vociferous
C. complacency	F. hesitant

2. The film suffered from numerous (i) _________ flaws. Although it was set in the 1920s, it contained several (ii) _________, such as cars that were not manufactured until the 1960s. Furthermore, the acting lacked (iii) _________, making it difficult to believe the characters were real people.

Blank (i)	Blank (ii)	Blank (iii)
A. trivial	D. anomalies	G. affluence
B. crucial	E. allusions	H. eccentricity
C. inconsequential	F. anachronisms	I. authenticity

For Questions 3–9, choose only one answer choice unless otherwise indicated.

Questions 3–5 are based on the following passage.

Smiling involves a complex group of facial movements. It may suffice to remind the reader of such characteristic changes as the drawing back and slight lifting of the corners of the mouth, the raising of the upper lip, which partially uncovers the teeth, and the curving of the furrows betwixt the corners of the mouth and the nostrils (the naso-labial furrows) which these movements involve. To these must be added the formation of wrinkles under the eyes—a most characteristic part of the expression—which is a further result of the first movements. The increased brightness of the eyes is probably the effect of their tenseness, due to the contraction of the adjacent muscles and the pressure of the raised cheek, though an acceleration of the circulation within the eyeball may have something to do with it.

These facial changes are common to the smile and to the laugh, though in the more violent forms of laughter the eyes are apt to lose under their lachrymal suffusion the sparkle which the smile brings.

As a characteristic group of facial movements the smile is excellently well suited for its purpose—the primitive and most universal expression of a pleasurable or happy state of mind. It forms, in respect of certain of its features at least, a marked contrast to the expression of opposite feelings. Thus it is far removed, and so easily distinguishable, from the facial expression during weeping, *viz.*, the firmly closed eyelids and the wide opening of the mouth in the form of a squarish cavity; as also from the face's betrayal of low spirits and "crossness," in the depressed corners of the mouth, the oblique eyebrows and the furrowed forehead.

—Excerpt from *Laughter* by James Sully

3. In the first paragraph, the author most likely mentions the physical movements involved in smiling to emphasize that

   A. the face endures a degree of strain in order to smile.

   B. smiling is a relatively simple physiological process.

   C. smiling involves much more than just the mouth.

   D. smiling can be the result of tension rather than joy.

   E. showing teeth while smiling implies greater joy than a tight-lipped smile.

4. In the context in which it appears, "drawing" (line 2) most nearly means

   A. pulling.

   B. sketching.

   C. selecting.

   D. illustration.

   E. depicting.

For Question 5, consider each answer individually and select all choices that apply.

5. Based on the passage, with which of the following statements might the author likely agree?

   A. Smiling is easy to distinguish from expressions that convey sadness.

   B. There are numerous physical similarities between smiling and laughing.

   C. There are several components to smiling.

Questions 6 and 7 are based on the following passage.

Nothing can be known to *exist* except by the help of experience. That is to say, if we wish to prove that something of which we have no direct experience exists, we must have among our premises the existence of one or more things of which we have direct experience. Our belief that the Emperor of China exists, for example, rests upon testimony, and testimony consists, in the last analysis, of sense-data seen or heard in reading or being spoken to. Rationalists believed that, from general consideration as to what *must* be, they could deduce the existence of this or that in the actual world. In this belief they seem to have been mistaken. All the knowledge that we can acquire *a priori* concerning existence seems to be hypothetical: it tells us that *if* one thing exists, another must exist, or, more generally, that *if* one proposition is true, another must be true. This is exemplified by the principles we have already dealt with, such as '*if* this is true, and this implies that, then that is true', or '*if* this and that have been repeatedly found connected, they will probably be connected in the next instance in which one of them is found'. Thus the scope and power of *a priori* principles is strictly limited. All knowledge that something exists must be in part dependent on experience. When anything is known immediately, its existence is known by experience alone; when anything is proved to exist, without being known immediately, both experience and *a priori* principles must be required in the proof. Knowledge is called *empirical* when it rests wholly or partly upon experience. Thus all knowledge which asserts existence is empirical, and the only *a priori* knowledge concerning existence is hypothetical, giving connections among things that exist or may exist, but not giving actual existence.

—Excerpt from *The Problems of Philosophy* by Bertrand Russell

6. Select the sentence that supports the author's opinion that all *a priori* principles are limited.
   - A. Nothing can be known to *exist* except by the help of experience.
   - B. Rationalists believed that, from general consideration as to what must be, they could deduce the existence of this or that in the actual world.
   - C. In this belief they seem to have been mistaken.
   - D. Thus the scope and power of *a priori* principles is strictly limited.
   - E. '*If* this is true, and this implies that, then that is true.'

7. The author of the passage suggests which of the following about Rationalists?
   - A. Their beliefs contradict those of people who trust in the importance of empirical knowledge.
   - B. They secretly have faith in the principles of empirical knowledge.
   - C. They did not see any difference between *a priori* thought and empirical knowledge.
   - D. They do not believe something exists simply because they can experience it.
   - E. They will believe anything anyone tells them regardless of the existence of evidence.

Questions 8 and 9 are based on the following passage.

In the summer of 2021, during a mission to excavate sections of the ancient Mayan city Palenque, archeologists found a partial visage of an ancient statue in which a chin, nose, and parted mouth are visible. In 2022, researchers from Mexico's National Institute of Anthropology and History asserted that the partial statue shows the likeness of Hun Hunahpu, the Mayan god associated with maize.

Maize, or corn, is indigenous to the areas of Central America the Maya had inhabited. It was not only a staple of the Mayan diet but also a critical symbol of the Maya people's spiritual relationship with the earth. Perhaps most important, the Mayans believed that humankind itself had come from maize since their creation folklore included the idea that humans had been fashioned by the gods using white and yellow corn. In short, maize was linked to virtually all aspects of Mesoamerican culture.

Because of the god's association with such an important resource, the Maya worshipped Hun Hunahpu devoutly. Beliefs associated with Hun Hunahpu include the idea that every autumn, when the harvest came, the god would be decapitated, only to be reborn when spring came. This deep connection to the cycle of life and death as well as the changing of the seasons meant both Hun Hunahpu and the maize with which the god was associated were central to Mayan concepts of time itself.

The discovery of this partial statue in Palenque was momentous for researchers in that it is the first of its magnitude from the dig site. Archaeologists believe the stucco comes from the Late Classic Period, which would place its origin somewhere between 700 and 850 B.C.E. The statue was found in a preserved pond area likely devoted to Hun Hunahpu, who researchers identified based on the items found around the statue and the maize-like appearance of the statue's visible hair. The statue's head also appeared to be intentionally separated from the original statue's body, suggesting it depicted Hun Hunahpu in the decapitated state. Researchers also believe that the statue's placement was important; its gaze would have aligned with rows of maize at dawn and its orientation at the foot of a pond likely signified the deity's close relationship with the underworld.

For Question 8, consider each answer individually and select all choices that apply.

8. Select the quotation(s) from the passage that best explain(s) why researchers believe the statue found in Palenque depicts Hun Hunahpu.

   A. "This deep connection to the cycle of life and death as well as the changing of the seasons meant both Hun Hunahpu and the maize with which the god was associated were central to Mayan concepts of time itself." (lines 12–14)

   B. "The statue's head also appeared to be intentionally separated from the original statue's body. . . ." (lines 19–20)

   C. "Researchers also believe that the statue's placement was important; its gaze would have aligned with rows of maize at dawn. . . ." (lines 21–23)

9. In the context in which it appears, "fashioned" (line 8) most nearly means

   A. illustrated.

   B. created.

   C. imagined.

   D. influenced.

   E. destroyed.

For Questions 10–12, choose the two answers that best fit the meaning of the sentence as a whole and result in two completed sentences that are alike in meaning.

10. The company had to call in a third party to ________ the dispute between the workers and their employers.

   A. accelerate

   B. mediate

   C. facilitate

   D. triumvirate

   E. arbitrate

   F. intercede

11. While many popular songs are actually quite complex, this one is utterly ________.

   A. byzantine
   B. inspired
   C. insipid
   D. convoluted
   E. tortuous
   F. trite

12. She decided to amend her usual ________ habits when she moved in with her first roommate.

   A. meticulous
   B. slovenly
   C. fastidious
   D. disorderly
   E. persnickety
   F. insouciant

STOP!

IF YOU FINISH BEFORE THE TIME IS UP, YOU MAY CHECK YOUR WORK IN THIS SECTION ONLY.

SECTION 3: VERBAL REASONING

23 minutes—15 questions

For each question, follow the specific directions and choose the best answer.

For Questions 1–3, choose one answer for each blank. Select from the appropriate column for each blank. Choose the answer that best completes the sense of the text.

1. Some dedicated vegetarians regard eating meat to be downright ________.

A. acceptable
B. laudable
C. palliative
D. pernicious
E. dauntless

2. This novel may be too (i) ________ for readers who prefer a traditional, (ii) ________ narrative.

Blank (i)	Blank (ii)
A. mellifluous	D. impenetrability
B. enigmatic	E. warranted
C. entrepreneurial	F. straightforward

3. This modern artist is considered to be at the (i) ________ of an exciting new aesthetic movement despite the fact he spent his early career in (ii) ________ facing what, at the time, seemed to be insurmountable (iii) ________.

Blank (i)	Blank (ii)	Blank (iii)
A. forerunner	D. notoriety	G. impetuses
B. paradox	E. obscurity	H. conceits
C. vanguard	F. obliquity	I. encumbrances

For Questions 4–9, choose only one answer choice unless otherwise indicated.

Questions 4–6 are based on the following passage.

Of the thousands of people who consider themselves lovers of music, it is surprising how few have any real appreciation of it. It is safe to say that out of any score of persons gathered to hear music, whether it be hymn, song, oratorio, opera, or symphony, ten are not listening at all, but are looking at the others, or at the performers, or at the scenery or program, or are lost in their own thoughts. Five more are basking in the sound as a dog basks in the sun—enjoying it in a sleepy, languid way, but not actively following it at all. For them music is, as a noted critic has said, "a drowsy reverie, relieved by nervous thrills." Then there are one or two to whom the music is bringing pictures or stories: visions of trees, cascades, mountains, and rivers fill their minds, or they dream of princesses in old castles, set free from magic slumber by brave heroes from afar. Perhaps also there is one who takes a merely scientific interest in the music: he is so busy analyzing themes and labeling motives that he forgets to enjoy. Only two out of the twenty are left, then, who are actively following the melodies, living over again the thoughts of the composer, really appreciating, by vigorous and delightful attention, the beauties of the music itself.

—Excerpt from *The Appreciation of Music* by Thomas Whitney Surette and Daniel Gregory Mason

4. The author most likely includes the final sentence (lines 10–12) to

   A. emphasize that music is not enjoyable to everyone.

   B. question those who cannot actively follow a musical composition.

   C. analyze the factors that contribute to someone developing a true appreciation for a composition.

   D. illustrate that only a fraction of listeners can appreciate the music in the same way a composer might.

   E. ponder how one's degree of attentiveness to a composition affects one's ultimate enjoyment of it.

5. Which of the following sentences would serve as the most logical and relevant addition to the paragraph?

   A. If people behaved less like dogs and more like human beings, they would have a greater appreciation for music.

   B. Music is a great deal like science and should be heard with a scientist's level of attention.

   C. True music appreciation is dependent on knowledge of music's various qualities and keen powers of concentration.

   D. Only by studying music appreciation for a minimum of four years will anyone learn to truly love the music they hear.

   E. Much like music, art is an art form that tends to go unappreciated due to the lack of concentration of museum visitors.

6. The passage suggests that the author would agree with which of the following about the subject of music appreciation?

   A. If you listen to better-quality music, you will appreciate it more.

   B. If you learn to play an instrument, you will naturally appreciate music more.

   C. Surround yourself only with people who truly appreciate music.

   D. One is wisest to give up on trying to truly appreciate music.

   E. One should listen to music in settings without distractions.

Questions 7–9 are based on the following passage.

Sleep seldom, if ever, is a condition of utter unconsciousness. We so frequently have at least a vague recollection, when we wake, of dreaming—whether or not we remember the dream material—that we are inclined to accept sleep as always a state of some kind of mental activity, though waking so often wipes the slate clean . . . we describe sleep as a state of rest of the conscious mind made possible as weariness overpowers the *censor*, and this guard at the gate naps. The censor is merely that mental activity which forces the mind to keen, alert, constructive attention during our waking hours, a guard who *censors* whatever enters the conscious mind and compares it with reality, forcing back all that is not of immediate use, or that is undesirable, or that contradicts established modes of life or thought. In sleep we might say that the censor, wearied by long vigilance, presses all the material—constantly surging from the unconscious into consciousness, there to meet and establish relations with matter—back into the unconscious realms, and locks the door, and lies and slumbers. Then the half-thoughts, the disregarded material, the unfit, the unexpressed longings or fears, the forbidden thoughts; in fact, the whole accumulation of the disregarded or forgotten, good, bad, and indifferent—for the unconscious has no moral sense—seize their opportunity. The guard has refused to let them pass. He is now asleep. And the more insistent of them pick the lock and slip by, masquerading in false characters, and flit about the realms of the sleeping consciousness as ghosts in the shelter of darkness. If the guard half-wakes he sleepily sees only legitimate forms; for the dreams are well disguised. His waking makes them scurry back, sometimes leaving no trace of their lawless wanderings. So the unconscious thoughts of the day have become sleep-consciousness by play acting.

—Excerpt from *Applied Psychology for Nurses* by Mary F. Porter

7. The author's primary intention in this passage is most likely to

   A. explain that the brain functions differently when asleep than it does when awake, but it still functions.

   B. make the process of sleeping and dreaming seem particularly vivid and exciting.

   C. amuse the reader with an absurd scenario in which a guard is failing to prevent certain thoughts from bothering a sleeping person.

   D. argue that we are more thoughtful when we are asleep than we are when we are awake.

   E. describe how our most consequential thoughts occur when we are sleeping.

8. Based on the passage, what is the purpose of the censor?

   A. To stop the mind from worrying about unpleasant circumstances while sleeping and dreaming
   B. To prevent the mind from thinking of unimportant, undesirable, or unrealistic matters during waking hours
   C. To keep a sleeping person from becoming overly anxious at bedtime so that a good night's sleep can be achieved
   D. To help people to focus on matters that allow them to complete work during waking hours
   E. To prevent people from having unrealistic fantasies during their waking hours

9. Which sentence from the passage explains the main reason most people accept the idea that the mind remains at work while sleeping?

   A. Sentence 2 ("We so frequently . . . at the gate naps.")
   B. Sentence 3 ("The censor is . . . life or thought.")
   C. Sentence 4 ("In sleep we might . . . lies and slumbers.")
   D. Sentence 5 ("Then the half-thoughts . . . seize their opportunity.")
   E. Sentence 8 ("And the more insistent . . . shelter of darkness.")

Questions 10 and 11 are based on the following passage.

The great mistake most artists make when they have a large wall-space to decorate with figures, is to proceed in the same way as they would for an easel picture. Elaborate finish, powerful light and shade, expression and individuality in the heads, are all excellent qualities in an easel picture, but they are by no means necessary in decorative work.

On the other hand, a well-balanced and harmonious composition, a pure and grand style of drawing, and great breadth and luminosity of coloring are absolutely essential for good decorative work.

These are all qualities which are never got by dexterity of hand, dodges about color, or chance, to which much of the fascination of oil-painting on canvas must be attributed. They are only attainable by patient and laborious work.

—Excerpt from *Lectures on Painting* by Edward Armitage

10. "Composition" (line 5) most nearly means

   A. demeanor.
   B. harmony.
   C. rhythm.
   D. writing.
   E. arrangement.

For Question 11, consider each answer individually and select all choices that apply.

11. Which of the following might be an artistic strategy that would satisfy the author of the passage?

A. Honestly evaluating one's own skills

B. Considering the specifics of the medium

C. Taking stock of the materials available

Question 12 is based on the following passage.

Goffman's dramaturgical theory, or Goffman's dramaturgical model, is a sociological theory proposed by Erving Goffman in his 1959 book *The Presentation of Self in Everyday Life*. The term *dramaturgy*, which is usually associated with the world of theatre, means "the practice and theory of composing drama." Goffman borrowed from his study of the dramatic arts, saying that theatrical drama is a good metaphor to represent the way people playact to present themselves a certain way to the rest of society.

Social interactions then, in this model, are like scenes of dialogue in which the actors (humans in a society) are constantly acting and reacting to the norms and values communicated to them by others. Whether they follow those rules and norms or not is a matter of character, manner, and temperament, all of which are curated by the individual at both the conscious and subconscious levels to create a particular version of the self to present to society. One of the ways they do so is through what Goffman calls "impression management." For instance, when a person gets dressed up and ensures that they look their best for a first date or job interview, they do so in hopes of assuring themselves a good first impression.

12. Which of the following can be inferred from the passage?

A. Goffman's theories are applicable to the field of neuroscience as well.

B. Human beings are generally skeptical of first impressions and tend to reserve judgment.

C. Human beings can only control first impressions on a conscious level.

D. Human beings are never consciously aware of the kind of first impression they are making.

E. A person who is meeting a significant other's parents for the first time will likely try to control the first impression they make.

For Questions 13–15, choose the two answers that best fit the meaning of the sentence as a whole and result in two completed sentences that are alike in meaning.

13. Even though he had recently suffered a tragedy, he was so ________ that it was impossible to tell how the hardships affected him.

A. impassive

B. emotive

C. dynamic

D. deadpan

E. didactic

F. insolvent

14. Her extreme ________ makes her an ideal presidential candidate.

 A. inscrutability
 B. integrity
 C. rectitude
 D. abstruseness
 E. conviviality
 F. deplorability

15. Before enacting these strict new requirements, we must first consider their ________ thoroughly.

 A. obstructions
 B. tipulations
 C. adversaries
 D. monograms
 E. ramifications
 F. consequences

STOP!

IF YOU FINISH BEFORE THE TIME IS UP, YOU MAY CHECK YOUR WORK IN THIS SECTION ONLY.

SECTION 4: QUANTITATIVE REASONING

21 minutes—12 questions

For each question, follow the specific directions and choose the best answer.

The test maker provides the following information that applies to all questions in the Quantitative Reasoning section of the GRE General Test:

- All numbers used are real numbers.
- All figures are assumed to lie in a plane unless otherwise indicated.
- Geometric figures, such as lines, circles, triangles, and quadrilaterals, *are not necessarily* drawn to scale. That is, you should *not* assume that quantities such as lengths and angle measures are as they appear in a figure. You should assume, however, that lines shown as straight are actually straight, points on a line are in the order shown, and more generally, all geometric objects are in the relative positions shown. For questions with geometric figures, you should base your answers on geometric reasoning, not on estimating or comparing quantities by sight or by measurement.
- Coordinate systems, such as *xy*-planes and number lines, *are* drawn to scale. Therefore, you can read, estimate, or compare quantities in such figures by sight or by measurement.
- Graphical data presentations, such as bar graphs, circle graphs, and line graphs, *are* drawn to scale. Therefore, you can read, estimate, or compare data values by sight or by measurement.

For Questions 1–5, compare Quantity A and Quantity B. Some questions will have additional information above the two quantities to use in determining your answer.

1. $x^{2/3} = (y - 1)^{1/3}$

Quantity A	Quantity B
y	0

A. Quantity A is greater.

B. Quantity B is greater.

C. The two quantities are equal.

D. The relationship cannot be determined from the information given.

2. A fair six-sided die is rolled twice.

Quantity A	Quantity B
The probability that the sum of both rolls is 5	The probability that each roll is at least 5

A. Quantity A is greater.

B. Quantity B is greater.

C. The two quantities are equal.

D. The relationship cannot be determined from the information given.

3. Polygon *ABCD* is a parallelogram.

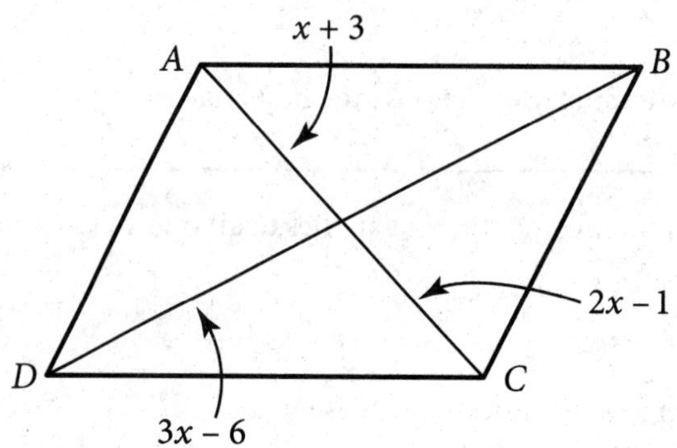

Quantity A	Quantity B
The length *AC*	The length *BD*

A. Quantity A is greater.
B. Quantity B is greater.
C. The two quantities are equal.
D. The relationship cannot be determined from the information given.

4. Six men have a mean height of 70". Seven women have a mean height of 65".

Quantity A	Quantity B
The height of the tallest man	The height of the tallest woman

A. Quantity A is greater.
B. Quantity B is greater.
C. The two quantities are equal.
D. The relationship cannot be determined from the information given.

5. A car rental company charges $25 per day, plus 9 cents for every mile driven.

Quantity A	Quantity B
The total cost of renting a car for 4 days and driving 978 miles	$200

A. Quantity A is greater.
B. Quantity B is greater.
C. The two quantities are equal.
D. The relationship cannot be determined from the information given.

Questions 6–12 have several formats. Unless the directions state otherwise, choose one answer choice. For the Numeric Entry questions, follow the instructions below.

Numeric Entry Questions

The following items are the same for both the actual GRE General Test and the test presented in this book. However, the actual GRE General Test will have additional information about entering answers in decimal and fraction boxes on the computer screen. To take the test in this book, enter your answers in boxes or answer grids.

- Your answer may be an integer, a decimal, or a fraction, and it may be negative.
- If a question asks for a fraction, there will be two boxes. One box will be for the numerator, and one will be for the denominator.
- Equivalent forms of the correct answer, such as 2.5 and 2.50, are all correct.
- Enter the exact answer unless the question asks you to round your answers.

Questions 6 and 7 refer to the chart below.

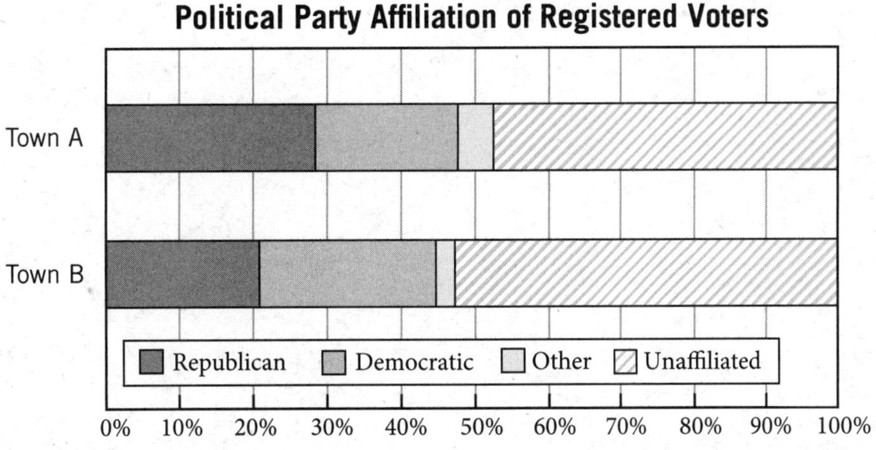

6. What is the most common party affiliation status in both towns?

A. Republican

B. Democratic

C. Other

D. Unaffiliated

E. The most common party affiliation is different for the two towns.

7. If Town A has 2,100 registered voters, which of the following is the best approximation for the number of voters in Town A who are unaffiliated?

   A. 700

   B. 800

   C. 900

   D. 1,000

   E. 1,100

8. The length of a rectangle is twice its width. If the perimeter of the rectangle is 72 feet, what is its area in square feet?

   A. 72

   B. 144

   C. 288

   D. 576

   E. 1,152

9. A bicycle is on sale for 20% off. A 6.5% sales tax is added to the sale price. If the total amount paid for the bicycle is $371.05, what was the original price?

   A. $281.10

   B. $278.72

   C. $316.13

   D. $435.50

   E. $627.12

For question 10, indicate all answers that apply.

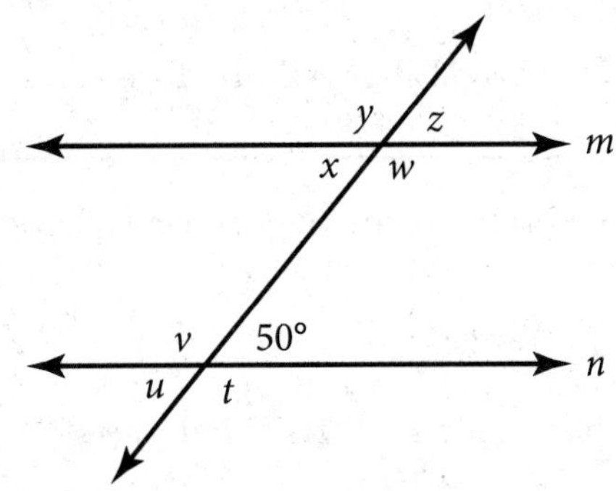

10. If lines m and n are parallel, which angles measure 50 degrees?

A. t

B. u

C. v

D. w

E. x

F. y

G. z

For questions 11 and 12, enter your answers in the boxes.

11. If the solutions to the equation $ax^2 + x - c = 0$ are $x = \frac{2}{3}$ and $x = -\frac{3}{4}$, what is the value of $\frac{c}{a}$? Give your answer as a fraction in lowest terms.

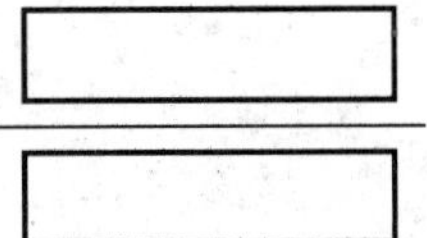

12. A cake batter recipe has flour, sugar, and butter in the ratio $\frac{5}{2}:\frac{3}{2}:1$. In a certain large batch of this recipe, there are a combined total of 12 cups of flour and sugar. How many cups of flour are there? Give your answer as a fraction in lowest terms.

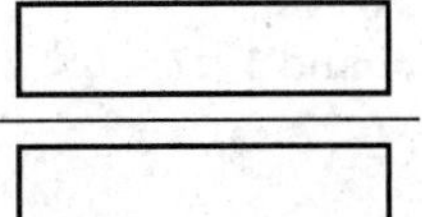

STOP!

IF YOU FINISH BEFORE THE TIME IS UP, YOU MAY CHECK YOUR WORK IN THIS SECTION ONLY.

SECTION 5: QUANTITATIVE REASONING

26 minutes—15 questions

For each question, follow the specific directions and choose the best answer.

The test maker provides the following information that applies to all questions in the Quantitative Reasoning section of the GRE General Test:

- All numbers used are real numbers.
- All figures are assumed to lie in a plane unless otherwise indicated.
- Geometric figures, such as lines, circles, triangles, and quadrilaterals, *are not necessarily* drawn to scale. That is, you should *not* assume that quantities such as lengths and angle measures are as they appear in a figure. You should assume, however, that lines shown as straight are actually straight, points on a line are in the order shown, and more generally, all geometric objects are in the relative positions shown. For questions with geometric figures, you should base your answers on geometric reasoning, not on estimating or comparing quantities by sight or by measurement.
- Coordinate systems, such as *xy*-planes and number lines, *are* drawn to scale. Therefore, you can read, estimate, or compare quantities in such figures by sight or by measurement.
- Graphical data presentations, such as bar graphs, circle graphs, and line graphs, *are* drawn to scale. Therefore, you can read, estimate, or compare data values by sight or by measurement.

For Questions 1–6, compare Quantity A and Quantity B. Some questions will have additional information above the two quantities to use in determining your answer.

1. $-4F + 8 > -12$

Quantity A	Quantity B
$F - 2$	3

A. Quantity A is greater.
B. Quantity B is greater.
C. The two quantities are equal.
D. The relationship cannot be determined from the information given.

2. $0 < b - a < 1$ and $1 < c - b < 2$

Quantity A	Quantity B
The mean of a, b, and c	The median of a, b, and c

A. Quantity A is greater.
B. Quantity B is greater.
C. The two quantities are equal.
D. The relationship cannot be determined from the information given.

3. $p \geq 2$

Quantity A	Quantity B
p^3	3^p

A. Quantity A is greater.

B. Quantity B is greater.

C. The two quantities are equal.

D. The relationship cannot be determined from the information given.

4. On a certain week, the average high temperature for the first five days was 52°F. The average high temperature over all seven days was 50°F.

Quantity A	Quantity B
The average high temperature for the last two days of the week	42°F

A. Quantity A is greater.

B. Quantity B is greater.

C. The two quantities are equal.

D. The relationship cannot be determined from the information given.

5. $$5+\frac{20V}{3V+2W}=9$$

Quantity A	Quantity B
V	W

A. Quantity A is greater.

B. Quantity B is greater.

C. The two quantities are equal.

D. The relationship cannot be determined from the information given.

6. A shop sells cylindrical candles in three sizes: small candles are 4.4 centimeters (cm) in diameter, medium candles are 6.2 cm in diameter, and large candles are 8.8 cm in diameter. All candles in the shop have the same height.

Quantity A	Quantity B
The volume of two small candles	The volume of one large candle

A. Quantity A is greater.

B. Quantity B is greater.

C. The two quantities are equal.

D. The relationship cannot be determined from the information given.

Questions 7–15 have several formats. Unless the directions state otherwise, choose one answer choice. For the Numeric Entry questions, follow the instructions below.

Numeric Entry Questions

The following items are the same for both the actual GRE General Test and the test presented in this book. However, the actual GRE General Test will have additional information about entering answers in decimal and fraction boxes on the computer screen. To take the test in this book, enter your answers in boxes or answer grids.

- Your answer may be an integer, a decimal, or a fraction, and it may be negative.
- If a question asks for a fraction, there will be two boxes. One box will be for the numerator, and one will be for the denominator.
- Equivalent forms of the correct answer, such as 2.5 and 2.50, are all correct.
- Enter the exact answer unless the question asks you to round your answers.

7. The mean of a, b, c, and d is x, and the mean of a and b is y. Which of the following is the mean of c and d?

   A. $\frac{2x-y}{2}$

   B. $x-y$

   C. $4x-2y$

   D. $2x-y$

   E. y

Questions 8 and 9 refer to the graph below.

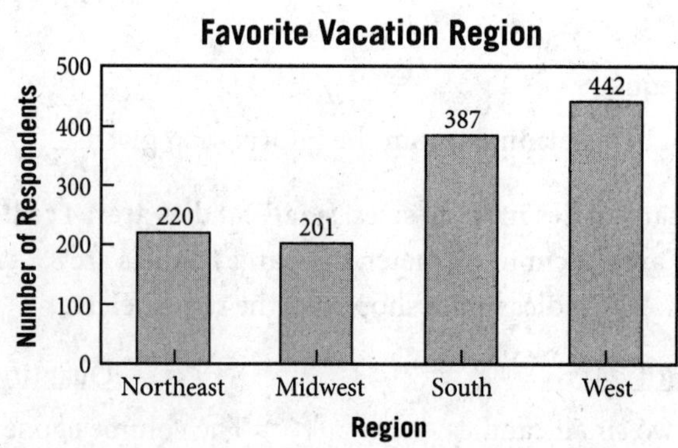

8. A pie chart is to be made to display these data, with four sections corresponding to the four regions specified. What should be the size of the central angle of the section corresponding to the South?

   A. 31°

   B. 58°

   C. 63°

   D. 111°

   E. 249°

9. Suppose 1,000 additional people are surveyed, and 292 of these additional respondents prefer the Northeast region. Would the percentage of total respondents who prefer the Northeast increase or decrease, and by how much?

A. Increase by 5%

B. Decrease by 5%

C. Increase by 18%

D. Increase by 29%

E. Decrease by 29%

10. How many positive integers less than 100 are divisible by 2, 3, and 5?

A. 1

B. 3

C. 19

D. 33

E. 49

11. What is the size of the largest angle in this triangle?

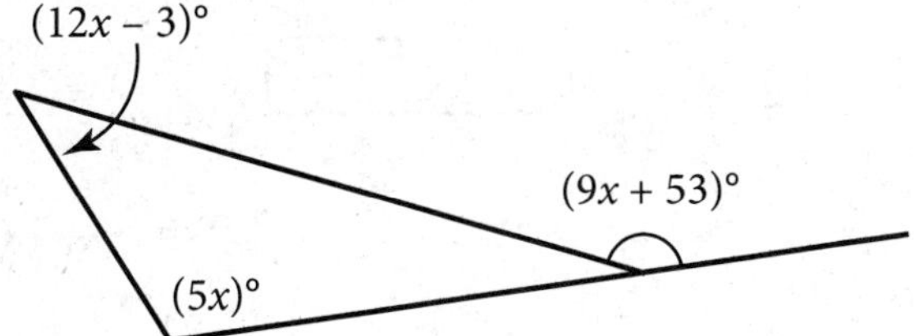

A. 7°

B. 35°

C. 64°

D. 81°

E. 116°

For questions 12 and 13, indicate <u>all</u> answers that apply.

12. Which of the following values are solutions of the equation $|3 + |x + 1|| = 4$?

A. –2

B. –1

C. 0

D. 1

E. 2

13. Line L passes through the point (3, 4) and has slope $-\frac{2}{3}$. Line L also passes through which of the following points?

A. (6, 6)

B. (0, 2)

C. (6, 2)

D. (0, 6)

E. (9, 0)

For questions 14 and 15, enter your answer in the box.

14. If $\left(\frac{(p^3)^4}{p^{-2}p^5}\right)^{-2} = p^{3t}$, then $t=$

15. Six different cards are dealt evenly to three players so that each receives two cards. If the order in which a player receives their cards doesn't matter, in how many distinct ways could the cards be dealt?

STOP!

IF YOU FINISH BEFORE THE TIME IS UP, YOU MAY CHECK YOUR WORK IN THIS SECTION ONLY.

ANSWER KEYS AND EXPLANATIONS

Section 1: Analytical Writing

To assist you with evaluating your writing, we have provided the following rubric, which is adapted from the official rubric used by ETS.* If you need more assistance evaluating your writing, consider the writing samples for essays at score levels 2, 4, and 6 as provided in Chapter 3.

ANALYTICAL WRITING SCORING RUBRIC SUMMARY		
Score Level	**Description**	**Characteristics of a Typical Response**
6 Outstanding	A sustained, insightful, organized, detailed analysis of well-developed, complex ideas supported by meaningful evidence and highly persuasive support. Utilizes a wide range of vocabulary and rhetorical methods while demonstrating a superior understanding of the conventions of Standard Written English. Very minor errors may be present but do not impact meaning.	• Presents a distinct and perceptive viewpoint regarding the issue as outlined in the given instructions • Expands meaningfully on the viewpoint with convincing rationales and/or compelling examples • Maintains focus, organization, and clarity while establishing meaningful connections between concepts • Seamlessly and accurately moves between concepts using a range of transitions, word choices, and sentence structures • Exhibits exceptional proficiency with the norms of Standard Written English, even if very minor errors are present
5 Strong	A thoughtful, generally organized, and focused analysis of nuanced ideas supported by sound reasoning and meaningful examples. Uses a range of rhetorical skills and conventions to demonstrate meaningful control of the conventions of Standard Written English. Minor errors may be present but do not impact meaning.	• Presents a lucid and carefully considered viewpoint regarding the issue as outlined in the given instructions • Elaborates on the viewpoint with logically coherent rationales and/or well-chosen examples • Maintains focus and exhibits general organization, establishing suitable connections between ideas • Communicates ideas clearly and effectively, employing fitting vocabulary and varying sentence structures • Exhibits proficiency with the norms of Standard Written English, though occasional minor errors may be present

(continues)

* The GRE General Test: Analytical Writing Measure Scoring," ETS, 2024, https://www.ets.org/gre/test-takers/general-test/prepare/content/analytical-writing/scoring.html.

ANALYTICAL WRITING SCORING RUBRIC SUMMARY (*CONTINUED*)		
Score Level	**Description**	**Characteristics of a Typical Response**
4 Adequate	A competent, considered analysis of meaningful ideas that ventures a main point and supports it with relevant evidence or reasoning. Ideas are organized in a satisfactory manner, clearly conveyed, and supported by adequate control of rhetorical skills and the conventions of Standard Written English. May have some minor errors that impact clarity of meaning.	• Presents a clear viewpoint regarding the issue as outlined in the given instructions • Develops the viewpoint with relevant reasoning and/or examples • Maintains adequate focus and organization • Demonstrates satisfactory command of language to articulate ideas with acceptable clarity • Exhibits general understanding of the norms of Standard Written English, albeit with occasional errors
3 Limited	A somewhat competent analysis that addresses specific required tasks and makes some effort to address main points. Rhetorical skills may be lacking or underdeveloped, and writing may be limited by weak structure, poor organization, or underdevelopment of ideas. Contains some errors that limit clarity of meaning and/or contribute to vagueness.	Exhibits **one or more** of the following concerns: • Shows vagueness or inadequacy in addressing the given instructions, presenting or developing a viewpoint, or both • Demonstrates weakness in employing relevant examples or rationales, or leans heavily on unsupported assertions • Exhibits limited focus and/or organization • Includes issues in language or sentence structure, contributing to lack of clarity • Contains either occasional major errors or frequent minor errors in grammar, usage, and/or mechanics of Standard Written English, impeding comprehension
2 Seriously Flawed	A weak analysis that does not adequately address specific required tasks and/or that is underdeveloped, disorganized, or unclear. Frequent issues with rhetorical skills and/or the conventions of Standard Written English obfuscate meaning and limit clarity. Frequent errors make it difficult to parse.	Exhibits **one or more** of the following concerns: • Exhibits a lack of clarity or serious limitation in addressing the given instructions, developing a viewpoint on the issue, or both • Offers few, if any, relevant rationales or examples to support assertions • Lacks focus and/or organization • Includes serious issues in language or sentence structure, frequently obstructing clarity or contributing to outright confusion • Contains serious errors in grammar, usage, or mechanics that frequently obscure meaning

ANALYTICAL WRITING SCORING RUBRIC SUMMARY (*CONTINUED*)		
Score Level	**Description**	**Characteristics of a Typical Response**
1 Fundamentally Deficient	A deficient analysis that contains fundamental errors and fails to communicate a meaningful main point. Content may be incomprehensible or extremely difficult to parse and/or may be irrelevant to the task at hand. Frequent and pervasive errors render the analysis incomprehensible or incoherent.	Exhibits **one or more** of the following concerns: • Demonstrates little or no evidence of grasping the given instructions or the issue at hand • Shows minimal or no evidence of the ability to craft an organized response, often appearing disorganized and/or excessively concise • Suffers from severe issues in language and sentence structure, consistently hindering comprehension • Contains widespread errors in grammar, usage, and mechanics, leading to incoherence
0	An analysis that cannot be evaluated because it does not address any aspect of the specified task. It may copy parts of the prompt in lieu of developing concepts or may be written in a foreign language or otherwise incomprehensible.	Exhibits **one or more** of the following concerns: • Demonstrates zero awareness of the given instructions or the issue at hand • Fully off topic • Merely copies the topic • Incomprehensible • Written in a foreign language • Consists only of random keystrokes or nonsensical inputs
NS	Blank essays will receive a score of NS, meaning no score.	

Section 2: Verbal Reasoning

1. C, E	4. A	7. A	9. B	11. C, F
2. B, F, I	5. A, B, C	8. B, C	10. B, E	12. B, D
3. C	6. A			

1. **The correct answers are C and E.** Answer Blank (i): The second half of the sentence suggests a contradiction to the first half, so the word in the blank should suggest the opposite of taking action—*complacency* means "the state of inaction."

   Answer Blank (ii): The word in the blank should suggest a mood bordering on violence, and *vociferous* means "raucous."

2. **The correct answers are B, F, and I.** Answer Blank (i): When something suffers, it is usually from major problems. *Crucial* means "major," so it is the best word for the first blank. Choices A and C both mean "minor," which is the opposite of the correct answer, and the fact that *trivial* (choice A) and *inconsequential* (choice C) share the same exact meaning means they should be eliminated simply because they cancel each other out.

   Answer Blank (ii): The problem described in the second sentence is one of historical mistakes, so the word in the second blank should be the name of such mistakes. *Anachronisms* are historical mistakes. *Anomalies* (choice D) means "irregularities," and its lack of specificity makes choice D a weaker answer than choice F. *Allusions* (choice E) means "references," which are not necessarily flaws.

   Answer Blank (iii): The final sentence also refers to a flaw, and a potential major flaw of a film would be poor acting that is hard to believe. *Authenticity* means "believability," so it is the closest choice.

3. **The correct answer is C.** The author spends the first paragraph enumerating the different parts of the face involved in smiling, so it's reasonable to infer that they did so in order to emphasize that much more than just the mouth is involved in the process. The complexity of movement described contradicts the idea that smiling is a simple process (choice B), but there is no indication that this complex process strains the face (choice A). Nothing in the first paragraph relates to the statements made in choices D and E.

4. **The correct answer is A.** While each answer choice can be used as a synonym for "drawing," only choice A makes sense in this context since the author uses the word to describe how the corners of the mouth pull back when smiling. The word is not used to refer to the act of drawing a picture, so choices B and E can be eliminated. It does not make sense to say that the corners of the mouth "selected" back, so choice C is incorrect. The author uses the word *drawing* as a verb, yet the word *illustration* is a noun, so choice D can be eliminated too.

5. **The correct answers are choices A, B, and C.** The passage provides support for each answer choice. Lines 14–16 support choice A. Information throughout the second paragraph supports choice B. Information throughout the first paragraph supports choice C.

6. **The correct answer is A.** This sentence distills the limitations of *a priori* knowledge, which does not require direct knowledge to gain experience, by indicating that direct experience is the only way to acquire knowledge. Choice B is a general statement about Rationalists, not support for the author's opinion about the limitations of *a priori* principles. Choice C is an opinion about Rationalists, not support for the author's opinion about the limitations of *a priori* principles. Choice D is the opinion itself, not support for that opinion. Choice E is an example of Rationalist thought.

7. **The correct answer is A.** Based on evidence in the passage, Rationalists believe knowledge can be gained outside of empirical evidence, which supports choice A and eliminates choice C. Choice B suggests something the passage never implies.

Choices D and E are extreme and unrealistic interpretations of Rationalism.

8. **The correct answers are B and C.** While the quotation in choice A does provide context on who Hun Hunahpu is and how they related to Mayan culture, it does not provide any information about how researchers were able to match the statue to descriptions of Hun Hunahpu. Choices B and C, by contrast, describe specific details from the statue which, given the context of the rest of the passage, can be linked to Hun Hunahpu.

9. **The correct answer is B.** The word *fashioned* means created, formed, or constructed. If the Mayans believed that humans had been fashioned out of white and yellow corn by the gods, as the passage states, then that means the Mayans believed that the gods had created humans from maize.

10. **The correct answers are B and E.** A third party is one not directly involved in a dispute. To work between opposing sides of a dispute is to *mediate* or *arbitrate* that dispute. *Intercede* (choice F) also means "mediate," but it is a word that requires a preposition (e.g., "intercede in"), and the lack of such a preposition in this sentence means that choice F is not the best answer. The other answer choices simply do not make sense in this context.

11. **The correct answers are C and F.** The introductory word *while* suggests that the second half of this sentence will contradict the first half, and it is the word *complex* that requires an antonym. Both *insipid* and *trite* mean the opposite of *complex.* Choices A, D, and E all share the same meaning as *complex. Inspired* (choice B) means "stimulated," and it does not work in this context as well as choices C and F do.

12. **The correct answers are B and D.** It is commonly believed that neatness is an important quality to possess when living with someone, so one would "amend" ways that are the opposite of neat before moving in with a first roommate. Both *slovenly* and *disorderly* are antonyms for *neat.* Choices A, C, and E can all be eliminated because they are synonyms of *neat.* Choice F is not a strong answer since *insouciant* merely means "carefree" and does not have the negative connotations that *slovenly* and *disorderly* do.

NOTES

Section 3: Verbal Reasoning

1. D	4. D	7. A	10. E	13. A, D
2. B, F	5. C	8. B	11. B	14. B, C
3. C, E, I	6. E	9. A	12. E	15. E, F

1. **The correct answer is D.** Someone extremely dedicated to never eating animals might have very strong and negative opinions regarding the eating of meat, so the most logical answer is *pernicious* since it means injurious, destructive, or immoral. Choices A and B are essentially the opposite since *acceptable* means "worthy of being accepted" and *laudable* means "worthy of being celebrated." The other responses do not fit the context.

2. **The correct answers are B and F.** Answer Blank (i): A traditional narrative tends to follow a logical pattern, so you are looking for a term that means something like "not logical"—*enigmatic* is a synonym for *puzzling*. The other answer choices simply would not be used to describe any kind of narrative since *mellifluous* (choice A) means "smooth" and *entrepreneurial* (choice C) means "industrious."

   Answer Blank (ii): You need a word that works in concert with "traditional," and *straightforward* is such a word since its synonyms include *plain* and *direct*. *Impenetrability* (choice D), meaning "the quality of being confusing," is almost the opposite of the correct answer. *Warranted* (choice E) means "necessary," and it does not suit this context as well as choice F does.

3. **The correct answers are C, E, and I.** Answer Blank (i): In the world of art, it is noteworthy to be at the front of a new artistic movement, and *vanguard* means "at the front." While *forerunner* (choice A) describes someone who is at the front, it does not describe the position of being at the front, which is what the sentence requires. *Paradox* (choice B) means "something that seems to contradict itself" and simply does not make sense in this context.

   Answer Blank (ii): A word meaning "the state of being unknown" is required, and *obscurity* fits. *Notoriety* (choice D) is the opposite of that since it means "fame." *Obliquity* (choice F) means "ambiguity," which is a synonym for another meaning of *obscurity*, but it does not fit in this context.

   Answer Blank (iii): Something described as "insurmountable" is most often a challenge of some sort, so *encumbrances* fits best here. *Impetuses* (choice G) describes the opposite since its synonyms include *incentives* and *stimuli*. *Conceits* (choice H) means "delusions," so it does not fit the context.

4. **The correct answer is D.** The author's main thrust throughout the passage is that the only way to truly appreciate music is to specifically focus on its intrinsic qualities. To make this point, the author mentions all the different types of listeners who might enjoy a piece before coming to the final sentence, wherein the author implies that only "two out of twenty" people are capable of "actively following the melodies" and "really appreciating, by vigorous and delightful attention" the choices a composer has made. This is most consistent with the statement in choice D, which suggests that only a fraction of listeners are capable of deeply appreciating the music in the way a composer might.

5. **The correct answer is C.** The sentence "True music appreciation is dependent on knowledge of music's various qualities and keen powers of concentration" distills the author's main idea in a way that helps the reader focus on the skills they would need to sharpen to appreciate music better. Therefore, it would be a fine addition to the passage. Choice A focuses too much on a passing example in the passage and would not add anything of value to the discussion. The example in lines 9–10

contradicts the likelihood that the author shares the belief in choice B. Choice D is unnecessarily specific. Choice E shifts the topic in a way that renders it irrelevant to this particular discussion of music appreciation.

6. **The correct answer is E.** The author seems to believe that distractions are a key barrier to fully appreciating music. The author draws no correlations between listening to certain kinds of music and the ability to truly appreciate music, so choice A is a weak answer. There is no evidence to support choice B since the author never discusses learning to play an instrument. Choice C lacks evidence as well. While the author does present the goal of truly appreciating music as something of a challenge, choice D expresses a very extreme reaction to that challenge.

7. **The correct answer is A.** Throughout the passage, the author is primarily concerned with explaining that the brain functions differently when asleep than it does when awake, but it still functions. While the scenario involving a guard may be vivid or even amusing, choices B and C misunderstand the main point behind that scenario. Choices D and E both reach extreme conclusions that the passage does not really support.

8. **The correct answer is B.** The author defines the censor in lines 5–8. According to the author, the censor is at work during waking hours, not sleeping hours, so choices A and C are incorrect. Choices D and E are too specific to interpret lines 5–8 accurately.

9. **The correct answer is A.** Sentence 2 explains that the fact that people remember at least a little of their dreams after waking is the reason most people accept the idea that the mind remains at work while sleeping. Choices B and C merely explain what the censor does. Choices D and E explain how thoughts occur during sleep, but they do not explain anything about why people accept the idea that the mind remains active during sleeping hours.

10. **The correct answer is E.** While each answer choice can be used as a synonym for *composition*, *arrangement* makes the most sense in this context since the author is discussing how shapes, colors, and patterns are arranged in a piece of art. *Demeanor* (choice A) is a word better used to describe a person than a piece of art. Choices B and C are better used to describe music than art. A painting is not a piece of writing, so choice D makes little sense.

11. **The correct answer is B.** The passage is mainly about how different mediums—canvases versus walls, for example—require different artistic choices. This passage never discusses matters of the artist's skills (choice A) or the materials they have in stock (choice C).

12. **The correct answer is E.** Goffman's discussion of impression management toward the end of the second paragraph makes it clear that a person who is going to meet a significant other's parents for the first time is likely to present the best version of themselves. All the other statements can be contradicted or clarified by context from the passage.

13. **The correct answers are A and D.** One tends to become clearly sad after suffering a tragedy, but this sentence seems to draw a contrast with that usual behavior. So someone who does not show emotion so easily would be *impassive* or *deadpan*. Choice B suggests the opposite of the correct answers since *emotive* means "emotional." *Dynamic* (choice C) means "energetic," which implies something quite different from the state of being unemotional. The other answer choices have nothing to do with showing emotions at all. *Didactic* (choice E) means "educational," and *insolvent* (choice F) means "bankrupt."

14. **The correct answers are B and C.** The word in the blank should describe a quality of an ideal leader. Most people would agree that such a quality is extreme goodness, and that is what *integrity* and *rectitude* mean. Choices A and D both describe the quality of being difficult to understand, which is not usually considered to be a very positive quality. While *conviviality*, or "friendliness," is a good

quality, the lack of another answer choice with the same meaning eliminates choice E. *Deplorability* (choice F) is the quality of being disgraceful, and no sensible person would want a president with such a quality, so choice F is incorrect.

15. **The correct answers are E and F.** This sentence suggests the considerations taken before instating new rules, and the most obvious such considerations are thinking about everything that may result from those rules. *Ramifications* and *consequences* both mean "results." *Obstructions* (choice A) means "blockades," so choice A makes little sense in this context. *Stipulations* (choice B), meaning "conditions," makes more sense, but the lack of another answer choice with that meaning renders choice B an answer that should be eliminated. *Adversaries* (choice C) might also make sense if not for the fact that no other answer choice means "rivals." *Monograms* (choice D) means "initials," which simply does not make sense in this context.

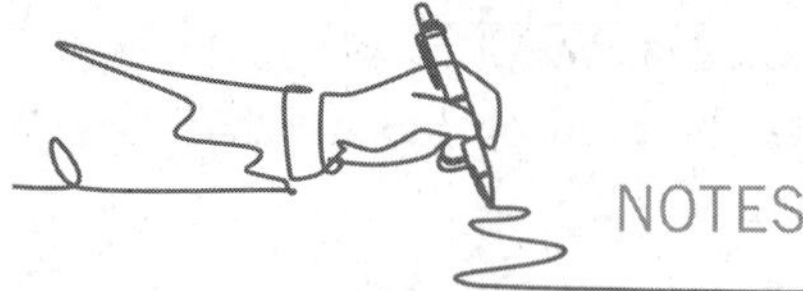

NOTES

Section 4: Quantitative Reasoning

1. A	4. D	7. D	9. D	11. $\frac{1}{2}$
2. C	5. B	8. C	10. B, E, G	12. $\frac{15}{2}$
3. A	6. D			

1. **The correct answer is A.** Raise each side of the equation to the power of 3:

$$(x^{2/3})^3 = ((y-1)^{1/3})^3$$
$$x^{6/3} = (y-1)^{3/3}$$
$$x^2 = y-1$$

Solving for y yields $y = x^2 + 1$. Since x^2 cannot be negative, $y = x^2 + 1$ must be positive.

2. **The correct answer is C.** The sum of both rolls is 5 if the results of each roll were 1 and 4 in some order or 2 and 3 in some order. If both rolls are at least 5, then the results of each roll were 5 and 5, 6 and 6, or 5 and 6 in some order. There are four distinct possibilities corresponding to each outcome, so their probabilities are equal.

3. **The correct answer is A.** The quantities $x + 3$ and $2x - 1$ are equal, as the diagonals of a parallelogram always bisect each other. Set $x + 3 = 2x - 1$ and solve to see that $x = 4$. Therefore, $x + 3$ and $2x - 1$ are both equal to 7, and the diagonal AC has length 14. Diagonal BD, on the other hand, has a length that is twice the value of $3x - 6$. But this is $3(4) - 6 = 6$, so BD has length 12. Therefore, Quantity A is greater.

4. **The correct answer is D.** The mean height, and therefore total height, of the men is greater. However, this tells us nothing at all about the height of any particular man or woman. So the relationship cannot be determined from the information given.

5. **The correct answer is B.** The 4-day rental costs $4 \times \$25 = \$100$ plus the cost of 978 miles. Rounding both the miles driven and cost per mile up, 1,000 miles at 10 cents per mile would be an additional \$100. Since 978 is less than 1,000, and 9 cents is less than 10 cents, the total cost is certainly less than \$200, so Quantity B is greater.

6. **The correct answer is D.** For both towns, the last portion of the bar, representing Unaffiliated, is the largest section.

7. **The correct answer is D.** The percentage of registered voters in Town A who are unaffiliated is shown in the chart to be between 40% and 50% but closer to 50%. 40% of 2,100 is 840, while 50% of 2,100 is 1,050. Therefore, the answer should be between 840 and 1,050 but closer to 1,050. 1,000 is the best approximation among the given choices.

8. **The correct answer is C.** If W is the width of the rectangle, then its length is $2W$. An equation involving the perimeter can then be written and solved:

$$2L + 2W = 72$$
$$2(2W) + 2W = 72$$
$$6W = 72$$
$$W = 12$$

The width is 12, so the length is 24. The area is then $12 \times 24 = 288$ ft.^{2}.

9. **The correct answer is D.** \$371.05 is 106.5% of the discounted price, so the discounted price is $\frac{\$371.05}{1.065} = \$348.40$. But this reflects a 20% discount, so it is 80% of the original price. The original price was therefore $\frac{\$348.40}{0.8} = \$435.50$.

10. **The correct answers are B, E, and G.** When parallel lines are crossed by a transversal, all of the acute angles are congruent, all of the obtuse angles are congruent, and the measurements of these sum to 180°. In this case, the acute angles all measure 50°, and the obtuse angles all measure $180° - 50° = 130°$. Angles u, x, and z are the acute angles. Choices A, C, D, and F are all incorrect because they are 130°.

11. **The correct answer is $\frac{1}{2}$.** Since $x = \frac{2}{3}$, $3x - 2 = 0$. Therefore, $3x - 2$ is a factor of the quadratic. Similarly, we can find that $4x + 3$ is a factor. The quadratic equation is therefore $(3x - 2)(4x + 3) = 0$. Expanding, $12x^2 + x - 6 = 0$. Matching up with the form $ax^2 + x - c = 0$, we see that $a = 12$ and $c = 6$. Therefore, $\frac{c}{a} = \frac{6}{12} = \frac{1}{2}$.

12. **The correct answer is $\frac{15}{2}$.** Since the flour, sugar, and butter have a ratio of $\frac{5}{2} : \frac{3}{2} : 1$, the actual quantities in any given batch of this recipe can be represented by $\frac{5}{2}x$, $\frac{3}{2}x$, and 1x, respectively. Therefore, for the scenario given, we have $\frac{5}{2}x + \frac{3}{2}x = 12$. This simplifies to $4x = 12$, so $x = 3$. The number of cups of flour is then given by $\frac{5}{2}x = \frac{5}{2}(3) = \frac{15}{2}$.

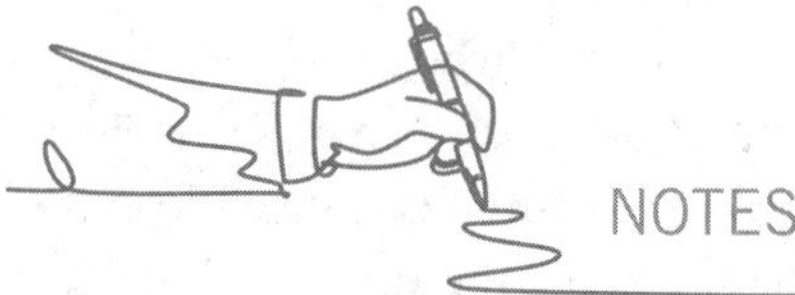

NOTES

Section 5: Quantitative Reasoning

1. B	4. A	7. D	10. B	13. C, D, E
2. A	5. C	8. D	11. D	14. -6
3. D	6. B	9. A	12. A, C	15. 90

1. **The correct answer is B.** Dividing both sides of the inequality by –4, and remembering to reverse the direction of the inequality, yields the following:

$$-4F+8>-12$$
$$F-2<3$$

So Quantity B is greater.

2. **The correct answer is A.** First, note that from the inequalities given, b is greater than a and less than c, so $a < b < c$. Therefore, the median of a, b, and c is b.

Next, consider the mean of the three numbers. The inequalities given are equivalent to $a < b < a + 1$ and $b + 1 < c < b + 2$. This shows that the distance of a from b is less than 1, whereas the distance of c from b is greater than 1. When calculating the mean, the value of c will have a larger effect than the value of a. Therefore, the mean of the numbers is closer to c than to a. In other words, the mean will be larger than b, so the mean of the numbers is greater than the median of the numbers.

3. **The correct answer is D.** We are given that $p \geq 2$, so let's try plugging in some numbers to the quantities.

With $p = 2$, Quantity A is $p^3 = 2^3 = 8$, and Quantity B is $3^p = 3^2 = 9$, so Quantity B is greater.

With $p = 3$, Quantity A is $p^3 = 3^3 = 27$, and Quantity B is $3^P = 3^3 = 27$, so the two quantities are equal.

The relationship cannot be determined from the information given, since the relationship changes depending on the value of p.

4. **The correct answer is A.** The average high temperature for the week is 50°F, so the sum of the high temperatures from all seven days is 7(50) = 350. The average high temperature for the first five days was 52°F, so the sum of the high temperatures from the first five days is 5(52) = 260. Therefore, the average high temperature for the last two days is $\frac{350-260}{2}=\frac{90}{2}=45°\text{F}$.

5. **The correct answer is C.** Solve the given equation for one of the variables:

$$5+\frac{20V}{3V+2W}=9$$
$$\frac{20V}{3V+2W}=4$$
$$20V=4(3V+2W)$$
$$20V=12V+8W$$
$$8V=8W$$
$$V=W$$

This shows that V and W are the same even though we do not know what their common value is.

6. **The correct answer is B.** The formula for the volume of a cylinder is $V=\pi r^2h$. The volume of two small candles is $2\pi r_s^2h$ cm^3, where $r_s=\frac{4.4}{2}=2.2$ cm. Since large candles have the same height and twice the radius of small candles, the volume of one large candle is $\pi(2r_s)^2h=4\pi r_s^2h$ cm^3, which is greater than the volume of two small candles.

7. **The correct answer is D.** The mean of a, b, c, and d is x, so $\frac{a+b+c+d}{4}=x$. Similarly, the mean of a and b is y, so $\frac{a+b}{2}=y$. Multiplying the latter equation by 2, we get $a + b = 2y$, which can be used to substitute for $a + b$ in the first equation: $\frac{2y+c+d}{4}=x$. Multiply by 4 and subtract $2y$ to isolate $c + d$: $c + d = 4x - 2y$. Since the sum of c and d is $4x - 2y$, their mean is $\frac{4x-2y}{2}=2x-y$.

ANSWERS: PRACTICE TEST 1

8. **The correct answer is D.** The fraction of respondents who prefer a given region must be equal to the fraction of the circle that is taken up by the corresponding section of the pie chart. In the case of the South, this gives the following equation: $\frac{387}{1,250}=\frac{x}{360}$, where x is the degree measure to be determined.

   Cross-multiplying and solving, we get the following:

$$1,250x = 139,320$$
$$x \approx 111$$

   Therefore, the section of the pie chart should have an angle measuring 111°.

   Choice A is incorrect since 31 is the percentage of respondents who prefer the South, not the angle that the corresponding section of the pie chart should measure. Choices B, C, and E are the angle measures for the sections of the pie chart corresponding to Midwest, Northeast, and West, respectively.

9. **The correct answer is A.** From the original set of 1,250 respondents, 220 prefer the Northeast, which is $\frac{220}{1,250} \approx 18\%$. After including the additional 1,000 people, there are a total of 1,250 + 1,000 = 2,250 respondents, and 220 + 292 = 512 prefer the Northeast. This gives a new percentage of $\frac{512}{2,250} \approx 23\%$. The percentage increased by approximately 5%.

10. **The correct answer is B.** If a number is divisible by 2, 3, and 5, it is also divisible by their product, which is 30. Conversely, if a number is divisible by 30, it is also divisible by 2, 3, and 5. Therefore, the numbers that are divisible by 2, 3, and 5 are exactly those that are divisible by 30. There are only 3 positive numbers less than 100 that satisfy this: 30, 60, and 90.

11. **The correct answer is D.** An external angle of a triangle is always equal to the sum of the two opposite interior angles. In the triangle shown, this means that $9x + 53$ is equal to the sum of $12x - 3$ and $5x$. Set up and solve this equation.

$$(12x-3)+5x = 9x+53$$
$$17x-3 = 9x+53$$
$$8x = 56$$
$$x = 7$$

   Now substitute this value back into the angles shown:

$$5x = 5\times 7 = 35$$
$$12x-3 = 12\times 7-3 = 81$$
$$9x+53 = 9\times 7+53 = 116$$

   The angle of the triangle that is not shown is supplementary to 116°, so it is 180° – 116° = 64°. The three angles of the triangle are therefore 35°, 81°, and 64°. The largest one is 81°.

12. **The correct answers are A and C.** We have an absolute value equal to 4, which means that the quantity inside can be either 4 or –4. Examining the quantity inside the absolute value, $3 + |x + 1|$, we see that it can be 4 if $|x + 1| = 1$, and it can be –4 if $|x + 1| = 7$. The latter, however, is impossible since an absolute value is always nonnegative. We are left with the possibility that $|x + 1| = 1$. Using similar reasoning, this can happen if $x + 1 = 1$ or if $x + 1 = -1$. Solving each of these gives solutions $x = 0$ and $x = -2$, so choices A and C are correct. The other answer choices will fail when substituted into the equation.

13. **The correct answers are C, D, and E.** If line L passes through point (x, y), the slope between (x, y) and (3, 4) must be $-\frac{2}{3}$. In other words, values x and y must satisfy the equation $\frac{y-4}{x-3}=-\frac{2}{3}$. Check each answer choice to see if the slope formed with the point (3, 4) is $-\frac{2}{3}$:

   Choice A: $\frac{6-4}{6-3}=\frac{2}{3}$

   Choice B: $\frac{2-4}{0-3}=\frac{2}{3}$

   Choice C: $\frac{2-4}{6-3}=-\frac{2}{3}$

Choice D: $\frac{6-4}{0-3}=-\frac{2}{3}$

Choice E: $\frac{0-4}{9-3}=-\frac{2}{3}$

The choices that work are C, D, and E.

14. **The correct answer is –6.** Use the rules of exponents: the numerator is $(p^3)^4 = p^{12}$, and the denominator is $p^{-2}p^5 = p^3$, so the fraction simplifies to $\frac{p^{12}}{p^3} = p^9$. This is raised to the –2 power, leaving $(p^9)^{-2} = p^{-18}$. Since this is equal to p^{3t}, $-18 = 3t$, so $t = -6$.

15. **The correct answer is 90.** Call the three players A, B, and C. There are $6 \times 5 = 30$ ways to deal two out of six cards to player A, but since the order in which the cards are received doesn't matter, divide by 2 to avoid counting each pair twice. Therefore, there are $\frac{30}{2}=15$ ways to choose a pair of cards for player A.

Assuming two cards have been dealt to player A, there are $\frac{4\times3}{2}=6$ ways to choose two of the four remaining cards for player B. Player C receives the two remaining cards. Thus, the total number of ways to deal the cards is $15 \times 6 = 90$.

CHAPTER

Practice Test 2

PRACTICE TEST 2

OVERVIEW

DIRECTIONS FOR PRACTICE TEST 2

Practice Test 2 contains the five scored sections you will encounter on the actual GRE General Test.

On pages 379–385, we've provided sheets for planning and composing your Analytical Writing response, followed by an answer sheet for filling in your responses in the Verbal Reasoning and Quantitative Reasoning sections. Before you begin the test, remove or photocopy these pages.

As on the actual GRE General Test, each test section has its own time allocation. During that time period you may work on only that section. Be sure to use a timer for each section so you can accurately simulate the test-day experience. Total testing time is approximately 1 hour and 58 minutes.

Following Section 5, you will be provided tools to help you assess your response to the Analytical Writing task. An answer key and a comprehensive explanation follow for each test question in the Verbal Reasoning and Quantitative Reasoning sections.

Answer sheets for this test can be found on pages 379–385.

SECTION 1: ANALYTICAL WRITING

30 minutes

The time for this Analyze an Issue task is 30 minutes. You must plan and draft a response that evaluates the issue given below. If you do not respond to the specific issue, your score will be zero. Your response must be based on the accompanying instructions, and you must provide evidence for your position. You may use support from reading, experience, observations, and/or coursework.

The surest indicator of a great nation is represented not by the achievements of its rulers, artists, or scientists but the general welfare of its people.

*Write a response that expresses the degree to which you agree or disagree with the claim and the reason or reasons that underlie the claim. As you present, develop, and explain your position, discuss when and how the statement might or might not hold true. Explain how those possibilities provide support for your own point of view.**

STOP!

IF YOU FINISH BEFORE THE TIME IS UP, YOU MAY CHECK YOUR WORK IN THIS SECTION ONLY.

* All of the Analytical Writing prompts in the practice tests of this book come directly from the list of prompts for the GRE, which can be found at https://www.ets.org/pdfs/gre/issue-pool.pdf.

DIRECTIONS FOR THE VERBAL REASONING AND QUANTITATIVE REASONING SECTIONS

On test day, you will find information here about the question formats for the Verbal Reasoning and Quantitative Reasoning sections as well as information about how to use the software program. You will also receive important information about how these two sections are scored. Every correct answer earns a point, but points are not subtracted for incorrect answers, so it is better to guess if you aren't sure of an answer than to leave a question unanswered.

All multiple-choice questions will have answer options preceded by either blank ovals or blank squares, depending on the question type.

For your convenience in answering questions and checking answers in this paper-based practice test, answer choices are shown as lettered options. This notation makes it easier to check your answers against the answer keys and explanations.

NOTES

SECTION 2: VERBAL REASONING

18 minutes—12 questions

For each question, follow the specific directions and choose the best answer.

For Questions 1 and 2, choose one answer for each blank. Select from the appropriate column for each blank. Choose the answer that best completes the sense of the text.

1. The brains of all mammals are (i) _________ in three membranes known as the meninges. These membranes (ii) _________ the arachnoid mater, the dura mater, and the pia mater.

Blank (i)	Blank (ii)
A. lathered	D. involve
B. enveloped	E. comprise
C. paralleled	F. contain

2. Zydeco is a musical genre (i) _________ from Louisiana. This lively form (ii) _________ such other musical modes as jazz, blues, country and western, and rhythm and blues. Among the instruments most closely (iii) _________ with Zydeco are the accordion and the *vest frottoir* or rub board.

Blank (i)	Blank (ii)	Blank (iii)
A. burgeoning	D. electrifies	G. congenerous
B. emanating	E. synthesizes	H. fungible
C. absconding	F. adulterates	I. affiliated

For Questions 3–9, choose only one answer choice unless otherwise indicated.

Questions 3 and 4 are based on the following passage.

In undertaking a study of insects it is well first of all to know something about what they are, their general nature, appearance, habits and development. The insects comprise the largest group of animals on the globe. There are about four times as many different kinds of insects as all other kinds of animals combined. Insects vary greatly in size. Some are as large as small birds, while others are so small that a thousand placed in one pile would not equal the size of a pea.

Insects are commonly spoken of as "bugs." This term, however, is properly used only when referring to the one order of insects which includes the sap and blood-sucking insects such as the chinch bug, bedbug, squash bug, and the like. Then too, there are many so-called "bugs" which are not insects at all. Spiders, thousand-legs, crawfishes and even earthworms are often spoken of as bugs.

Insects are variously formed, but as a rule the mature ones have three and only three pairs of legs, one pair of feelers, one pair of large eyes, and one or two pairs of wings. The body is divided into a head, thorax and abdomen. The head bears the eyes, feelers and mouth, the thorax bears the legs and wings, and the abdomen is made up of a number of segments. The presence of wings at once decides whether or not it is an insect, for, aside from bats and birds, insects alone have true wings.

—Excerpt from *Elementary Study of Insects* by Leonard Haseman

3. As used in the passage, "order" (line 7) most likely means

A. command.
B. instruction.
C. stability.
D. class.
E. arrange.

4. In the context of this passage, what is significant about the number of legs a mature insect has?

A. It helps insects to move quickly.
B. It makes insects more stable when climbing.
C. It is the most distinctive part of the insect's anatomy.
D. It helps one tell the difference between birds and insects.
E. It distinguishes insects from other creatures.

Questions 5 and 6 are based on the following passage.

The validity of emotional support animals (ESAs) continues to be a subject of debate in academic and societal circles. Skepticism surrounding the validity of ESAs emerges from the lack of standardized criteria and scientific evidence supporting their therapeutic efficacy. While proponents argue that ESAs offer essential emotional support for individuals grappling with mental health challenges, the subjective nature of emotional well-being makes it difficult to establish clear parameters for determining the necessity of such animals. Moreover, the rise in instances of individuals obtaining ESA certifications without legitimate medical need raises questions about the potential misuse of the system. Critics contend that the widespread acceptance of emotional support animals without stringent oversight may compromise the integrity of the concept, potentially diminishing the rights and accommodations for those with genuine disabilities. Consequently, a critical examination of the scientific foundation and practical implementation of ESAs is essential to ensure their validity and prevent unintended consequences in both academic and societal contexts. Balancing the genuine need for emotional support with concerns about abuse and the potential infringement on the rights of those without disabilities remains a complex challenge, making the validity of emotional support animals a nuanced and multifaceted topic worthy of careful consideration and continued discussion.

5. Based on this passage, with which of the following statements about emotional support animals (ESAs) might the author likely agree?

A. Their usefulness is unsubstantiated and therefore invalid.
B. They fill an essential need for those grappling with mental health challenges.
C. Their implementation is a drain on public resources.
D. Their validity is a topic worthy of further consideration and further discussion.
E. Some animals are better suited to be ESAs than others.

6. As used in the passage, "stringent" (line 8) most nearly means

A. derelict.

B. insistent.

C. sanctioned.

D. labile.

E. strict.

Questions 7–9 are based on the following passage.

It is commonly said that everybody can sing in the bathroom; and this is true. Singing is very easy. Drawing, though, is much more difficult. I have devoted a good deal of time to Drawing, one way and another; I have to attend a great many committees and public meetings, and at such functions I find that Drawing is almost the only Art one can satisfactorily pursue during the speeches. One really cannot sing during the speeches; so as a rule I draw. I do not say that I am an expert yet, but after a few more meetings I calculate that I shall know Drawing as well as it can be known.

The first thing, of course, is to get on to a really good committee; and by a good committee I mean a committee that provides decent materials. An ordinary departmental committee is no use: generally they only give you a couple of pages of lined foolscap and no white blotting-paper, and very often the pencils are quite soft. White blotting-paper is essential. I know of no material the spoiling of which gives so much artistic pleasure—except perhaps snow. Indeed, if I was asked to choose between making pencil-marks on a sheet of white blotting-paper and making foot-marks on a sheet of white snow I should be in a thingummy.

—Excerpt from "On Drawing" by A. P. Herbert

7. The author of this passage mentions his experiences at committees and public meetings in order to

A. prove that singing is very easy as a use of time at meetings.

B. illustrate that practice allows one to draw well through a personal example.

C. describe the materials one needs to draw and the ideal environment for the practice.

D. argue that singing during speeches is difficult.

E. entertain the reader with a silly story about drawing during speeches.

For Questions 8 and 9, consider each answer individually and select all choices that apply.

8. Select the sentence in the passage that does NOT directly add support to the main idea.

A. It is commonly said that everybody can sing in the bathroom; and this is true.

B. One really cannot sing during the speeches; so as a rule I draw.

C. White blotting-paper is essential.

9. Which of the following, if it were true, would weaken the author's argument?

   A. While one may be born with the ability to draw, it takes education to sharpen that skill.

   B. Attendees at meetings rarely pay attention to what others are doing.

   C. The author of the passage is not a famous artist.

   D. The author of the passage is both a great singer and a great artist.

   E. It is not necessary to have quality art materials to improve one's skill at drawing.

For Questions 10–11, choose the two answers that best fit the meaning of the sentence as a whole and result in two completed sentences that are alike in meaning.

10. An area with "wilderness character" is legally defined as land that is _________ and affords the opportunity for solitude.

    A. eradicated

    B. natural

    C. cleared

    D. untrammeled

    E. razed

    F. gashed

11. Italy's election of 2018 was particularly _________, with three viable candidates representing the severely different ideologies of a highly divided country.

    A. fractious

    B. unified

    C. shattered

    D. acrimonious

    E. insipid

    F. vapid

Question 12 is based on the following passage.

Music's universality transcends cultural, linguistic, and geographical boundaries, serving as a fundamental mode of human expression and communication. Across diverse civilizations and epochs, music has been an integral part of rituals, celebrations, and daily life, reflecting the values, emotions, and experiences of individuals and communities. Its power lies in its ability to evoke profound emotions and connect people on a visceral level, bypassing linguistic barriers and fostering empathy and understanding. From the rhythmic beats of African drumming to the intricate melodies of classical symphonies, music resonates with universal themes of love, joy, sorrow, and triumph, offering a shared language that unites humanity in its collective experiences. Moreover, technological advancements in communication and digital media have further facilitated the global exchange and dissemination of music, amplifying its role as a catalyst for cultural exchange and mutual appreciation. Thus, music's universality not only enriches our individual lives but also serves as a bridge that fosters cross-cultural understanding and fosters a sense of interconnectedness in an increasingly diverse and interconnected world.

For Question 12, consider each answer individually and select all choices that apply.

12. Which of the following might provide a statement on the value of music that would satisfy the author?

   A. Music's influence crosses over both man-made and natural boundaries.

   B. The power of music lies in its ability to evoke profound emotions and connect people.

   C. Technology has allowed for the global exchange of music, which expands appreciation for new cultures.

STOP!

IF YOU FINISH BEFORE THE TIME IS UP, YOU MAY CHECK YOUR WORK IN THIS SECTION ONLY.

SECTION 3: VERBAL REASONING

23 minutes—15 questions

For each question, follow the specific directions and choose the best answer.

For Questions 1–3, choose one answer for each blank. Select from the appropriate column for each blank. Choose the answer that best completes the sense of the text.

1. The area of the brain called the hippocampus earned its unusual name due to its ________ to the mythical creature of the same name: a sea horse that pulled Poseidon's chariot in the epic poem *The Iliad.*

A. affinity
B. adjacency
C. identical
D. similitude
E. acquiescence

2. Sweep is a particular form of the competitive sport of rowing. It (i) ________ each rower using both hands to pull a single oar. Sculling is the (ii) ________ in which a rower pulls two oars, holding one in each hand.

Blank (i)	Blank (ii)
A. entails	D. variant
B. exemplifies	E. difference
C. affixes	F. feature

3. Of the six pyramids in Giza, the Great Pyramid is the oldest. While its (i) ________ is difficult to pinpoint precisely, the most popular theory is that Fourth Dynasty ruler Khufu (ii) ________ its creation. In the Western world, Khufu is better known by the (iii) ________Cheops.

Blank (i)	Blank (ii)	Blank (iii)
A. birth	D. commissioned	G. moniker
B. primeval	E. oppugned	H. entitle
C. genesis	F. commenced	I. nominal

For Questions 4–15, choose only one answer choice unless otherwise indicated.

Questions 4–6 are based on the following passage.

Science is knowledge; it is what we know. But mere knowledge is not science. For a bit of knowledge to become a part of science, its relation to other bits of knowledge must be found. In botany, for example, bits of knowledge about plants do not make a science of botany. To have a science of botany, we must not only know about leaves, roots, flowers, seeds, etc., but we must know the relations of these parts and of all the parts of a plant to one another. In other words, in science, we must not only *know*, we must not only have *knowledge*, but we must know the significance of the knowledge, must know its *meaning*. This is only another way of saying that we must have knowledge and know its relation to other knowledge.

A scientist is one who has learned to organize his knowledge. The main difference between a scientist and one who is not a scientist is that the scientist sees the significance of facts, while the non-scientific man sees facts as more or less unrelated things. As one comes to hunt for causes and inquire into the significance of things, one becomes a scientist. A thing or an event always points beyond itself to something else. This something else is what goes before it or comes after it—is its cause or its effect. This causal relationship that exists between events enables a scientist to prophesy.

—Excerpt from *The Science of Human Nature* by William Henry Pyle

4. The author of the passage discusses the relationship between knowledge and science most likely in order to

   A. explain what constitutes science and scientists.

   B. prove that science is knowledge.

   C. define the term *scientist*.

   D. contrast the term *knowledge* with *meaning*.

   E. show what the science of botany requires.

5. Which of the following, if it were true, would weaken the author's argument?

   A. A scientist must have knowledge of facts.

   B. A botanist is a scientist who studies plant life.

   C. Sometimes non-scientific jobs require one to see the significance of facts.

   D. Inquiry is a component of many occupations and is not unique to scientists.

   E. Scientists are often fascinated by puzzles and problem-solving.

6. The author of the passage suggests that the ways scientists use their knowledge

   A. cannot be truly comprehended by non-scientists.

   B. can seem almost mystical to a layperson.

   C. are more important than their ability to deduce meaning.

   D. appear to be more complex than they really are.

   E. can be learned by any non-scientist.

Questions 7–9 are based on the following passage.

Technical disasters, despite their devastating immediate consequences, often serve as catalysts for significant advancements in technology and safety protocols. These disasters prompt thorough investigations, leading to the identification of design flaws, operational errors, or unforeseen risks, thereby providing valuable lessons for engineers, scientists, and policymakers. For instance, the Space Shuttle *Challenger* disaster in 1986 spurred comprehensive reviews of NASA's safety protocols, resulting in substantial improvements to space shuttle designs and launch procedures. Similarly, the Fukushima Daiichi nuclear accident in 2011 prompted reevaluations of nuclear safety standards worldwide, leading to advancements in reactor design, emergency response protocols, and risk mitigation strategies. Thus, while technical disasters inflict tremendous human and environmental costs, they also stimulate innovation and drive progress in technology and safety measures.

However, the ethical implications of relying on technical disasters to drive technological advancements raise profound questions. Imagine the impact—just hours after the *Challenger* disaster, surviving family and friends who witnessed the explosion were being told consolingly by their nation's leader, "It's all part of the process of exploration and discovery . . . of taking a chance and expanding man's horizons. The future doesn't belong to the fainthearted; it belongs to the brave." It is morally questionable to accept the loss of lives and environmental devastation as inevitable byproducts of technological progress. Moreover, the notion of leveraging disasters as learning opportunities may inadvertently create complacency or undermine proactive efforts to prevent catastrophes in the first place. Ethical considerations also arise concerning the distribution of benefits derived from advancements resulting from disasters, particularly if vulnerable communities disproportionately bear the brunt of technological failures. Therefore, while technical disasters undoubtedly contribute to technological evolution, ethical deliberations are imperative to ensure that such progress is pursued responsibly and with due consideration for human welfare and environmental sustainability.

7. Based on the passage, the author evidently believes that

   A. the lessons learned from technical disasters are well worth the sacrifices made.

   B. technical disasters should not be used as learning opportunities.

   C. technical disasters such as the *Challenger* explosion and the Fukushima Daiichi plant accident were inevitable byproducts of technological progress.

   D. benefits from technological advancements should be rewarded only to those responsible for the advancements.

   E. striving for technological progress must be balanced with ethical considerations for human and environmental safety.

8. What function does the quotation (lines 13–15) in the second paragraph serve in this argument?

   A. It supports the idea of relying on technical disasters to drive technological advancements.

   B. It provides a counterargument to the author's main point.

   C. It illustrates how the loss of life can be portrayed as an inevitability of technological progress and a learning opportunity.

   D. It summarizes the main idea of the passage.

   E. It defines a term the author introduced.

9. In the passage, "mitigation" (line 8) most nearly means

   A. eradication.

   B. preparation.

   C. augmentation.

   D. compensation.

   E. reduction.

Questions 10 and 11 are based on the following passage.

Pudon: Consider mangrove restoration; these coastal ecosystems sequester carbon dioxide at a remarkable rate, mitigating climate change impacts. Preserving and enhancing mangroves not only safeguards biodiversity but also provides a natural defense against rising sea levels and storm surges. Research suggests that investing in mangrove restoration could significantly reduce greenhouse gas emissions and bolster coastal resilience. Integrating such nature-based solutions into climate strategies is vital for combating the impending crisis. Let's embrace these measures to secure a sustainable future for generations to come.

Warschau: While mangrove restoration shows promise, it's crucial to acknowledge its limitations. For instance, the effectiveness of mangroves in carbon sequestration may vary depending on factors like location and ecosystem health. Additionally, investments in mangrove restoration might divert resources from other climate solutions with potentially greater impact. There is clearly an even greater need for holistic approaches addressing systemic issues like deforestation and fossil fuel consumption, so balancing various strategies is essential for comprehensive climate action.

For Question 10, consider each answer individually and select all choices that apply.

10. Based on Pudon's argument, which of the following is a benefit of mangrove restoration?

    A. Increased sequestration of carbon dioxide

    B. Natural protection against storm surges

    C. Improved resilience of coastal ecosystems

11. Warschau responds to Pudon's argument by doing which of the following?

    A. Refuting the idea that mangrove restoration would serve as a comprehensive solution to excess carbon dioxide

    B. Advocating for alternative solutions that do not involve mangrove restoration

    C. Disproving the idea that mangrove restoration is an effective way to combat climate change

    D. Critiquing the scientific accuracy of Pudon's assertions

    E. Questioning the veracity of scientific studies regarding the efficacy of mangrove restoration

For Questions 12–14, choose the two answers that best fit the meaning of the sentence as a whole and result in two completed sentences that are alike in meaning.

12. *The Twilight Zone* is among the most ________ of fantastical television series; it inspired other series such as *Tales from the Crypt* and *Black Mirror* to adopt both its anthology format and its shocking, twist endings.

A. seminal

B. worn

C. constant

D. ubiquitous

E. acclaimed

F. influential

13. Drupes include such ________ treats as cherries, peaches, and plums, as well as more savory items such as olives and almonds.

A. succulent

B. scrumptious

C. cloying

D. savory

E. putrid

F. delectable

14. The suburban gothic is a(n) ________ of American film and literature that is centered on the idea that suburban neighborhoods may not be as safe and idyllic as they seem.

A. segment

B. category

C. subgenre

D. link

E. compartment

F. exemplary

Question 15 is based on the following passage.

The group of birds usually known as the *Raptores*, or Rapacious Birds, embraces three well-marked divisions, namely, the Owls, the Hawks, and the Vultures. In former classifications they headed the Class of Birds, being honored with this position in consequence of their powerful organization, large size, and predatory habits. But it being now known that in structure they are less perfectly organized than the *Passeres* and *Strisores*, birds generally far more delicate in organization, as well as smaller in size, they occupy a place in the more recent arrangements nearly at the end of the Terrestrial forms.

The complete definition of the order *Raptores*, and of its subdivisions, requires the enumeration of a great many characters; and that their distinguishing features may be more easily recognized by the student, I give first a brief diagnosis, including their simplest characters, to be followed by a more detailed account hereafter.

—Excerpt from *A History of North American Birds, vol. 3*
by S. F. Baird, T. M. Brewer, and R. Ridgway

15. Based on the passage, what will be the most significant result of the author giving the distinguishing features of certain birds?

A. The author will help the reader to be more imaginative.

B. The author will help the reader to know which birds are dangerous.

C. The author will have explained the meaning of the term *Raptores*.

D. The author will have explained the simplest features of rapacious birds.

E. The author will help students to identify rapacious birds.

STOP!

IF YOU FINISH BEFORE THE TIME IS UP, YOU MAY CHECK YOUR WORK IN THIS SECTION ONLY.

SECTION 4: QUANTITATIVE REASONING

21 minutes—12 questions

For each question, follow the specific directions and choose the best answer.

The test maker provides the following information that applies to all questions in the Quantitative Reasoning section of the GRE General Test:

- All numbers used are real numbers.
- All figures are assumed to lie in a plane unless otherwise indicated.
- Geometric figures, such as lines, circles, triangles, and quadrilaterals, *are not necessarily* drawn to scale. That is, you should *not* assume that quantities such as lengths and angle measures are as they appear in a figure. You should assume, however, that lines shown as straight are actually straight, points on a line are in the order shown, and more generally, all geometric objects are in the relative positions shown. For questions with geometric figures, you should base your answers on geometric reasoning, not on estimating or comparing quantities by sight or by measurement.
- Coordinate systems, such as *xy*-planes and number lines, *are* drawn to scale. Therefore, you can read, estimate, or compare quantities in such figures by sight or by measurement.
- Graphical data presentations, such as bar graphs, circle graphs, and line graphs, *are* drawn to scale. Therefore, you can read, estimate, or compare data values by sight or by measurement.

For Questions 1–5, compare Quantity A and Quantity B. Some questions will have additional information above the two quantities to use in determining your answer.

1.

Quantity A	Quantity B
12% of 17% of x	34% of 6% of x

A. Quantity A is greater.
B. Quantity B is greater.
C. The two quantities are equal.
D. The relationship cannot be determined from the information given.

2.

Quantity A	Quantity B
$\frac{1}{2^{25}}$	$\frac{1}{\sqrt{2}^{51}}$

A. Quantity A is greater.
B. Quantity B is greater.
C. The two quantities are equal.
D. The relationship cannot be determined from the information given.

3. The faces of a cube are painted with different colors so that no two faces that share an edge have the same color.

Quantity A	Quantity B
The minimum number of colors required to paint the cube	3

A. Quantity A is greater.

B. Quantity B is greater.

C. The two quantities are equal.

D. The relationship cannot be determined from the information given.

4.

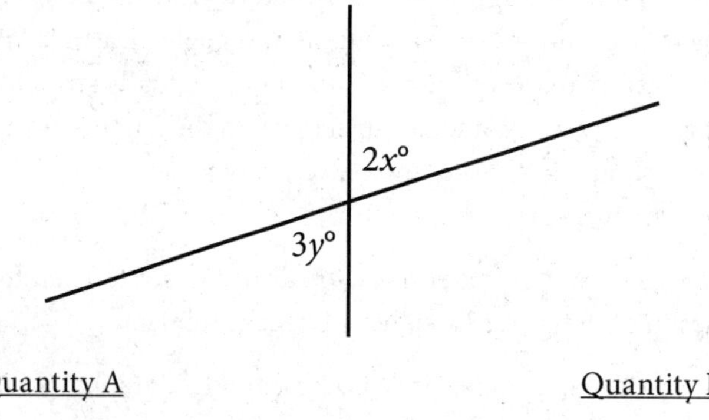

Quantity A	Quantity B
x	y

A. Quantity A is greater.

B. Quantity B is greater.

C. The two quantities are equal.

D. The relationship cannot be determined from the information given.

5. Fran is older than John, John is younger than Beth, and Beth is younger than Tabitha.

Quantity A	Quantity B
Fran's age	Tabitha's age

A. Quantity A is greater.

B. Quantity B is greater.

C. The two quantities are equal.

D. The relationship cannot be determined from the information given.

Questions 6–12 have several formats. Unless the directions state otherwise, choose one answer choice. For the Numeric Entry questions, follow the instructions below.

Numeric Entry Questions

The following items are the same for both the actual GRE General Test and the test presented in this book. However, the actual GRE General Test will have additional information about entering answers in decimal and fraction boxes on the computer screen. To take the test in this book, enter your answers in boxes or answer grids.

- Your answer may be an integer, a decimal, or a fraction, and it may be negative.
- If a question asks for a fraction, there will be two boxes. One box will be for the numerator, and one will be for the denominator.
- Equivalent forms of the correct answer, such as 2.5 and 2.50, are all correct.
- Enter the exact answer unless the question asks you to round your answers.

Questions 6 and 7 refer to the graph below.

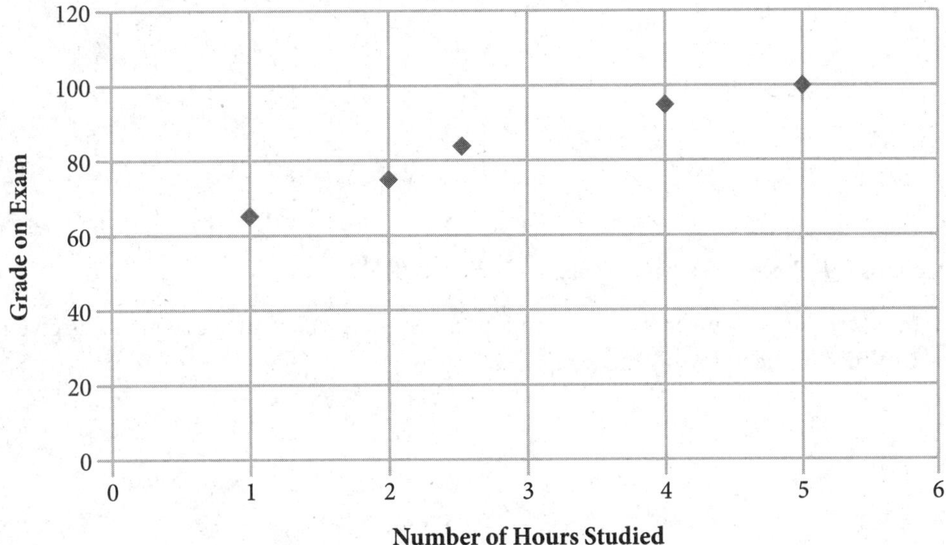

6. What kind of correlation exists between the number of hours studied and a grade on an exam?

   A. Positive

   B. Negative

   C. None

   D. Quadratic

   E. Exponential

7. Which of the following is the best estimate for the grade a student would receive if she studied for 3 hours?

A. 60

B. 70

C. 80

D. 90

E. 100

8. A rectangular garden measures 12 feet by 16 feet. If it is enlarged on all sides by 2 feet, what is the area of the new garden?

A. 192 square feet

B. 240 square feet

C. 252 square feet

D. 256 square feet

E. 320 square feet

9. The wholesale price of a laptop is $600. A retailer marks it up by 15% but then puts it on sale for 10% off. What percentage of the wholesale price does it sell for?

A. 76.5%

B. 90%

C. 93.5%

D. 103.5%

E. 126.5%

For Question 10, choose all the answers that apply.

10. The first term of a sequence is given by $a_1 = 2$, and for $n > 1$, the nth term of the sequence is given by $a_n = 2a_{n-1} - 1$. Which of the following are terms of the sequence?

A. 3

B. 4

C. 5

D. 9

E. 12

F. 17

G. 33

H. 60

For Questions 11 and 12, enter your answers in the boxes.

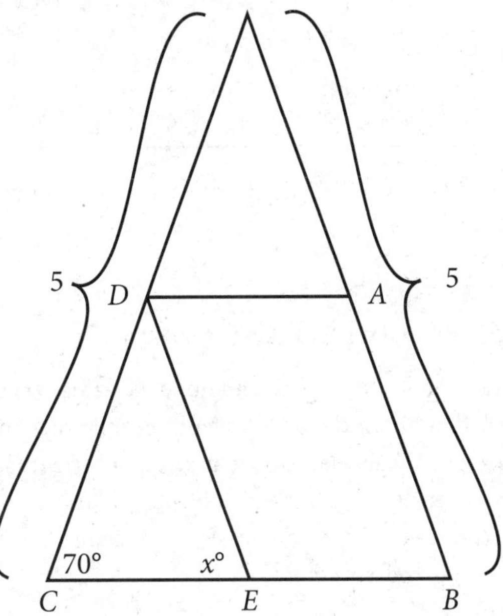

11. If $\overline{AB}$ is parallel to $\overline{DE}$, what is the value of x?

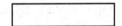

12. A recording artist rents a studio for a week to record an album. If the rental fee was $5,400, and she sells albums for $12.50, how many must she sell to cover the cost of the rental?

STOP!

IF YOU FINISH BEFORE THE TIME IS UP, YOU MAY CHECK YOUR WORK IN THIS SECTION ONLY.

SECTION 5: QUANTITATIVE REASONING

26 minutes—15 questions

For each question, follow the specific directions and choose the best answer.

The test maker provides the following information that applies to all questions in the Quantitative Reasoning section of the GRE General Test:

- All numbers used are real numbers.
- All figures are assumed to lie in a plane unless otherwise indicated.
- Geometric figures, such as lines, circles, triangles, and quadrilaterals, *are not necessarily* drawn to scale. That is, you should *not* assume that quantities such as lengths and angle measures are as they appear in a figure. You should assume, however, that lines shown as straight are actually straight, points on a line are in the order shown, and more generally, all geometric objects are in the relative positions shown. For questions with geometric figures, you should base your answers on geometric reasoning, not on estimating or comparing quantities by sight or by measurement.
- Coordinate systems, such as *xy*-planes and number lines, *are* drawn to scale. Therefore, you can read, estimate, or compare quantities in such figures by sight or by measurement.
- Graphical data presentations, such as bar graphs, circle graphs, and line graphs, *are* drawn to scale. Therefore, you can read, estimate, or compare data values by sight or by measurement.

For Questions 1–5, compare Quantity A and Quantity B. Some questions will have additional information above the two quantities to use in determining your answer.

1. $d < e < f < g$

Quantity A	Quantity B
$g - f$	$e - d$

A. Quantity A is greater.
B. Quantity B is greater.
C. The two quantities are equal.
D. The relationship cannot be determined from the information given.

2. *ABCD* is a convex quadrilateral. Sides *AB* and *CD* are parallel.

Quantity A	Quantity B
The average degree value of angles *A*, *B*, and *C*	60

A. Quantity A is greater.
B. Quantity B is greater.
C. The two quantities are equal.
D. The relationship cannot be determined from the information given.

3. Consultant A charges an initial fee of $300, plus $75 for every hour spent working on a project. Consultant B charges an initial fee of $200, plus $85 per hour spent working. An organization estimates that a project will take 15 hours to complete.

Quantity A	Quantity B
The estimated cost of hiring consultant A for the project	The estimated cost of hiring consultant B for the same project

A. Quantity A is greater.
B. Quantity B is greater.
C. The two quantities are equal.
D. The relationship cannot be determined from the information given.

4. A circle has a circumference of 8π, and a square has a perimeter of 30.

Quantity A	Quantity B
The area of the circle	The area of the square

A. Quantity A is greater.
B. Quantity B is greater.
C. The two quantities are equal.
D. The relationship cannot be determined from the information given.

5. In a certain town, if it snows on Monday, the probability that it will also snow on Tuesday is 40%. If it does not snow on Monday, the probability of snow on Tuesday is 10%. Assume there is a 20% chance of snow on Monday.

Quantity A	Quantity B
The probability that it snows on Tuesday, but not Monday	The probability that it snows on both days

A. Quantity A is greater.
B. Quantity B is greater.
C. The two quantities are equal.
D. The relationship cannot be determined from the information given.

Questions 6–15 have several formats. Unless the directions state otherwise, choose one answer choice. For the Numeric Entry questions, follow the instructions below.

Numeric Entry Questions

The following items are the same for both the actual GRE General Test and the test presented in this book. However, the actual GRE General Test will have additional information about entering answers in decimal and fraction boxes on the computer screen. To take the test in this book, enter your answers in boxes or answer grids.

- Your answer may be an integer, a decimal, or a fraction, and it may be negative.
- If a question asks for a fraction, there will be two boxes. One box will be for the numerator, and one will be for the denominator.
- Equivalent forms of the correct answer, such as 2.5 and 2.50, are all correct.
- Enter the exact answer unless the question asks you to round your answers.

6. Payal can shovel the snow from a driveway in 12 minutes, and Shreya can shovel the snow from the same driveway in 18 minutes. Working together, how long will it take for them to shovel the driveway? Round to the nearest minute.

   A. 6 minutes
   B. 7 minutes
   C. 12 minutes
   D. 15 minutes
   E. 30 minutes

7. 12 miles per hour is equivalent to how many feet per second?

   A. 1.47
   B. 8.18
   C. 12
   D. 17.6
   E. 1,056

Questions 8 and 9 refer to the figure below.

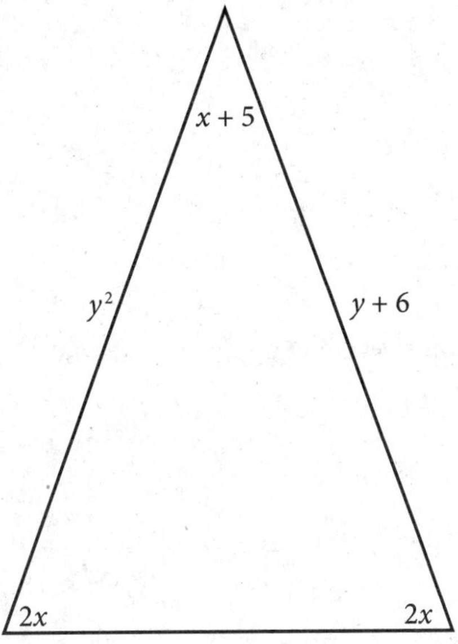

8. What is the value of x?

   A. 5

   B. 19

   C. 35

   D. 36

   E. 45

9. What is the value of y?

   A. 0

   B. 1

   C. 2

   D. 3

   E. 3 or –2

10. If $A = \{7, 9, 11, 13\}$ and $B = \{6, 8, 12, 14\}$, which of the following are true?

    A. A and B have the same mean and the same standard deviation.

    B. A and B have different means but the same standard deviation.

    C. A and B have different means and different standard deviations.

    D. A and B have the same mean, but A has a larger standard deviation.

    E. A and B have the same mean, but B has a larger standard deviation.

11. Maureen invests \$4,500 in an account earning 3.5% annual interest, compounded monthly. What is the value of the account after 2 months?

A. \$4,513.13

B. \$4,526.25

C. \$4,526.29

D. \$4,657.50

E. \$4,766.33

For Questions 12 and 13, choose all the answers that apply.

12. If a is even and b is odd, which of the following are even?

A. $a + b$

B. $a - b$

C. ab

D. a^b

E. b^a

13. Suppose $a_1 = 3$ and for $n > 1$, $a_n = 2 - a_{n-1}$. Which of the following numbers will appear as terms of this sequence?

A. −1

B. 1

C. −2

D. 2

E. −3

F. 3

G. −4

H. 4

For Questions 14 and 15, enter your answers in the boxes.

14. If $x = 2a$, $a = 3b$, $b = 7y$, and $x = ky$, find k.

15. The surface area and volume of a cube are numerically equal. What is the length of a side of the cube?

STOP!

IF YOU FINISH BEFORE THE TIME IS UP, YOU MAY CHECK YOUR WORK IN THIS SECTION ONLY.

ANSWER KEYS AND EXPLANATIONS

Section 1: Analytical Writing

To assist you with evaluating your writing, we have provided the following rubric, which is adapted from the official rubric used by ETS.* If you need more assistance evaluating your writing, consider the writing samples for essays at score levels 2, 4, and 6 as provided in Chapter 3.

ANALYTICAL WRITING SCORING RUBRIC SUMMARY		
Score Level	**Description**	**Characteristics of a Typical Response**
6 Outstanding	A sustained, insightful, organized, detailed analysis of well-developed, complex ideas supported by meaningful evidence and highly persuasive support. Utilizes a wide range of vocabulary and rhetorical methods while demonstrating a superior understanding of the conventions of Standard Written English. Very minor errors may be present but do not impact meaning.	• Presents a distinct and perceptive viewpoint regarding the issue as outlined in the given instructions • Expands meaningfully on the viewpoint with convincing rationales and/or compelling examples • Maintains focus, organization, and clarity while establishing meaningful connections between concepts • Seamlessly and accurately moves between concepts using a range of transitions, word choices, and sentence structures • Exhibits exceptional proficiency with the norms of Standard Written English, even if very minor errors are present
5 Strong	A thoughtful, generally organized, and focused analysis of nuanced ideas supported by sound reasoning and meaningful examples. Uses a range of rhetorical skills and conventions to demonstrate meaningful control of the conventions of Standard Written English. Minor errors may be present but do not impact meaning.	• Presents a lucid and carefully considered viewpoint regarding the issue as outlined in the given instructions • Elaborates on the viewpoint with logically coherent rationales and/or well-chosen examples • Maintains focus and exhibits general organization, establishing suitable connections between ideas • Communicates ideas clearly and effectively, employing fitting vocabulary and varying sentence structures • Exhibits proficiency with the norms of Standard Written English, though occasional minor errors may be present

(continues)

* The GRE General Test: Analytical Writing Measure Scoring," ETS, 2024, https://www.ets.org/gre/test-takers/general-test/prepare/content/analytical-writing/scoring.html.

ANALYTICAL WRITING SCORING RUBRIC SUMMARY (*CONTINUED*)		
Score Level	**Description**	**Characteristics of a Typical Response**
4 Adequate	A competent, considered analysis of meaningful ideas that ventures a main point and supports it with relevant evidence or reasoning. Ideas are organized in a satisfactory manner, clearly conveyed, and supported by adequate control of rhetorical skills and the conventions of Standard Written English. May have some minor errors that impact clarity of meaning.	• Presents a clear viewpoint regarding the issue as outlined in the given instructions • Develops the viewpoint with relevant reasoning and/or examples • Maintains adequate focus and organization • Demonstrates satisfactory command of language to articulate ideas with acceptable clarity • Exhibits general understanding of the norms of Standard Written English, albeit with occasional errors
3 Limited	A somewhat competent analysis that addresses specific required tasks and makes some effort to address main points. Rhetorical skills may be lacking or underdeveloped, and writing may be limited by weak structure, poor organization, or underdevelopment of ideas. Contains some errors that limit clarity of meaning and/or contribute to vagueness.	Exhibits **one or more** of the following concerns: • Shows vagueness or inadequacy in addressing the given instructions, presenting or developing a viewpoint, or both • Demonstrates weakness in employing relevant examples or rationales, or leans heavily on unsupported assertions • Exhibits limited focus and/or organization • Includes issues in language or sentence structure, contributing to lack of clarity • Contains either occasional major errors or frequent minor errors in grammar, usage, and/or mechanics of Standard Written English, impeding comprehension
2 Seriously Flawed	A weak analysis that does not adequately address specific required tasks and/or that is underdeveloped, disorganized, or unclear. Frequent issues with rhetorical skills and/or the conventions of Standard Written English obfuscate meaning and limit clarity. Frequent errors make it difficult to parse.	Exhibits **one or more** of the following concerns: • Exhibits a lack of clarity or serious limitation in addressing the given instructions, developing a viewpoint on the issue, or both • Offers few, if any, relevant rationales or examples to support assertions • Lacks focus and/or organization • Includes serious issues in language or sentence structure, frequently obstructing clarity or contributing to outright confusion • Contains serious errors in grammar, usage, or mechanics that frequently obscure meaning

ANALYTICAL WRITING SCORING RUBRIC SUMMARY (*CONTINUED*)		
Score Level	**Description**	**Characteristics of a Typical Response**
1 Fundamentally Deficient	A deficient analysis that contains fundamental errors and fails to communicate a meaningful main point. Content may be incomprehensible or extremely difficult to parse and/or may be irrelevant to the task at hand. Frequent and pervasive errors render the analysis incomprehensible or incoherent.	Exhibits **one or more** of the following concerns: • Demonstrates little or no evidence of grasping the given instructions or the issue at hand • Shows minimal or no evidence of the ability to craft an organized response, often appearing disorganized and/or excessively concise • Suffers from severe issues in language and sentence structure, consistently hindering comprehension • Contains widespread errors in grammar, usage, and mechanics, leading to incoherence
0	An analysis that cannot be evaluated because it does not address any aspect of the specified task. It may copy parts of the prompt in lieu of developing concepts or may be written in a foreign language or otherwise incomprehensible.	Exhibits one or more of the following concerns: • Demonstrates zero awareness of the given instructions or the issue at hand • Fully off topic • Merely copies the topic • Incomprehensible • Written in a foreign language • Consists only of random keystrokes or nonsensical inputs
NS	Blank essays will receive a score of NS, meaning no score.	

Section 2: Verbal Reasoning

1. B, E	4. E	7. B	9. E	11. A, D
2. B, E, I	5. D	8. A, B	10. B, D	12. A, B, C
3. D	6. E			

1. **The correct answers are B and E.** Answer Blank (i): The correct word is a verb that belongs with the preposition *in*, and *enveloped*, in this context, means a "natural enclosing covering," such as a membrane. While something can be lathered in a substance, *lathered* (choice A) is usually used to indicate a soapy or frothy covering, and this would not be an accurate way to describe a membrane. *Paralleled* (choice C) is incorrect because one does not say that something is paralleled *in* something else—it is paralleled *with* something else.

   Answer Blank (ii): While the terms in the list that follows the blank are likely unfamiliar to you, the structure of the sentence indicates that these terms are included in a list of membranes. *Comprise* means "include." *Involve* (choice D) is less concrete a synonym for *include* than *comprise*. The word *contain* (choice F) makes it sound as though the membranes are a physical container that holds the arachnoid mater, the dura mater, and the pia mater, which does not make sense since the sentence already indicated that these membranes cover the brain.

2. **The correct answers are B, E, and I.** Answer Blank (i): Specific types of music, such as Zydeco, originate from specific locations, such as Louisiana. *Emanating* means "originating."

   Answer Blank (ii): The list of musical styles indicates that Zydeco is a combination of all these styles and *synthesizes* means "combines." *Electrifies* (choice D) and *adulterates* (choice F) suggest that Zydeco directly affected these other musical styles, for better or worse, which is the opposite of the truth.

   Answer Blank (iii): The final sentence of the paragraph refers to instruments used to play Zydeco, and such instruments would be affiliated with the genre. It does not make sense to say that a musical style and instruments are "similar" (*congenerous*, choice G) or "exchangeable" (*fungible*, choice H).

3. **The correct answer is D.** While the word *order* can be used as a synonym for any of the answer choices, only *class* makes sense in this context. The term *bugs* describes a type or class of insects. Choices A, B, and C simply do not make sense in this context. The correct answer also must be a noun, and *arrange* (choice E) is a verb.

4. **The correct answer is E.** The passage mentions that determining the number of legs an insect has is a way to identify insects and distinguish them from other creatures. Choices A and B may be true, but these are not significant reasons the author mentions about the number of legs mature insects have in this passage. The number of legs a mature insect has is just one of the distinguishing features listed in this passage, so choice C is not the best answer. The author mentions wings only when comparing insects to birds, so choice D is not the best answer either.

5. **The correct answer is D.** The author presents an objective view about ESAs, relating, for the most part, the opinions of others, apart from acknowledging at the end of the paragraph that the validity of ESA use is a "nuanced and multifaceted topic worthy of careful consideration and continued discussion" (lines 14–15). Choice A is incorrect because although the paragraph mentions that skepticism regarding ESA use emerges from a "lack of standardized criteria and scientific evidence supporting their therapeutic efficacy," it does not take such an extremely negative stance. Choice B is incorrect because the paragraph also does not claim that ESAs are essential to those

with mental health issues. Choices C and E are not addressed in the passage.

6. **The correct answer is E.** The word *stringent* refers to the oversight required to verify the legitimate medical need for ESAs, so the oversight should be strict and adhere closely to a set of standards. *Derelict* (choice A) means "neglectful," and *labile* (choice D) means "unstable"; both are antonyms of *stringent.* Although the oversight needed would likely be officially approved, *sanctioned* (choice C) is not synonymous with *stringent. Insistent* (choice B) is a synonym of *strident*, a word close in spelling but far different in meaning from *stringent.*

7. **The correct answer is B.** The point of the first paragraph of the passage is that one needs to practice a lot to draw well. Choice A is just one detail in the paragraph, and it isn't a very important detail. Choice C is the point of the second paragraph, not the first one. Choice D is another individual detail from the first paragraph. While the passage is fairly humorous, there is a greater purpose than merely entertaining the reader, so choice E is not the best answer.

8. **The correct answers are A and B.** The passage is mainly about the materials and mindset one needs to learn how to draw, and the sentences in choices A and B do not support this main idea directly. Choice C is an instruction for obtaining the right materials for drawing, so it is relevant.

9. **The correct answer is E.** The author spends a good deal of time specifying materials that he requires to practice his drawing. As a result, learning that specific materials aren't necessary to develop one's practice would contradict the author. Choice A supports the author's argument that one must work to sharpen his or her drawing skills. If attendees at meetings paid close attention to what other attendees were doing, the author would not be able to practice drawing at them, so choice B does not weaken the author's argument. One does not need to be a famous artist to be a good one, so choice C is incorrect, and choice D would do nothing to weaken the author's argument, as it is largely irrelevant to his ideas about how to develop as an artist.

10. **The correct answers are B and D.** Wilderness land is, by definition, natural and untrammeled by human development. *Eradicated* (choice A), *cleared* (choice C), and *razed* (choice E) would all refer to land that people have altered for development or other purposes, and such land would no longer be classified as wilderness. *Gashed* (choice F) is not a word one would use to describe an area of land in any event.

11. **The correct answers are A and D.** Phrases such as "severely different ideologies" and "highly divided" are clues that the election was one in which tempers were bad, and *fractious* and *acrimonious* would indicate such a testy atmosphere. *Unified* (choice B) implies a peaceful atmosphere. *Shattered* (choice C) is not a word one would use to describe the atmosphere surrounding a political election. *Insipid* (choice E) and *vapid* (choice F) are terms denoting a lack of energy or interest, and they do not portray the testiness of the election in question.

12. **The correct answers are A, B, and C.** The passage states that music's universality transcends cultural, linguistic, and geographical boundaries (choice A) with a shared language that unites humanity through its collective experiences (choice B). It further discusses how technological advancements in communication and digital media have further facilitated the global exchange and dissemination of music, fostering cross-cultural understanding (choice C).

Section 3: Verbal Reasoning

1. D	4. A	7. E	10. A, B, C	13. A, B, F
2. A, D	5. D	8. C	11. A	14. B, C
3. C, D, G	6. B	9. E	12. A, F	15. E

1. **The correct answer is D.** This sentence deals with how a part of the brain looks like a mythical creature, and *similitude* indicates that two things share some trait, such as appearance. *Affinity* (choice A) means "affection," and *adjacency* (choice B) refers to a physical closeness, so neither relates to shared traits. *Identical* (choice C) indicates too much similarity, and it is also an adjective when this sentence requires a noun. *Acquiescence* (choice E) is "obedience" and does not make sense in this context.

2. **The correct answers are A and D.** Answer Blank (i): The second sentence of the paragraph explains what the sport of sweep involves, and *entails* means "involves." *Exemplifies* (choice B) means "represents," and *affixes* (choice C) means "attaches." Neither word makes sense in this context.

   Answer Blank (ii): The third sentence describes a form of rowing slightly different from sweep, and *variant* means "a different form." *Difference* (choice E) relates to *variant*, but it is not a synonym. *Feature* (choice F) indicates nothing about difference.

3. **The correct answers are C, D, and G.** Answer Blank (i): The paragraph discusses how the Great Pyramid of Giza was first created, and *genesis* indicates the beginning of something. One would not describe a pyramid as being born, so *birth* (choice A) is an odd word for this context. *Primeval* (choice B) means "primitive," and something does not need to be primitive to have an origin or genesis.

   Answer Blank (ii): One can deduce from the context that Khufu was responsible for having the Great Pyramid built, and when one is responsible for having something created, that person can be said to have commissioned the thing's creation. It would be contradictory to the context to say that Khufu *oppugned*, or opposed, the pyramid's creation, so choice E is not the best answer. It is unlikely that a ruler such as Khufu would personally begin construction on a pyramid, so choice F, *commenced*, is not the best answer either.

   Answer Blank (iii): The final sentence of the paragraph explains an alternate name by which Khufu is known, and *moniker* means "name." The other two terms not only do not conceptually fit the context but also do not fulfill the need for a noun to replace the answer blank.

4. **The correct answer is A.** The first paragraph of the passage explains what constitutes a science, and the second paragraph explains what constitutes a scientist. While the idea that "science is knowledge" is directly in the first words of the passage, the rest of the passage expands on this idea to the degree that choice B is an insufficient explanation of the passage's main point. Choice C makes the passage seem like a dictionary entry. The terms in choice D are not actually contrasted in the passage. Choice E focuses on just one supporting detail in the passage instead of explaining the point of the passage as a whole.

5. **The correct answer is D.** The author defines a scientist as one who has come to "hunt for causes and inquire into the significance of things." This constitutes a wide definition of scientists which would include many professions outside of what some might envision when thinking of a scientist. However, challenging the perception that this form of inquiry was unique to scientists—rather than a component of many different occupations—would weaken the author's argument about how to define a scientist. The author does state that scientists must have knowledge of facts, but he says that this is not all that a scientist must do, so choice A is not

the best answer. The idea that non-scientific jobs require one to see the significance of facts (choice C) is not specific enough to weaken the author's argument. The other answer choices are all things that would support the author's argument regarding science and scientists, not weaken it.

6. **The correct answer is B.** The ability to make prophesies, or see the future, is a mystical ability, so by stating that the way scientists use knowledge to comprehend causal relationships "enables a scientist to prophesy" supports choice B. While the author draws distinctions between scientists and non-scientists, he does not make the extreme implication that is in choice A. The author also stresses the important relationship between knowledge and meaning and does not necessarily indicate that one side of that relationship is more important than the other, so choice C is not the best answer. There is no strong support for the inferences in choices D or E.

7. **The correct answer is E.** The author's statement that "while technical disasters undoubtedly contribute to technological evolution, ethical deliberations are imperative to ensure that such progress is pursued responsibly and with due consideration for human welfare and environmental sustainability" (lines 20–23) supports the conclusion in choice E. The author recognizes that technical disasters serve as opportunities to stimulate innovation and drive progress in technology and safety measures, which is ultimately beneficial, but they also assert that spinning these disasters as learning opportunities is morally distasteful, so choice B is incorrect. Choices A, C, and D directly conflict with what the author states in the passage.

8. **The correct answer is C.** The author uses the quotation because it voices a questionable underlying attitude toward loss of life in the pursuit of technological advancement. The quotation references the *Challenger* explosion, asking the reader to imagine the impact on the loved ones who survived the astronauts, who were told that the accident was "all part of the process." Choice A can be eliminated because the quotation doesn't address reliance on disasters but rather accepting them. The quotation does not serve as a counterargument to the argument (choice B); it serves as an example to support the author's argument that challenges the morality of accepting the loss of life in the name of technological progress. The quotation supports the argument, but it does not summarize it (choice D). The quotation does not define a term either (choice E).

9. **The correct answer is E.** The word *mitigation* means "reduction," and advanced strategies to ensure a reduction in risk were developed after the Fukushima Daiichi accident. While risk *eradication* (choice A), or elimination altogether would be ideal, risk *reduction* is the more realistic plan and thus a more accurate term. Similarly, preparation (choice B) would be part of a mitigation plan, but these two words are not interchangeable. *Augmentation* means "to increase or add to," which is the opposite intent of what's being discussed, so choice C is incorrect. Making up for risks is a nonsensical strategy, so *compensation* (choice D) is incorrect.

10. **The correct answers are A, B, and C.** Pudon's section includes all three choices as potential benefits of mangrove restoration.

11. **The correct answer is A.** Warschau's response centers on the idea that mangrove restoration is neither the only solution to climate change nor the most important. It is therefore not a comprehensive solution to climate change. Using a process of elimination, you'll recognize that there is no attempt to disprove (choice C) or critique (choice D) Pudon's ideas, nor does Warschau call into question the scientific studies upon which Pudon based their claims about mangrove restoration (choice E). The word *not* is key to understanding why choice B is incorrect, since at no point does Warschau claim that mangrove restoration is a bad idea, only that other solutions should take higher priority and that any measure to combat climate change should be part of a balanced and comprehensive plan that attacks the issue from multiple angles.

12. **The correct answers are A and F.** The sentence describes how *The Twilight Zone* affected other television series, and something that is *seminal* or *influential* affects the things that follow it. *Worn* (choice B) has negative connotations and does not fit this context. *Constant* (choice C) is not specifically related to affecting other things. *Ubiquitous* (choice D) means "inescapable" and does not have much to do with being influential or seminal. Something can be *acclaimed*, or well loved, without necessarily affecting anything else, so choice E is not the best answer.

13. **The correct answers are A, B, and F.** The word *treats* is a clue that the needed adjective should indicate qualities that make a particular food taste good enough to be considered a treat. *Scrumptious* and *delectable* both mean "delicious" and are qualities that would make a food a treat. *Succulent*, meaning "full of juice" or "moist and tasty," is also a correct answer. *Cloying* (choice C) means "overly sweet" and has somewhat negative connotations. The sentence draws a contrast between two lists of foods, and since the second list is already defined as savory foods, a different term is needed to define the first list, so choice D can be eliminated. *Putrid* (choice E) means "disgusting," so it should be eliminated as well.

14. **The correct answers are B and C.** The correct answers should indicate that the suburban gothic is a kind of American film and literature, and terms such as *strain* and *subgenre* are often used to mean "kind" when discussing aspects of a larger category. *Segment* (choice A) and *compartment* (choice E) have similar connotations, but these terms are not typically used when discussing literary or cinematic genres since they suggest a physical subsection of something larger. One would not say that something is a link *of* anything else, so choice D should be eliminated. *Exemplary* may seem correct because it resembles *example*, which would fit the blank, but *exemplary* is an adjective and the blank requires a noun.

15. **The correct answer is E.** In the second paragraph of the passage, the author indicates that giving the distinguishing features of certain birds will help define them as *Raptores*, or rapacious birds. Picturing something that actually exists would not really help anyone to be more imaginative, so choice A is not a very strong answer. While some rapacious birds may be dangerous, the author never implies that choice B is the purpose behind describing their appearances. The author already explained the meaning of the term *Raptores*, so choice C is incorrect. While choice D is true in itself, it is not the most significant result of giving the distinguishing features of certain birds.

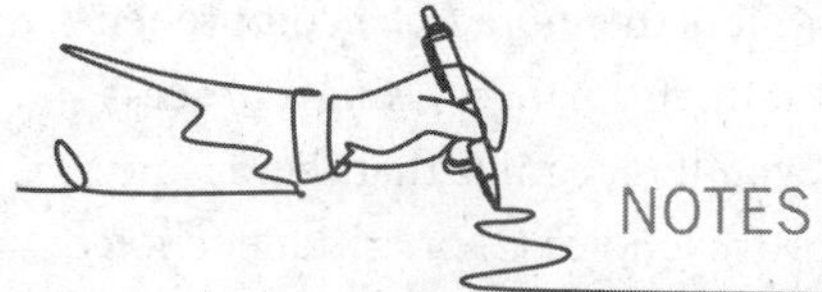
NOTES

Section 4: Quantitative Reasoning

1. C	4. A	7. D	9. D	11. 70
2. A	5. D	8. E	10. A, C, D, F, G	12. 432
3. C	6. A			

1. **The correct answer is C.** 12% of 17% of x is (0.12)(0.17)x. 34% of 6% of x is $(0.34)(0.06)x = (0.34 \times 0.5)(0.06 \times 2)x = (0.17)(0.12)x$. Therefore, the quantities are equal.

2. **The correct answer is A.** First, break down Quantity B:

$$\frac{1}{\sqrt{2}^{51}} = \frac{1}{\sqrt{2} \times \sqrt{2}^{50}} = \frac{1}{\sqrt{2} \times (2)^{25}} = \frac{1}{\sqrt{2}} \times \frac{1}{2^{25}}$$

But $\frac{1}{\sqrt{2}} < 1$, so Quantity B is less than $\frac{1}{2^{25}}$.

3. **The correct answer is C.** Suppose the cube is painted red, blue, and yellow such that each pair of opposite faces shares a color. This satisfies the requirement of no two adjacent faces sharing the same color, so three colors are sufficient. Two colors are not sufficient, since for any two adjacent faces of a cube, a third face shares edges with both. Thus, the minimum number of colors required is 3 and quantities A and B are equal.

4. **The correct answer is A.** Opposite angles formed by the intersection of two lines have equal measure. The image shows that $2x = 3y$, so $x = \frac{3}{2}y$. Thus, x is greater than y.

5. **The correct answer is D.** The information given is consistent with any relationship between the ages of Fran and Tabitha. For example, if John is 5, Beth is 6, and Tabitha is 10, then Fran could be 7, 10, or 11 (along with other possibilities).

6. **The correct answer is A.** The points on the graph clearly approximate a line with a positive slope. Choice B is incorrect since the line rises to the right instead of falling to the right. Choice C is incorrect because there is, in fact, a clear pattern visible in the graph. Choices D and E are incorrect since the points approximately form a line, not another shape.

7. **The correct answer is D.** The graph shows a consistent increase in grade as the number of hours studied increases. Therefore, the estimated grade for studying 3 hours should be between the values associated with 2.5 and 4 hours. The only answer choice that satisfies this condition is 90.

8. **The correct answer is E.** Each of the dimensions increases by 4 feet, since the expansion applies on all sides. The new dimensions are 16 feet by 20 feet, so the area is (16)(20) = 320 square feet. Choice A is incorrect because 192 square feet is the area of the original garden, not the expanded one. Choices B and D are the result of incorrectly increasing only one of the dimensions, not both. Choice C is the result of incorrectly increasing each dimension by 2 instead of 4.

9. **The correct answer is D.** The retail price is (1.15)(600) = 690, and the discount is (0.10)(690) = 69, so it sells for 690 – 69 = 621. This is $\frac{621}{600} = 1.035 = 103.5\%$ of the wholesale price.

10. **The correct answers are A, C, D, F, and G.** Each term is one less than twice the previous term, so the sequence is 2, 3, 5, 9, 17, 33, 65, 129. It always increases, so all the other answers will never be part of the sequence.

11. **The correct answer is 70.** The large triangle is isosceles since two of its sides are equal. Therefore, angle ABE is equal to angle DCE, so it is 70°. Since $\overline{AB}$ and $\overline{DE}$ are parallel, their corresponding angles are congruent, so $x = 70$.

12. **The correct answer is 432.** Divide 5,400 by 12.50 to get 432.

Section 5: Quantitative Reasoning

1. D	4. B	7. D	10. E	13. A, F
2. A	5. C	8. C	11. C	14. 42
3. B	6. B	9. E	12. C, D	15. 6

1. **The correct answer is D.** The information given tells us only that both quantities are positive, since $f < g$ and $d < e$. It does not give any indication of how far apart these are from each other though, so there is no way to know which difference is greater, or if they are equal.

2. **The correct answer is A.** The angles in a quadrilateral always add up to 360°. Since the quadrilateral is convex, angle D measures less than 180°, so the sum of the degree values of A, B, and C is greater than 360 – 180 = 180. Therefore, the average degree value of angles A, B, and C is greater than $\frac{180}{3} = 60$.

3. **The correct answer is B.** The cost of hiring consultant A for a 15-hour project would be $300 + 15($75) = $1,425. The cost of hiring consultant B for the same amount of time would be $200 + 15($85) = $1,475. The estimated cost of hiring consultant B is greater.

4. **The correct answer is B.** Circumference is given by $2\pi r$, so the radius of the circle is 4, and its area is $\pi r^2 = 16\pi \approx 50.24$. If the perimeter of the square is 30, its side length is 7.5, so its area is $7.5^2 = 56.25$.

5. **The correct answer is C.** The chance of snow on Tuesday, given that there was no snow on Monday, is 10%, or 0.1. Since the probability of no snow on Monday is 1 – 0.2 = 0.8, the probability that it snows only on Tuesday is (0.8)(0.1) = 0.08.

   If it snows on Monday, then the chance of snow on Tuesday is 40%, or 0.4. The probability that it snows on both days is therefore (0.2)(0.4) = 0.08. The two probabilities are equal.

6. **The correct answer is B.** Payal completes $\frac{1}{12}$ of the driveway per minute, and Shreya completes $\frac{1}{18}$ of the driveway per minute. Together, then, they complete $\frac{1}{12}+\frac{1}{18}=\frac{5}{36}$ of the driveway per minute. The entire driveway will therefore take $\frac{36}{5} = 7.2$ minutes, rounded to 7.

7. **The correct answer is D.**

$$\frac{12\text{ miles}}{1\text{ hour}} \times \frac{5{,}280\text{ feet}}{1\text{ mile}} \times \frac{1\text{ hour}}{60\text{ seconds}} \times \frac{1\text{ minute}}{60\text{ seconds}} = \frac{63{,}360}{3{,}600} = \frac{17.6\text{ feet}}{1\text{ second}}$$

8. **The correct answer is C.** The angles in a triangle add up to 180, so:

$$2x + 2x + (x + 5) = 180$$

   Solving the equation gives you $x = 35$.

9. **The correct answer is E.** Since two of the angles are equal, the triangle is isosceles, and therefore $y^2 = y + 6$, or $y^2 - y - 6 = 0$. This factors as $(y - 3)(y + 2) = 0$, so $y = 3$ or -2. Choosing $y = 3$ results in side lengths of 6, and choosing $y = -2$ results in a triangle with side lengths of 4. Choice A is incorrect since that would make the side length of the triangle 0, which is impossible. Choice B is the result of incorrectly setting $y^2 = y$ but forgetting the 6. Choice C is the result of solving $y^2 + y + 6 = 0$ instead of $y^2 - y - 6 = 0$. Choice D is incorrect because while answer 3 is correct, another correct answer was left out.

10. **The correct answer is E.** A and B both have a sum of 40, so both have a mean of 10. The numbers in B are farther away from the mean of 10 compared to the numbers in A, so B has a larger standard deviation.

11. **The correct answer is C.** After the first month, the value is:

$$4{,}500\left(1+\frac{0.035}{12}\right) = 4{,}513.13$$

After the second month, it is

$$4{,}513.13\left(1+\frac{0.035}{12}\right)=4{,}526.29$$

12. **The correct answers are C and D.** The product of an even number with any other number is even. The sum or difference of an even and an odd number is odd, so choices A and B are incorrect. The product of an odd number with an odd number is odd, so choice E is incorrect.

13. **The correct answers are A and F.** $2 - 3 = -1$ and $2 - (-1) = 3$, so the sequence will always alternate between 3 and -1. These are the only numbers that will ever appear.

14. **The correct answer is 42.** $x = 2a = 2(3b) = 2(3(7y)) = 42y$. But $x = ky$, so $42y = ky$, and $k = 42$.

15. **The correct answer is 6.** The surface area of a cube with side length x is $6x^2$, and the volume is x^3. Therefore, we need to solve $6x^2 = x^3$. This is equivalent to $6x^2 - x^3 = 0$, which factors as $x^2(6 - x) = 0$, so $x = 0$ or $x = 6$. A cube cannot have sides of length 0, so the answer is 6.

CHAPTER

Practice Test 3

PRACTICE TEST 3

OVERVIEW

DIRECTIONS FOR PRACTICE TEST 3

Practice Test 3 contains the five scored sections you will encounter on the actual GRE General Test.

On pages 387–393, we've provided sheets for planning and composing your Analytical Writing response, followed by an answer sheet for filling in your responses in the Verbal Reasoning and Quantitative Reasoning sections. Before you begin the test, remove or photocopy these pages.

As on the actual GRE General Test, each test section has its own time allocation. During that time period you may work on only that section. Be sure to use a timer for each section so you can accurately simulate the test-day experience. Total testing time is approximately 1 hour and 58 minutes.

Following Section 5, you will be provided tools to help you assess your response to the Analytical Writing task. An answer key and a comprehensive explanation follow for each test question in the Verbal Reasoning and Quantitative Reasoning sections.

Answer sheets for this test can be found on pages 387–393.

SECTION 1: ANALYTICAL WRITING

30 minutes

The time for this Analyze an Issue task is 30 minutes. You must plan and draft a response that evaluates the issue given below. If you do not respond to the specific issue, your score will be zero. Your response must be based on the accompanying instructions, and you must provide evidence for your position. You may use support from reading, experience, observations, and/or coursework.

Claim: Universities should require every student to take a variety of courses outside the student's major field of study.

Reason: Acquiring knowledge of various academic disciplines is the best way to become truly educated.

*Write a response in which you discuss the extent to which you agree or disagree with the claim and the reason on which the claim is based.**

STOP!

IF YOU FINISH BEFORE THE TIME IS UP, YOU MAY CHECK YOUR WORK IN THIS SECTION ONLY.

* All of the Analytical Writing prompts in the practice tests of this book come directly from the list of prompts for the GRE, which can be found at https://www.ets.org/pdfs/gre/issue-pool.pdf.

DIRECTIONS FOR THE VERBAL REASONING AND QUANTITATIVE REASONING SECTIONS

On test day, you will find information here about the question formats for the Verbal Reasoning and Quantitative Reasoning sections as well as information about how to use the software program. You will also receive important information about how these two sections are scored. Every correct answer earns a point, but points are not subtracted for incorrect answers, so it is better to guess if you aren't sure of an answer than to leave a question unanswered.

All multiple-choice questions will have answer options preceded by either blank ovals or blank squares, depending on the question type.

For your convenience in answering questions and checking answers in this paper-based practice test, answer choices are shown as lettered options. This notation makes it easier to check your answers against the answer keys and explanations.

NOTES

SECTION 2: VERBAL REASONING

18 minutes—12 questions

For each question, follow the specific directions and choose the best answer.

For Questions 1 and 2, choose one answer for each blank. Select from the appropriate column for each blank. Choose the answer that best completes the sense of the text.

1. The victory proved to be ________, given that immediately afterward, the team was disqualified for having a player test positive for a banned substance.

A. ephemeral
B. procedural
C. epidural
D. epochal
E. unequivocal

2. Hamlet's "to be or not to be" (i) ________ in Act 1 is one of the most famous scenes in all of theatre history. In it, the (ii) ________ Prince of Denmark asks himself whether he should continue on with life, despite the pain and agony. Gone is the playful, (iii) ________ prince he had been before his father's death.

Blank (i)	Blank (ii)	Blank (iii)
A. dialogue	D. sanguineous	G. candid
B. soliloquy	E. morose	H. fretful
C. manifesto	F. foolhardy	I. mirthful

For Questions 3–9, choose only one answer choice unless otherwise indicated.

Questions 3 and 4 are based on the following passage.

In 1963, when anthropologists first stumbled upon the archaeological site in Turkey now known as Göbekli Tepe, they initially thought the limestone slabs protruding from the ground were grave markers. Decades passed with the assumption that the site was merely a cemetery abandoned sometime during the medieval period. Then, in 1994, a German archaeologist named Klaus Schmidt encountered the so-called cemetery and began examining it more closely, suspecting there might be more to it. To say he was correct is a significant understatement.

What Schmidt ultimately revealed is Göbekli Tepe, an ancient gathering space, potentially of religious significance, widely acknowledged as the oldest human monument in the world. The discoveries made and ongoing at Göbekli Tepe, which means "belly hill" in Turkish, are evidence of the earliest manifestations of human civilization. The site dates back at least 11,000 years, making it millennia older than other human monuments like Stonehenge and the Great Pyramid of Giza.

Perhaps the most astonishing aspect of the human-like stone figures and other carvings erected at Göbekli Tepe is that they predate the invention of pottery and metal tools. This raises questions about how prehistoric humans were able to produce such a multitude of artifacts using only stone tools. Additionally, findings at the site shed light on how early hunter-gatherers might have begun to settle more permanently around identifiable landmarks.

The discovery of animal bones from wild species rather than domesticated animals at the Göbekli Tepe site provides concrete evidence that the monument likely resulted from collaboration among nomadic peoples. This conclusion is supported by the substantial labor required to construct a monument of this scale during the Neolithic era and the absence of evidence for plant or animal domestication at the site. Schmidt suggests that the site may have served as a sacred meeting place for widely dispersed nomadic tribes, possibly used for feasts and other gatherings. It's even conceivable that this site was the first of its kind ever created.

For Questions 3 and 4, consider each answer individually and choose all choices that apply.

3. Which of the following pieces of evidence offered by the author support(s) the claim that Göbekli Tepe was created and used by nomadic peoples?

   A. The site was initially assumed to be a sacred place for burying the dead.

   B. Archaeologists have evidence that the site was created using only stone tools.

   C. The site contains an abundance of archaeological evidence from wild animal species.

4. Select the sentence in the passage that does NOT add to the support for the main idea of the passage.

   A. "Decades passed with the assumption that the site was merely a cemetery abandoned sometime during the medieval period." (lines 3–4)

   B. "What Schmidt ultimately revealed is Göbekli Tepe, an ancient gathering space, potentially of religious significance, widely acknowledged as the oldest human monument in the world." (lines 7–8)

   C. "Perhaps the most astonishing aspect of the human-like stone figures and other carvings erected at Göbekli Tepe is that they predate the invention of pottery and metal tools." (lines 12–13)

Questions 5–7 are based on the following passage.

But it is in the new monarchy that difficulties really exist. Firstly, if it is not entirely new, but a member as it were of a mixed state, its disorders spring at first from a natural difficulty which exists in all new dominions, because men change masters willingly, hoping to better themselves; and this belief makes them take arms against their rulers, in which they are deceived, as experience shows them that they have gone from bad to worse. This is the result of another very natural cause, which is the necessary harm inflicted on those over whom the prince obtains dominion, both by his soldiers and by an infinite number of other injuries unavoidably caused by his occupation.

Thus you find enemies in all those whom you have injured by occupying that dominion, and you cannot maintain the friendship of those who have helped you to obtain this possession, as you will not be able to fulfil their expectations, nor can you use strong measures with them, being under an obligation to them; for which reason, however strong your armies may be, you will always need the favour of the inhabitants to take possession of a province. It was from these causes that Louis XII of France, though able to occupy Milan without trouble, immediately lost it, and the forces of Ludovico alone were sufficient to take it from him the first time, for the inhabitants who had willingly opened their gates to him, finding themselves deluded in the hopes they had cherished and not obtaining those benefits that they had anticipated, could not bear the vexatious rule of their new prince.

—Excerpt from *The Prince* by Niccolo Machiavelli

5. Select the sentence that restates the premise of the author's argument.

   A. A prince can trust only his subjects after he takes over.

   B. A new ruler has very little support that he can rely upon.

   C. Supportive friends are the key to maintaining power.

   D. Inhabitants rarely change their minds about the leader they want.

   E. Once a ruler is in power, it is easy to maintain that role.

6. "Vexatious" (line 16) most nearly means

   A. well-liked.

   B. bothersome.

   C. frightening.

   D. lengthy.

   E. cruel.

7. The passage implies that a new prince's rule is

   A. natural.

   B. inherited.

   C. impossible.

   D. unstable.

   E. unhappy.

Questions 8 and 9 are based on the following passage.

Neither the purpose nor the effect of punishment has ever been definitely agreed upon, even by its most strenuous advocates. So long as punishment persists it will be a subject of discussion and dispute. No doubt the idea of punishment originated in the feeling of resentment and hatred and vengeance that, to some extent at least, is incident to life. The dog is hit with a stick and turns and bites the stick. Animals repel attack and fight their enemies to death. The primitive man vented his hatred and vengeance on things animate and inanimate. In the tribes no injury was satisfied until some member of the offending tribe was killed. In more recent times family feuds have followed down the generations and were not forgotten until the last member of a family was destroyed. Biologically, anger and hatred follow fear and injury, and punishment follows these in turn. Individuals, communities and whole peoples hate and swear vengeance for an injury, real or fancied. Punishments, even to the extent of death, are inflicted where there can be no possible object except revenge. Whether the victim is weak or strong, old or young, sane or insane, makes no difference; men and societies react to injury exactly as animals react.

—Excerpt from *Crime: Its Cause and Treatment* by Clarence Darrow

For Question 8, consider each answer individually and select all choices that apply.

8. What does the author's comparison of humans and animals suggest?

   A. Punishment cannot overcome biological urges.

   B. Punishment is the only thing that separates humans and animals.

   C. Vengeance is a natural reaction to injury.

9. "Incident" (line 4) most nearly means

   A. event.

   B. confrontation.

   C. unusual.

   D. natural.

   E. dependent.

For Questions 10 and 11, choose the two answers that best fit the meaning of the sentence as a whole and result in two completed sentences that are alike in meaning.

10. The Peace of Westphalia is the collective name for a series of ________ that ended the Thirty Years' War and the Eighty Years' War.

    A. settling

    B. disputes

    C. treaties

    D. accords

    E. amity

    F. retaliations

11. As part of the tax audit, Mark is required to submit all documents ________ to his income for the past six years.

    A. pertaining

    B. concerning

    C. relating

    D. inapplicable

    E. converted

    F. indebted

Question 12 is based on the following passage.

Modern chivalry, though evolved from its medieval origins, continues to resonate in contemporary society through its emphasis on honor, respect, and kindness. In today's context, chivalry is not confined to knights in shining armor, but rather manifests in everyday interactions, reflecting a code of conduct that promotes courtesy, empathy, and gallantry. It encompasses gestures such as holding the door open for others, offering a seat to someone in need, or treating individuals with dignity and compassion regardless of gender or social status. Furthermore, modern chivalry extends beyond acts of politeness to encompass advocacy for gender equality, consent, and inclusivity. It involves standing up against injustice and discrimination. Thus, modern-day chivalry represents a contemporary interpretation of traditional values, emphasizing the importance of decency, empathy, and integrity in fostering a more respectful and equitable society.

12. It can be inferred from the passage that the author believes that

A. modern chivalry does not exist.

B. medieval chivalry was more romantic than modern chivalry.

C. modern chivalry eschews traditional values.

D. chivalry has no context in today's society.

E. the scope of medieval chivalry was limited.

STOP!

IF YOU FINISH BEFORE THE TIME IS UP, YOU MAY CHECK YOUR WORK IN THIS SECTION ONLY.

SECTION 3: VERBAL REASONING

23 minutes—15 questions

For each question, follow the specific directions and choose the best answer.

For Questions 1–3, choose one answer for each blank. Select from the appropriate column for each blank. Choose the answer that best completes the sense of the text.

1. Many blamed voter _________ for the low turnout in last November's special election to fill the departing senator's seat.

A. indignation
B. apathy
C. enthusiasm
D. puritanism
E. attendance

2. A mysterious maple syrup smell that would occasionally (i) _________ over New York City was determined to be caused by a New Jersey fragrance processing plant. This knowledge (ii) _________ nervous New Yorkers, who worried it might be a chemical attack.

Blank (i)	Blank (ii)
A. migratory	D. assaulted
B. waft	E. assuaged
C. outbreak	F. asserted

3. During the (i) _________ at the funeral, the pastor spoke at length about the deceased, waxing (ii) _________ about her life although they had never met and he had acquired only _________ information about her.

Blank (i)	Blank (ii)	Blank (iii)
A. trilogy	D. loquacious	G. surreptitious
B. travelogue	E. gregarious	H. secondhand
C. eulogy	F. mendacious	I. disparaging

For Questions 4–15, choose only one answer choice unless otherwise indicated.

Questions 4–6 are based on the following passage.

Often enough, staying in a hotel in a foreign town, I have wished to sally forth and to dine or breakfast at the typical restaurant of the place, should there be one. Almost invariably I have found great difficulty in obtaining any information regarding any such restaurant. The proprietor of the caravanserai at which one is staying may admit vaguely that there are eating-houses in the town, but asks why one should be anxious to seek for second-class establishments when the best restaurant in the country is to be found under his roof. The hall-porter has even less scruples, and stigmatizes every feeding-place outside the hotel as a den of thieves, where the stranger foolishly venturing is certain to be poisoned and then robbed. This book is an attempt to help the man who finds himself in such a position. His guide-book may possibly give him the names of the restaurants, but it does no more. My co-author and myself attempt to give him some details—what his surroundings will be, what dishes are the specialties of the house, what wine a wise man will order, and what bill he is likely to be asked to pay.

—Excerpt from *The Gourmet's Guide to Europe* by Algernon Bastard and Lieutenant Colonel Newnham-Davis

4. It can be inferred from the passage that the author

   A. has had frustrating dining experiences while traveling to foreign places.

   B. is the proprietor of a caravanserai and wants to attract travelers.

   C. is very picky when it comes to choosing restaurants when traveling.

   D. does not trust the opinions of hall-porters who recommend restaurants.

   E. has been both poisoned and robbed while traveling to foreign places.

5. Which of the following is likely to be the most reliable source for information, according to the author?

   A. Hotel staff

   B. Word-of-mouth recommendations

   C. Crime reports

   D. An impartial guidebook

   E. The author's travel memoir

6. What is the primary purpose of the phrase "wise man" in line 10?

   A. It insinuates the reader is unintelligent.

   B. It insults the hotel proprietor.

   C. It flatters the reader.

   D. It emphasizes the author's feeling of inferiority.

   E. It stigmatizes ordering wine.

Questions 7–9 are based on the following passage.

The distinctive features of Millet's art are so marked that the most inexperienced observer easily identifies his work. As a painter of rustic subjects, he is unlike any other artists who have entered the same field, even those who have taken his own themes. We get at the heart of the matter when we say that Millet derived his art directly from nature. "If I could only do what I like," he said, "I would paint nothing that was not the result of an impression directly received from nature, whether in landscape or in figure." His pictures are convincing evidence that he acted upon this theory. They have a peculiar quality of genuineness beside which all other rustic art seems forced and artificial.

The human side of life touched him most deeply, and in many of his earlier pictures, landscape was secondary. Gradually he grew into the larger conception of a perfect harmony between man and his environment. Henceforth landscape ceased to be a mere setting or background in a figure picture, and became an organic part of the composition. As a critic once wrote of the *Shepherdess*, "the earth and sky, the scene and the actors, all answer one another, all hold together, belong together." The description applies equally well to many other pictures and particularly to the *Angelus*, the *Sower*, and the *Gleaners*. In all these, landscape and figure are interdependent, fitting together in a perfect unity.

As a painter of landscapes, Millet mastered a wide range of the effects of changing light during different hours of the day. The mists of early morning in *Filling the Water-Bottles*; the glare of noonday in the *Gleaners*; the sunset glow in the *Angelus* and the *Shepherdess*; the sombre twilight of the *Sower*; and the glimmering lamplight of the *Woman Sewing*, each found perfect interpretation. Though showing himself capable of representing powerfully the more violent aspects of nature, he preferred as a rule the normal and quiet.

—Excerpt from *John Francois Millet* by Estelle M. Hurll

7. All the following are stated or implied in the passage EXCEPT that Millet

   A. was primarily a landscape painter.
   B. had an affinity for nature.
   C. prioritized human subjects over nature.
   D. captured the rustic charm of his subjects.
   E. valued authenticity in his art.

8. Which of the following statements is supported by the passage?

   A. Human subjects are insignificant compared to landscapes.
   B. Rustic art is boring and outdated.
   C. Even experienced critics underestimate Millet.
   D. Distinctive style can sometimes hide subtle touches.
   E. Millet's landscape work was stronger than his portraits.

9. "Impression" (line 5) most nearly means a(n)

   A. difference.

   B. feeling.

   C. imitation.

   D. indentation.

   E. premonition.

Questions 10 and 11 are based on the following passage.

Nwadike: Our research shows that implementing artificial intelligence (AI) in medical settings revolutionizes patient care. For one, AI algorithms analyze vast amounts of medical data with unprecedented speed and accuracy, enabling early disease detection and personalized treatment plans. Additionally, AI-powered diagnostic tools enhance clinical decision-making, leading to improved patient outcomes and reduced healthcare costs. With all this in mind, it's time that industry leaders begin investing in a workable AI infrastructure.

Rocha: While that may be true, it concerns me that the study may have overlooked the importance of patient privacy. Issues concerning data security loom large in the medical industry. The collection and analysis of sensitive medical information raises ethical dilemmas, including potential breaches of confidentiality and misuse of patient data for profit.

For Question 10, consider each answer individually and select <u>all</u> choices that apply.

10. Which of the following strategies does Nwadike use to relay their argument?

    A. Relaying the results of recent studies regarding the efficacy of using AI in medical settings

    B. Elucidating the benefits of and necessity for investing in AI infrastructure

    C. Alleviating concerns that AI poses ethical dilemmas regarding patient privacy

11. Rocha responds to Nwadike's argument by doing which of the following?

    A. Highlighting ethical concerns that may result from the use of AI in medical settings

    B. Proposing ideas for increased research into alternative medical technologies

    C. Advocating for the use of stored patient data to detect diagnostic trends across demographic groups

    D. Disproving the effectiveness of AI algorithms in medical diagnosis

    E. Critiquing the potential impact of AI on the role of healthcare professionals

For Questions 12–14, choose the two answers that best fit the meaning of the sentence as a whole and result in two completed sentences that are alike in meaning.

12. After the actress's foul-mouthed ________ against her assistant went viral, she was fired from her TV show.

A. confab

B. tirade

C. commendation

D. harangue

E. agitate

F. tribute

13. The late New York Yankees catcher Yogi Berra is famous for his slightly off-center ________ like, "If you come to a fork in the road, take it!"

A. aphids

B. apocrypha

C. maxims

D. dictations

E. dictums

F. anecdotes

14. After keeping passengers stuck on the tarmac for more than two hours, the airline attempted to ________ passengers with an extra round of free snacks.

A. mollify

B. mortify

C. prevaricate

D. placate

E. fabricate

F. confound

Question 15 is based on the following passage.

Government implies the power of making laws. It is essential to the idea of a law, that it be attended with a sanction; or, in other words, a penalty or punishment for disobedience. If there be no penalty annexed to disobedience, the resolutions or commands which pretend to be laws will, in fact, amount to nothing more than advice or recommendation. This penalty, whatever it may be, can only be inflicted in two ways: by the agency of the courts and ministers of justice, or by military force; by the coercion of the magistracy, or by the coercion of arms. The first kind can evidently apply only to men; the last kind must of necessity, be employed against bodies politic, or communities, or States. It is evident that there is no process of a court by which the observance of the laws can, in the last resort, be enforced. Sentences may be denounced against them for violations of their duty; but these sentences can only be carried into execution by the sword. In an association where the general authority is confined to the collective bodies of the communities, that compose it, every breach of the laws must involve a state of war; and military execution must become the only instrument of civil obedience. Such a state of things can certainly not deserve the name of government, nor would any prudent man choose to commit his happiness to it.

—Excerpt from *Federalist Paper #15* by Alexander Hamilton

For Question 15, consider each answer individually and select <u>all</u> choices that apply.

15. Which statement(s) summarize(s) an aspect of Hamilton's stances on laws?

A. A law is not a law unless it is connected to a reasonable consequence for failure to heed it.

B. It is not possible to create a law that can justly be applied to an entire population.

C. Punishments can only be exacted through force, or the agency of a court designated for the sanctioning of laws.

STOP!

IF YOU FINISH BEFORE THE TIME IS UP, YOU MAY CHECK YOUR WORK IN THIS SECTION ONLY.

SECTION 4: QUANTITATIVE REASONING

21 minutes—12 questions

For each question, follow the specific directions and choose the best answer.

The test maker provides the following information that applies to all questions in the Quantitative Reasoning section of the GRE General Test:

- All numbers used are real numbers.
- All figures are assumed to lie in a plane unless otherwise indicated.
- Geometric figures, such as lines, circles, triangles, and quadrilaterals, *are not necessarily* drawn to scale. That is, you should *not* assume that quantities such as lengths and angle measures are as they appear in a figure. You should assume, however, that lines shown as straight are actually straight, points on a line are in the order shown, and more generally, all geometric objects are in the relative positions shown. For questions with geometric figures, you should base your answers on geometric reasoning, not on estimating or comparing quantities by sight or by measurement.
- Coordinate systems, such as *xy*-planes and number lines, *are* drawn to scale. Therefore, you can read, estimate, or compare quantities in such figures by sight or by measurement.
- Graphical data presentations, such as bar graphs, circle graphs, and line graphs, *are* drawn to scale. Therefore, you can read, estimate, or compare data values by sight or by measurement.

For Questions 1–5, compare Quantity A and Quantity B. Some questions will have additional information above the two quantities to use in determining your answer.

1. a and b are integers.
$a < 0$

Quantity A	Quantity B
a^b	a^{2b}

A. Quantity A is greater.
B. Quantity B is greater.
C. The two quantities are equal.
D. The relationship cannot be determined from the information given.

2. Bank A pays 3% simple annual interest. Bank B pays 4% simple annual interest.

Quantity A	Quantity B
\$100 invested at Bank A for 4 years	\$100 invested at Bank B for 3 years

A. Quantity A is greater.
B. Quantity B is greater.
C. The two quantities are equal.
D. The relationship cannot be determined from the information given.

3. x, y, and z are consecutive integers.

Quantity A	Quantity B
xz	y^2

A. Quantity A is greater.
B. Quantity B is greater.
C. The two quantities are equal.
D. The relationship cannot be determined from the information given.

4.

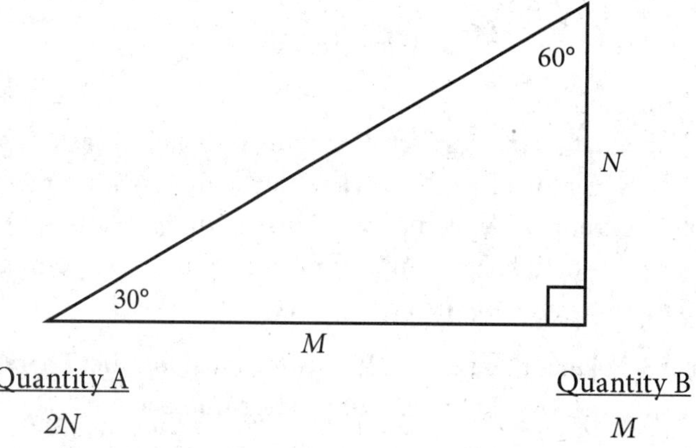

Quantity A	Quantity B
$2N$	M

A. Quantity A is greater.
B. Quantity B is greater.
C. The two quantities are equal.
D. The relationship cannot be determined from the information given.

5. Team A has 12 wins and has won 60% of its games.
Team B has 14 wins and has lost 30% of its games.

Quantity A	Quantity B
The number of games played by Team A	The number of games played by Team B

A. Quantity A is greater.
B. Quantity B is greater.
C. The two quantities are equal.
D. The relationship cannot be determined from the information given.

Questions 6–12 have several formats. Unless the directions state otherwise, choose one answer choice. For the Numeric Entry questions, follow the instructions below.

Numeric Entry Questions

The following items are the same for both the actual GRE General Test and the test presented in this book. However, the actual GRE General Test will have additional information about entering answers in decimal and fraction boxes on the computer screen. To take the test in this book, enter your answers in boxes or answer grids.

- Your answer may be an integer, a decimal, or a fraction, and it may be negative.
- If a question asks for a fraction, there will be two boxes. One box will be for the numerator, and one will be for the denominator.
- Equivalent forms of the correct answer, such as 2.5 and 2.50, are all correct.
- Enter the exact answer unless the question asks you to round your answers.

6. The distance from one corner of a square plot of land to its center is $10\sqrt{2}$ meters. What is the perimeter of the plot of land, in meters?

   A. 20
   B. 40
   C. 80
   D. 100
   E. 400

7. A car rental company charges $14 per day plus $0.25 per mile. Another company charges $40 per day but does not have an additional mileage charge. If you are renting a car for 6 days, how many miles would you have to drive for the costs of renting from the two companies to be equal?

   A. 39
   B. 104
   C. 208
   D. 624
   E. 904

8. Line A passes through the points (3, 7) and (–2, 1). Line B is perpendicular to line A and passes through the origin. Which of the following equations represents line B?

A. $y=-\frac{5}{6}x$

B. $y=-\frac{6}{5}x$

C. $y=\frac{6}{5}x$

D. $y=\frac{5}{6}x$

E. $y=\frac{5}{6}x+1$

Questions 9 and 10 refer to the table below.

x	$f(x)$	$g(x)$
–1	–4	–5
0	1	–1
1	8	0
2	3	2
3	2	1

9. Evaluate $f(g(0))$.

A. –5

B. –4

C. –1

D. 0

E. 8

10. What is the average rate of change of $g(x)$ between $x=-1$ and $x=3$?

A. –5

B. $-\frac{3}{2}$

C. 1

D. $\frac{3}{2}$

E. 6

For Question 11, choose all that apply.

11. Which of the following values are NOT in the domain of $h(x)=\frac{\sqrt{x+5}}{x-1}$?

A. –7

B. –5

C. –3

D. –1

E. 1

F. 3

G. 5

H. 7

For Question 12, enter your answer in the box.

12. The height of a ball thrown upwards from a height of 6 feet at a speed of 96 feet per second is given by the function $h(t) = -16t^2 + 96t + 6$, where t is the time in seconds since the ball was thrown and h is its height in feet. What is the maximum height reached by the ball, in feet?

[ ] feet

STOP!

IF YOU FINISH BEFORE THE TIME IS UP, YOU MAY CHECK YOUR WORK IN THIS SECTION ONLY.

SECTION 5: QUANTITATIVE REASONING

26 minutes—15 questions

For each question, follow the specific directions and choose the best answer.

The test maker provides the following information that applies to all questions in the Quantitative Reasoning section of the GRE General Test:

- All numbers used are real numbers.
- All figures are assumed to lie in a plane unless otherwise indicated.
- Geometric figures, such as lines, circles, triangles, and quadrilaterals, *are not necessarily* drawn to scale. That is, you should *not* assume that quantities such as lengths and angle measures are as they appear in a figure. You should assume, however, that lines shown as straight are actually straight, points on a line are in the order shown, and more generally, all geometric objects are in the relative positions shown. For questions with geometric figures, you should base your answers on geometric reasoning, not on estimating or comparing quantities by sight or by measurement.
- Coordinate systems, such as *xy*-planes and number lines, *are* drawn to scale. Therefore, you can read, estimate, or compare quantities in such figures by sight or by measurement.
- Graphical data presentations, such as bar graphs, circle graphs, and line graphs, *are* drawn to scale. Therefore, you can read, estimate, or compare data values by sight or by measurement.

For Questions 1–7, compare Quantity A and Quantity B. Some questions will have additional information above the two quantities to use in determining your answer.

1.

Quantity A	Quantity B
$\frac{1}{2^{-3}}$	$\frac{1}{3^{-2}}$

A. Quantity A is greater.

B. Quantity B is greater.

C. The two quantities are equal.

D. The relationship cannot be determined from the information given.

2.

$S = \{19, 21, 23, 25, 27\}$

Quantity A	Quantity B
The mean of the numbers in S	The median of the numbers in S

A. Quantity A is greater.

B. Quantity B is greater.

C. The two quantities are equal.

D. The relationship cannot be determined from the information given.

3. $x > 20$

Quantity A	Quantity B
$\sqrt[5]{32}$	$\sqrt[4]{x}$

A. Quantity A is greater.
B. Quantity B is greater.
C. The two quantities are equal.
D. The relationship cannot be determined from the information given.

4. At a music school, 40% of students play piano, 30% play guitar, and 25% play violin.

Quantity A	Quantity B
The probability that a randomly chosen student does not play piano	The probability that at least one of two randomly chosen students plays piano

A. Quantity A is greater.
B. Quantity B is greater.
C. The two quantities are equal.
D. The relationship cannot be determined from the information given.

5. A circle has a radius of 12.

Quantity A	Quantity B
The area of a 60° sector of the circle	The perimeter of the circle

A. Quantity A is greater.
B. Quantity B is greater.
C. The two quantities are equal.
D. The relationship cannot be determined from the information given.

6. A rectangle has a perimeter of 20.

Quantity A	Quantity B
The area of the rectangle	20

A. Quantity A is greater.
B. Quantity B is greater.
C. The two quantities are equal.
D. The relationship cannot be determined from the information given.

7. Quantity A: $4^{(3^2)}$ Quantity B: $(4^3)^2$

A. Quantity A is greater.

B. Quantity B is greater.

C. The two quantities are equal.

D. The relationship cannot be determined from the information given.

Questions 8–15 have several formats. Unless the directions state otherwise, choose one answer choice. For the Numeric Entry questions, follow the instructions below.

Numeric Entry Questions

The following items are the same for both the actual GRE General Test and the test presented in this book. However, the actual GRE General Test will have additional information about entering answers in decimal and fraction boxes on the computer screen. To take the test in this book, enter your answers in boxes or answer grids.

- Your answer may be an integer, a decimal, or a fraction, and it may be negative.
- If a question asks for a fraction, there will be two boxes. One box will be for the numerator, and one will be for the denominator.
- Equivalent forms of the correct answer, such as 2.5 and 2.50, are all correct.
- Enter the exact answer unless the question asks you to round your answers.

8. Starting from her house, Kendra walks 3 miles north, 6 miles east, 1 mile south, and 1 mile west. How far from her house is she?

A. 5.39 miles

B. 6.71 miles

C. 7.00 miles

D. 8.06 miles

E. 29.00 miles

9. Among the 450 students in a high school senior class, 150 take AP Calculus, 78 take AP Chemistry, and 49 take both. How many students do not take either AP Calculus or AP Chemistry?

A. 130

B. 173

C. 179

D. 222

E. 271

Questions 10 and 11 refer to the chart below.

Cars Counted in a Large Parking Lot

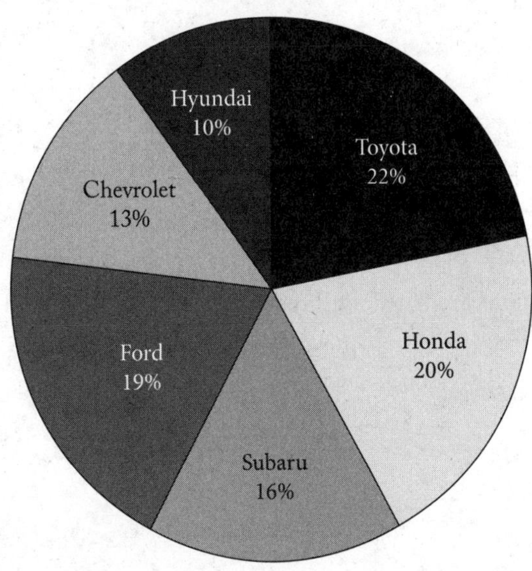

10. If there were 600 cars in the parking lot, how many Hyundai and Toyota cars were there?

A. 60

B. 132

C. 192

D. 408

E. 600

11. What is the ratio of Hyundai cars to Honda cars?

A. $\frac{1}{10}$

B. $\frac{1}{5}$

C. $\frac{5}{11}$

D. $\frac{1}{2}$

E. $\frac{2}{1}$

For Questions 12 and 13, choose all that apply.

12. If $x^2(x-5)^2 = 36$ and $x^3 > 0$, which of the following could be the value of x?

    A. −6

    B. −1

    C. 1

    D. 2

    E. 3

    F. 6

13. Which of the following equations are true for all real-number values of x and y?

    A. $x + y = y + x$

    B. $x - 2y = y - 2x$

    C. $xy + x + 1 = (x + 1)(y + 1) - y$

    D. $\sqrt{xy} = \sqrt{x}\sqrt{y}$

    E. $(x + y)^2 = x^2 + y^2$

For Questions 14 and 15, enter your answers in the boxes.

14. Brittany is 5 years older than Marla. When the sum of their ages is 45, Marla will be twice as old as Brittany is now. How old is Marla now?

    [ ] years old

15. Srikar can speed-read 45 pages in 25 minutes. To the nearest minute, how long will it take him to read a 98-page book?

    [ ] minutes

STOP!

IF YOU FINISH BEFORE THE TIME IS UP, YOU MAY CHECK YOUR WORK IN THIS SECTION ONLY.

ANSWER KEYS AND EXPLANATIONS

Section 1: Analytical Writing

To assist you with evaluating your writing, we have provided the following rubric, which is adapted from the official rubric used by ETS.* If you need more assistance evaluating your writing, consider the writing samples for essays at score levels 2, 4, and 6 as provided in Chapter 3.

ANALYTICAL WRITING SCORING RUBRIC SUMMARY		
Score Level	**Description**	**Characteristics of a Typical Response**
6 Outstanding	A sustained, insightful, organized, detailed analysis of well-developed, complex ideas supported by meaningful evidence and highly persuasive support. Utilizes a wide range of vocabulary and rhetorical methods while demonstrating a superior understanding of the conventions of Standard Written English. Very minor errors may be present but do not impact meaning.	• Presents a distinct and perceptive viewpoint regarding the issue as outlined in the given instructions • Expands meaningfully on the viewpoint with convincing rationales and/or compelling examples • Maintains focus, organization, and clarity while establishing meaningful connections between concepts • Seamlessly and accurately moves between concepts using a range of transitions, word choices, and sentence structures • Exhibits exceptional proficiency with the norms of Standard Written English, even if very minor errors are present
5 Strong	A thoughtful, generally organized, and focused analysis of nuanced ideas supported by sound reasoning and meaningful examples. Uses a range of rhetorical skills and conventions to demonstrate meaningful control of the conventions of Standard Written English. Minor errors may be present but do not impact meaning.	• Presents a lucid and carefully considered viewpoint regarding the issue as outlined in the given instructions • Elaborates on the viewpoint with logically coherent rationales and/or well-chosen examples • Maintains focus and exhibits general organization, establishing suitable connections between ideas • Communicates ideas clearly and effectively, employing fitting vocabulary and varying sentence structures • Exhibits proficiency with the norms of Standard Written English, though occasional minor errors may be present

(continues)

* The GRE General Test: Analytical Writing Measure Scoring," ETS, 2024, https://www.ets.org/gre/test-takers/general-test/prepare/content/analytical-writing/scoring.html.

ANALYTICAL WRITING SCORING RUBRIC SUMMARY (*CONTINUED*)		
Score Level	**Description**	**Characteristics of a Typical Response**
4 Adequate	A competent, considered analysis of meaningful ideas that ventures a main point and supports it with relevant evidence or reasoning. Ideas are organized in a satisfactory manner, clearly conveyed, and supported by adequate control of rhetorical skills and the conventions of Standard Written English. May have some minor errors that impact clarity of meaning.	• Presents a clear viewpoint regarding the issue as outlined in the given instructions • Develops the viewpoint with relevant reasoning and/or examples • Maintains adequate focus and organization • Demonstrates satisfactory command of language to articulate ideas with acceptable clarity • Exhibits general understanding of the norms of Standard Written English, albeit with occasional errors
3 Limited	A somewhat competent analysis that addresses specific required tasks and makes some effort to address main points. Rhetorical skills may be lacking or underdeveloped, and writing may be limited by weak structure, poor organization, or underdevelopment of ideas. Contains some errors that limit clarity of meaning and/or contribute to vagueness.	Exhibits **one or more** of the following concerns: • Shows vagueness or inadequacy in addressing the given instructions, presenting or developing a viewpoint, or both • Demonstrates weakness in employing relevant examples or rationales, or leans heavily on unsupported assertions • Exhibits limited focus and/or organization • Includes issues in language or sentence structure, contributing to lack of clarity • Contains either occasional major errors or frequent minor errors in grammar, usage, and/or mechanics of Standard Written English, impeding comprehension
2 Seriously Flawed	A weak analysis that does not adequately address specific required tasks and/or that is underdeveloped, disorganized, or unclear. Frequent issues with rhetorical skills and/or the conventions of Standard Written English obfuscate meaning and limit clarity. Frequent errors make it difficult to parse.	Exhibits **one or more** of the following concerns: • Exhibits a lack of clarity or serious limitation in addressing the given instructions, developing a viewpoint on the issue, or both • Offers few, if any, relevant rationales or examples to support assertions • Lacks focus and/or organization • Includes serious issues in language or sentence structure, frequently obstructing clarity or contributing to outright confusion • Contains serious errors in grammar, usage, or mechanics that frequently obscure meaning

ANALYTICAL WRITING SCORING RUBRIC SUMMARY (*CONTINUED*)		
Score Level	**Description**	**Characteristics of a Typical Response**
1 Fundamentally Deficient	A deficient analysis that contains fundamental errors and fails to communicate a meaningful main point. Content may be incomprehensible or extremely difficult to parse and/or may be irrelevant to the task at hand. Frequent and pervasive errors render the analysis incomprehensible or incoherent.	Exhibits **one or more** of the following concerns: • Demonstrates little or no evidence of grasping the given instructions or the issue at hand • Shows minimal or no evidence of the ability to craft an organized response, often appearing disorganized and/or excessively concise • Suffers from severe issues in language and sentence structure, consistently hindering comprehension • Contains widespread errors in grammar, usage, and mechanics, leading to incoherence
0	An analysis that cannot be evaluated because it does not address any aspect of the specified task. It may copy parts of the prompt in lieu of developing concepts or may be written in a foreign language or otherwise incomprehensible.	Exhibits **one or more** of the following concerns: • Demonstrates zero awareness of the given instructions or the issue at hand • Fully off topic • Merely copies the topic • Incomprehensible • Written in a foreign language • Consists only of random keystrokes or nonsensical inputs
NS	Blank essays will receive a score of NS, meaning no score.	

Section 2: Verbal Reasoning

1. A	4. A, B	7. D	10. C, D
2. B, E, I	5. B	8. A, C	11. A, C
3. C	6. B	9. D	12. E

1. **The correct answer is A.** *Ephemeral* describes something that lasts for a very short time—which fits with the rest of the sentence. *Epochal* (choice D) describes a significant or momentous period of time, and the rest of the sentence does not support the idea that the victory was momentous—just temporary. None of the other choices link the first part of the sentence with the context provided in the latter half.

2. **The correct answers are B, E, and I.** Answer Blank (i): The context suggests that Hamlet is the only one speaking, which makes *dialogue* (choice A) unlikely. A *manifesto* (choice C) can be the work of a solo person, but given that *soliloquy* means a monologue, it fits the theater context more directly.

   Answer Blank (ii): Hamlet is considering a painful choice, so *morose* (meaning sad or depressed) fits the tone best out of the options. *Sanguineous* (choice D) means "optimistic," and *foolhardy* (choice F) means "reckless," which both seem to be the opposite of Hamlet's mood.

   Answer Blank (iii): The writer is setting up a juxtaposition between what Hamlet was like before and who he is now, so *mirthful* (meaning joyful) is the best option to illustrate how much Hamlet has changed.

3. **The correct answer is C.** All three statements are true about the archeological site, but only choice C is described as evidence that the site was created and used by nomadic peoples. Specifically, the passage states that "The discovery of animal bones from wild species rather than domesticated animals at the Göbekli Tepe site provides concrete evidence that the monument likely resulted from collaboration among nomadic peoples" (lines 17–19).

4. **The correct answers are A and B.** The key to understanding this question is paying close attention to the wording. Here, you are looking for any answer that does NOT express a supporting detail for the main idea of the passage. Choice A provides historical context, but that context is not intended to support the main idea so much as introduce the topic. Choice B states the main idea of the passage—it is not itself a supporting detail. Choice C, by contrast, provides an explicit detail that helps support the main idea, so it is the only answer that can be eliminated.

5. **The correct answer is B.** The second paragraph outlines the ways in which enemies, former friends, and new subjects can't be trusted to help a new ruler maintain power. The sentence "A new ruler has very little support that he can rely upon" supports the premise of the author's argument in the first paragraph that "men change masters willingly" (line 3).

6. **The correct answer is B.** The root verb *vex* means "to bother or irritate," so *vexatious* most nearly means "bothersome." *Well-liked* (choice A) can be eliminated as it has the opposite meaning. The sentence describes how the inhabitants feel about the prince and, given that the passage talks about how fickle they can be, it is unlikely that the rule is *lengthy* (choice D). Choices C and E are unlikely given the context—the passage is more about the political issues than the personal qualities of the prince himself, and there is no information that suggests he is *frightening* or *cruel.*

7. **The correct answer is D.** The passage talks about how a prince in a new monarchy is subject to pressure and dangers on virtually all sides. You can infer that this destabilizes the role, making *unstable* the best option. The second sentence

suggests that the natural state is chaos and change, rather than willing acceptance of new leadership, so choice A can be eliminated. While the prince may feel unhappy with the challenges of his new monarchy, and the rule is difficult, the author does not discuss the prince's personal feelings (choice E) or suggest that ruling is impossible (choice C).

8. **The correct answers are A and C.** Choices A and C emphasize the writer's idea that the reactions to punishment and injury are not necessarily rational but are instinctual like an animal's. Choice B is incorrect because the author is using animals to highlight the nature of human reactions, not necessarily to judge or compare humans and animals.

9. **The correct answer is D.** Although the usual definition of the word *incident* is an occurrence, you need to make sure you're considering the context of the passage. In this instance, the author is using the word as an adjective, which eliminates both *event* (choice A) and *confrontation* (choice B). *Unusual* (choice C) means the opposite of what the author is saying (that resentment and vengeance are unavoidable in life). *Dependent* (choice E) doesn't work because resentment and vengeance do not depend on life, they exist in it.

10. **The correct answers are C and D.** *Treaties* and *accords* are synonyms that mean "peaceful agreements." *Settling* (choice A) does not make sense because the word in the blank needs to be a noun that represents a series of something such as an agreement. Choices B and F don't make sense because disputes and retaliations are typically among the causes of wars, not the solutions. *Amity* (choice E), meaning "friendly relations between nations," is incorrect because it is not a type of agreement.

11. **The correct answers are A and C.** The documents Mark is required to submit need to pertain to or relate to his income, so *pertaining* and *relating* are correct. While tax documents can concern income items, the present participle form of *concerning* (choice B) is not used with the preposition *to* and thus does not fit into the sentence. Although *inapplicable* (choice D), *converted* (choice E), and *indebted* (choice F) fit the sentence grammatically, these choices do not make sense in the context of the sentence.

12. **The correct answer is E.** It can be inferred that the author feels the scope of medieval chivalry was limited. This is because the passage begins by making the comparison between medieval and modern chivalry, describing medieval chivalry as "confined to knights in shining armor," thus pointing out its limited scope. You can also infer from the ways the author describes modern chivalry as more expansive (such as by not limiting behaviors along gender lines) that the medieval form would also have been more limited. The passage focuses on modern chivalry and how it is displayed, so Choice A is incorrect. The author did not make any other comparisons between medieval and modern chivalry beyond their scope, so choice B is incorrect. Choices C and D are incorrect because they contradict information stated or described in the paragraph.

Section 3: Verbal Reasoning

1. B	4. A	7. A	10. A, B	13. C, E
2. B, E	5. D	8. D	11. A	14. A, D
3. C, D, H	6. C	9. B	12. B, D	15. A, C

1. **The correct answer is B.** The word in the blank is a noun that describes something that would cause people to stay away from the polls, so *apathy* (meaning indifference) is the best choice. *Indignation* (choice A) and *enthusiasm* (choice C) are unlikely to cause a low turnout. *Puritanism* (choice D) could work if there were specific details given about the election, but *apathy* works better given the context of the sentence. *Attendance* (choice E) does not make sense in the sentence.

2. **The correct answers are B and E.** Answer Blank (i): All three options suggest movement, but *waft* (which means "to drift") fits the best, as it has the correct tense and the best approximate meaning given the context of the sentence. Moreover, *waft* is often used in association with smells. *Migratory* (choice A) is not a verb. *Outbreak* (choice C) is not usually used as a verb and is usually associated with diseases or medical issues.

   Answer Blank (ii): *Assuaged* means "reassured," so choice E works best with the sentence. *Assaulted* (choice D) carries an aggressive tone that does not fit with the rest of the sentence. *Asserted* (choice F) doesn't work with the sentence, as smells are not usually associated with the verb "to assert."

3. **The correct answers are C, D, and H.** Answer Blank (i): A *eulogy* is a speech given at a funeral, so that option matches the context of the sentence. A *trilogy* (choice A) is a series of three things, such as books or movies. A *travelogue* (choice B) is a story about one's travels.

   Answer Blank (ii): "Spoke at length" is the key context phrase here. *Loquacious* means "highly verbal" or "talkative," which works best with the rest of the sentence. *Gregarious* (choice E) means "sociable," which doesn't fit as well with the funeral setting. *Mendacious* (choice F) means "dishonest," and there is no information given that suggests the pastor was lying.

   Answer Blank (iii): Knowing that the pastor was unacquainted with the deceased provides the clue that any information he acquired about her could very well be from secondhand (choice H) sources. Given that the information was being used in a eulogy, it is unlikely to have been either *surreptitious* (choice G), meaning "secret," or *disparaging* (choice I), meaning "slanderous."

4. **The correct answer is A.** This question asks you to identify the author's perspective on the events described in the passage. The author uses humorous examples (possibly exaggerated) to show the need for a guidebook that gives useful information about local restaurants. Choice A is best supported by the passage, particularly the last three sentences. All the other options are either unsupported or not supported as directly as choice A.

5. **The correct answer is D.** The author is describing the purpose of the book, and in lines 9–11 he states that "My co-author and myself attempt to give him some details—what his surroundings will be, what dishes are the specialties of the house, what wine a wise man will order, and what bill he is likely to be asked to pay." This suggests that the guidebook is the most valuable insight of all when it comes to recommending restaurants. Choices A and B are unlikely because much of the passage is spent describing how unreliable personal recommendations can be. And although the author humorously mentions a "den of thieves" (lines 6–7) and being poisoned and robbed, it's clear that these suggestions are meant facetiously, not literally, so choice C doesn't work. The author does not give specific details about his own travels (choice E).

6. **The correct answer is C.** The author uses the phrase "wise man" to suggest that the book is offering savvy advice for a reader who wants to be that wise man. It's not a comparison between the author and the reader (choice A), nor is it a judgment of the hotel proprietor (choice B). The author is trying to present his book as a superior source of information, and there is nothing in the passage to suggest that he feels inferior (choice D). Choice E is incorrect because the author is suggesting that wise men order particular wines, while the usage of the word *stigmatizes* suggests a negative judgment.

7. **The correct answer is A.** The passage does not state or imply that Millet was primarily a landscape painter. To confirm this answer, though, you need to make sure you're looking deeper, because the author describes Millet's work in landscaping at several points. However, in the second paragraph the author makes it clear that Millet was also a figure painter.

8. **The correct answer is D.** Although the passage starts with a discussion of Millet's distinctive style, most of the passage is about the subtle touches that elevate Millet's art. Choices A and E are incorrect because the passage describes Millet's figure painting as equivalent to his landscape painting. Choice B is incorrect because the author only describes rustic art in relation to Millet's rustic art versus everyone else's—there is no specific judgment about rustic art in general. Choice C is incorrect because the author is not judging other critics in this passage; rather, they are mentioned to show how easily Millet's work is identified.

9. **The correct answer is B.** The author uses the word *impression* to describe the feelings and inspiration Millet received from nature. While choices A, C, D, and E are all alternative meanings for *impression*, none of these answer choices fit the context of the sentence.

10. **The correct answers are A and B.** Nwadike very clearly relays the results of recent studies on the efficacy of using AI in a medical setting (choice A) and elucidates the benefits of and necessity for investing in AI infrastructure (choice B)—both points are core tenets of their brief argument. However, though Rocha's counterargument centers on the ethical concerns raised by the use of AI in medical settings, Nwadike never actually makes any attempt to refute that point.

11. **The correct answer is A.** Though Nwadike mentions several potential benefits of using AI in medical settings, Rocha's counterargument focuses on the myriad potential ethical dilemmas that AI poses for the medical industry. Rocha makes no attempt to advocate for alternative medical technologies (choice B), disprove the effectiveness of AI algorithms (choice D), or critique AI for its potential impact on the healthcare profession (choice E). Choice C is actually contradictory to Rocha's stance, since such an undertaking would involve ignoring the very ethical dilemmas that Rocha mentions.

12. **The correct answers are B and D.** Your clearest context clue is "foul-mouthed," so the words you need are unlikely to be positive. The words *tirade* and *harangue* are the best choices. *Confab* (choice A) means "an informal meeting," which doesn't quite match the tone of the sentence. *Commendation* (choice C) is positive in tone and therefore not the best answer choice in this context. *Agitate* (choice E) could match tone-wise, but the word needed for the blank is a noun, not a verb. A tribute is typically given to convey someone's worth, so choice F doesn't make sense in this context.

13. **The correct answers are C and E.** Maxims and dictums are short statements that represent truisms about life. Aphids (choice A) are insects, apocrypha (choice B) are statements of uncertain origin, dictations (choice D) are writings based on speech, and anecdotes (choice F) are usually short narratives rather than statements; none of these choices fit the context of the sentence.

14. **The correct answers are A and D.** *Mollify* and *placate* both mean "to appease." None of the other words have meanings that fit the context of the

sentence, nor can they be arranged into pairs of synonyms, which is a necessity for correct answers of this question type.

15. **The correct answers are A and C.** Choice A can be supported by Hamilton's assertion that "It is essential to the idea of a law, that it be attended with a sanction; or, in other words, a penalty or punishment for disobedience" (lines 1–2). Choice C can be supported by Hamilton's assertion that "This penalty, whatever it may be, can only be inflicted in two ways: by the agency of the courts and ministers of justice, or by military force; by the coercion of the magistracy, or by the coercion of arms" (lines 4–6). While a cursory reading of the latter half of the excerpt may make choice B seem correct, close reading makes it clear that Hamilton never makes such a claim.

NOTES

Section 4: Quantitative Reasoning

1. D	4. A	7. D	9. B	11. A, E
2. C	5. C	8. A	10. D	12. 150
3. B	6. C			

1. **The correct answer is D.** We know that a is negative, so a^b is negative if b is an odd integer. In that case, $a^b < a^{2b}$. However, if b is a negative even integer, then a^b may be greater than a^{2b}. For example, if $a = -3$ and $b = -2$, then $a^b = (-3)^{-2} = \frac{1}{(-3)^2} = \frac{1}{9}$ whereas $a^{2b} = (-3)^{-4} = \frac{1}{(-3)^4} = \frac{1}{81} < \frac{1}{9}$. Therefore, the relationship cannot be determined from the information given.

2. **The correct answer is C.** At Bank A, a \$100 investment earns \$3 per year, so the investment will be worth \$112 after 4 years. At Bank B, \$100 earns \$4 per year, so the investment will be worth \$112 after 3 years.

3. **The correct answer is B.** Since x, y, and z are consecutive integers, $x = y - 1$ and $z = y + 1$. So $xz = (y - 1)(y + 1) = y^2 - 1$, which is less than y^2.

4. **The correct answer is A.** Since the triangle has angles measuring 30, 60, and 90 degrees, its hypotenuse is twice the length of its shortest side (to see why, divide an equilateral triangle into two 30-60-90 triangles by drawing a line from one corner to the midpoint of the opposite side). The side with length M is shorter than the hypotenuse, so M is less than $2N$.

5. **The correct answer is C.** For Team A, 12 represents 60% of their games, so they've played a total of $\frac{12}{0.6} = 20$ games. For Team B, 14 represents 70% of their games, so they've played a total of $\frac{14}{0.7} = 20$ games as well.

6. **The correct answer is C.** The plot of land has a diagonal of length $2(10\sqrt{2}) = 20\sqrt{2}$ meters. The diagonal of a square is always $\sqrt{2}$ times its side length, so the length of one side is 20 meters. Therefore, the perimeter is $4(20) = 80$ meters.

7. **The correct answer is D.** The cost of renting from the first company will be $6(14) + 0.25m$ where m is the number of miles you drive. The cost of renting from the second company will be $6(40) = 240$. Set these expressions equal to each other and solve:

$$84 + 0.25m = 240$$
$$0.25m = 156$$
$$m = 624$$

The cost will be the same when you drive 624 miles over the course of 6 days.

8. **The correct answer is A.** The slope of line A is $\frac{7-1}{3-(-2)} = \frac{6}{5}$. The slope of a line perpendicular to this has the opposite reciprocal slope, or $-\frac{5}{6}$. Since line B passes through the origin, its y-intercept is 0, so its equation is $y = -\frac{5}{6}x$. All of the other answer choices are incorrect as they have the wrong slope. Additionally, choice E has an incorrect y-intercept.

9. **The correct answer is B.** The table shows that $g(0) = -1$, so $f(g(0)) = f(-1) = -4$.

10. **The correct answer is D.** The average rate of change of $g(x)$ between -1 and 3 is $\frac{g(3)-g(-1)}{3-(1)} = \frac{1-(-5)}{3-(-1)} = \frac{6}{4} = \frac{3}{2}$.

11. **The correct answers are A and E.** There are two unrelated restrictions to the domain of $h(x)$. First, since $x + 5$ is in a square root, it must be greater than or equal to 0, so x must be at least -5. Choice A is the only value that does not satisfy this. Second, the denominator cannot be 0, so x cannot be 1. This means that choice E is also a correct answer.

12. **The correct answer is 150.** The vertex of the function $ax^2 + bx + c$ occurs when $x = -\frac{b}{2a}$. In this case, it occurs after $t = -\frac{96}{2(-16)} = \frac{-96}{-32} = 3$ seconds. Substitute $t = 3$ into the function: $h(3) = -16(3)^2 + 96(3) + 6 = 150$.

Section 5: Quantitative Reasoning

1. B	4. B	7. A	10. C	13. A, C
2. C	5. C	8. A	11. D	14. 5
3. B	6. D	9. E	12. D, E, F	15. 54

1. **The correct answer is B.** Evaluate each expression. $\frac{1}{2^{-3}} = 2^3 = 8$, and $\frac{1}{3^{-2}} = 3^2 = 9$. Therefore, Quantity B is greater.

2. **The correct answer is C.** The mean of the numbers is $(19 + 21 + 23 + 25 + 27) \div 5 = 23$, and the median is also 23, since the list is in order and 23 is in the middle.

3. **The correct answer is B.** $\sqrt[5]{32} = 2$, since $2^5 = 32$. Also, $2^4 = 16$, and x is certainly greater than 16, so $\sqrt[4]{x} > 2$.

4. **The correct answer is B.** The probability that a randomly chosen student does not play piano is $1 - 0.4 = 0.6$. If two students are selected at random, the probability that neither plays piano is $(0.6)(0.6) = 0.36$, so the probability that at least one plays piano is $1 - 0.36 = 0.64$. Thus, Quantity B is greater.

5. **The correct answer is C.** The area of the entire circle is $\pi(12)2 = 144\pi$. A 60° sector is $\frac{1}{6}$ of the circle, so its area is $\frac{144\pi}{6} = 24\pi$. The perimeter of the circle is $2\pi(12) = 24\pi$.

6. **The correct answer is D.** The area of the rectangle might be greater than or less than 20. For example, the dimensions could be 9 by 1, in which case the area would be 9, or they could be 5 by 5, in which case the area is 25. Because of this variability, the answer cannot be determined.

7. **The correct answer is A.** $4^{(3^2)} = (2^2)^9 = 2^{18}$, and $(4^3)^2 = (2^2)^6 = 2^{12}$, so Quantity A is certainly greater.

8. **The correct answer is A.** After walking the distances described, Kendra is 2 miles north and 5 miles east of her house. By the Pythagorean theorem, her distance is $\sqrt{2^2 + 5^2} = \sqrt{29} = 5.39$ miles.

9. **The correct answer is E.** Since 49 students take both AP Calculus and AP Chemistry, there are $150 - 49 = 101$ students who take *only* AP Calculus, and $78 - 49 = 29$ students who take *only* AP Chemistry. Combined with the 49 students who take both, there are $101 + 29 + 49 = 179$ students in these two classes combined. Therefore, there are $450 - 179 = 271$ students who do not take either class.

10. **The correct answer is C.** Hyundai and Toyota combine to account for $10 + 22 = 32\%$ of the cars, and $0.32(600) = 192$.

11. **The correct answer is D.** Hyundai accounts for 10% of the cars, and Honda for 20%, so the ratio is $\frac{10}{20} = \frac{1}{2}$.

12. **The correct answers are D, E, and F.** Take the square root of both sides of $x^2(x - 5)^2 = 36$:

$$\sqrt{x^2(x-5)^2} = \sqrt{36}$$
$$x(x-5) = -6$$
$$x^2 - 5x = -6$$

Since $\sqrt{36}$ could be positive or negative, we are left with two quadratic equations: either $x^2 - 5x - 6 = 0$, or $x^2 - 5x + 6 = 0$. Solve each quadratic:

$$x^2 - 5x - 6 = (x+1)(x-6) = 0 \Rightarrow x = -1, 6$$
$$x^2 - 5x + 6 = (x-2)(x-3) = 0 \Rightarrow x = 2, 3$$

Since $x^3 > 0$, x must be positive, leaving 2, 3, and 6

as the possible values of x.

13. **The correct answers are A and C.** Choice A is correct since addition of real numbers is commutative. Choice C is also correct since $(x + 1)(y + 1) - y = (xy + x + y + 1) - y = xy + x + 1$. Choice B is only true when $x = y$. Choice D will

only be true when both x and y are non-negative. Choice E is only true when either x or y is 0.

14. **The correct answer is 5.** Brittany is 5 years older than Marla, so when the sum of their ages is 45, Brittany will be 25 and Marla will be 20. If Marla were twice as old as Brittany is now, then Brittany must be 10 now. Finally, Marla is 5 years younger than Brittany, so she must be 5 years old now.

15. **The correct answer is 54.** Set up a proportion and solve:

$$\frac{45}{25}=\frac{98}{x}$$
$$45x=2,450$$
$$x=\frac{2,450}{45}$$
$$x=54$$

APPENDIXES

A | Common Errors in Grammar and Mechanics

B | Frequently Confused and Confusing Words

APPENDIX A

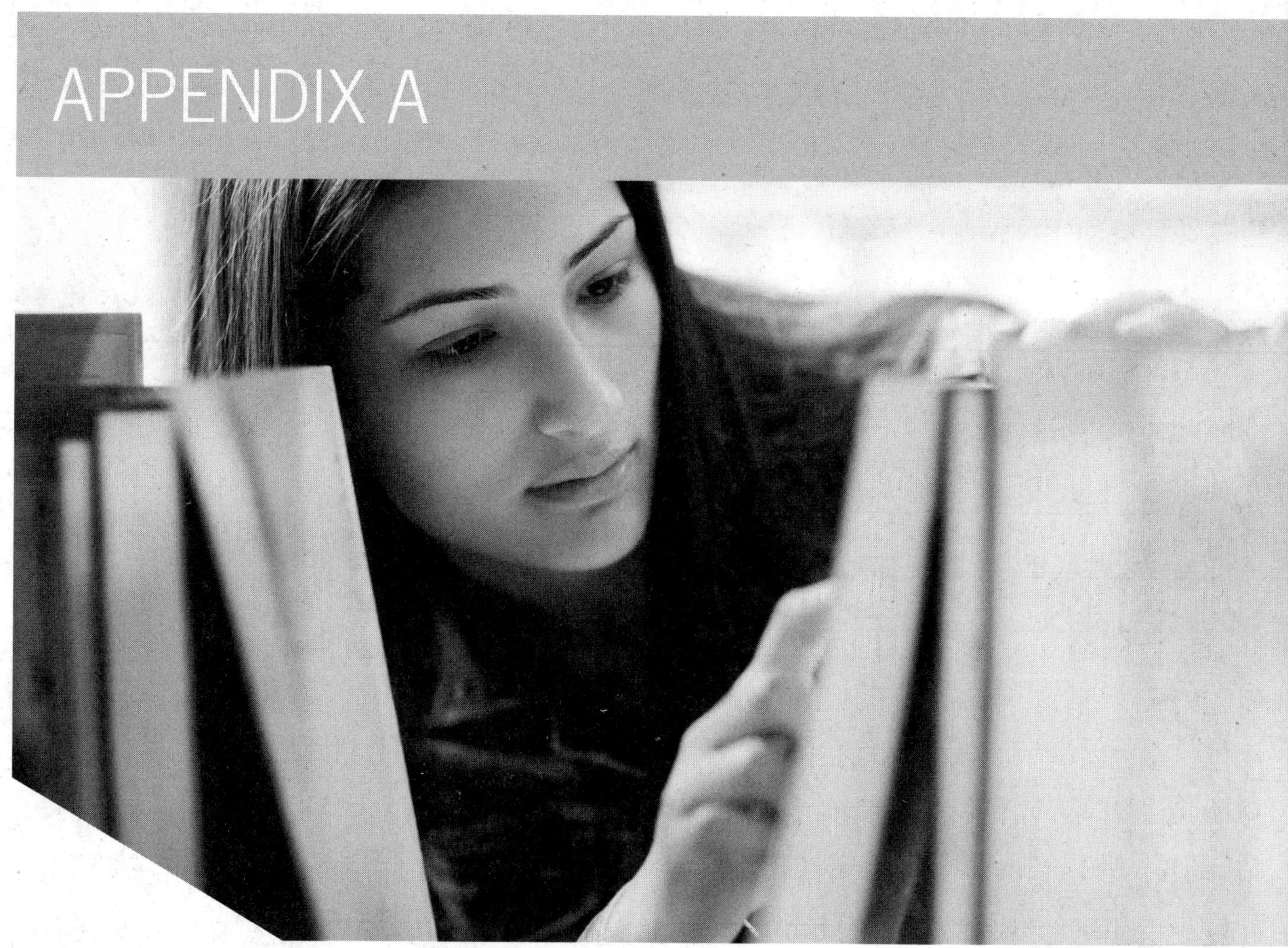

COMMON ERRORS IN GRAMMAR AND MECHANICS

The rubric for the Analytical Writing section has expectations with regards to both grammar and mechanics. While even the highest scoring band of 6 allows for minor errors that do not impede meanings, one of the ways a writer can gain a score of 6 is to demonstrate an exceptional understanding of the conventions of Standard Written English (i.e., grammar, usage, and mechanics). The question is: How "minor" are minor errors? ETS's official rubric, which can be found at **https://www.ets.org/gre/test-takers/general-test/prepare/content/analytical-writing/scoring.html**, indicates that errors will be judged according to the degree to which they interfere with a reader's ability to understand what you've written. This means that small spelling errors and missing commas likely will hurt you less than, say, improperly conjugated verbs or misplaced modifiers, simply because the latter two impact intended meaning more. Certain errors can stop a reader and interrupt the flow of the ideas that you want to get across. Certain "minor errors" can force the reader to reread the sentence or even a couple of sentences to try to figure out what you mean. Your best policy is to strive to make as few errors as possible and to ensure that you reserve time to edit your writing for errors.

A

As a graduate school candidate, you're likely already quite familiar with the conventions of Standard Written English, so this section is neither extensive nor exhaustive, but it focuses on the common problems with sentence construction that trip up many writers —occasionally, even the best of writers. This information should help you avoid some of the errors that can throw your meaning into question and detract from your analysis. It also highlights some problems with pronouns that, if consistently present, may detract from your score. You won't have much time to edit your response, so concentrate on possible problems in the order that we've presented them here:

- Sentence faults
- Misplaced modifiers
- Subject-verb agreement
- Pronoun problems

After we discuss these four key areas, we'll offer some additional advice to help you make the most of your writing.

SENTENCE FAULTS

The most important idea to take away from this section on sentence faults is that fixing these problems is not just a matter of cleaning up grammar; it's a matter of making it easier for your reader to understand your ideas. There are three common sentence faults, or problems with sentence constructions, that you should be aware of as you write and proofread your responses. You won't have time to do much editing, so concentrate on finding and correcting these three problems foremost. They can seriously detract from meaning and hinder your reader's understanding of your thesis.

Comma Splice

A comma splice occurs when two or more independent clauses are joined only by a comma.

> Sam decided to go back for his ***umbrella, Jack*** thought he would get his, too.

You can fix a comma splice by separating the two clauses completely with a period, or by separating them less completely with a semicolon. In the example sentence, the ideas are so closely related that a semicolon could be considered the better choice.

> Sam decided to go back for his ***umbrella; Jack*** thought he would get his, too.

You can also fix a comma splice by using a coordinating or a subordinating conjunction to join the two clauses.

> With a coordinating conjunction, the two clauses remain equal in importance.
>
> With a subordinating conjunction, one clause becomes subordinate to the other.

This decision isn't just a matter of grammar; it's a matter of meaning. It's a choice that you, as the writer, need to make. Are the ideas equally important? Is there one idea that you want to emphasize over the other? Perhaps you decide that the two ideas are equally important, and you choose to use a coordinating conjunction to connect the two ideas/clauses.

TIP

The names of the parts of speech are irrelevant. What you need to remember are the different problems you might run into in your writing and how to solve them.

Coordinating Conjunctions		
The coordinating conjunctions are as follows:		
and	nor	so
but	or	yet
for		

With a coordinating conjunction:

Sam decided to go back for his umbrella, ***and*** Jack thought he would get his, too.

If you decide that one idea is more important than the other, then you need to emphasize that idea. That idea becomes the main clause of the new sentence, and the second idea becomes the dependent, or subordinate, clause. In that case, you need to use a subordinating conjunction to fix the comma splice.

Subordinating Conjunctions		
The following are commonly used subordinating conjunctions:		
after	if	until
although	in case that	unless
as far as	in order that	when
as soon as	no matter how	whenever
as if	now that	where
as though	once	whereas
because	provided that	wherever
before	rather than	whether
even if	since	while
even though	so that	why
how	though	

With subordinating conjunction:

When Sam decided to go back for his umbrella, Jack thought he would get his, too.

Run-on Sentence

A run-on sentence has two or more independent clauses that are not connected by either punctuation or a conjunction.

Sam took his roommate's yellow ***umbrella he*** couldn't find his when he left for work.

As with a comma splice, you can fix a run-on sentence by separating the two clauses with a period if the ideas are equal in importance. If the ideas are equal in importance and closely related, then use a semicolon between the two clauses.

Sam took his roommate's yellow ***umbrella; he*** couldn't find his when he left for work.

If the sentences are not equal in importance, the easiest way to correct the problem is with a subordinating conjunction.

Sam took his roommate's yellow umbrella ***because*** he couldn't find his when he left for work.

However, there are additional ways to solve the problem with a run-on sentence. You could use a conjunctive adverb or a transitional phrase. Both may require some rewriting of the original sentence.

With a conjunctive adverb:

Sam couldn't find his umbrella when he left for work; ***consequently***, he took his roommate's yellow umbrella.

With a transitional phrase:

Sam couldn't find his umbrella when he left for work. ***As a result***, he took his roommate's yellow umbrella.

There are a variety of conjunctive adverbs and transitional phrases you can use to solve run-on sentence problems.

Conjunctive Adverbs		
also	incidentally	now
anyhow	indeed	otherwise
anyway	likewise	similarly
besides	meanwhile	still
consequently	moreover	then
finally	nevertheless	therefore
furthermore	next	thus
however	nonetheless	
Transitional Phrases		
after all	as a result	even so
as a consequence	at any rate	for example
	at the same time	in addition
	by the way	in fact

Like fixing comma splices, fixing run-on sentences is not just a matter of cleaning up a grammar problem. It's a matter of deciding what you want to say—what's important—and choosing the best solution to make your meaning clear.

Sentence Fragment

A sentence fragment is a group of words that has a period at the end but does not express a complete thought. It may have a verb form—that is, a verbal such as a participle—but that's not the same as a verb.

> Sam ***carrying*** a yellow umbrella to the office.

The following are possible corrections of the problem, depending on time:

> Sam ***is carrying*** a yellow umbrella to the office.
>
> Sam ***carries*** a yellow umbrella to the office.
>
> Sam ***was carrying*** a yellow umbrella to the office.
>
> Sam ***carried*** a yellow umbrella to the office.

There are several types of sentence fragments in addition to the previous example and several ways to correct them.

An improperly connected subordinate clause:

> ***Because he thought it would rain.*** Sam was carrying his umbrella.

Rewritten as a connected subordinate clause:

> ***Because he thought it would rain,*** Sam was carrying his umbrella.

A phrase:

> Sam was ready for rain. ***First, his umbrella and then his raincoat.***

Rewritten as a sentence:

> Sam was ready for rain. ***First, he took out his umbrella and then his raincoat.***

A verbal phrase:

> Sam was impatient for the bus to come. ***Kept looking up the street for it.***

Combined and rewritten as a single new sentence:

> ***Sam, impatient for the bus to come, kept looking up the street for it.***

This is an example of a writer's judgment. The writer can make any number of decisions based on what they want to emphasize in the sentence.

Using Dashes

Use dashes sparingly. They often mark the work of writers who don't have a command of standard English, don't know how to develop ideas clearly, or have little to say. Use dashes if you want to show a break in thought or to emphasize a parenthetical idea.

EXAMPLE

These are only some of the many reasons that so many new teachers leave the field within five years—the profession is simply no longer worth the headache.

MISPLACED MODIFIERS

A misplaced modifier is any word, phrase, or clause that does not refer clearly and logically to other words or phrases in the sentence. There are two problems involving misplaced modifiers.

The first occurs when a word, phrase, or clause is not close to the part of the sentence that it refers to, thus confusing the reader. Let's look at a few examples:

EXAMPLES

> Sam ***wrote*** that he was taking her umbrella ***in the note he left his roommate***.

A clearer version is:

> Sam ***wrote in the note he left his roommate*** that he was taking her umbrella.

> Sam's ***roommate*** was annoyed because now she didn't have an umbrella ***who is usually very easy-going***.

A clearer version is:

> Sam's ***roommate, who is usually very easy-going***, was annoyed because now she didn't have an umbrella.

> At the bus stop, Sam didn't see the ***bus trying to stay dry under his umbrella***.

A clearer version is:

> At the bus stop, ***Sam, trying to stay dry under his umbrella***, didn't see the bus.

The second and more serious problem with misplaced modifiers occurs when a phrase introduced by a verbal (a word formed from a verb but functioning as a different part of speech), such as a participle, doesn't relate clearly to another word or phrase in the sentence. The problem is often the result of a lack of a clear relationship between the subject of the sentence and the phrase.

EXAMPLES

> ***Holding the umbrella sideways, the car*** splashed him anyway.

In this sentence, the true subject is missing. It seems that the car was holding the umbrella sideways when the writer meant:

> ***Holding the umbrella sideways, Sam*** was splashed by the car anyway.

> ***On entering the bus, there*** were no seats.

Who entered the bus? To be clearer:

> ***On entering the bus, Sam saw*** there were no seats.

> ***Hot and tired, that*** was the perfect end to a perfect day, thought Sam ironically.

What? Try instead:

> ***Hot and tired, Sam*** thought ironically that it was the perfect end to a perfect day.

TIP

An easy way to recognize a participle is by the *-ing* ending. Not all participles end in *-ing* in English, but many do.

You'll notice that we continue to use simple examples so that you can easily see the problem and the correction. However, the essay you write will likely be more complex than the example sentences we've provided. The following example paragraph better approximates what can happen when a writer writes quickly to get thoughts down. See if you can spot the errors in this excerpt from a response to an Issue Task and how you think they should be fixed.

> The arts make an important contribution to the economy of communities across the nation this is true. Even when the economy is in trouble. Governments should fund arts programs. When arts programs thrive, tax receipts flow into government coffers. It's not just the artists who make money. But people who work in allied businesses. For example, my small city has a live theater company that produces three plays a year plus has several concerts and dance programs. Having no other theater for a 75-mile radius, it brings in people from the region. These people go to dinner at local restaurants they park in a garage near the theater if they come early, they shop in local stores. All this brings in money to stores and restaurants that have to hire people to serve these theatergoers. Every sale means sales tax for the city and for the state, jobs and income taxes for the state and the federal government.

A revised version might read like this:

> The arts make an important contribution to <u>a community's economy. Across</u> the nation this is true. Even when the economy is in <u>trouble, governments</u> should fund arts programs. When arts programs thrive, tax receipts flow into government coffers. It's not just the artists who make <u>money, but</u> also people who work in allied businesses. For example, my small city has a live theater company that produces three plays a year plus has several concerts and dance programs. <u>Having no other theater for a 75-mile radius, people come to my city from across the region.</u> These people go to dinner at local <u>restaurants and park</u> in a garage near the <u>theater. If</u> they come early, they shop in local stores. All this brings in money to stores and restaurants that have to hire people to serve these theatergoers. Every sale means sales tax for the city and the <u>state, and jobs</u> and income taxes for the state and the federal government.

While this essay isn't perfect, and there are likely more improvements a writer could make if given time, this is a significant improvement over the first version. As you can see from the examples in this section, it is often necessary to rework sentences to establish the clear relationship between the misplaced word, phrase, or clause and the word it modifies. Keep this in mind as you revise your practice drafts so that on test day, you'll be able to spot problems quickly and know a range of options for correcting them.

SUBJECT-VERB AGREEMENT

The following are probably two rules that you've heard a thousand times:

1. A singular subject takes a singular verb.
2. A plural subject takes a plural verb.

However, the correct subject-verb agreement can still elude a writer when several words, phrases, or even a subordinate clause comes between the subject and the verb. This is especially true when the subject is singular but a plural noun ends a prepositional phrase just before the verb, or vice versa. Such an error usually doesn't impede understanding, and one or two won't hurt your score, but try to avoid this problem as much as possible. Consider the following example.

> Incorrect: Sam's ***umbrella*** along with his briefcase and gym shoes ***were*** under his desk.

> Correct: Sam's ***umbrella*** along with his briefcase and gym shoes ***was*** under his desk.

Here's a plural subject-verb agreement problem:

> The ***umbrellas***, which belonged to Sam and Jack and were a riot of color, ***was*** a welcome sight on the gray day.

In this example, the comma after *color* should clue you in that *color* can't be the subject of the verb.

> The ***umbrellas***, which belonged to Sam and Jack and were a riot of color, ***were*** a welcome sight on the gray day.

Pronoun Problems

There are a variety of pronouns and a variety of problems you can get into when using them. The most common problems involve using incorrect forms, having unclear antecedents, and confusing pronouns with other words. A couple minor pronoun issues likely won't hurt you, but consistent mistakes throughout your response could cause you to lose a point. Unclear antecedents are a meaning issue; if the reader can't tell to whom or what you're referring, that can affect meaning.

Unclear Antecedents for Pronouns

The antecedent is the word that the pronoun refers to, or stands in for, in the sentence. When you review your essay, check for any problems with clarity so that the reader will have no difficulty in telling to whom or what the pronouns refer.

> Jack and Sam went back to their offices to get their umbrellas because it was starting to rain. They were gone for a few minutes because ***theirs*** were across the floor from the elevator.

Here, it is unclear whether *theirs* refers to their offices or their umbrellas. A clearer version is:

> Jack and Sam went back to their offices to get their umbrellas because it was starting to rain. They were gone for a few minutes because ***their offices*** were across the floor from the elevator.

Incorrect Forms

Is it *I* or *me*, *she* or *her*, *he* or *him*, *we* or *them*? Most people don't have trouble figuring out which pronoun to use when the subject of a sentence or clause is singular. The trouble comes when the subject is plural.

The following sentences show incorrect forms.

> ***Her*** and I went. ***Him*** and I went. We and ***them*** went, or even, ***us*** and ***them*** went.

The sentences should read:

> ***She*** and I went. ***He*** and I went. ***We*** and ***they*** went.

Objects of verbs and prepositions (*of, for, in, on, etc.*) are another problem area for pronoun forms. The following sentences show incorrect forms.

> The umbrellas belong to ***him*** and ***I*** (or to ***he*** and ***I***).
>
> The umbrellas belong to ***her*** and ***I*** (or to ***she*** and **I**).
>
> The umbrellas belong to ***them*** and ***I*** (or to ***they*** and ***I***).

The correct sentences are:

> The umbrellas belong to ***him*** and ***me***.
>
> The umbrellas belong to ***her*** and ***me***.
>
> The umbrellas belong to ***them*** and ***me***.

Confusing Pronoun Forms with Other Words

You've probably heard these rules in every English/language arts class you've ever taken, but they're worth repeating because many writers still make these errors.

it's or its

- *It's* is a contraction that stands for *it is*: ***It's*** raining. (***It is*** raining.)
- *Its* is an adjective that modifies a noun to show possession: The dog got ***its*** coat wet because ***it's*** raining.

An easy way to test which word you should use is to substitute *it is* in the sentence: The dog got ***it is*** coat wet because ***it is*** raining. "It is coat" doesn't make sense, so it must be "***its*** coat."

who's or whose

This pair of often-confused words is similar to the problem with *it's* and *its*.

- *Who's* is a contraction that stands for *who is*: ***Who's*** going to take an umbrella? (***Who is*** going to take an umbrella?)
- *Whose* is an interrogative pronoun that shows possession: ***Whose*** umbrella will we take?

Like testing out *it's* and *its*, substitute *who is* into the sentence: ***Who is*** going to take ***who is*** umbrella? "Who is umbrella" doesn't make sense, so it must be "***whose*** umbrella."

they're, their, or there

- *They're* is a contraction that stands for *they are*: ***They're*** going to take umbrellas. (***They are*** going to take umbrellas.)

- *Their* is a possessive adjective that shows possession or ownership: Jack and Sam are taking ***their*** own umbrellas.
- *There* is a pronoun that is used to introduce a clause or a sentence when the subject comes after the verb: ***There*** were no umbrellas in the closet.

Substitute *they are* in a sentence to see if the substitution makes sense: ***They are*** looking in ***they are*** desks for umbrellas. "They are desks" makes no sense, so it must be "***their*** desks."

Knowing the difference between ***there*** and the other two forms is something you must learn; there's no easy solution, which brings up the issue of ***there's*** and ***theirs***.

- *Theirs* is a form of the personal pronoun that shows ownership in the third person (as opposed to the first person [*mine, ours*] or the second person [*yours*]): Those umbrellas are ***theirs***. (The umbrellas belong to certain people.)
- *There's* is a contraction that stands for *there is*: ***There's*** no umbrella in the closet. (***There is*** no umbrella in the closet.)

Substitute *there is* in the sentence: ***There is*** one umbrella, but I doubt that it's either one of ***there is***. "There is" at the end of the sentence doesn't make sense, so it must be ***theirs***, meaning something belonging to two or more.

A FEW ADDITIONAL WORDS OF ADVICE

Please keep these ideas in mind as you write and revise your responses:

- **Use Active Voice Whenever Possible.** Passive voice (when the object of an action is the subject of a sentence) can weaken your writing. Use the active voice to emphasize who or what is doing the action. Consider the following examples.
    - **Passive Voice:** Ticket sales were adversely affected by the singer's recent scandal.
    - **Active Voice:** The singer's recent scandal adversely affected ticket sales.
- **Get Rid of Redundancies.** Avoid wordiness and redundancies that just fill up space. It's the quality of your thoughts that counts toward your score, not the length of your response. Repetition and wordiness can mask a good analysis.
- **Don't Use Jargon, Clichés, and Slang.** Jargon (words and phrases used by a certain group of people, usually in a specific profession) doesn't fit the tone and style required to answer either an issue or an argument task. The use of clichés (trite or overused expressions or ideas) can indicate that the writer is (1) not a very original thinker or (2) trying to fill up space. Slang doesn't fit the tone or style either.
- **Use Transition Words Thoughtfully.** Make sure that the transition words you choose help guide your reader and clarify your argument. As you edit, you may need to adjust your transition words to keep the essay clear.

Three Steps to Help You Practice Your Grammar Skills

1. To practice what you've learned about correcting common errors that can affect your comprehension, choose four pieces of writing that you've done recently that are about the same length as the Analytical Writing tasks on the GRE General Test. Review each one to see if you have any of the errors that are described in this section. Revise any errors that you find.
2. Review the two tasks on the Diagnostic Test and any of the Practice Tests (if you have already taken them). Correct any errors that you find.
3. Keep the concepts from this review in mind as you write any of the remaining writing tasks on the Practice Tests. After you evaluate and score each one, go back and correct any errors. The fewer the errors in Standard English, the better the chance of a score of 5 or 6 on the GRE General Test and the better presentation you'll make in any written document in your professional life.

If you need more help practicing your writing skills, revisit Chapter 3.

APPENDIX B

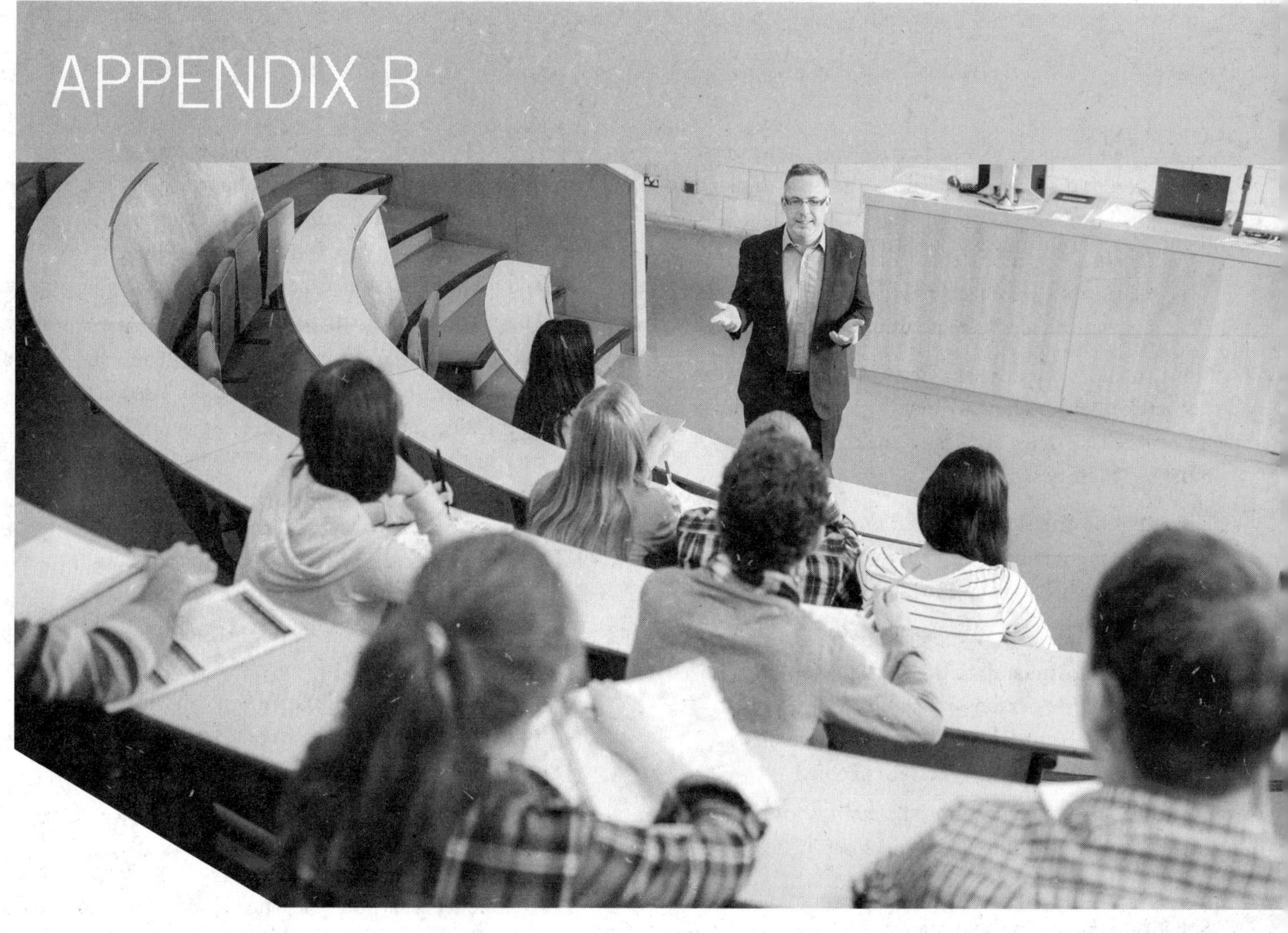

FREQUENTLY CONFUSED AND CONFUSING WORDS

The confusion with these words may not come from a misunderstanding of their meaning, but rather from a problem of misspelling. As you review the word pairs in this section, pay special attention to the spelling of each word as well as its meaning.

B

A

accept/except

accept: (verb) to receive

except: (preposition) excluding or omitting; (conjunction) other than, but

He bought all the tulips *except* the white ones.

He would have *accepted* the award in person *except* he was in Hong Kong.

accuse/allege

accuse: (verb) to blame

allege: (verb) to state as a fact something that has yet to be proven

He was *accused* of white-collar theft and was *alleged* to have stolen $5 million.

adopt/adapt/adept

adopt: (verb) to take as one's own

adapt: (verb) to change

adept: (adjective) very skilled

Adept at organizational design, she *adopted* the plan and then *adapted* it to her unit's needs.

advice/advise

advice: (noun) opinion

advise: (verb) to guide or recommend concerning future action

He *advised* the accused on his rights, but his *advice* was ignored.

affect/effect

affect: (verb) to influence; to pretend

effect: (noun) result or outcome; (verb) to bring about (less common usage)

He was able to *affect* her decision, but the *effect* was minimal.

Determined to conceal the devastating *effect* of losing the contest, Paul forced himself to *affect* indifference to the situation.

Her arrogance *affected* her downfall.

aggregate/total

aggregate: (noun) collection of separate parts into a whole; (verb) to combine into one

total: (noun) a whole without regard to its parts; (verb) to add up

The *aggregate* budget deficits for the five largest cities *totaled* more than $100 billion; the *total* was staggering.

allude/elude

allude: (verb) to refer indirectly to a person, object, or event

elude: (verb) to evade or slip away from

The candidate *alluded* to her opponent by mimicking his answer that "the nuances of the Iran policy *elude*" some who would serve on the Foreign Affairs Committee.

allusion/illusion

allusion: (noun) reference or mention of something or someone

illusion: (noun) mistaken perception of reality

In an effort to create the *illusion* of erudition in his paper, the student used many *allusions* to Shakespearian characters and themes.

alternate/alternative

alternate: (adjective) happening in turns, first one and then the other; (verb) to take turns

alternative: (noun) choice between two mutually exclusive options

Rather than always meeting on the third Thursday of the month, the *alternative* was to *alternate* between third Thursdays and Tuesdays.

ambivalent/ambiguous

ambivalent: (adjective) holding conflicting wishes, unable to decide, unsure

ambiguous: (adjective) difficult to understand, having more than one interpretation

He was *ambivalent* about the promotion because the new job description was *ambiguous* about to whom he actually reported: the CFO or the COO.

anachronism/anomaly

anachronism: (noun) person or object placed in the wrong time

anomaly: (noun) departure from the norm something; peculiar, irregular, abnormal

The play had a number of *anachronisms*, but the worst was the presence of a telephone in an 1850s parlor; then there was the greatest *anomaly*: a zombie as the house maid.

arbitrate/mediate

arbitrate: (verb) to settle a dispute in a legal sense

mediate: (verb) to act as a go-between, to negotiate between parties

Jack was called in to *arbitrate* between management and the union when the judge ordered an injunction against the strikers.

Will had to *mediate* a dispute between his sons over whose turn it was to have the car.

authoritarian/authoritative

authoritarian: (adjective) having complete power, expecting complete obedience

authoritative: (adjective) official, very reliable; exercising power

The president was *authoritarian* in his manner because the military backed him up.

The president had a very *authoritative* manner in dealing with his ministers.

This edition of the play is the *authoritative* version; no scholar questions that it represents the author's complete changes.

C

complaisant/complacent

complaisant: (adjective) tending to consent to others' wishes

complacent: (adjective) pleased with one's self

The members up for re-election were *complacent*, thinking their record in office was sufficient for re-election. They saw no need to be *complaisant* toward the voters and were soundly defeated as a result.

complement/compliment

complement: (noun) completing a whole, satisfying a need; (verb) to complete a whole, to satisfy a need

compliment: (noun) praise; (verb) to praise

The full *complement* of engineers who worked on the project was *complimented* for meeting the tight deadline.

The work of the engineers *complemented* the work of the programmers—all of whom received *compliments* on their work.

condemn/condone

condemn: (verb) to express disapproval

condone: (verb) to excuse, to overlook; to forgive

The dictator *condemned* the protesters as criminals, but he *condoned* the methods his soldiers used to suppress the protesters.

contention/contentious

contention: (noun) a point made in an argument; dispute, controversy, quarrel

contentious: (adjective) quarrelsome, always ready to argue

The board meeting turned *contentious* with the *contention* by the new member that the director was out of order.

continual/continuous/constantly

continual: (adjective) recurring regularly or frequently

continuous: (adjective) occurring without interruption

constantly: (adverb) regularly recurring

The faucet was leaking *constantly*, and I couldn't stand the *continual* drip-drip; it was worse than the sound of a *continuous* stream of water would have been.

credible/credulous

credible: (adjective) believable, plausible

credulous: (adjective) too ready to believe, gullible

The plaintiff's testimony that she had bought drugs on the street thinking they were incense was *credible* only to the *credulous* member of the jury who had recently moved to the city.

D

defective/deficient

defective: (adjective) faulty, flawed

deficient: (adjective) lacking some essential part, inadequate

The *defective* part didn't work; it was *deficient*.

deterrent/detriment

deterrent: (noun) something that keeps another from doing something

detriment: (noun) something that causes harm or loss

Although intended to be a *deterrent* to continued bad behavior, expulsion of the student proved to be a *detriment* to his social development.

disinterested/uninterested

disinterested: (adjective) impartial

uninterested: (adjective) bored

The mediator was a *disinterested* party to the dispute between the couple, one of whom yawned constantly and seemed *uninterested* in the proceedings.

discrete/discreet

discrete: (adjective) separate, distinct, unconnected

discreet: (adjective) prudent, unobtrusive, diplomatic

The scientist was examining *discrete* bits of evidence and finding that they did not support his colleague's theory, but he was *discreet* about his findings until he was sure.

distinct/distinctive

distinct: (adjective) unmistakable, clear

distinctive: (adjective) something that sets a person or thing apart from everything else, characteristic

I had the *distinct* impression that she wore a red scarf with every outfit to maintain a *distinctive* appearance in a roomful of her peers.

E

elicit/illicit

elicit: (verb) to draw out, to call forth

illicit: (adjective) unlawful

The lawyer was able to *elicit* from the witness information about the *illicit* bank transactions.

endemic/epidemic

endemic: (adjective) prevalent in a particular area or among a particular group or region

epidemic: (adjective) spreading rapidly; (noun) outbreak of a contagious disease

Some *endemic* diseases can develop more effective transmissibility over time. When this occurs, case loads can surge to *epidemic* proportions.

TIP

Want more help with vocabulary on the GRE? Sign up at **www.petersons.com/gre** to receive even more help with the GRE. You'll find online lessons and practice tests and a variety of helpful interactive activities like flash cards to help you review these words and other important vocabulary terms.

energize/enervate

energize: (verb) to give energy to, to invigorate

enervate: (verb) to weaken

I find that exercise *energizes* me rather than *enervates* me; I find that I am more alert and ready to tackle work after a good run.

expatiate/expiate

expatiate: (verb) to enlarge on, to speak or write at length

expiate: (verb) to make amends for, to make up for

The professor *expatiated* on his favorite poet, oblivious to the growing restlessness in his class. In an effort to *expiate* for his digression, the professor dismissed the class early.

expedient/expeditiously

expedient: (adjective) suitable, appropriate; (noun) means to an end

expeditiously: (adjective) acting quickly and efficiently

The *expedient* thing to do was to process the woman's visa request as *expeditiously* as possible so she could visit her ill mother.

F

fortuitous/fortunate

fortuitous: (adjective) occurring by chance or accident; happening by a lucky chance

fortunate: (adjective) being lucky, having good luck

Jack's winning the lottery was *fortuitous* because it means he'll be *fortunate* enough to begin his career with no debt.

H

humane/humanitarian

humane: (adjective) marked by mercy, kindness, or compassion

humanitarian: (adjective) having the best interests of humankind at heart; (noun) philanthropist

Mother Theresa was a great *humanitarian*; she believed that everyone, even the poorest of the poor, deserved *humane* care.

hypercritical/hypocritical

hypercritical: (adjective) excessively critical, overcritical

hypocritical: (adjective) insincere, expressing feelings or virtues that one doesn't have

The review panel's analysis was *hypercritical*, finding fault even with the feeding times used. The chief reviewer expressed sympathy with the lead researcher, who thought him *hypocritical* because the two often competed for the same grants.

I

imply/infer

imply: (verb) to suggest indirectly

infer: (verb) to draw a conclusion from

The report *implied* that the deal was fraudulent, and I *inferred* from the details that the executive was the culprit.

incipient/insipid

incipient: (adjective) beginning to appear, emergent

insipid: (adjective) lacking spirit, dull, boring; lacking taste or flavor

The *incipient* revolt was quashed by the army before it could attract many followers.

Lacking in flavor, the tea was as *insipid* as the dull host's conversation was boring.

---

ingenious/ingenuous/ingénue

ingenious: (adjective) inventive, skillful; clever; shrewd

ingenuous: (adjective) candid, frank, straightforward; showing a childlike innocence or simplicity

ingénue: (noun) naïve young woman or girl

Casting the college student as the *ingénue* was *ingenious*; she is perfect for the part of an *ingenuous* newcomer to Broadway.

---

insoluble/insolvent

insoluble: (adjective) unable to dissolve; unable to solve

insolvent: (adjective) unable to pay debts, bankrupt

When mixed together, the two chemicals were *insoluble* in water, and determining exactly why this occurred proved an *insoluble* problem for the researchers.

The company was *insolvent* and filed for Chapter 11 bankruptcy.

---

intense/intensive

intense: (adjective) extreme, using great effort

intensive: (adjective) concentrated, making heavy use of something

The six-week *intensive* Spanish course was a very *intense* experience.

J

judicial/judicious

judicial: (adjective) relating to the courts

judicious: (adjective) showing good judgment

Certain *judicial* appointments below the Supreme Court require Senate confirmation, and presidents attempt to be *judicious* in selecting nominees who will win confirmation without heated debate.

M

marshal/martial

marshal: (verb) to arrange in order; to solicit, to guide

martial: (adjective) relating to war or a fighter

Before applying for a license, the businessman *marshaled* support for his *martial* arts studio from the other storefront businesses.

N

negligible/negligent

negligible: (adjective) insignificant, unimportant

negligent: (adjective) lacking attention to something, careless

The attorney was *negligent* in not telling his witness of the change in court dates. However, the effect on the case was *negligible*.

P

populace/populous

populace: (noun) general public, population

populous: (adjective) having a large population

Much of the *populace* lived in the *populous* suburbs of the three major cities.

---

precede/proceed

precede: (verb) to go before

proceed: (verb) to continue

He waved for the woman to *precede* him through the door, and then they *proceeded* down the hall together.

FYI

Though the dictionary now accepts the figurative use of *literally* to mean the same as *virtually*, this use of *literally* should generally be avoided in academic writing.

precipitate/precipitous

precipitate: (verb) to cause to happen sooner than expected

precipitous: (adjective) hasty, acting without thinking

The prime minister's refusal to fire his cabinet secretary *precipitated* a call for elections in June rather than September. The opposition may find that the move was *precipitous* because its poll numbers are falling steadily.

prescribe/proscribe

prescribe: (verb) to establish a rule or guide; to order medicine

proscribe: (verb) to forbid, to prohibit

The doctor *prescribed* an antibiotic for the infection.

The judge *proscribed* any further contact between the two parties to the lawsuit.

proceeding/preceding

proceeding: (noun) course of action, sequence of events, legal action

preceding: (adjective) coming before

The juvenile *proceeding* took place in the judge's chamber, *preceding* the regular court cases for the day.

R

reversal/reversion

reversal: (noun) turning around

reversion: (noun) turning back

The *reversal* of the appeal required a *reversion* of the patent to the company's former employee.

S

simple/simplistic

simple: (adjective) not involved or complicated; unpretentious; humble

simplistic: (adjective) making complex problems overly simple

The explanation of the motivations of the antagonist was *simplistic*, but then the critic tended to look at most motivations as *simple* issues of right and wrong.

stultify/stupefy

stultify: (verb) to make useless or worthless; to take away strength or efficiency

stupefy: (verb) to make dull or stupid; to confuse or astound

Many experts fear that the hours of television that children watch every day *stultifies* their brains.

A woman born in 1900 would be *stupefied* by the gadgets available today in most US kitchens.

subtitle/subtle

subtitle: (noun) second part of a title, often an explanation of the title

subtle: (adjective) not obvious, difficult to detect or understand

The *subtitle* of the report was not *subtle* in describing the author's opinion.

T

than/then

than: (conjunction) used to show deviation in type, manner, or identity; (preposition) in comparison to someone or something

then: (adverb) at a given time; next or soon after a given time; besides or additionally

I used to think that I was stronger *than* my brother, but *then* he beat me at arm wrestling.

theory/hypothesis

theory: (noun) a principle or set of principles considered logical, plausible, and scientifically sound; an idea or belief used to determine an action or set of actions

hypothesis: (noun) a tentative assumption ventured for the purpose of testing its logic

At the start of her experiment, Iliana based her *hypothesis* on a prominent new *theory* in the field of quantum mechanics.

V

virtually/literally

virtually: (adverb) nearly; almost completely; practically speaking

literally: (adverb) with complete accuracy; exactly

Virtually everyone in town had come to the sold-out event, so *literally* every seat in the stadium was occupied.

Y

your/you're

your: (adjective) of or relating to one or oneself

you're: (contraction) you are

You said *you're* going to buy *your* mother a gift.

ANSWER SHEETS

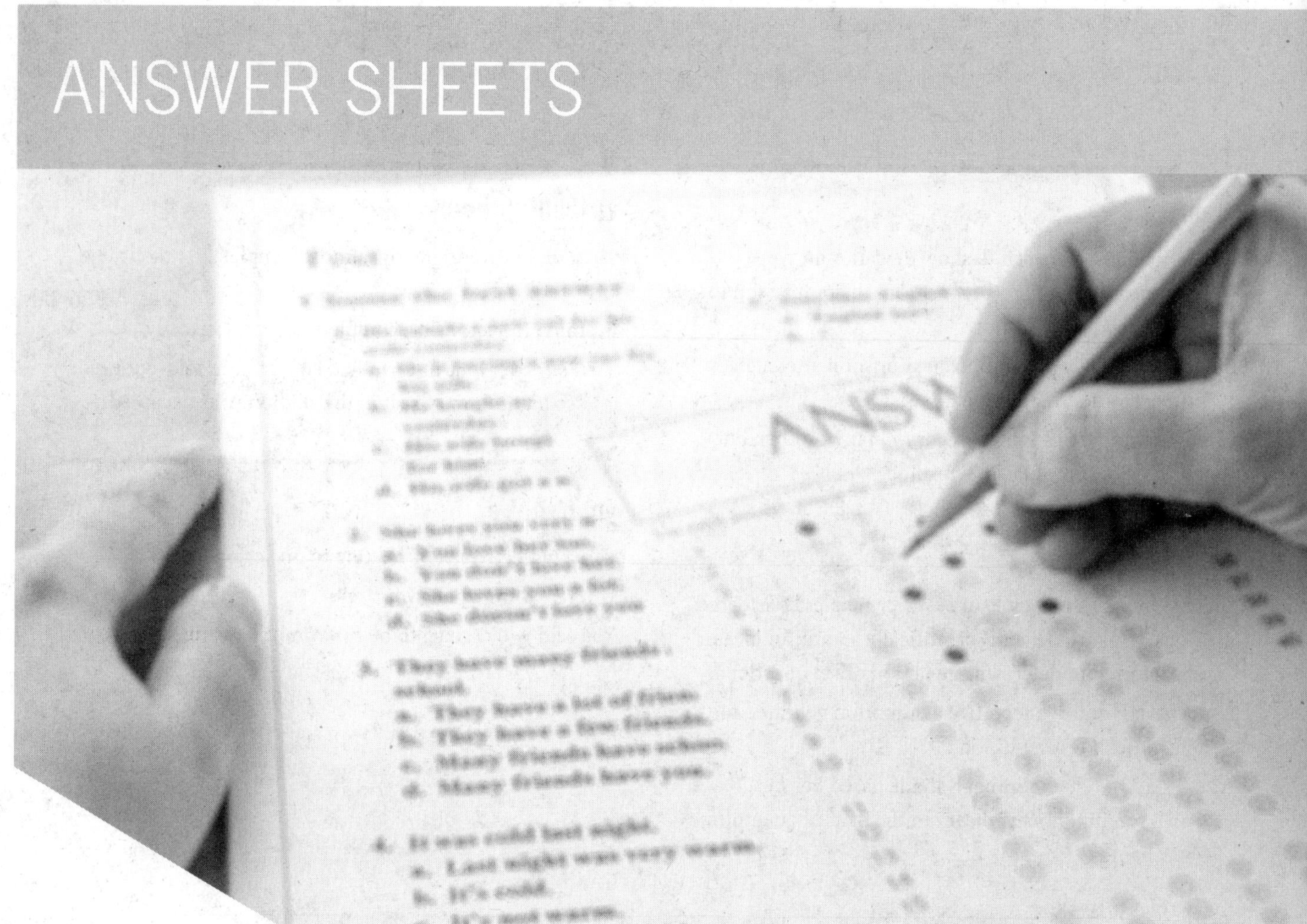

DIAGNOSTIC TEST

Section 1: Analytical Writing

DIAGNOSTIC TEST

Section 2: Verbal Reasoning

1. Ⓐ Ⓑ Ⓒ Ⓓ Ⓔ
2. Ⓐ Ⓑ Ⓒ Ⓓ Ⓔ Ⓕ
3. Ⓐ Ⓑ Ⓒ Ⓓ Ⓔ Ⓕ Ⓖ Ⓗ Ⓘ
4. Ⓐ Ⓑ Ⓒ
5. Ⓐ Ⓑ Ⓒ
6. Ⓐ Ⓑ Ⓒ
7. Ⓐ Ⓑ Ⓒ
8. Ⓐ Ⓑ Ⓒ
9. Ⓐ Ⓑ Ⓒ Ⓓ Ⓔ
10. Ⓐ Ⓑ Ⓒ Ⓓ Ⓔ Ⓕ
11. Ⓐ Ⓑ Ⓒ Ⓓ Ⓔ Ⓕ
12. Ⓐ Ⓑ Ⓒ Ⓓ Ⓔ

Section 3: Verbal Reasoning

1. Ⓐ Ⓑ Ⓒ Ⓓ Ⓔ
2. Ⓐ Ⓑ Ⓒ Ⓓ Ⓔ Ⓕ
3. Ⓐ Ⓑ Ⓒ Ⓓ Ⓔ Ⓕ Ⓖ Ⓗ Ⓘ
4. Ⓐ Ⓑ Ⓒ Ⓓ Ⓔ
5. Ⓐ Ⓑ Ⓒ
6. Ⓐ Ⓑ Ⓒ Ⓓ Ⓔ
7. Ⓐ Ⓑ Ⓒ
8. Ⓐ Ⓑ Ⓒ Ⓓ Ⓔ
9. Ⓐ Ⓑ Ⓒ Ⓓ Ⓔ
10. Ⓐ Ⓑ Ⓒ Ⓓ Ⓔ Ⓕ
11. Ⓐ Ⓑ Ⓒ Ⓓ Ⓔ Ⓕ
12. Ⓐ Ⓑ Ⓒ Ⓓ Ⓔ Ⓕ
13. Ⓐ Ⓑ Ⓒ Ⓓ Ⓔ
14. Ⓐ Ⓑ Ⓒ Ⓓ Ⓔ
15. Ⓐ Ⓑ Ⓒ

DIAGNOSTIC TEST

Section 4: Quantitative Reasoning

1. Ⓐ Ⓑ Ⓒ Ⓓ
2. Ⓐ Ⓑ Ⓒ Ⓓ
3. Ⓐ Ⓑ Ⓒ Ⓓ
4. Ⓐ Ⓑ Ⓒ Ⓓ
5. Ⓐ Ⓑ Ⓒ Ⓓ
6. Ⓐ Ⓑ Ⓒ Ⓓ Ⓔ
7. Ⓐ Ⓑ Ⓒ Ⓓ Ⓔ
8. Ⓐ Ⓑ Ⓒ Ⓓ Ⓔ Ⓕ Ⓖ Ⓗ
9. Ⓐ Ⓑ Ⓒ Ⓓ Ⓔ
10. Ⓐ Ⓑ Ⓒ Ⓓ Ⓔ
11. Ⓐ Ⓑ Ⓒ Ⓓ Ⓔ Ⓕ Ⓖ Ⓗ
12. Ⓐ Ⓑ Ⓒ Ⓓ Ⓔ

Section 5: Quantitative Reasoning

1. Ⓐ Ⓑ Ⓒ Ⓓ
2. Ⓐ Ⓑ Ⓒ Ⓓ
3. Ⓐ Ⓑ Ⓒ Ⓓ
4. Ⓐ Ⓑ Ⓒ Ⓓ
5. Ⓐ Ⓑ Ⓒ Ⓓ
6. Ⓐ Ⓑ Ⓒ Ⓓ
7. Ⓐ Ⓑ Ⓒ Ⓓ Ⓔ
8. Ⓐ Ⓑ Ⓒ Ⓓ Ⓔ
9. Ⓐ Ⓑ Ⓒ Ⓓ Ⓔ
10. Ⓐ Ⓑ Ⓒ Ⓓ Ⓔ
11. Ⓐ Ⓑ Ⓒ Ⓓ Ⓔ
12. Ⓐ Ⓑ Ⓒ Ⓓ Ⓔ
13. Ⓐ Ⓑ Ⓒ Ⓓ Ⓔ
14. Ⓐ Ⓑ Ⓒ Ⓓ Ⓔ Ⓕ
15. $\frac{\boxed{}}{\boxed{}}$

PRACTICE TEST 1

Section 1: Analytical Writing

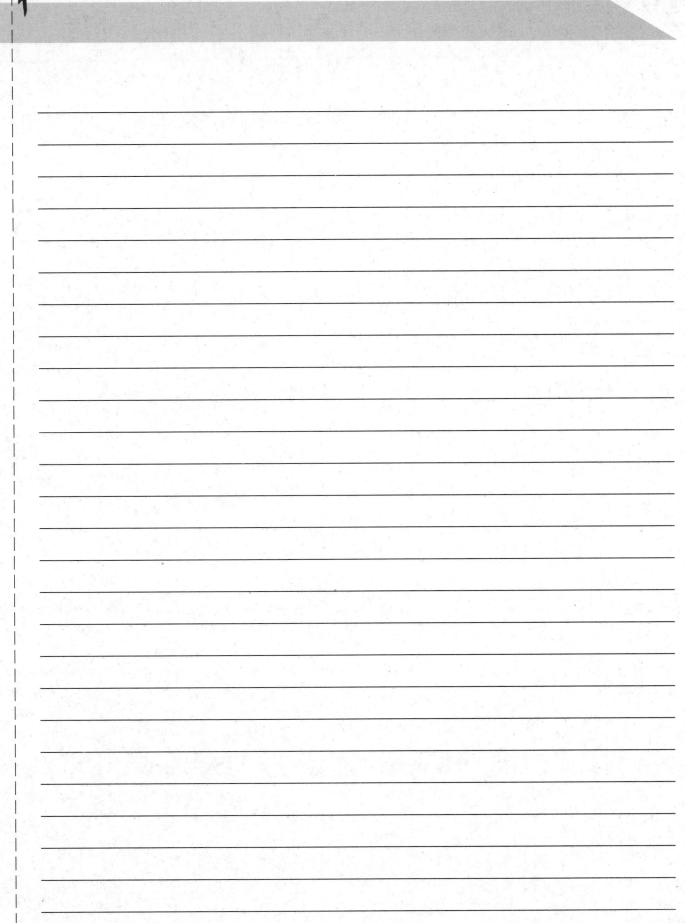

PRACTICE TEST 1

Section 2: Verbal Reasoning

1. Ⓐ Ⓑ Ⓒ Ⓓ Ⓔ Ⓕ
2. Ⓐ Ⓑ Ⓒ Ⓓ Ⓔ Ⓕ Ⓖ Ⓗ Ⓘ
3. Ⓐ Ⓑ Ⓒ Ⓓ Ⓔ
4. Ⓐ Ⓑ Ⓒ Ⓓ Ⓔ
5. Ⓐ Ⓑ Ⓒ
6. Ⓐ Ⓑ Ⓒ Ⓓ Ⓔ
7. Ⓐ Ⓑ Ⓒ Ⓓ Ⓔ
8. Ⓐ Ⓑ Ⓒ
9. Ⓐ Ⓑ Ⓒ Ⓓ Ⓔ
10. Ⓐ Ⓑ Ⓒ Ⓓ Ⓔ Ⓕ
11. Ⓐ Ⓑ Ⓒ Ⓓ Ⓔ Ⓕ
12. Ⓐ Ⓑ Ⓒ Ⓓ Ⓔ Ⓕ

Section 3: Verbal Reasoning

1. Ⓐ Ⓑ Ⓒ Ⓓ Ⓔ
2. Ⓐ Ⓑ Ⓒ Ⓓ Ⓔ Ⓕ
3. Ⓐ Ⓑ Ⓒ Ⓓ Ⓔ Ⓕ Ⓖ Ⓗ Ⓘ
4. Ⓐ Ⓑ Ⓒ Ⓓ Ⓔ
5. Ⓐ Ⓑ Ⓒ Ⓓ Ⓔ
6. Ⓐ Ⓑ Ⓒ Ⓓ Ⓔ
7. Ⓐ Ⓑ Ⓒ Ⓓ Ⓔ
8. Ⓐ Ⓑ Ⓒ Ⓓ Ⓔ
9. Ⓐ Ⓑ Ⓒ Ⓓ Ⓔ
10. Ⓐ Ⓑ Ⓒ Ⓓ Ⓔ
11. Ⓐ Ⓑ Ⓒ
12. Ⓐ Ⓑ Ⓒ Ⓓ Ⓔ
13. Ⓐ Ⓑ Ⓒ Ⓓ Ⓔ Ⓕ
14. Ⓐ Ⓑ Ⓒ Ⓓ Ⓔ Ⓕ
15. Ⓐ Ⓑ Ⓒ Ⓓ Ⓔ Ⓕ

PRACTICE TEST 1

Section 4: Quantitative Reasoning

1. Ⓐ Ⓑ Ⓒ Ⓓ
2. Ⓐ Ⓑ Ⓒ Ⓓ
3. Ⓐ Ⓑ Ⓒ Ⓓ
4. Ⓐ Ⓑ Ⓒ Ⓓ
5. Ⓐ Ⓑ Ⓒ Ⓓ
6. Ⓐ Ⓑ Ⓒ Ⓓ Ⓔ
7. Ⓐ Ⓑ Ⓒ Ⓓ Ⓔ
8. Ⓐ Ⓑ Ⓒ Ⓓ Ⓔ
9. Ⓐ Ⓑ Ⓒ Ⓓ Ⓔ
10. Ⓐ Ⓑ Ⓒ Ⓓ Ⓔ Ⓕ Ⓖ
11.
12.

Section 5: Quantitative Reasoning

1. Ⓐ Ⓑ Ⓒ Ⓓ
2. Ⓐ Ⓑ Ⓒ Ⓓ
3. Ⓐ Ⓑ Ⓒ Ⓓ
4. Ⓐ Ⓑ Ⓒ Ⓓ
5. Ⓐ Ⓑ Ⓒ Ⓓ
6. Ⓐ Ⓑ Ⓒ Ⓓ
7. Ⓐ Ⓑ Ⓒ Ⓓ Ⓔ
8. Ⓐ Ⓑ Ⓒ Ⓓ Ⓔ
9. Ⓐ Ⓑ Ⓒ Ⓓ Ⓔ
10. Ⓐ Ⓑ Ⓒ Ⓓ Ⓔ
11. Ⓐ Ⓑ Ⓒ Ⓓ Ⓔ
12. Ⓐ Ⓑ Ⓒ Ⓓ Ⓔ
13. Ⓐ Ⓑ Ⓒ Ⓓ Ⓔ
14.
15.

PRACTICE TEST 2

Section 1: Analytical Writing

PRACTICE TEST 2

Section 2: Verbal Reasoning

1. Ⓐ Ⓑ Ⓒ Ⓓ Ⓔ Ⓕ
2. Ⓐ Ⓑ Ⓒ Ⓓ Ⓔ Ⓕ Ⓖ Ⓗ Ⓘ
3. Ⓐ Ⓑ Ⓒ Ⓓ Ⓔ
4. Ⓐ Ⓑ Ⓒ Ⓓ Ⓔ
5. Ⓐ Ⓑ Ⓒ Ⓓ Ⓔ
6. Ⓐ Ⓑ Ⓒ Ⓓ Ⓔ
7. Ⓐ Ⓑ Ⓒ Ⓓ Ⓔ
8. Ⓐ Ⓑ Ⓒ
9. Ⓐ Ⓑ Ⓒ Ⓓ Ⓔ
10. Ⓐ Ⓑ Ⓒ Ⓓ Ⓔ Ⓕ
11. Ⓐ Ⓑ Ⓒ Ⓓ Ⓔ Ⓕ
12. Ⓐ Ⓑ Ⓒ

Section 3: Verbal Reasoning

1. Ⓐ Ⓑ Ⓒ Ⓓ Ⓔ
2. Ⓐ Ⓑ Ⓒ Ⓓ Ⓔ Ⓕ
3. Ⓐ Ⓑ Ⓒ Ⓓ Ⓔ Ⓕ Ⓖ Ⓗ Ⓘ
4. Ⓐ Ⓑ Ⓒ Ⓓ Ⓔ
5. Ⓐ Ⓑ Ⓒ Ⓓ Ⓔ
6. Ⓐ Ⓑ Ⓒ Ⓓ Ⓔ
7. Ⓐ Ⓑ Ⓒ Ⓓ Ⓔ
8. Ⓐ Ⓑ Ⓒ Ⓓ Ⓔ
9. Ⓐ Ⓑ Ⓒ Ⓓ Ⓔ
10. Ⓐ Ⓑ Ⓒ
11. Ⓐ Ⓑ Ⓒ Ⓓ Ⓔ
12. Ⓐ Ⓑ Ⓒ Ⓓ Ⓔ Ⓕ
13. Ⓐ Ⓑ Ⓒ Ⓓ Ⓔ Ⓕ
14. Ⓐ Ⓑ Ⓒ Ⓓ Ⓔ Ⓕ
15. Ⓐ Ⓑ Ⓒ Ⓓ Ⓔ

PRACTICE TEST 2

Section 4: Quantitative Reasoning

1. Ⓐ Ⓑ Ⓒ Ⓓ
2. Ⓐ Ⓑ Ⓒ Ⓓ
3. Ⓐ Ⓑ Ⓒ Ⓓ
4. Ⓐ Ⓑ Ⓒ Ⓓ
5. Ⓐ Ⓑ Ⓒ Ⓓ
6. Ⓐ Ⓑ Ⓒ Ⓓ Ⓔ
7. Ⓐ Ⓑ Ⓒ Ⓓ Ⓔ
8. Ⓐ Ⓑ Ⓒ Ⓓ Ⓔ
9. Ⓐ Ⓑ Ⓒ Ⓓ Ⓔ
10. Ⓐ Ⓑ Ⓒ Ⓓ Ⓔ Ⓕ Ⓖ Ⓗ
11. ☐
12. ☐

Section 5: Quantitative Reasoning

1. Ⓐ Ⓑ Ⓒ Ⓓ
2. Ⓐ Ⓑ Ⓒ Ⓓ
3. Ⓐ Ⓑ Ⓒ Ⓓ
4. Ⓐ Ⓑ Ⓒ Ⓓ
5. Ⓐ Ⓑ Ⓒ Ⓓ
6. Ⓐ Ⓑ Ⓒ Ⓓ Ⓔ
7. Ⓐ Ⓑ Ⓒ Ⓓ Ⓔ
8. Ⓐ Ⓑ Ⓒ Ⓓ Ⓔ
9. Ⓐ Ⓑ Ⓒ Ⓓ Ⓔ
10. Ⓐ Ⓑ Ⓒ Ⓓ Ⓔ
11. Ⓐ Ⓑ Ⓒ Ⓓ Ⓔ
12. Ⓐ Ⓑ Ⓒ Ⓓ Ⓔ
13. Ⓐ Ⓑ Ⓒ Ⓓ Ⓔ Ⓕ Ⓖ Ⓗ
14. ☐
15. ☐

PRACTICE TEST 3

Section 1: Analytical Writing

PRACTICE TEST 3

Section 2: Verbal Reasoning

1. Ⓐ Ⓑ Ⓒ Ⓓ Ⓔ
2. Ⓐ Ⓑ Ⓒ Ⓓ Ⓔ Ⓕ Ⓖ Ⓗ Ⓘ
3. Ⓐ Ⓑ Ⓒ
4. Ⓐ Ⓑ Ⓒ
5. Ⓐ Ⓑ Ⓒ Ⓓ Ⓔ
6. Ⓐ Ⓑ Ⓒ Ⓓ Ⓔ
7. Ⓐ Ⓑ Ⓒ Ⓓ Ⓔ
8. Ⓐ Ⓑ Ⓒ
9. Ⓐ Ⓑ Ⓒ Ⓓ Ⓔ
10. Ⓐ Ⓑ Ⓒ Ⓓ Ⓔ Ⓕ
11. Ⓐ Ⓑ Ⓒ Ⓓ Ⓔ Ⓕ
12. Ⓐ Ⓑ Ⓒ Ⓓ Ⓔ

Section 3: Verbal Reasoning

1. Ⓐ Ⓑ Ⓒ Ⓓ Ⓔ
2. Ⓐ Ⓑ Ⓒ Ⓓ Ⓔ Ⓕ
3. Ⓐ Ⓑ Ⓒ Ⓓ Ⓔ Ⓕ Ⓖ Ⓗ Ⓘ
4. Ⓐ Ⓑ Ⓒ Ⓓ Ⓔ
5. Ⓐ Ⓑ Ⓒ Ⓓ Ⓔ
6. Ⓐ Ⓑ Ⓒ Ⓓ Ⓔ
7. Ⓐ Ⓑ Ⓒ Ⓓ Ⓔ
8. Ⓐ Ⓑ Ⓒ Ⓓ Ⓔ
9. Ⓐ Ⓑ Ⓒ Ⓓ Ⓔ
10. Ⓐ Ⓑ Ⓒ
11. Ⓐ Ⓑ Ⓒ Ⓓ Ⓔ
12. Ⓐ Ⓑ Ⓒ Ⓓ Ⓔ Ⓕ
13. Ⓐ Ⓑ Ⓒ Ⓓ Ⓔ Ⓕ
14. Ⓐ Ⓑ Ⓒ Ⓓ Ⓔ Ⓕ
15. Ⓐ Ⓑ Ⓒ

PRACTICE TEST 3

Section 4: Quantitative Reasoning

1. Ⓐ Ⓑ Ⓒ Ⓓ
2. Ⓐ Ⓑ Ⓒ Ⓓ
3. Ⓐ Ⓑ Ⓒ Ⓓ
4. Ⓐ Ⓑ Ⓒ Ⓓ
5. Ⓐ Ⓑ Ⓒ Ⓓ
6. Ⓐ Ⓑ Ⓒ Ⓓ Ⓔ
7. Ⓐ Ⓑ Ⓒ Ⓓ Ⓔ
8. Ⓐ Ⓑ Ⓒ Ⓓ Ⓔ
9. Ⓐ Ⓑ Ⓒ Ⓓ Ⓔ
10. Ⓐ Ⓑ Ⓒ Ⓓ Ⓔ
11. Ⓐ Ⓑ Ⓒ Ⓓ Ⓔ Ⓕ Ⓖ Ⓗ
12. [ ]

Section 5: Quantitative Reasoning

1. Ⓐ Ⓑ Ⓒ Ⓓ
2. Ⓐ Ⓑ Ⓒ Ⓓ
3. Ⓐ Ⓑ Ⓒ Ⓓ
4. Ⓐ Ⓑ Ⓒ Ⓓ
5. Ⓐ Ⓑ Ⓒ Ⓓ
6. Ⓐ Ⓑ Ⓒ Ⓓ
7. Ⓐ Ⓑ Ⓒ Ⓓ
8. Ⓐ Ⓑ Ⓒ Ⓓ Ⓔ
9. Ⓐ Ⓑ Ⓒ Ⓓ Ⓔ
10. Ⓐ Ⓑ Ⓒ Ⓓ Ⓔ
11. Ⓐ Ⓑ Ⓒ Ⓓ Ⓔ
12. Ⓐ Ⓑ Ⓒ Ⓓ Ⓔ Ⓕ
13. Ⓐ Ⓑ Ⓒ Ⓓ Ⓔ
14. [ ]
15. [ ]

NOTES

NOTES